Business Administration and Managerial Economics

Business Administration and Managerial Economics

Edited by
Swena Lesley

Willford Press
www.willfordpress.com

Published by Willford Press,
118-35 Queens Blvd., Suite 400,
Forest Hills, NY 11375, USA

ISBN: 978-1-68285-601-7

Cataloging-in-Publication Data

Business administration and managerial economics / edited by Swena Lesley.
p. cm.
Includes bibliographical references and index.
ISBN 978-1-68285-601-7
1. Industrial management. 2. Managerial economics. 3. Management. I. Lesley, Swena.
HD31.2 .B87 2019
658--dc23

For information on all Willford Press publications
visit our website at www.willfordpress.com

Willford Press

Printed in China.

Contents

Preface

Business administration and managerial economics are two important fields that are significant to the success of a business. While business administration refers to the study of the administrative aspects of a business, managerial economics is the application of economic principles and models to solve practical problems in a business. Business administration is concerned with the management of varied business operations, decision-making, human resource organization, material allocation, etc. Techniques of managerial economics are most commonly applied to risk analysis, production analysis, pricing analysis and capital budgeting. This book sheds light on the fundamental theories and concepts of each discipline. Some of the diverse topics covered in this book address the varied branches that fall under this category. Students, researchers, experts, managers, economists and all associated with business administration and managerial economics will benefit from this book.

Various studies have approached the subject by analyzing it with a single perspective, but the present book provides diverse methodologies and techniques to address this field. This book contains theories and applications needed for understanding the subject from different perspectives. The aim is to keep the readers informed about the progresses in the field; therefore, the contributions were carefully examined to compile novel researches by specialists from across the globe.

Indeed, the job of the editor is the most crucial and challenging in compiling all chapters into a single book. In the end, I would extend my sincere thanks to the chapter authors for their profound work. I am also thankful for the support provided by my family and colleagues during the compilation of this book.

Editor

A Data Analytical Study of the Japanese Equity Market over a Lengthy Period

Jarrett JE[1]* and Li Y[2]

[1]*Management Science and Finance, University of Rhode Island, Kingston, RI, USA*
[2]*Doctoral Student (Finance), University of Rhode Island, USA*

Abstract

The primary goal is to examine the time series of the Japanese equity market over a lengthy period of time to determine aspects of this time series as it moves and what are the factors that may determine its. We study the Index of the Tokyo Exchange over nearly four decades by data analytical methods also known as exploratory data analysis with some principle methods of statistical testing. The aim is to put to rest some arguments concerning the applicability in long range memory modeling some use of methods based serial correlation in the data over this nearly four decades of monthly observations. Those in the past have indicated that Japanese time series of equity prices contain only small percentages of permanent and temporary components. Also, Japanese stock prices are often characterized by "bubbles" in their movements. The data analytics attempts to validate this phenomena over the length of this study.

Keywords: Japan equity market; Long memory models; Bubbles; Data analytics; Exploratory data analysis

Intoduction

Japan as a nation exhibited great growth followed by stagnation with intermittent bubbles of economic activity. Studies of the Japanese equity market. Studies such as Kang and Stulz [1,2] concluded the relation to its banks contributed to the stagnation in the Japanese economy. Furthermore, Peek and Rosengren [3] argued that Japanese corporate affiliations and the main bank system proved to be an effective strategy to increase credit availability with several drawbacks. Reducing agency costs made it more difficult for needed economic restructuring of the Japanese economy. These factors led to shielding competitors from market mechanisms that would be imposed by creditors. Hence, many competitors still received credit when their financial health should have led to the stopping of these practices. Many firms did recover who were thought to be dying, Fukuda and Nakamura [4].

Since stock prices reflect overall performance of financial markets, the focus of this here will be on the analytics of data collected over a roughly forty year performance of the index of closing prices on the Tokyo Stock Exchange. We begin by examining the data on during this period and previous studies of forecasting aspects of these closing prices. Following the initial comprehension of the mean of the data, we compare the change in closing prices in Tokyo to find differences in the behavior of prices during each decade of the lengthy period on Japanese data. Finally, we try to assess the characteristics of Japanese prices by decade, to determine if one can easily find some method for forecasting the general movement of prices.

Previous studies of Japanese equity markets include Hamao, Mei and Xu [5], where changes in the Japanese equity markets were documented as having relationships to the manner in which the Japanese banking systems environment. Regulations in the environment often resulted in "bubbles" in a long-term stagnation in the Japanese equity markets. The particular methods that Japan employed to stimulate and regulate the Japanese banking systems and general economy resulted in this stagnation and were related to the so-call bubbles in its economy. For example, Bayonne and Collyns [6] documented the era when Japan went from great growth in its asset prices to virtual stagnation producing the worst crises in Japan since the outcome of the Second World War. Furthermore, Ray, Jarrett and Chen [7] produced evidence of both temporary and permanent components in the time series of a sample of listed Japanese equities. The last study using ARFIMA time series methods identified these components but also indicted some of the great difficulties in predicting prices of Japanese securities. They indicated that the inclusion of the temporary component in a sample of 15 individual listed Japanese firms. I addition, listed equities of the Tokyo Exchange contain at most 5 to 15% of permanent components and, thus, there may be a small amount of predictability in listed equity prices. Nagayasu [8] using the ARFIMA-FGARCH model studied the efficiency of the Japanese equity market by examining the statistical properties of the return and volatility of the Nikkei 225. He found also, some evidence of a long range dependence. This differs from the notion of the efficient market hypothesis (EMH) and is valid for the sample studied and the period of the data. This suggests that Japan's market reform of the early 2000's resulted in no significant efficiency improvements.

Others have made similar studies in other equity markets. These studies include Agiakloglou [9] Baillie [10]; Baillie [11], Barkoulas [12], Bollerslev [13], Lo [14], Lo [15], Mills [16], Sadique [17], Davidson [18], and Shi [19]. In all, these studies conclude that predicting closing prices of listed stocks is exceptionally difficult.

Goals of this study

The motivation in this study is to examine past data on the Japanese equity markets based on the inability of financial forecasters to predict accurately both the direction and size of change in the principle Japanese equity market and see what may cause predictions to be accurate. We examine the evidence concerning the lack of long memory or serial in a roughly period of time series data on returns to

***Corresponding author:** Jarrett JE, Professor, Management Science and Finance, University of Rhode Island, Kingston, RI, USA
E-mail: jejarrett133@gmail.com

the Japanese equity market. As a number previous studies, we collected data over almost four decades from the PACAP Databases on Japanese equity markets kept at the University of Rhode Island/CBA. The data include the closing prices of the Tokyo Stock Exchange from 1975 until and including 2012. They are denoted as decade (group) 1, 2, 3 and 4.

Our purpose of this study is to determine what factors in the time series of Japanese equity prices that may cause this great difficulty in prediction. We propose to study the value weighted and equal weighted monthly return over a lengthy period to explain the lack of ability of predicting accurately Japanese equity prices.

Data analytics and exploratory data analysis

By graphically exploring data, the research presents a great deal of information about the time series of the closing prices. Examine Figure 1 which shows the variation in the data of the nearly 40 years by month. The advantage of using monthly data is reduce the seasonal effect of daily fluctuations or hourly fluctuation in prices which would tend to diminish what one learn from the data. Figure 1 is a time series plot of closing prices of the Tokyo Stock Exchange (Figure 1).

The figure indicates what the earlier studies concluded that the Japanese equities grew rapidly until about month180 and thereafter dropped significantly until the latest periods studied. Naturally, there were significant ups and downs of the closing prices often referred to "bubbles" by previous authors noted before. Stagnation is the term used to describe the variation observed in the data reducing the expectations of greater growth in the Japanese economy. If we attempt to utilize time series decomposition we would observe the results in Figure 2. [Time Series decomposition is discussed in Jarrett, 1987 and 1991 and in other sources.

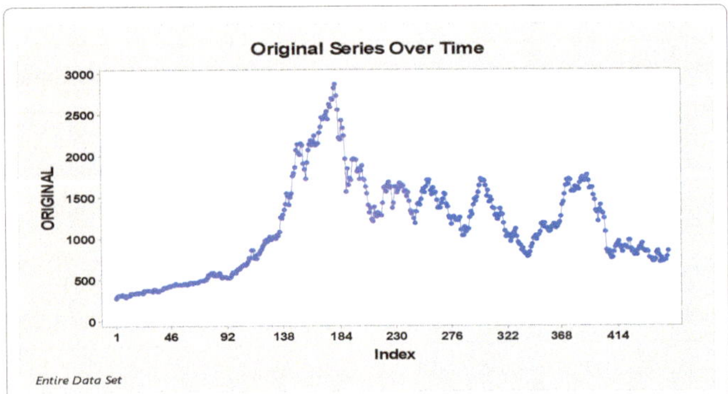

Figure 1: Original Series over Time.

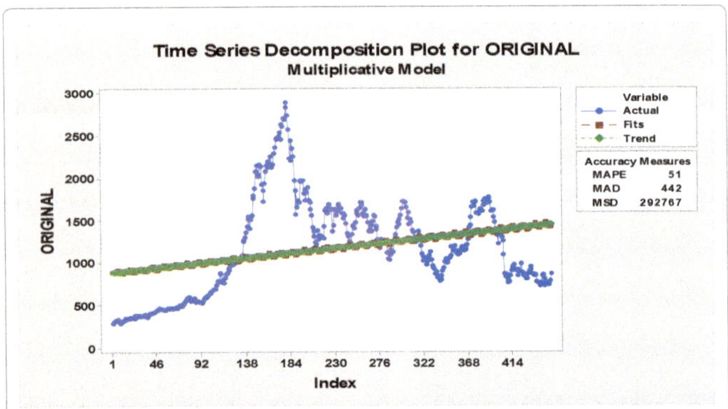

Figure 2: Time series decomposition plot for original.

As you can observe, the multiplicative decomposition model indicates a solid trend in the data over time, but it does predict month to month movements which vary greatly from the trend. There is obviously cycles in the data and some seasonality as well. Movements do not tend to be long term as characterizing the data over the entire period studies. Changes occurred and did seem to ignite the stagnation felt in the equity market with the "bubbles" related to the ups and downs of the market.

To determine and compare the changes in the Tokyo stock market over a lengthy period of time the data collected over the almost four decade era are in turn analyzed to summarize the information therein. The following setoff tables provide the information observed for the Tokyo Stock Index during this period (Tables 1A-1E).

The above Table 1 contains a set of panels denoted by letters A, B, …E where each panel produces the information or data analysis where one possess vital information about the time series of the Tokyo Stock Index for the near forty period studied. Note in A that we possess 456 observations with a mean of about 1167 and standard deviation

N	456	Sum Weights	456
Mean	1167.37285	Sum Observations	532322.02
Std Deviation	566.401138	Variance	320810.249
Skewness	0.47374152	Kurtosis	-0.2241792
Uncorrected SS	767386938	Corrected SS	145968663
Coeff Variation	48.5193002	Std Error of Mean	26.5241635

Table 1A: The PROC UNIVARIATE Procedure Output Variable LSTVAL (All Obs.) Moments.

Location		Variability	
Mean	1167.373	Std Deviation	566.40114
Median	1134.615	Variance	320810
		Range	2592
		Interquartile Range	831.60500

Table 1B: Basic Statistical Measures.

Test	Statistic		p-value	
Student's t	t	44.01167	Pr. >abs t	<0.0001
Sign	M	228	Pr.≥ abs M	<0.0001
Signed Rank	S	52098	Pr≥ abs. S	<0.0001

Table 1C: Tests for Location: μ=0.

100% Maximum	2881.370
99%	2692.650
95%	2195.390
90%	1859.120
75% Q3	1571.480
50% Median	1134.615
25% Q1	739.875
10%	438.180
5%	357.900
1%	317.00
0% Minimum	288.880

Table 1D: Quantiles.

Lowest Value	Obs.	Highest Value	Obs.
288.88	1	2692.65	178
291.63	9	2702.22	177
306.10	8	2737.57	181
Above 313.36	2	2929.54	179
317.00	10	2881.37	180

Table 1E: Extreme Observations.

of about 566. The skewness coefficient is about 0.4737 indicating a movement over time in the upward direction and a lack of normality in the distribution of the data. The Kurtosis coefficient of about -0.2242. Kurtosis is a measure of whether the data are heavy-tailed or light-tailed relative to a normal distribution. Stated differently, data with high kurtosis tend to have heavy tails, or outliers. Data with low kurtosis tend to have light tails, or lack of outliers. A uniform distribution would be the extreme case. Normal distributions have a Kurtosis of approximately 3. Hence, the data are certainly far form normally distributed. Further the coefficient of variation is 48.519 indicating that the mean is slightly more than twice the size of the standard deviation. This corroborate the picture one observes after calculating the measures of skewness and kurtosis.

Panel B above, contains the descriptive measures estimated from the data of the Tokyo Stock Index. Note the mean and median are relatively close in value, i.e., 1167 versus 1134. The mean is larger indicating that the tail of the distribution is in the positive direction The standard deviation and variance are the same values as before the range is large (2592) and interquartile range (the first quartile minus the third quartile) is 831.605 which determines the middle fifty percent of the data distribution which will be utilized later in observing and interpreting the Boxplots.

Observing Panel C, we accomplish tests for location to determines if the mean of the distribution equals zero or not, i.e., $\mu=0$ or $\mu \neq 0$. We reject the null hypothesis at less than .0001 for the test using Student t-statistic, Sign M and the Signed Rank statistics. The latter two tests are done since the assumption of normality in the Student t-statistic methods is probably not valid. Again this indicates the mean of data does not have a zero value and indicates the movement over the nearly four decade period exists.

Observe Panel D where the distribution of the data is displayed in a table where one can conclude that the data is not normal nor is it uniformly distributed around the median. The median is not equidistant from the maximum and minimum nor is it equidistant from the First and Third Quartiles. Finally, Panel E produces data on the extremes of the distribution which corroborates the information observed in earlier panels (Table 2).

Table 2 ,also, contains a set of panels denoted by letters A, B, …E where each panel produces the information or data analysis where one possess vital information about the time series of the Tokyo Stock Index for the first decade period studied. Note in A that we possess 120 observations with a mean of about 498 and standard deviation of about 150. The skewness coefficient is about 0.4737 indicating a movement over time in the upward direction and a lack of normality in the distribution of the data. The Kurtosis coefficient of about -0.2242. Kurtosis is a measure of whether the data are heavy-tailed or light-tailed relative to a normal distribution. Stated differently, data with high kurtosis tend to have heavy tails, or outliers. Data with low kurtosis tend to have light tails, or lack of outliers. A uniform distribution would be the extreme case. Normal distributions have a Kurtosis of approximately 3. Hence, the data are certainly far form normally distributed. Further the coefficient of variation is 48.519 indicating that the mean is slightly more than twice the size of the standard deviation. This corroborate the picture one observes after calculating the measures of skewness and kurtosis.

Panel B above, contains the descriptive measures estimated from the data of the Tokyo Stock Index. Note the mean and median are relatively close in value, i.e., 498 versus 464. The mean is larger indicating that the tail of the distribution is in the positive direction The standard deviation and variance are the same values as before the range is large (624.49) and interquartile range (the first quartile minus the third quartile) is 196.95 which determines the middle fifty percent of the data distribution which will be utilized later in observing and interpreting the Boxplots.

N	120	Sum Weights	120
Mean	497.93075	Sum Observations	59751.69
Std Deviation	149.797132	Variance	22439.1808
Skewness	0.94179031	Kurtosis	0.26689446
Uncorrected SS	32422466.3	Corrected SS	2670262.51
Coeff Variation	30.08392288	Std Error of Mean	13.6745447

Table 2A: The PROC UNIVARIATE Procedure Output Variable LSTVAL (Decade 1) Moments.

Location		Variability	
Mean	497.9308	Std Deviation	149.79713
Median	464.1050	Variance	22439
		Range	624.49000
		Interquartile Range	196.95000

Table 2B: Basic Statistical Measures.

Test	Statistic		p-value	
Student's t	t	36.41297	Pr. >abs t	<0.0001
Sign	M	60	Pr.≥ abs M	<0.0001
Signed Rank	S	3630	Pr≥ abs. S	<0.0001

Table 2C: Tests for Location: μ=0.

100% Maximum	913.370
99%	875.810
95%	819.710747.715
90%	574.335
75% Q3	464.105
50% Median	377.385
25% Q1	377.385
10%	336.420
5%	318.015
1%	291.630
0% Minimum	288.880

Table 2D: Quantiles.

Lowest Value		Highest Value	
Value	Obs.	Value	Obs.
288.88	1	860.44	118
291.63	9	862.10	112
306.10	8	871.32	111
313.36	2	875.81	119
317.00	10	913.37	120

Table 2E: Extreme Observations.

Observing Panel C, we accomplish tests for location to determines if the mean of the distribution equals zero or not, i.e., $\mu=0$ or $\mu \neq 0$. We reject the null hypothesis at less than 0.0001 for the test using Student t-statistic, Sign M and the Signed Rank statistics. The latter two tests are done since the assumption of normality in the Student t-statistic methods is probably not reliable. Again this indicates the mean of data does not have a zero value and indicates the movement over the first decade period exists.

Observe Panel D where the distribution of the data is displayed in a table where one can conclude that the data is not normal nor is it uniformly distributed around the median. The median is not equidistant from the maximum and minimum nor is it equidistant from the First and Third Quartiles. Finally, Panel E produces data on the extremes of the distribution which corroborates the information observed in earlier panels. The lowest extreme observation occur for number 1,2,8,9 and 10 and the highest extreme observations occur for 111, 112 118, 119 and 120. This would indicate large deviations over the decade (Table 3).

Similar to the above tables, Table 3 contains the data analysis to the second decade of the study. The date table contains five panels denoted by letters A, B,…E with every panel giving evidence of the distribution of data each panel produces the information or data analysis where one possess vital information about the time series of the Tokyo Stock Index for the second decade period studied. Note in A that we possess 120 observations with a mean of about 1755 and standard deviation of about 480. The mean and standard deviation are both larger than in the previous decade. The skewness coefficient is about 0.3004 indicating a movement over time in the upward direction and again a lack of normality in the distribution of the data. The Kurtosis coefficient of about -0.6030. As stated earlier, Kurtosis is a measure of whether the data are heavy-tailed or light-tailed relative to a nor mal distribution. Stated differently, data with high kurtosis tend to have heavy tails, or outliers. Data with low kurtosis tend to have light tails, or lack of outliers. A uniform distribution would be the extreme case. Normal distributions have a Kurtosis of approximately 3. Hence, the data are certainly far form normally distributed. Further the coefficient of variation is about 27.3304 indicating that the mean is slightly less than four times the size of the standard deviation. This corroborate the picture one observes after calculating the measures of skewness and kurtosis.

Moments			
N	**120**	**Sum Weights**	**120**
Mean	1755.00383	Sum Observations	210600.46
Std Deviation	479.64879	Variance	230062.961
Skewness	0.3003654	Kurtosis	-0.602961
Uncorrected SS	396982107	Corrected SS	27377492.4
Coeff Variation	27.3303557	Std Error of Mean	43.7857436

Table 3A: The PROC UNIVARIATE Procedure Output Variable LSTVAL (Decade 2).

Location		**Variability**	
Mean	1755.004	Std Deviation	479.64879
Median	1677.910	Variance	230063
		Range	1950
		Interquartile Range	735.86000

Table 3B: Basic Statistical Measures.

Test	**Statistic**		**p-value**	
Student's t	t	40.08163	Pr. >abs t	<0.0001
Sign	M	60	Pr.≥ abs M	<0.0001
Signed Rank	S	3630	Pr≥ abs. S	<0.0001

Table 3C: Tests for Location: μ=0.

100% Maximum	2881.37
99%	2829.54
95%	261614
90%	2457.11
75% Q3	2132.60
50% Median	1677.91
25% Q1	1396.74
10%	1045.51
5%	1003.79
1%	967.28
0% Minimum	931.06

Table 3D: Quantiles.

Lowest Value		**Highest Value**	
Value	**Obs.**	**Value**	**Obs.**
931.06	121	2692.65	178
967.28	124	2702.22	177
977.30	122	2737.57	181
992.13	127	2829.54	179
997.03	125	2881.37	180

Table 3E: Extreme Observations.

Panel B above, contains the descriptive measures estimated from the data of the Tokyo Stock Index. Note the mean and median are relatively close in value, i.e., 1755 versus 1677. These values are both larger than the mean and median found in Table 2. Again, the mean is larger indicating than the tail of the distribution is in the positive direction. The standard deviation and variance are the same values as in Panel A, but the range is larger as that found in Table 2 (1950 versus 624.49). The interquartile range and interquartile range (the first quartile minus the third quartile) is almost 736 and is much greater than the similar statistics in Table 2 which determines the middle fifty percent of the data distribution. These values will be reflected in the figure on Boxplots to be analyzed later.

Observing Panel C, we accomplish tests for location to determines if the mean of the distribution equals zero or not as before, i.e., μ=0 or μ ≠ 0. We reject the null hypothesis at less than 0.0001 for the test using Student t-statistic, Sign M and the Signed Rank statistics. The latter two tests are done because the assumption of normality in the Student t-statistic methods is probably not valid. Again this indicates the mean of data does not have a zero value and indicates the movement over the first decade period exists.

Observe Panel D where the distribution of the data is displayed in a table where one can conclude that the data is not normal nor is it uniformly distributed around the median. The median is not equidistant from the maximum and minimum nor is it equidistant from the First and Third Quartiles. Finally, Panel E produces data on the extremes of the distribution which corroborates the information observed in earlier panels that the distribution is not symmetrical. The lowest extremes are observation numbers from 121 to 127 and largest extremes lie in 177 to 181 (Table 4).

To reduce redundancy, we observe only the large changes Decade 3 from the previous decades. Note in Panel A the mean and standard deviation became more disparate then in the earlier decades and the coefficients of variation is now only approximately 19.250. This indicates that the standard deviation is now about five times larger than the mean. Any forecasting model would probably been wrong during this decade and we can suspect that the Boxplot to be examined later will by much larger between the third and first quartile. Panel B gives evidence of some symmetry in the distribution of the data since the mea and median are relatively close in value (1270.400 and 1267.365 respectively. The interquartile range and the range are also not small but not the larges values. Hence, in Panel C the null hypothesis of the mean equaling zero is also rejected at p-values of less than 0.0001.

Panel D indicates another phenomena that differs from the other decades studied. The median is roughly equidistant from the maximum and minimum. The same appears to be roughly the same

N	120	Sum Weights	120
Mean	1270.40017	Sum Observations	152448.02
Std Deviation	344555884	Variance	59807.5804
Skewness	0.02989492	Kurtosis	-0.8845272
Uncorrected SS	200787092	Corrected SS	71177102.06
Coeff Variation	19.2503032	Std Error of Mean	22.3247957

Table 4A: The PROC UNIVARIATE Procedure Output Variable LSTVAL (Decade 3) Moments.

Location		Variability	
Mean	1270.400	Std Deviation	244.55588
Median	1267.365	Variance	59808
		Range	934.20000
		Interquartile Range	385.04500

Table 4B: Basic Statistical Measures.

Test	Statistic		p-value	
Student's t	t	56.90534	Pr. >abs t	<0.0001
Sign	M	60	Pr.≥ abs M	<0.0001
Signed Rank	S	3630	Pr≥ abs. S	<0.0001

Table 4C: Tests for Location: μ=0.

100% Maximum	1722.2000
99%	1718.940
95%	1693.225
90%	1602.355
75% Q3	1467.310
50% Median	1267.365
25% Q1	1082.265
10%	953.320
5%	852.765
1%	796.560
0% Minimum	788.000

Table 4D: Quantiles.

Lowest Value	Obs.	Highest Value	Obs.
788.00	339	1707.96	301
796.56	340	1712.42	256
818.73	338	1712.45	258
821.18	337	1718.94	302
837.70	341	1722.20	300

Table 4E: Extreme Observations.

for the distance between the median and first quartile and the distance between the median and the third quartile. This is even amplified by examining the extreme observations in Panel E. All the lowest extremes include observations 337 through 341. This appears to corroborate the "bubble" observed by earlier studies. The largest extremes include two observations of 256 and 258 and another trio at 300 through 302. Analyzing data in this way certainly reinforces the conclusions of some earlier researchers who made these observations but did not present the analysis of this type (Table 5).

The fourth period studied includes 96 observations based on the latest data available at the start and finish of this data analysis. We observe only important changes Period 4 which contains eight years of time series data. Note in Panel A the mean and standard deviation became more like Decades 1 and 2 than Decade 3. In Period 4 as in earlier decades, the coefficients of variation is now only approximately 31.472. This indicates that the standard deviation is now slightly more than three times larger than the mean. Although not like Decade 3, forecasting models would probably have difficulty during this decade and we can suspect that the Boxplot to be examined later will differ than Decade 3. Panel C indicates the same results as in all other periods (decades). Panel D shows that the median is no longer equidistant from the limits of the first and third quartiles and the distance from the median to the maximum and minimum are equal at all. . Finally, Panel E indicates the low extremes are in observations 443 to 552 and extremes in the highest direction are in the observations of 375 to 390. Theses extreme values indicate wide extreme in the data and therefore my also give evidence in "bubbles" in stock prices in the Tokyo market.

In the next section, Boxplots by decades will provide additional evidence of the difficulty to forecast or totally use data analytics to produce accurate and totally informative diagnostics of the lengthy period studied.

Exploratory data analysis with boxplots

A box-plot [20] is an underrated method of conveying location, variation and skewness for information contained in a data set. The purpose is often used to determine and detect and illustrate location

N	96	Sum Weights	96
Mean	1140.8526	Sum Observations	109527.85
Std Deviation	359.04822	Variance	128915.624
Skewness	0.4857672	Kurtosis	-1.3766822
Uncorrected SS	137195272	Corrected SS	12246984.3
Coeff Variation	31.4719201	Std Error of Mean	36.6452055

Table 5A: The PROC UNIVARIATE Procedure Output Variable LSTVAL (Decade 4) Moments.

Location		Variability	
Mean	1140.853	Std Deviation	359.04822
Median	958.500	Variance	128916
		Range	1055
		Interquartile Range	694.83500

Table 5B: Basic Statistical Measures.

Test	Statistic		p-value	
Student's t	t	31.13238	Pr. >abs t	<0.0001
Sign	M	48	Pr.≥ abs M	<0.0001
Signed Rank	S	2328	Pr≥ abs. S	<0.0001

Table 5C: Tests for Location: μ=0.

100% Maximum	1774.88
99%	1774.88
95%	1721.96
90%	1701.00
75% Q3	1534.05
50% Median	958.50
25% Q1	839.21
10%	761.17
5%	736.31
1%	719.49
0% Minimum	719.49

Table 5D: Quantiles.

Lowest Value	Obs.	Highest Value	Obs.
719.49	449	1721.96	385
728.46	443	1728.16	375
728.61	444	1752.74	386
731.64	452	1755.68	389
736.31	451	1774.88	390

Table 5E: Extreme Observations.

variation changes with different groups in a data set. Figure 3 are the boxplots of the variable Original (Tokyo Stock Exchange Index) for the four groups (decade or period) which summarizes the data analytics performed in the previous section. Group 1 has the narrowest middle interval, Group 2 has the widest middle interval with Group 3 having middle interval that appears having the first and third quartile limits that are equidistant from the median with a mean virtually equal to the median. Group 4 has a mean that is much great than the median with the limit of the third quartile being very much greater than the median. There is no doubt that the groups are not like each other and those of long term memory models may not be very useful in explaining or forecasting the variation in data across time (Figure 3).

Some additional comments about normality and autocorrelation

Now, we plot the entire data set data against a theoretical normal distribution in such a way that the points should form an approximate straight line. When the plot indicates departures from this straight line, the conclusion suggests that the observations depart from normality. Again, [20] points out that the normal probability plot is used to answer the following questions; "Are the data normally distributed?" From Figure 4, the normal probability plot suggests that there are series departure from normality in the data especially at the early and latter parts of the time series (Figures 4 and 5).

One can observe an additional point in Figure 5 concerning the relationship between the residuals and fitted values. Note, autocorrelation also known as serial correlation, is the correlation of an observation or value in a time series with itself at different points in time. From the plot of residuals versus the Originals, one easily observes the pattern in the plot indicating that autocorrelation is present. If autocorrelation was not present, we would see that the plot would have no pattern. Durbin-Watson Statistic and other test would show the absence of pattern. Although not shown here, the results are obvious from Figures 4 and 5 [21].

Conclusion

The study included a thorough data analysis using modern analytics and exploratory data analysis to permit us to ascertain aspects of the Tokyo (Japan) Stock Index to determine reactions to claims of researchers in previous years. Like any stock exchange, Tokyo's stock prices change from period to period and do not fluctuate in the same manner from decade to decade. The ability to predict future prices of Tokyo securities is related to other Asia-Pacific economies as well as its trading partners in North America, Europe and other parts of the world. The analytics included an exhaustive analysis of data to determine if long memory modeling was recommended by the analysis for predicting future events and economic factors that genuinely influence prices on the Japanese equity Market. Earlier studies did suggest reasons for the difficulty in predicting Japanese stock prices including an exhaustive one measuring the permanent and temporary

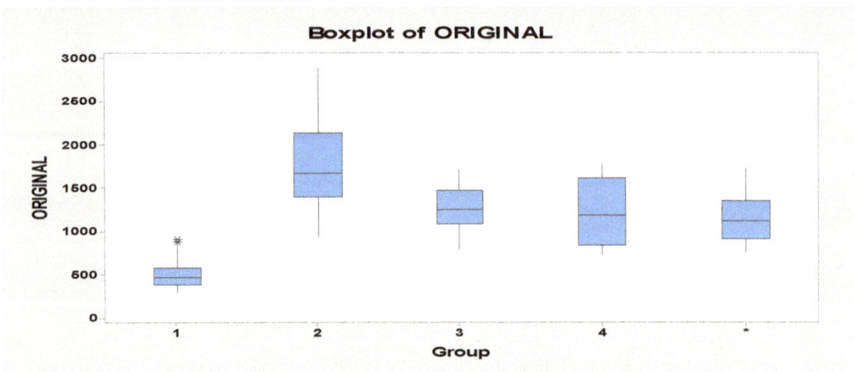

Figure 3: Box plot of original.

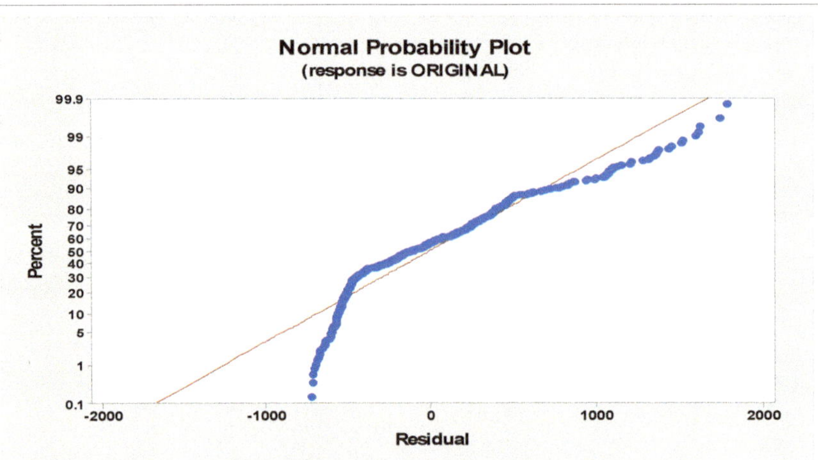

Figure 4: Normal probability plot.

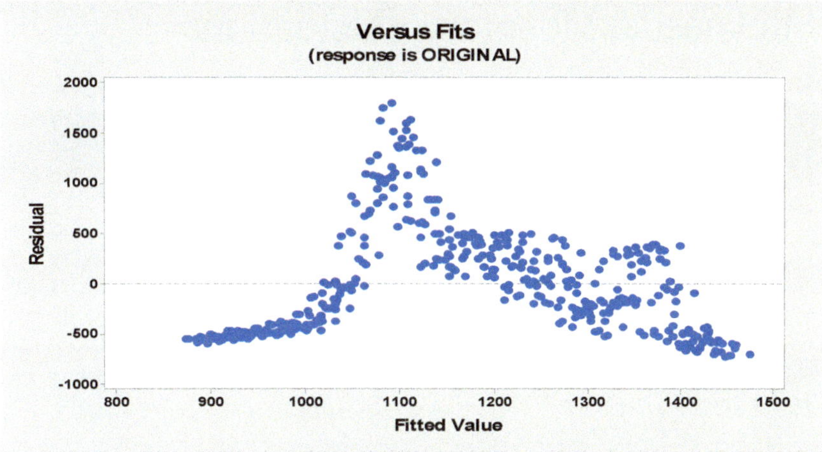

Figure 5: Versus Fits.

components in Japanese stock prices of individual firms. The 'bubbles" in Japanese security prices concluded by others earlier are given greater support from this study. Lessons for other Asia-Pacific economies are subject to similar activity as Japan when study other Pacific Basin economies.

References

1. Kang JK, Stulz R (2000) Do Banking Shocks Affect Borrowing Firm Performance? An Analysis of the Japanese Experience. Journal of Business 73: 1-23.
2. Morck R, Nakamura M (1999) Banks and Corporate Control in Japan. Journal of Finance 54: 319-339.
3. Peek J, Rosengren E (2005) Unnatural Selection: Perverse Incentives and the Misallocation of Credit in Japan. American Economic Review 95: 1144-1166.
4. Fukuda S, Nakamura J (2010) Why did 'zombie' firms recover in Japan? The World Economy 34: 1124-1137.
5. Hamao Y, Xu Y (2007) Unique Symptoms of Japanese Stagnation: An Equity Market Perspective. Journal of Money Credit and Banking 39: 1538-4616.
6. Bayoumi T, Collyns C (2000) Post-Bubbles Blues: How Japan Responded to Asset Price Collapse, International Monetary Fund.
7. Ray K, Jarrett JE, Chen S (1997) Identifying Permanent and Temporary Components in Japanese Stock Prices. Financial Engineering and the Japanese Markets 4: 233-256.
8. Nagayasu J (2003) The Efficiency of the Japanese Equity Market. International Monetary Fund. IMF Working Papers.
9. Agiakloglou C, Newbold P, Wohar M (1993) Bias in an Estimator of the Fractional Difference Parameter. Journal a/f Time Series Analysis 14: 235-246.
10. Richard BT, (1996) Long Memory Processes and Fractional Integration in Econometrics. Journal of Econometrics 73: 5-59.
11. Richard BT, Bollerslev T, Mikkelsen HO (1996) Fractionally Integrated Generalized Autoregressive Conditional Heteroskedasticity. Journal of Econometrics 74: 3-30.
12. Barkoulas JT, Baum CF, Travlos N (2000) Long Memory in the Greek Stock Market. Applied Financial Economics 10: 177-184.
13. Tim B, Mikkelsen HO (1996) Modeling and Pricing Long Memory in Stock Market Volatility. Journal of Econometrics 73: 151-184.
14. Andrew LW (1991) Long-Term Memory in Stock Market Prices. Econometrica 59: 1279-1313.
15. Andrew LW (1997) Fat Tails, Long Memory, and the Stock Market since the 1960s. Economic Notes 26: 219-252.
16. Mills TC (1993) Is There Long-Term Memory in UK Stock Returns? Applied Financial Economics. 3: 303-306.
17. Sadique S, Silvapulle P, Li X (2001) Long-Term Memory in Stock Market Returns: International Evidence. International Journal of Finance and Economics 6: 59-67.
18. Davidson J, Li X (2015) Strict stationarity, persistence and volatility forecasting in ARCH (∞) processes. Journal of Empirical Finance 9.
19. Yi S, Ho KY (2015) Long memory and regime switching: A simulation study on the Markov regime-switching ARFIMA model. Journal of Banking and Finance 61: S189-S204.
20. Chambers J, Cleveland W, Kleiner B, Tukey P (1983) Graphical Methods for Data Analysis, Wadsworth.
21. Jarrett J (1987) Business Forecasting Methods Performance? An Analysis of the Japanese Experience. Journal of Business 73: 1-23.

Investigation on Keynesian Monetary Fluctuations

Byung Woo K*

Korea National University ofTransportation (KNUT), Korea

Abstract

We examined money-output regression (St. Louis equation) considering econometric problem, macroeconomic theory, and policy implications. Our results reveal that increases in money affects real variables like output over a few quarters. These results ascertain Keynesian macroeconomic view that price-wage rigidity cause output to respond to nominal shocks like shifts in money demand.

Out derivation adds contribution to the original empirical results with regard to; endogeneity of money, lags from monetary shocks on output, and serial correlation in output disturbances (persistence), and fundamental equilibrium relationship (co-integration), etc.

Keywords: St. Louis equation; Real business-Keynesian theories; Structural VAR; IS-MP model

JEL Classification: E32, O30

Introduction

Keynesian economic theory assumes that there is rigidity in price and wage [1]. Hence, we need to know aggregate supply to determine output level. In this model, monetary disturbances have real effects on employment and output. In contrast, real-business cycle models argue that purely monetary disturbances have no real effects [2]. One of the methods to determine which is right is famous St. Louis equation (Anderson and Jordan, 1968).

Friedman and Schwartz [3] analyzed the sources of movements in the money and concluded that financial development is main source of fluctuations of money rather than real developments. Blanchard and Quah [4] show that aggregate demand shock in money supply equation has transitory effect on output in contrast to the fact that supply shock has permanent effect. Cecchtti and Rich (2001) presented a structural VAR that provides two-equation model of inflation and output. They calculated the sacrifice ratio, which is the amount of decrease in GDP for disinflationary policy. This was used to study the long-run real effects of monetary policy.

In classical economists, money plays only the role of determining the price level. It cannot affect real variables like output. This phenomenon is called as the neutrality of money. Money determines aggregate demand, but not production, since output (aggregate supply) is fixed at the full employment level. New classical economists including real-business fluctuation theory also has the same view. In contrast, Keynesian economists argue that money affects output through transmission mechanism.

In this study, we investigate these issues with regard to output regression method. The following questions should be answered to determine the existence of real effects of money stock from St. Louis equation estimation. This equation is important in that it is important to know the actual effect of monetary policy in boosting the economy. Since 2008 global financial crisis, worldwide recession caused the government to think on appropriate instrument for stabilizing the national economy.

First, does causation run from money to output? Full understanding for monetary policy requires the path through which output and money affect each other including transmission mechanism.

Second, what are the determinants of monetary policy? Policy may be preemptive (discretionary) or of rule.

Third, we should consider the shift of money demand due to deregulation and financial innovation. In 1980s, financial innovation affected money demand with regard to transaction costs, etc.

Fourth, are there any other sophisticated statistical methods than ordinary regression? Recently, various econometric models like error correction, GARCH, and polynomial distributed lagged model, etc., have been developed rapidly.

Sixth, we solve several econometric problems related with money-output regression like St. Louis equation. These are problems of autocorrelation, endogeneity, omitted variables and reverse causation (Cooley and LeRoy, 1985).

We compare macroeconomic structures of the economies through comparison of estimation results. Our research is mainly based on graduate textbook level like Romer [5]. Figure 1 shows the growth of money and output in graph. Money stock seems to be procyclical and leading variable. It is well known that M1 is procyclical and leading in Korea. Its volatility is about three times higher than that of GDP. M1 includes cash, demand deposit, MMDA (money market deposit account) and MMF (money market fund).

Recently, Federal Reserve performed QE (quantitative easing) policy for providing liquidity for markets and its tapering. In general, short-run stabilization of macroeconomy in most countries is performed by monetary policy rather than fiscal policy. We summarize the aspects of monetary policy in brief. *Fisher equation*, which shows the relation between interest rate and inflation, is expressed as follows; $R=r+\pi(e)$.

Inflation coming from the increase of money stock in short-run is called *liquidity effect*. It lowers nominal interest rates in negative

***Corresponding author:** ByungWoo K, Korea National University of Transportation (KNUT), 72 DaehangNo, ChungJu, Korea-380-702, E-mail: byungw@cjnu.ac.kr

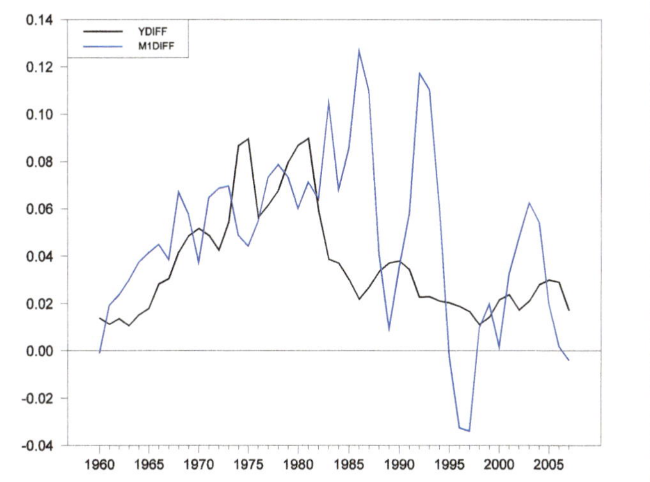

Figure 1: Growth in M1 and GDP in the U.S.

direction. But, in long run, the change in money stock affects nominal rates one-for-one; *Fisher effect*. We assume that real interest rate is unaffected by inflation. But, if we allow the real interest rate to change, then liquidity effects also imply the real rates being able to decrease.

Monetarist Friedman argues that the increase in money stock causes the nominal income to increase responsively. We want to know how much the real income to increase in response to monetary shocks. Neutrality of money asserts that one-time increase in nominal money stock doesn't affect the real sector variables.

Monetary-business cycle theory presents the mechanism through which monetary shock affects output. It emphasizes the misperception of workers, which leads to the illusion between real and nominal wages.

Econometric Model of Monetary Policy

Interest rates, output and monetary policy

First, we construct IS-MP diagram. [5]

Y=C(Y-T)+I(r)+G

M/P=L(r+πe, Y) (2-1)

In this simple model, money is considered as high-powered money, that is, the sum of currency and reserves. We can analyze the mechanism through which money affects the interest rate and output.

The second equation shows the equilibrium condition in the money (financial) market. It expresses inflation as a function of the money stock.

P=M/L(R, Y)

If there is permanent increase in money growth, the price level grows at the same rate. Although real interest rate is constant in short-run, nominal rate shows the path changing after some pattern. Main determinant of inflation is money growth. The fluctuation of nominal interest rate comes from expected inflation component. Short-term variation of real rate is limited. Meanwhile, if price is incompletely flexible, effects on nominal rate is important.

In this study, we mainly study the paths of output and nominal interest rate after IS-MP macroeconomic model. We follow the response path of output and nominal rate due to increase in money.

Distributed lags (DL); policy analysis

We use structural VAR for estimating the effects of money on GDP. This model overcomes the disadvantage of reduced VAR, among which the depletion of theoretical component is most serious. So many economic researches are based on this model [2].

First, we examine the relationships between monetary changes and business cycle. The following results show that monetary disturbances implies future boom in the economy.

$$y_t = f(x_t, x_{t-1}, x_{t-2}, \ldots) \qquad (2\text{-}2)$$

where x: M1, y: real GDP

Data used in regression are money and output in the U.S. during 1947-2007.

A natural test of real business vs. Keynesian theories was performed by Anderson and Jordan (1968). This regression of output growth on money growth is known as St. Louis equation.

This specification is called finite distributed lags (FDLs) in econometrics. The sum of the coefficients on the current and two lagged values of money growth are 0.16, with a standard error of 0.07. It means that 1% increase in the money stock is associated with (1/6) increase in output over the two quarters later.

It is important to note that in the presence of autocorrelation, OLS estimator is no longer best. It means that hypothesis testing can be misleading in St. Louis equation.

Second degree PDL takes the form:

$$Y = \Sigma(a + bx + c^{x^2})\,X$$

We estimated delay multipliers and drawn their graph in Figure 2. It seems to coincide with the estimates for DL model (Tables 1 and 2).

We use VAR for defining Granger no causality (strong exogeneity) of money, when lagged values of M do not provide information about the conditional mean of Y.

$$E\left[Y\,(t)\mid Y\,(t-1)\,M\,(t-1)\,M\,(t-2)\ldots\right] = E\left[Y\,(t)\mid Y\,(t-1)\right]$$

The test for this no causality is performed for testing zero coefficients using F-test.

Vector autoregression (VAR); policy analysis

We use structural VAR for estimating the effects of money on GDP. This model overcomes the

Second, Let's see the standard form of reduced VAR.

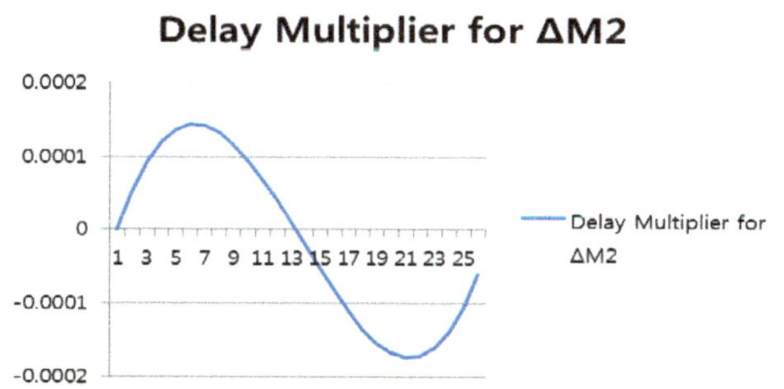

Figure 2: Delay multiplier in polynomial lags model: St. Louis Equation.

OLS	
Null Hypothesis : The following coefficients are zero (non causality)	
ΔM1	**Lag(s) 0 to 2**
F(3,196)	2.0 with significance level 0.11
Summary of linear combination of coefficients(interim multiplier)	
ΔM1	**Lag(s) 0 to 2**
Value	0.15
Standard error	0.07
Durbin-Watson statistic	1.3
t-statistic	2.2
Signif level	0.02**
GLS considering autocorrelation (Cochrane-Orcutt procedure)	
Null Hypothesis : The following coefficients are zero (non causality)	
M1DIFF	**Lag(s) 0 to 2**
F(3,194)	3.56 with significance level 0.01
Summary of linear combination of coefficients(interim multiplier)	
M1DIFF	**Lag(s) 0 to 2**
Value	0.22
Standard error	0.09
t-statistic	2.31
Signif level	0.02**

Table 1: Causality in finite distributed lags model with and without autocorrelation: St. Louis Equation.

Exogeneity of nominal variables (M2 P)
Log determinants: 20.8 21.4
Chi-squared(24)=86.6 with significance level 0.00
Null hypothesis: The following coefficients are zero ΔM2 Lag 0 to 12
F(13,126)=1.83 with significance level 0.04

Table 2: Reduced form VAR model; Exogeneity.

$$y_t = A_1 y_{t-1} + \ldots + A_p y_{t-p} + Bx_t + \epsilon_t \qquad (2\text{-}3)$$

The structural error is obtained from linear transformation of reduced form error. If we transform the notation of the structural error into u and reduced form error into e:

$$A\,e_t = B\,u_t$$

Main advantage of structural VAR is that we can impose so many restrictions corresponding to theory (for example, supply side does not affect demand side in macroeconomy). The main idea is that we can overcome reduced form VAR devoided of structural or theoretical component. Economists made assumptions about the conduct of policy that allow the estimates of VAR to be mapped into policy's impact. These structural VARs were pioneered by Sims [6], Bernanke etc. Cecchtti and Rich (2001) presented a structural VAR for analyzing disinflationary policies of the Fed on output.

We can see this problem from different side:

$$y_t + \beta_1 x_t = \alpha_1 y_{t-1} + \alpha_2 x_{t-1} + e_t^y$$
$$x_t + \beta_2 y_t = \alpha_3 y_{t-1} + \alpha_4 x_{t-1} + e_t^x$$

structural VAR, e is not observed, but should be identified from observed reduced form error (or residuals).

$$y_t = \delta_1 y_{t-1} + \delta_2 x_{t-1} + v_t^y$$
$$x_t = \delta_3 y_{t-1} + \delta_4 x_{t-1} + v_t^x$$

: reduced form VAR

$$B = \begin{bmatrix} 1 & \beta_1 \\ \beta_2 & 1 \end{bmatrix}; \quad A = \begin{bmatrix} \alpha_1 & \alpha_2 \\ \alpha_3 & \alpha_4 \end{bmatrix}; \quad E = \begin{bmatrix} e_t^y \\ e_t^x \end{bmatrix}$$

$$C = B^{-1}A, \quad V = B^{-1}E$$

Identification condition is: B=I

We use this model for estimating impulse response function of GDP for the shock of the change in monetary aggregate. We used monthly data set from BEA website for the U.S. economy. Variables include real GDP(Y), consumption(C), physical investment (I), government purchases (G), money stock (M1) and inflation rate (P) from 1948 to 2007 (Figure 3).

We can approach more wide issues at this stage. First, we can construct AD-AS model with structural VARs as [4]. They do not consider explicitly the effects on output of money growth. Second, money-inflation relation is also important. We can decompose the effects of monetary policy into on output and the price level separately. Cecchtti and Rich (2001) presented a structural VAR that presents two-equation model of inflation and output. In structural VAR, the equation system is written by: [Δ (output), Δ (inflation)] the components of the disturbance (innovation) are identified as shocks to AS (aggregate supply) and AD, respectively. To calculate the impact of structural shocks, they use the VMA (vector moving average) form. Blanchard and Fischer [2] showed that aggregate demand shocks caused by changes in the money in the face of incomplete adjustment of wages and prices have transitory effects on output. Relative importance of aggregate demand and supply shocks are main theme of macroeconomics.

Aggregate demand and supply disturbances [4].

Macroeconomic model

$$y(t) = M(t) - P(t) + a.\theta(t),$$
$$y(t) = N(t) + \theta(t),$$
$$P(t) = W(t) - \theta(t),$$
$$W(t) = W \mid \{E_{t-1}N(t) = \bar{N}\}.$$

Y: output M: money P: price level θ: productivity

N: employment W: nominal wage

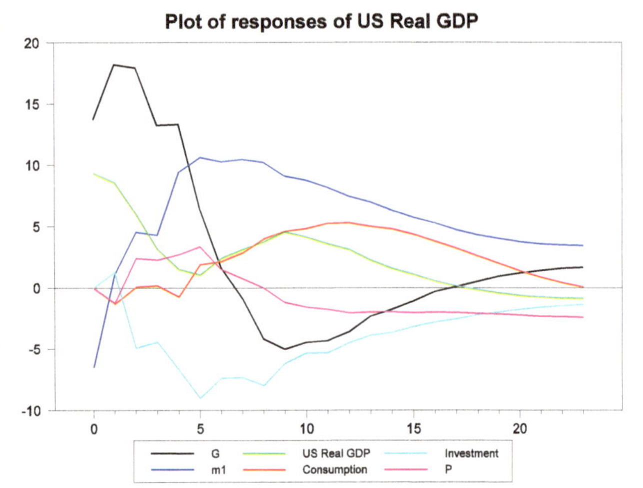

Figure: 3 Impulse response from reduced form (Ordering: G M1 Y C I P).

Sophisticated Statistical Evidence

In this study, we investigate the following issues:

- First, does causation run from money to output?

We performed exogeneity test using F and t tests. The lagged variables of money are significant at 5% level. The hypothesis of endogeneity is rejected at high level of significance. Our causality tests show that causation run bilaterally. King and Plosser [7] argue that when firms increase their production, they may increase money holdings. Measures of money, such as M1, are set by Federal Reserves. We can think that they increase high-powered money when there occurs economic boom. In addition, increase in money stock boosts economy through transmission mechanism. There are two different ways by which money affects aggregate demand; Keynesian vs. Monetarist. We need to know the accurate lags through which money and output affect each other. Our exogeneity tests show that the causation between money and output runs bilaterally. Romer [5] argues that there is possibility of causation from output to money, but we got empirical evidence for this argument (Table 3).

- Second, what are the determinants of monetary policy?

We can choose measures of monetary policy other than M1. The choice is Federal Funds Rate. Finite distributed lags model shows that interim multiplier has significant negative value. In addition to output, we can regard the determinants of policy as inflation. Karenken and Solow (1963) argue that we can observe fluctuations in money and stable output, if Federal Reserve's efforts to stabilize the economy are successful. Kuttner [8] observed that Federal Reserve's open market operations are associated with nominal interest rates. FRB's target is associated with actual funds rate, which shows strong evidence of causality from monetary policy to short-term interest rates. We found other factor, interest rate rather than money that influences aggregate output (Table 4 and Figure 4).

- Third, we should consider the shift of money demand stemming from deregulation and financial innovation.

According to Stock and Watson (2004), consumption smoothing due to financial innovation contributed to the Great Moderation. This affects interest rate, prices and output through shift of money demand. The great moderation is said to occur in the midtime of 1980s. Our Chow test shows that there is no equivalence of equations over two periods. This means that there have been a series of large shifts in the demand for money over the past three decades. Keynesian theory asserts that if there occurs positive money demand shocks, there is negative relation between money and output. That is, when Fed does not intervene in money market, increase in money stock and high interest rate coexists.

Exogeneity of real variables (GDP C I G) Chi-squared (24)=62.2 with significance level 0.00**
Exogeneity of nominal variables (P M2) Chi-squared (6)=23.4 with significance level 0.00**

Table 3: Exogeneity tests of real vs. nominal variables.

Summary of linear combination of coefficients	
FFED	**Lag(s) 0 to 12**
Value	-4.23e-04
Standard error	2.42e-04
t-statistic	-1.75
Signif level	0.08*

Table 4: Effects of federal funds rate on output.

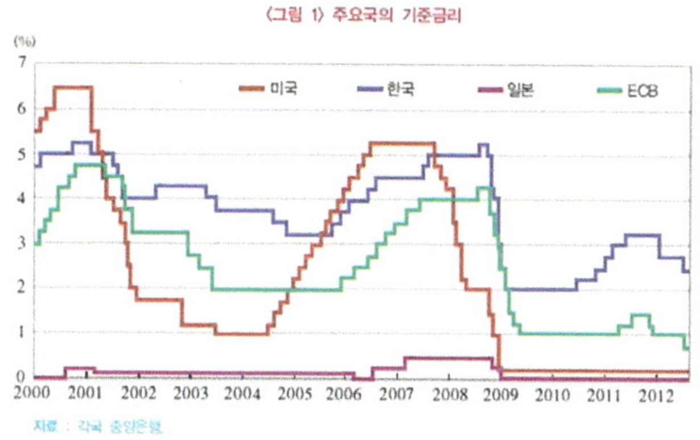

Note) 1 Cheong et al. (2015) Macroeconomics (Korean)

2 Red lines are for the US.

Figure 4: Trend of federal funds rate.

Korean case of money demand shift is summarized by Kim [9].

- Fourth, due to money demand shifts, estimation is sensitive to sample period, and measure of money.

We examined this argument by estimating equations through different sample periods and M1, M2, respectively. We know that changing measure of money from M1 to M2 causes the estimates in St. Louis equation to vary in significant amount.

- Fifth, is there any other sophisticated statistical method than ordinary regression?

Original St. Louis equation suffered from omitted variables, money-demand shifts and causation, etc. (Cooley and LeRoy, 1985). Money-output regression may suffer from endogeneity problem. In this case, OLS estimators are inconsistent. They do not converge to the true value even in the large sample.

Proper instrument variable should be correlated with money growth and not with the other factors that affect real output. We selected physical investment and Federal Funds Rate. Two-stage least squares estimation reduces to larger estimate than that of OLS. In finite distributed lags (FDLs) the sum of the coefficients on the current and two lagged values (over two months) of money growth is 0.16. It means that 1% increase in the money stock is associated with (1/6) increase in output over the two months later in contrast to 0.22 in GLS method. It is important to note that in the presence of autocorrelation, OLS estimator is no longer best. It means that hypothesis testing can be misleading in St. Louis equation. Allpying GLS cause the (estimated) standard error 0.9 to decrease to 0.7 [10-13].

Structural VARs allow the estimate of VAR parameters to be mapped into the results of policy impact estimates. We can set VAR model which allow causality from money, but not from output to money. This may envision the view that money demand cannot be shifted by short-term disturbances. In future study, we may use Marcov Switching model for ascertaining the shifts of the money demand function (Table 5) [14].

- Sixth, the impacts of monetary policy on financial markets are important.

Now, we review the Federal Reserve's Funds Rate Target more specifically. A very short-term rate, the Federal Funds rate is charged

Chow test for difference in moderation	
F(3,117)=9.60 with significance level 0.00 ΔY/ΔM1{0 to 24} 1950-1983 1984-2010	F(3,133)=19.9 with significance level 0.00 ΔY/ΔM2{0 to 24} 1950-1983 1984-2010

Table 5: Effects of financial innovation in 1980s on equation.

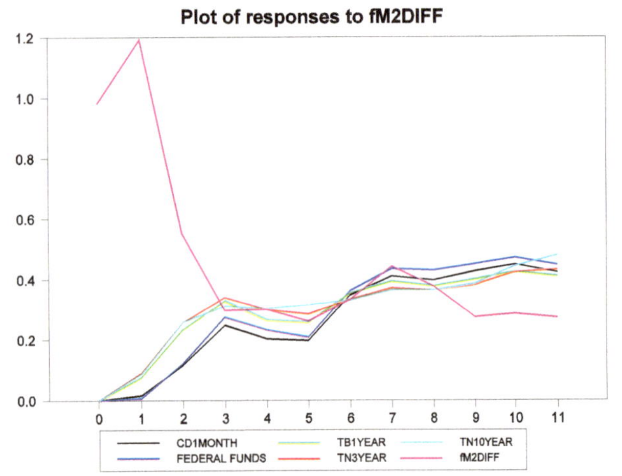

Figure 5: Effects of increase in money stock on nominal interest rates.

on another bank on one-day loans of reserves by one bank. Cook and Hahn (1989) confirmed that open-market operations affected relative prices like nominal interest rates [15].

Liquidity effect refers to the decrease in nominal and real interest rate in the short-run due to the increase in the growth rate of money stock. Fisher effect refers to one-to-one reflection in the nominal interest rate to the change in inflation. Our econometric analyses show that there are differences in the amount of the sum of liquidity and Fisher effects. Permanent increase in money increases short-term interest rate permanently. This coincides with impulse response function.

Now, let's see the effects of money growth on short and long term nominal interest rates.

$$(1+r_{0,2}) = \sqrt{(1+r_{0,1})(1+r^{e}_{1,1})} \quad \Leftrightarrow \quad r_{0,2} \approx \frac{r_{0,1}+r^{e}_{1,1}}{2} \qquad (2\text{-}4)$$

Where r_{ij} denotes return of j-period bond at time i.

Consider an investor who decides how to invest fund over the next two periods. Interest rate on long-term bond equals the average of (expected) rates on short-term bonds over two periods. This relationship implies that monetary expansion is likely to reduce short-term rates but increase long-term ones [5]. Impulse response graphs show that money growth increases both short and long term rates. This can be explained by the fact that liquidity effect for short-term interest rate is relatively small (Figure 5) [16].

Cook and Hahn (1989) investigated monetary policy (changing FFRs target)'s impact on bond interest rate of diverse maturities. They found that money growth increases nominal interest rates at all horizons (Table 6).

We also replicate Cook and Hahn (1989)'s investigation substituting FFRs target for money growth. We found similar significant coefficient estimates at high levels of significance. This supports the original idea of them (Table 7).

- Seventh, we can examine long-run equilibrium relationships between (real) money stock and output.

This supplements the previous literatures that focused on the short-term relationships between variables.

If shocks are not correlated and have no contemporaneous interactions, the identification and interpretation of impulse response and forecast error variance are straightforward. At first, we performed tests for stationarity of series (Tables 8 and 9) [17-19].

The form of econometric model analyzing long-run relation is as follows. Estimated cointegrating vector (long-run relationship) is:

$$\begin{aligned}\Delta(lnM_t - lnP_t) &= C + a\,(\Delta lnY_t) + bSR_t + cLR_t + d(lnM_{t-1} - lnP_{t-1} - lnY_{t-1})\Delta(REALM - INFLA)_t \\ &= C + a\,(\Delta LOGGDP) + bFEED + cFCM10 + d(REALM - INFLA - LOGGDP)_{t-1}\end{aligned} \qquad (2\text{-}5)$$

Estimated error correction coefficient is significant, but does not ascertain stability (has positive sign) (Tables 10 and 11).

2SLS Estimation	
Summary of linear combination of coefficients	
M1DIFF	**Lag(s) 0 to 2**
Value	0.22
Standard error	0.07
t-statistic	2.99
Signif level	0.00

Table 6: Effects of money stock on output: Endogeneity.

Summary of linear combination of coefficients on;			
M2DIFF		**Lag(s) 0 to 12**	
Five nominal interest rates		Federal funds rate	
1-Month		Certificates of deposit(CD)	
1-Year		Treasury bill	
3-Year		Treasury notes	
10-Year		Treasury notes	
Value	1.65	t-statistic	7.13
Standard error	0.23	Signif level	0.00**
Value	1.45	t-statistic	5.93
Standard error	0.24	Signif level	0.00**
Value	1.52	t-statistic	7.62
Standard error	0.19	Signif level	0.00**
Value	1.47	t-statistic	7.85
Standard error	0.18	Signif level	0.00**
Value	1.42	t-statistic	s8.01
Standard error	0.17	Signif level	0.00**

Table 7: Impact of monetary changes on nominal interest rates (Term-Structure).

Regression Run From 1960:04 to 2000:04 Observations 162 With intercept with 6 lags on the differences
Dickey-Fuller unit root test, Series REALM T-test statistic -1.99806
Dickey-Fuller Unit root test, Series LOGGDP T-test statistic -0.45701
Dickey-Fuller Unit root test, Series INFLA T-test statistic -2.73634
Dickey-Fuller Unit root test, Series FFED T-test statistic -2.71089
Dickey-Fuller Unit root test, Series FCM10 T-test statistic -1.69772
Critical values: 1%=-3.463 5%=-2.875 10%=-2.574

Table 8: Tests for stationarity and cointegration.

Likelihood based analysis of cointegration Unrestricted eigenvalues and -T log(1-lambda)					
Rank	EigVal	Lambda-max	Trace	Trace-95%	LogL
0					1608.2437
1	0.2629	49	121.2527	76	1632.9509
2	0.1583	27	71.8383	53	1646.9117
3	0.1337	23	43.9167	35	1658.5396
4	0.0779	13	20.6609	20	1665.1106
5	0.0454	7	7.5188	9	1668.8700

Table 9: Estimation of cointegration model.

Coeff		Std error	T-stat	Signif
EC1{1}	0.0016	0.000	3.036	0.002**

Table 10: Estimation of error-correction term.

Decomposition of variance for series REALM						
Step	Std error	REALM	LOGGDP	INFLA	FFED	FCM10
1	0.00622146	100.000	0.000	0.000	0.000	0.000
2	0.01249448	87.860	2.657	0.182	6.484	2.816
35	0.12321185	9.607	11.636	10.764	6.414	1.578
36	0.12567639	69.555	11.275	11.048	6.577	1.545

Table 11: Decomposition of forecast error variance decomposition.

For VEC model, explanatory power for dependent variable (real money stock) is strongest in output, then next inflation.

Summary and Conclusion

In this study, we investigated the following issues.

- First, we reexamined St. Louis equation (output-money regression) incorporating sophisticated econometric issues.

Results seem to coincide with previous literatures, but we can find some new insights into monetary macroeconomic policy.

- Second, hypothesis tests for real vs. Keynesian fluctuation theories could be tested by advanced econometric methods. This can contribute to deriving appropriate policy implications from past data sets.

Our improvements can be summarized: smaller standard error in GLS, applying distributed lags and polynomial distributed lags models rather than OLS in St. Louis equation, deriving impulse response of GDP (output) to monetary shocks directly rather than the estimate for the sum of coefficients, finding structural break in M-Y relationships due to financial innovation, and replication the analyses for term-structure for changes in monetary policy.

We can approach more wide issues in future research. First, we can construct AD-AS model with structural VARs as Blanchard and Quah [4]. They do not consider explicitly the effects on output of money growth. Second, we can modify money-output regression under fixed or floating exchange rates separately. Third, money-inflation relation is also important. We can decompose the effects of monetary policy into on output and the price level separately. Fourth, we can search natural experiments for determining the effects of monetary shocks. The death of the president of FRB of NY in 1928, brought monetary changes.

References

1. Romer C, Romer D (2000) Federal Reserve Information and the Behavior of Interest Rates. American Economic Review 90: 429-457.
2. Blanchard O, Fischer S (1989) Lectures on Macroeconomics. The MIT Press, Cambridge, London.
3. Friedman M, Schwarz A (1963) A Monetary History of the United States 1867-1960, Princeton University Press.
4. Blanchard O, Quah D (1989) The Dynamic Effects of Aggregate Demand and Supply Disturbances. American Economic Review 79: 655-673.
5. Romer D (2006) Advanced Macroeconomics (4thedn.) McGraw Hill.
6. Sims C (1986) Are Forecasting Models Usable for Policy Analysis? Federal Reserve Bank of Minneapolis Quarterly Review 10: 2-16.
7. King RG, Plosser C (1984) Money, Credit and Prices in a Real Business Cycle. American Economic Review 74: 363-380.
8. Kuttner KN (2001) Monetary Policy Surprises and Interest rates. Journal of Monetary Economics 47: 523-544.
9. Kim B (2014) Estimation of Money Demand Function of South Korea Considering Regime Switching. Chinese Business Review 13: 740-756.
10. Aghion P, Angleletos M, Banerjee A, Manova K (2005) Volatility and Growth: Financial Development and the Cyclical Behavior of the Composition of Investment. Harvard University.
11. Aghion P, Howitt P (2009) The Theory of Economic Growth. MIT Press, London.
12. Campbell J, Mankiw NG (1987) Permanent and Transitory Components in Macroeconomic Fluctuations. American Economic Review Proceedings.
13. Campbell J (1994) Inspecting the Mechanism: An analytical approach to the stochastic Growth. Journal of Monetary Economics 33: 463-506.
14. Christiano L, Eichenbaum M, Evans C (2003) Nominal Regidities and the Dynamic Effects of a Shock to Monetary Policy. Journal of Political Economy.
15. Cochrane J (1988) How Big is the Random Walk in GNP. Journal of Political Economy 96: 893-920
16. Cogley T (1990) International Evidence on the Size of the Random Walk in Output. Journal of Political Economy 98: 3.
17. Fatás A (2000) Do Business Cycles Cast Long Shadows? Short-Run Persistence and Economic Growth. Journal of Economic Growth 5: 147-162.
18. Nelson C, Plosser C (1982) Trends and Random Walks in Macroeconomic Time Series.
19. Prescott E (1986) Theory Ahead of Business Cycle Measurement. Federal Reserve Bank of Minneapolis Quarterly Review 10: 9-22.

Analysis of the Organizational Eco-Systemic Change in a Cooperative Society of Fishing Production

Vargas-Hernandez JG[1]*, Echeagaray JES[2] and Echeagaray TIS[2]

[1]University Center for Economic and Managerial Sciences, University of Guadalajara, Periferico Norte 799, Mexico
[2]Facultad de Ciencias Economico Administrativas de Mazatlán, Universidad Autonoma de Sinaloa, Av. Universidad s/n Ciudad Universitaria, Mexico

Abstract

This work aims to analyze the organizational change that has taken the Cooperative Society of Fishing Production "The Patole", S.C. of R.L. de C.V. It is assumed that as a result of having implemented systems theory, it has improved its organizational development and thus fulfillment of its objectives, being a source of employment and income for the cooperative. The main method used in this analysis is observing partners, gathering factual information and indicators and supported by the application of a Likert scale questionnaire. It is concluded that systems theory is related to the cooperative to be beneficial in the organizational development of the company.

Keywords: Organizational change; Fisheries production cooperatives; Systems theory

Introduction

In this twenty-first century businesses must try to maintain positioning in a competitive market. This is due to competition in the sector, rising inputs, climatic change, changing consumer mindset, etc. Companies are economic entities generating jobs and wealth for their owners.

The United Mexican States have a wealth of renewable and nonrenewable natural resources. In the fishing sector companies primarily engaged in the exploitation of marine products are cooperative societies. Cooperatives are supported entities in the cooperative philosophy that seeks the common good of the members, their families and society in general. The fishing sector is part of the productive sectors that support the economy of Mexico. Therefore, cooperatives are important to be sources of employment and income for their partners, families and society in general.

Cooperative societies to be part of the fisheries sector which in turn is part of the Mexican economy are systems. That is, the cooperative is a system within several other systems work together in social and economic benefit of the country. Herein lays the importance of the study of systems thinking in the Cooperative Society of Fishing Production "The Patole", S.C. of R.L. de C.V.

Background of the Problem

The current global environment is extremely competitive. Countries should support businesses to continue working in the market. Similarly, countries should use natural resources wisely so that future generations do not lack of these resources. The United Mexican States have a vast amount of resources that should use properly the good of its citizens.

Mexico has a land area of 1,964.375 square kilometers, corresponding 1,959.248 continental surface and 5,127 to islands. The extent of coastal is 11,122 square kilometers [1]. Marine species that inhabit the coasts are: anchovy, hake, squid, red crab, red snapper, grouper, sierra, sardines, tuna and shrimp [2]. The country's natural resources are outstanding and if properly exploited food and generate wealth for the population.

The state of Sinaloa is one of the leading producers of white shrimp (Penaeus vannamei). In 2014 according to National Institute of Statistics and Geography economic units in the country engaged in fishing were 4,230.745 [3]. Also it argues that farmed shrimp was 7,447.104 tons representing $507, 716.640 [4]. The shrimp was captured in estuaries 940.848 tons representing $62, 575.089. Service Information Agrifood and Fisheries (SIAP) reports in its monthly Bulletins the fish production by State in 2015. Production in the country was 26,617.59 tons and in the state of Sinaloa was 9295.26 [5]. This information shows the importance of the fisheries sector, especially shrimp in Mexico. The main operators of crustacean are cooperatives.

Cooperatives face several challenges to continue working. To name a few are the climatic change, competition, new market demands and environmental protection. It is seen as cooperatives are part of the Mexican and global economic system. This is the case of this article focuses on the case of the Cooperative Society of Fishing Production "The Patole", S.C. of R.L. de C.V. The Patole is a system that is within the economic system of the nation which in turn is part of a larger system the global economic system.

Delimitation of the Problem

This research is an investigation that was necessary to explain how organizational change was necessary at the Cooperative Society of Fishing Production "The Patole", S.C. of R.L. de C.V. in order to attain greater development in production volumes and growth. Plus it is affecting the entity, because a low impact business development in the social context where it is located. Low productivity affects employment generation causing no positive impact on fishing activity and the regional, state and national economy.

Organizational improvement in the cooperative system is crucial to the future of it. Cooperatives are founded figures that promote values such as solidarity and collective benefit. The cooperative philosophy is aimed at obtaining common good that benefits all members. In today's

***Corresponding author:** Vargas-Hernández JG, University Center for Economic and Managerial Sciences. University of Guadalajara, Periferico Norte 799, Mexico
E-mail: jvargas2006@gmail.com, jgvh0811@yahoo.com

competitive environment, it requires that cooperatives continue to be laboring jobs for partners within them. Such is the case study; the Patole is the source of employment for eighteen members and their families.

This study is based on a diagnosis that detected an organizational problem in the cooperative society that poses systemic model implementation to improve the functioning of the Cooperative Society of Fishing Production the Patole S.C. of R. L. of C. V. For the entity reconvenes philosophical principles of mutual assistance and common welfare and generate benefits in the members, their families and society in general.

Historical, Legal and Theoretical Background

The cooperative has its origins in 1844 when Rochdale cooperative, located in the county of Lancashire was founded. It consisted of workers who were weaving flannel together to purchase cheaper price staples [6]. In the late nineteenth century European immigrants brought the cooperative in southern Brazil, Uruguay and Argentina.

In the United Mexican States cooperatives were promoted in 1865 by a group of anarcho-syndicalist leaders. However, it would be until the 1930s when the movement would take shape under the government of President Lazaro Cardenas del Rio. The president support agrarian reform based on cooperatives [7]. Over the decades cooperatives continued their work consumption and production benefiting its members and society in general.

However, the change in society in the last decade of the twentieth century showed that an update was needed in legislation. On August 3, 1994 President Carlos Salinas de Gortari reformed the law and denominating General Law of Cooperative Societies (LGSC), the last update was on 13 August 2009. There is also another law regulating cooperatives in Latin America called Framework Law for Cooperatives in Latin America (LMCAL) that emerged in 1987 and was renovated in 2009. Both laws are in harmony.

The GLCC defines cooperative in its second article as a form of social organization composed of individuals based on common interests and the principles of solidarity, self-help and mutual aid, in order to meet individual and collective needs, through carrying out economic activities of production, distribution and consumption of goods and services.

While LMCAL in his third article defines cooperative as associations of persons united voluntarily to meet their common economic, social and cultural needs through a company owned jointly and managed democratically. They are private legal entities of social interest. The philosophy of mutual help and common benefit of the members of the cooperative is observed. In both laws cooperative principles are presented. In the LGSC in article six is exposed:

I. Freedom of association and voluntary retirement of partners;

II. Democratic administration;

III. III Limitation of interest to some partners' contributions will be agreed if so;

IV. Distribution of income in proportion to the participation of the partners;

V. Promoting cooperative education and education in the solidarity economy;

VI. Participation in cooperative integration;

VII. Respect the individual right of members to belong to any political party or religious association, and

VIII. Promotion of ecological culture.

While LMAL partnership presents it in his article four:

1. Voluntary and open membership;
2. Democratic management by partners;
3. Economic participation of the partners;
4. Autonomy and independence;
5. Education, training and information;
6. Cooperation between cooperatives;
7. Concern for the community.

The GLCC and MAL support the cooperative philosophy and support democracy, freedom and equality of each of its partners. Also education and training, this is done through cooperative education in which the partners motivate children of cooperative members and children of the community to study. Promoting ecological culture is extremely important especially in the issue of climate change that has occurred in recent decades.

As characteristics of cooperatives noted that partners are unlimited and can vary in number, their duration is indefinite, its capital is variable and unlimited, the organization presents political, racial and religious independence, the partners have equal rights and obligations, each partner is entitled to one vote regardless of their contributions and finally the social reserves are non-distributable.

In the LMCAL acts performed by cooperatives are regulated by the cooperative law. Cooperatives can serve external people from them always and when not on more favorable terms that partners and obtained surplus be devoted to cooperative education or reserve fund. Cooperatives can occur in various ways, consumers, associated and mixed without the prevalence of any criteria of classification and in any branch of the economy work [8].

Cooperatives are systems composed of partners who perform work for the benefit of themselves and their families. Therefore the general systems theory will be discussed. Aristotle was the first person to mention systems theory by stating that reality is addressed in general and not studying their parts separately to know their entirety. Rene Descartes in his philosophical book called Discourse on Method for conducting one's reason well and seek truth in science emphasizes the study of phenomena subdividing it into systems to examine the parties and relations between them [9].

System is defined as a set of interrelated parts to achieve certain goals [10]. Von Bertalanffy defines it as a complex organization composed of a combination of parts that constitute an intricate or unitary whole [11]. The Patole cooperative society is a system composed of people, partners who in turn are systems. Therefore this research sought the views of the eighteen cooperators to detect the problem and implement organizational systems theory in the organization.

The systemic model is an integrated model, consisting of parts that come together to achieve organizational objectives. Administrators try to convey to each subordinate how important they are for the system, so the administrator role transform itself to facilitate the achievement of the subordinate through various actions such as training in skills and appropriate behavior, concern true in relationships between people and feedback.

By the side of employees, they respond with mutual recognition of obligations to the cooperative organization. Employees go further than the self-discipline to achieve self-motivation in taking responsibility for their own goals and actions. The model provides individuals to achieve meeting a wide range of higher order needs, such as status, self-esteem, autonomy and personal fulfillment, which can result in the employee passion and commitment to the goals of the organization. The features of this model are extended in the following section [12].

The general systems theory arises from two approaches. The first is to observe the empirical universe and choose certain general phenomena to try to build a theoretical model that is relevant. Consider all systems (phenomena) seeking to reduce it to a more reasonable size. It is observed in the study on population for a given object of study, and researchers reduce the sample size, which is representative and possess the required characteristics.

The second approach sorts hierarchical empirical fields according to the complexity of the organization under review. This approach is more systematic and develops a system within a system. If a large organization is studied, there are sought departments as systems within the main system. In this way, it takes an order and the hierarchy is considered [13]. This article analyzes a case study and for this reason applies the second approach of systems theory.

In turn, there are two kinds of systems: Open systems and closed systems. In closed systems, nothing comes and nothing goes into them, everything happens within the system and communication with the outside is zero. Open systems require their environment to be. Examples of open systems are biological and social systems. Regarding the Ferguson, open systems states [14]:

"Some natural ways are open systems, that is, are involved in a continuous exchange of energy with the environment. A seed, a fertilized egg, a living being, are all open systems. There are also open systems manmade. Prigogine cites the example of a city: absorbs energy from the surrounding area (electricity, raw materials), transforms it into the factories, and returned to the environment."

For Goldfeder, an open system can only exist for the exchange of materials, information and energy with their environment, i.e., it performs the task of importing materials and transforms them to perform their internal maintenance and export the rest [15]. Open systems are registered within a larger system in which society must constantly relate to subsist. Rodriguez and Arnold indicate that systems are defined by a dynamic relationship between inputs (inputs) and outputs (outputs) [16]. The same system is responsible for processing the materials from the environment, for which have internal structure and organization.

Open systems require a balance between what they need to survive and what they cause. The inputs are the input elements whose form is money, materials, people, products, services and political and economic forces of the larger system. The outputs are what produce systems such as roses from a bush, the fruits of the trees, a software of a computer company, i.e., elements that can be inputs to other systems because all systems are interrelated between them to be part of a larger system.

Open systems have nine features mentioned below:

A. Energy imports. Companies are not self-sufficient for that reason need inputs from the medium or supra system.

B. Processing. The system processes the inputs doing work.

C. The product. It is the result of the transformation of inputs. The product is exported to supra system.

D. Cyclic operation. The continued cycle of exchange between the supra system and the system happens when the system continues to send products that serve as inputs to other systems and vice versa.

E. Negative entropy. It is the destructive energy of the system, controlled by importing more energy than necessary in order to store the surplus.

F. Inputs are information, negative feedback and the coding process. The information received to the system helps to understand the supra system and how their actions affect the environment. Negative information announces its faults to correct them. Using coding system will accept or reject the information relevant and necessary for its operation.

G. The system features a stable and constant state supported by entries selected for operation inputs.

H. Differentiation. Systems have specific characteristics that make it different from each other.

I. Equal finality. The system can achieve the ultimate state through different paths and initial states [17].

The Cooperative Society of Fishing Production "The Patole", S.C. of R.L. de C.V., is an open system that performs internal processes of transformation of its product. And it needs the external systems to perform its duties; it could not be closed by requiring others to its proper functioning system.

The general theory of systems avoids duplication of efforts that help the Patole organizational development to be a benefit to partners, its families and society in general [11]. The cooperative theory and systems theory are closely related; while the former seeks the common good of the partners that make up the cooperative the second analyzes the components of the company as a whole. The Patole is studied as an organization of people who are themselves systems. It is expected that following the example of the Patole other relevant sinaloenses cooperatives made organizational changes to increase their efficiency and their processes and obtain profits for their cooperative members, their families and society in general.

The Contextual Framework Patole

The Cooperative Society of Fishing Production S.C. the Patole RL de CV was founded in the late 1970s and derived from a draft collective social benefit, Mr. Jose Natividad Torres Salazar advised by Mr. Enrique Echeagaray Osuna, joined a group of people of Piaxtla de Abajo, San Ignacio, Sinaloa to form a cooperative society to come to jointly support the economy of the participants. The Cooperative Society of Fishing Production "The Patole", S. C. de R.L. of C.V. it was founded in order to help the inhabitants of the community of "Lomas del Mar Piaxtla" San Ignacio, Sinaloa to generate a source of employment because farming was insufficient to meet the needs of their families. This is because the agricultural activity was insufficient to continue being the source of family income.

On June 27, 1980 after completing legal formalities the company registration was obtained. The cooperative obtained the authorization to operate in protected waters, shrimp production, flake and oysters, as well as fishing off the coast of scale and shark. The corporate purpose of the cooperative is to extract, capture and fishing collectively in national and inland waters; as well as conducting sales, transportation and industrialization of the products obtained and aquaculture production of all kinds of shellfish, fish and crustaceans.

The mission of the cooperative is to produce shrimp aquaculture of excellent quality for local, national and international markets, seeking higher levels of profitability, with the highest overall development of the resources of society and especially the human resource and sustainable care of natural resources. Its vision is: The Patole Cooperative Society is an organization that develops a productive activity in the various economic and social fields, with proper management of resources and an efficient and competitive administration.

The cooperative has permission granted by the appropriate authorities of the Ministry of Environment and Natural Resources (SEMARNAT), the National Commission of Aquaculture and Fisheries (CONAPESCA) and the Secretariat of Agriculture, Livestock, Rural Development, Fisheries and Food (SAGARPA). The above government organizations are highly related to the primary sector supra systems fishing activity, Mexican economic system and ecological system.

The Patole has authorized areas that are marshlands called the Tazajal, the Patole, Banderillas and Los Muertos. The importance of Tazajal lies in direct communication that the estuary system has with the sea throughout the year. Its flooded area is three hundred hectares in the rainy season, in low-water period is about fifty hectares. The estuary the Tazajal like the fishing camp is located within the boundaries of the municipalities of San Ignacio and Mazatlan. Then in Figure 1 below a photo of the estuary the Tazajal is shown.

Access by the international road is at number fifteen to forty-eight kilometers from the port of Mazatlan. The route has thirty six kilometers of paved road and dirt road twelve kilometers from 1.5 kilometers away from the town of Mármol, Sinaloa. On the road Maxipista at twenty kilometers from Mazatlan to Culiacan and about ten kilometers of dirt road, as it is shown below in Figure 2.

The Patole is a system composed of sub systems that are the board of directors, the production manager, and the administrator. From the administrator depend on the auxiliary administrative sub systems. While from the production manager depend the accounting and administrative assistant subsystems, wages, cleaning and guard also depend on the systems. The organization is observed in Figure 3. A brief description of the positions was made.

A. Production Manager: It is responsible for the supervision and control of workers responsible for the production process. The manager must make periodic reports to the Assembly members.

B. Administrator: The person who takes control and makes decisions on minor issues in which it is not necessary to call the board. It is supported by an administrative assistant, who helps him in the record of the documents required for their duties.

Figure 1: The fishing camp "The Tazajal". Source: Internal information of the Cooperative Society of Fishing Production the Patole, S.C. of R.L. de C.V.

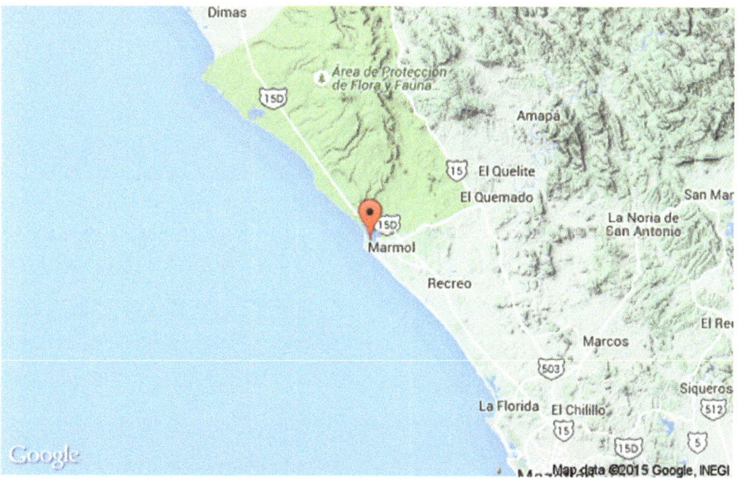

Figure 2: Location of the Cooperative Society The Patole with respect to the surrounding villages and the road network. Source: Google maps.

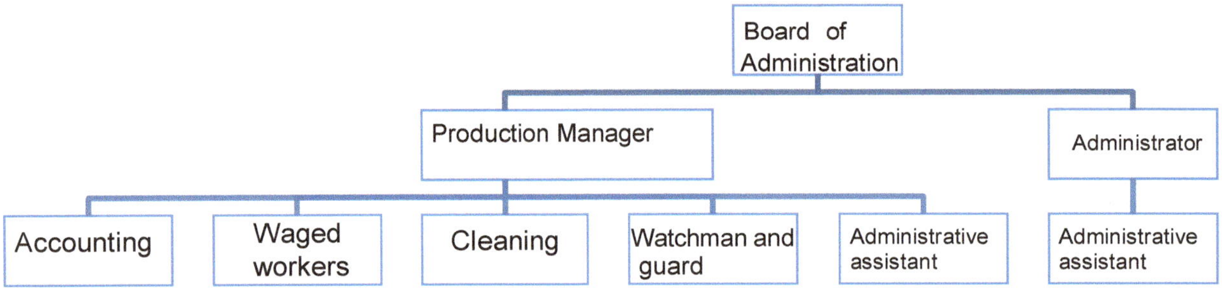

Figure 3: The Cooperative Society of Fishing Production the Patole, S.C. of R.L. de C.V. as a system within the Supra systems: Mexican economic system, primary sector, fishing activity and Mexican Ecological system.Source: Based on data provided by the Cooperative Society of Fishing Production the Patole, S.C. of R.L. de C.

C. Accounting: A person who takes control of accounting and financial records. Accounting manager must prepare monthly reports for the Production Manager.

D. Administrative Assistant. The person to support the production manager in administrative activities that have to do with receiving and selling the product.

E. Cleaning: It will be the person in charge of the cleanup of the plant.

F. Waged workers: Individuals who are responsible for monitoring the crop to harvest the shellfish. Wages serve the product to be ready for sale.

G. Watchman. The person responsible for protecting the safety of the place.

The structure discussed above performs the process of functioning of human resources as follows: The board of directors is the supreme body appointed by the assembly of members and makes decisions based on the reports from the production manager and administrator. The production manager is responsible for taking decisions and the entire production process. Meanwhile the administrator makes minor decisions based on administrative documentation for the best administrative operation of the cooperative.

The production manager and administrator meet to present their reports to the board of directors, who is making the major decisions that benefit the purpose and functioning of society. From the production manager depends hierarchically an administrative assistant and a counter on the first level and second level wages, a night watchman and a person responsible for grooming and cleaning.

The administrative assistant and accountant work together to present a report control of accounting records, financial and receipt and sale of the product is presented. This is done in order that the production manager can make the appropriate decisions to benefit The Patole. Wages, the night watchman and cleaning interact in the process of cultivation until harvest. Workers on wages serve the product to be ready for sale. While the watchman guards the safety of people who work and cleaning and toilet facilities are maintained in good condition. It can be seen that the cooperative turn, society is a system in Mexico's economic supra system in the primary industry supra system fishing activity and the Mexican ecological supra system, as it is shown below in Figure 3.

It can be seen that the cooperative turn, society is a system in Mexico's economic supra system in the primary industry supra system fishing activity and the Mexican ecological supra system, as it is shown in Figure 3. Earlier in the Figure 3 are seen how supra systems relate to the cooperative that is itself a system. From this fact lies the importance of the cooperative, being evident for several reasons:

A. It is a source of employment and income for partners and their families.

B. Generates indirect employment for temporary contracts that are required in certain specific times of the year such as preparation, production, lifting the harvest and marketing.

C. Drives the economy of the town.

D. Influences the primary sector fishing activity.

E. Influences the Mexican economic system.

F. Influences the Mexican ecological system.

The labor process of human resources in the structure of the Cooperative Society of Fishing Production the Patole, S.C. of R.L. de C.V. interacts with supra systems: Mexican economic system, primary sector, Mexican fishing activity and ecological system. These three supra systems cause uncertainty and complexity in the cooperative. It can be cited economic problems as the devaluation of the peso against the dollar affects purchasing inputs of society.

The primary sector fishing activity has its own characteristics dominated public by policy and market requirements, may be increased by consumption of shellfish or implementing regulations that protect the environment. This exposes the relationship between the primary sector of fishing activity and the Mexican ecological system in which the government issues the regulations required for the protection and proper exploitation of the environment. The decisions made by the manager and the production manager affect the board and therefore the functioning of society. Just the same way decisions made by administrator, the production manager and the board of directors influences fishing supra systems: Mexican economic system, primary sector activity and Mexican ecological system.

In this fact it is clearly observed the interactions between internal variables of the process that makes the structure of human resources of the cooperative and the uncertainty and complexity of the supra systems in which is located the Patole. Here lies the importance of the implementation of the systemic model in society, just because all human resources of the cooperative function as a single system can solve any problems that arise in the supra systems and take appropriate action measures.

The cooperative is a theory that seeks the common good of the people while the general systems theory seeks the relationship between different systems. The Patole complies with the cooperative theory and general systems theory, being an integrated supra systems mentioned above which are governed by the guidelines established by the philosophy of the cooperative system. The change in the economy and society has led to the cooperative facing competition from globalization, implementation of new technologies and the protection of the environment. For this reason it is necessary to detect any organizational problem so that can overcome external difficulties that arise and remain productive and competitive in the market.

Method

This article is a report of an investigation considered it is a process that, by applying the scientific method seeks to obtain relevant and reliable information to understand, verify, correct or apply knowledge [18]. All scientific research has to be sustained by serious work on a methodology that must submit a design or shape how it should be performed. It requires a design that marks a course of action, the nature of the research, study subjects, how to choose these subjects and the methodology to be used [19]. The researcher needs to point out the details of his study in order to shed correct and proper results. It is worth mentioning that there are different types of research to suit the needs of the various studies.

The methods used in obtaining the information were observing partners, gathering factual information and indicators and supported by the application, a Likert scale questionnaire. Observation for Hernandez is an accounting record of observable situations and using a set of categories and subcategories behaviors [17]. Observation was used to analyze the relationships between partners to identify organizational problems.

The documentary research was used to analyze internal documents to see if there have been profits in the Patole. Collection or analysis of secondary data is defined by Gilbert as the study of the original data collected by other researchers or institutions generally statistical in nature such as censuses and official government statistics. Being serious documents are reliable for use. In the same way any document prepared by a researcher is considered as secondary data, i.e. files are derived from previous research and may be useful for future research.

The third method is to apply a questionnaire to the partners, based on the Likert scale. Abascal mentions that the questionnaire performs the functions of the specific questions manage to move the objective of the investigation, the information obtained is homogenized because all respondents respond to the same formulated items, with proper design helps provide information and aid to effective treatment of the data collected [20].

Being standardized questionnaire helps in the statistical treatment of information obtained to be useful for research. Hernandez cites that was developed by Rensis Likert and consists of a set of five items presented as statements where it is required the participant to choose one of the items. Each item has a numerical value so that the participant gets a score that adds up until it is reached a final score. The design of the scale Likert manages to be easy to capture information in computer systems and being five items is practical to respond by study subjects.

The three methods relate to each other to achieve the desired research results. Not only applicable to the Patole but also to other cooperatives in the area and the state of Sinaloa. This is in order to maintain the cooperative democratic support and the relationship between the three supra systems in which the cooperative is related.

Analysis of Results

Taking up the point made by the cooperative theory, the partners have equalities and everyone works together for the common good. Systems theory supports the point that a system is composed of several parts that interact with each other for the common goal of the organization. Both theories apply to the Cooperative Society of Fishing Production "The Patole", S.C. of R.L. de C.V.

The successful implementation of the systemic model in the company depends on organizational design, the process of deciding on how to create, use and select the right combination of structures, control system and culture of the organization. Companies require supervise and monitor the design process to achieve outperformance [21].

In systemic approach it favors the cooperative because it establishes the conditions for participation in projects of external financing, provides reliable and timely information of the activities undertaken, and reduces costs and unnecessary expenses in establishing more efficient processes. Therefore, it manages the cooperative production processes can be more efficient. This coincides with the data provided by the partners in their questionnaires and comments.

According to the cooperative society studied, it is observed:

A. An initial resistance to the application of the systemic model. This fact because the partners were pleased with the performance of the leader. However, due to the current needs cooperators understood that the application of systems theory in the Patole was necessary.

B. Incentives to motivate members to work hard were implemented.

C. Feedback from partners to management of the cooperative was implemented.

D. Changes in the organizational structure and delegation of functions by the leader to the other partners were implemented.

E. Administrative controls are performed more precise and strict. Constant evaluation is performed so that the objectives are met.

F. The realization of agreements with buyers, in which they carry their refrigerated trucks to the fishing field so that the product remains fresh and frozen.

Reflections and Recommendations

This article is based on research and supported by the cooperative theory and systems theory has the following reflections and recommendations. The same reflections and recommendations can be abided by the any cooperative and any other organization wishing to implement the systemic model for more efficient activities.

The Cooperative Society of Fishing Production "The Patole", S.C. of R.L. de C.V. has implemented the systemic model based on:

A. The diversification of white shrimp supply and incorporating added value with biotechnological processes.

B. The cooperative philosophy based on mutual support, solidarity and cooperation among its members.

C. The objectives, mission and vision that support the daily work of the cooperative.

D. The correct and timely integration of partners to productive activities required in the process for obtaining white shrimp.

E. The feedback and relevant organizational restructuring which improved the efficiency of society.

F. The hiring of external personnel in strictly cases of administrative, accounting, legal advice, quality control and specialized care product activities, as can be the case that diseases are detected.

The above comments on the relevant recommendations derived:

A. The continued study of the Cooperative Society of Fishing Production "The Patole", S.C. of R.L. de C.V. in order to detect problems that afflict and may interfere with proper development and productivity.

B. Continue to involve partners in all activities that could affect the Patole. So that they can make appropriate decisions when problems arise in the supra systems: Mexican economic system, primary sector fishing activity and Mexican ecological system, affecting with its uncertainty and complexity the direct activities of the cooperative manner.

C. Conducting similar studies with this article in other cooperative societies in order to benefit the fishing sector.

D. Recommend among companies in general implementation of the systemic model in its functions.

It is observed the importance and benefits of the implementation of the ecosystem approach Cooperative Fish Production "The Patole" is observed, S.C. of R.L. de C.V. because the human resources that make up the entity in the process of its structure are active and make decisions that affect the organization. However, these decisions are influenced by interaction with supra systems: Mexican economic system, primary sector fishing activity and Mexican ecological system.

The Patole has internal interactions in the process of human resource structure supported through systems theory. Similarly, it maintains interactions among the three supra systems. It is therefore important to maintain a systemic organizational culture between the partners so that they can solve any problems that may affect the entity and remain competitive in the market for white shrimp.

This study is beneficial for the company as it can be for the other belonging to the fishing sector. As previously discussed, the cooperatives are a source of employment and income for cooperative members, their families, and the region where the cooperative and society in general is located. All of these are as a great system.

References

1. Schettino M (2002) Problemas sociales, políticos y económicos. Pearson educación.
2. Gutiérrez CA (2003) Entorno socioeconómico de México. México: Limusa.
3. INEGI (2015) Anuario estadístico y geográfico de los Estados Unidos Mexicanos. Aguascalientes, Aguascalientes.
4. INEGI (2014) Censos económicos. Resumen de los resultados definitivos. Aguascalientes, Aguascalientes.
5. SIAP (2016) Boletines de producción pesquera mensual por estado. México.
6. Morgado PP, Burgos RL (2006) Economía social y cooperativismo. Editorial Lex Nova.
7. Jaramillo MA (2005) Manual de cooperativismo y economía solidaria. Universidad Cooperativa de Colombia.
8. Mariño M (2009) Ley Marco para las Cooperativas de América Latina. Alianza Cooperativa Internacional.
9. Latorre EE (1996) Teoría General de Sistemas aplicada a la solución integral de problemas. Editorial Universidad del Valle.
10. Araya VHF, Solís VEH (1998). Evaluación e implantación de un sistema de calidad en instituciones educativas. San José, Costa Rica: Editorial Universidad Estatal a Distancia.
11. Von L (1989) Teoría general de los sistemas. Fondo de Cultura Económica.
12. Tirso JA (2008) Factores que influyen en el éxito personal. Chile, Smashwords Edition.
13. Johansen O (2004) Introducción a la teoría general de sistemas. Limusa: Noriega Editores.
14. Ferguson M (1994) La conspiración de acuario. Madrid, España: Editorial América Ibérica.
15. Goldfeder G, Aguilar E (2000) Planificación y Administración. Un enfoque integrador.
16. Rodríguez DAM (1990) Sociedad y teoría de sistemas. Editorial Universitaria.
17. Hernández SR, Fernández CC, Baptista LP (2010) Metodología de la investigación. McGraw Hill/Interamericana Editores.
18. Tamayo TM (2004) El proceso de la investigación científica. Limusa: Noriega Editores.
19. Nieto MS, Recamán PA (2010) En Investigación y evaluación educativa en la sociedad del conocimiento. Ediciones Universidad de Salamanca.
20. Fernández EA, Esteban IG (2009) Fundamentos y técnicas de investigación comercial. Escuela Superior de Gestión Comercial y Marketing (ESIC) Editorial.
21. Hill CWL, Jones GR (2009) Administración Financiera. McGraw-Hill/ Interamericana Editores SA de CV.

IPO Trading with Short-term & Intraday Temporal Functionalities

Vasiliki A Basdekidou*

Special Research FundAccount (ELKE)Aristotle University ofThessaloniki, Greece

Abstract

Trading is a temporal (i.e. time-based) historical living system with a number of functions, like: Initial Public Offerings (IPO), Seasoned Equity Offerings (SEO), stock (instrument) price action Gaps, Breakouts, etc. In this domain, a number of warning dynamics timing functionalities is available, like: On Open Gup-Ups (ooGUp), On Open Gup-Downs (ooGDn), Morning Breakouts (mB), etc. All these time-based functionalities are regarded as 2nd level functions (i.e. functions of functions; because of the timing involved) with great trading opportunities, and they are defined–for the first time in the corporate finance literature- by this paper as Temporal (timing) Trading Functionalities (TTF). In particular, the IPOs with the embedded TTF functionalities are great trading opportunities for the institutions, the individual (non-commercial) market investors, the swing traders, and the speculators. Data analysis shows that during the seasoned equity offerings time, shareowners significantly increase their share share-holding, including offerings that would be classified as overpriced at that time; hence, the involved trading volatility is increased resulting in great trading and profit opportunities. This paper contributes to corporate finance literature by examining the IPOs functions and define and document their inherit TTF functionalities. For this purpose, four categories of shareholders are regarded: The long-term institution and non-commercial traders (investors), the swing momentary institution traders (institutions), the short-term non-commercial traders (speculators) and the intraday non-commercial traders (speculators). Paper concludes that, in IPO/TTF trading, the swing traders(institutions), incorporating in their trading strategies the short-term TTF functionalities, are benefit at the expense of momentary and intraday speculators, while the long-term investors are not affected by the IPO offerings.

Keywords: Equity issue timing; Corporate ownership; Liquidity; Market timing; Initial public offerings; Temporal (timing) Trading functionalities

Introduction

Trading is regarded as a temporal historical living system [1,2] with a number of time-based company initiatives operating as trading functions. One of these company initiatives is the Initial Public Offering (IPO) which, like the Seasoned Equity Offering (IPO) initiative, has a great timing trading functionality [3-5], resulting in excellent profit and wealth growth opportunities [6,7]. In this domain, economics and finance literature reasoning that the companies time their SEOs and IPOs to months of relatively high stock prices, mainly because the CEOs and officers think that the prices of the shares (company stocks) will probably be overbought at such times (an encapsulated TTF functionality).

The observed mispricing concealed such as trading timing could be as the result of a lack of available TTF information for the investors, institutions and speculators for the embedded time-based behavioral biases dominant in equity, Forex and option markets. The reason that long-term investors (institutions) could buy overbought shares in IPOs/TTF is same with Edelen, Ince, and Kadlec [8], who provide evidences that long-term investors and speculators prefer to purchase shares classified as overbought (momentum trading psychology) based on a number of classical equities-trading strategies (trend-follow trading; without any TTF functionality in this case).

Corporate financing approach emphasizes that disengagement of holding and domination has as a result the clash of interest between outside shareowners, CEOs, and governors [9]. In this domain, the literature reasoning that big corporate shareowners can alleviate such as clashes by observing and controlling CEOs and governors [10]. Trading [11] and trading timing [12] theories of economics and financing try to clarify such as attitude assuming that the shares trading decisions (open/close positions; lot trade size, etc.) are formed for the regard of old non-speculative shareowners, who adequately take profit from IPO shares as a consequence of right-timing IPO initiatives/issues (IPO/TTF, SEO/TTF). The current paper agrees that the data are consistent with such as expectations as far as the timing for the company initiatives is regarded as a TTF functionality.

In the situation of equities and non-equities IPO timing (stocks, options, Forex, etc.), Cesari, et al. [13] argues on the effects of share-holding and stock liquidity on the SEO/TTF timing of repurchase and close (i.e. "buy" in case of a short position; and "sell" in case of a long position) transactions but no more details for TTF functionalities were given, and Demiralp, D'Mello, Schlingemann, and Subramaniam [5] state that old-issue shares returns and passive trading are both emphatically related to the coexisting old-issue changes in corporate holding for up to 3 weeks after the IPO/TTF time.

In this article, the author concludes that her results are persistent with the control acting of long-term passive-trading investors. Also, in this case the TTF functionalities were not discussed. Furthermore, Hao [14] states that companies with higher short-term non-commercial shareowners (speculators) experience more negative atypical returns at the report release (TTF timing) of IPOs and concludes that momentary corporate shareowners and speculators are not prompted to control the usage of the lifted trading capital and profit [4].

The current article is relevant to some other articles that investigate corporate share-holding under the prism of the IPO/TTF timing. In

***Corresponding author:** Vasiliki A. Basdekidou, Special Research Fund Account, Aristotle University of Thessaloniki, Greece
E-mail: Vasiliki.Basdekidou@gmail.com

this domain, some articles targeted on the information asset and stock-taking intelligence of corporate investors but no TTF information was given. Gibson, Safieddine, and Sonti [15] report that seasoned equity and option IPO initiatives, with the bigger boost in corporate share-holding, are detected between the (relative to IPO/TTF, IPO timing) quarters −1 and +1; these long-term investors reported that their positions outperform in the subsequent the IPO issue year and qualify this outperform to their competitive convenience asset position. Chemmanur, He, and Hu [16] find that long-term passive-trading investors (as opposed to non-commercial short-term investors and traders) are able to receive more share portions in IPOs hoping on better future returns (profit) and their post-IPO transactions somewhat greatly exceed a (even a well designed) passive "Buy-and-Hold" trading planning by the share-holding investors.

In contrast, Edelen, Ince, and Kadlec [8], who examined corporate trading and stock return abnormalities, found that corporate firms prefer to purchase shares categorized as overbought and that there is a negative association (i.e. relationship functionality) between corporate open-position and future trading (close-position) returns. Unlike these articles that spotlight on whether institutions are better-informed (i.e. insiders functionality), the current research article targets on the dominant relationship and the underlined trading functionalities between the corporate shareowners and the CEO/managers.

In disagreeing with these articles, Alti and Sulaeman [17] point to how company IPO issuing initiative is influenced by corporate and non-commercial trading. In their paper, they support that high stock returns and profit trading trigger equity derivation only when if it is connected with a great pre-issue initiative corporate investor demand, as it is regarded consistent by new corporate holdings (swing momentary traders). The Alti and Sulaeman clarify their results as logical and dependable with SEO initiatives using the corporate investor demand as a gauge of the market's interest in the company's equity SEO initiative. In this domain, the main target of the current article is disparate. Actually, I investigate whether old shareowners (as long-term investors), gain profit from the IPO/TTF timing. It is notable that, the results obtained are not dependable with the supposition and conclusion that IPOs/governors are gauged to sell overbought shares for the interest and profit of such kind of shareowners (corporate investors as opposed to non-commercial momentary speculators).

The rest of the article is organized as follows: next Section ("Share-holding and Trading Data") describes the share-holding data as the corporate share-holding variables; following Section ("Temporal (timing) Trading Functionality") documents the introduced TTF term by examining the relation between IPO timing and institutional and non-commercial share purchases, as well as the impact of corporate and non-commercial holdings on IPO timing; Finally, last Section ("Conclusions and Discussion") summarizes the conclusions and discusses paper's innovations and contributions.

Share-holding and Trading Data (Institutions And Non-Commercial Traders)

For the current paper, the Share-holding information, the changes in insider holdings and some sample profit/losses trading data (1990-2016) - used in this paper as the share-holding and profit variables-came from many resources. The Barron's information databases and sources, a Wall Street Journal affiliate [18]; the Stock Charts.com initiative; the Securities and Exchange Commission/SEC notices, releases and announcements; the Commitments of Traders (CoT)/CFTC speculative net positions reports; the Yahoo! Finance insiders data feed; the SEC EDGAR database; individual filings SEC's Forms 4 (CEO) and 14a (Directors and Officers); and the Thomson Financial corporate holdings SEC's Form 13f database, which reports corporate share-holdings and profit/losses on a calendar-quarter base ending in March 31st, June 30th, September 30th, and December 31st.

The United States SEC requires that all institutions with a total position greater than $100 million of securities or equities positions greater than 10,000 shares or positions in individual shares greater than $200,000, must report their holdings, using the SEC's Form 13f, quarterly.

In this paper, these numbers were used for back-testing purposes and estimation of the total corporate holdings and position changes. Also, current paper identifies long- and short-term corporate investors and speculators based on their average portfolio "share turnover" (defined as a measure of stock liquidity; calculated by dividing the total number of shares traded over a period by the average number of shares outstanding for that period. Obviously, the higher the "share turnover" number, the more liquid the share of the company) in the last four quarters [19].

Following, for each of the above 4 quarters, the traders involved in IPO were sorted into four categories according to their temporal (time-based) corporate holdings as the percentage of total shares outstanding at the end of each of these quarters. In the first category, I placed the institutions ranked in the bottom third after having the lowest "share turnover"; they are classified as Long-term corporate passive investors (LT share-holding) (Table 1). In the second category, I placed the institutions ranked in the top third after having the highest "share turnover"; they are classified as Momentary corporate swing-trading investors (swing ST institution share-holding) (Table 1). Then, the rest third is divided into two equal categories (third and fourth category). In the third category, I placed the individual traders involved in swing IPO trading (ST non-commercial share-holding) (Table 1). Finally, in the forth category the detected intraday individual traders were placed (Intraday non-commercial share-holding) (Table 1).

The result is an unbalanced panel, covering the sample time period from January 1st 2000 to June 30th 2016, with up to 100,000 observations, plus a number of more than 3,000 IPOs. The sample back-testing period starts from 2000 because from this year the data (share-holding, transaction, etc.) are available in a digital format with a relatively low cost.

While quarterly data allow me to better and more accurate to associate share-holding changes with IPO/TTF, time shorter (weekly) results are presented for two reasons. First, because they help me to understand how unusual the changes in ownership at the time of IPO they are; and Secondly, the annual (fiscal year) data provide firmness as well as flexibility but with some serious throwbacks, which are estimated using (fiscal year) annual data.

The statistics for the sample time period are presented in the following Table 1 which display the summary numbers of IPO initiatives and Non-IPO initiatives from 1st January 2000 to 30th June 2016 (IPO offerings are obtained from SEC/SDC).

Temporal (timing) Trading Functionalities (TTF)

In this section, the innovative term Temporal (timing) Trading Functionality (TTF) is introduced, analyzed and documented.

	Equity IPO initiatives				Non-IPO initiatives				Difference
	Obs.	Mean	Median	St. dev.	Obs.	Mean	Median	St. dev.	
Panel A. Firm characteristics									0.26*
Size	3105	4.54	4.74	1.72	100,005	4.80	4.87	2.15	
Return	3105	0.66	0.25	1.35	100,005	0.16	0.04	0.87	0.50
Market-to-book	3105	2.30	1.82	1.59	100,005	1.69	1.25	1.22	0.61
Total share-holding (%)	3105	51.62	49.88	26.50	100,005	35.04	39.80	26.92	16.58*
(1) LT share-holding (%)	3105	9.00	6.92	8.26	100,005	9.55	7.50	12.84	−0.55
(2) Swing ST institution share-holding (%)	3105	12.27	10.46	10.48	100,005	10.17	7.00	11.58	2.10
(3) ST non-commercial share-holding (%)	3105	14.70	11.41	12.54	100,005	11.70	7.57	12.35	3.00
(4) Intraday non-commercial share-holding (%)	3105	17.90	15.70	17.72	100,005	12.88	8.02	13.66	5.02
Panel B. Changes in share-holding (%)									
Continuing share-holding	3984	5.42	3.07	8.37	100,740	1.00	0.32	5.94	4.42
LT Continuing share-holding	3504	1.56	0.95	2.97	100,200	0.61	0.22	2.46	0.95
ST Continuing share-holding	3504	1.09	1.03	5.48	80,900	0.12	0.02	4.42	0.97
Liquidations	3809	−7.99	−6.19	6.99	100,230	−8.18	−5.27	9.15	0.19**
LT liquidations	2552	−1.19	−0.51	1.42	62,802	−1.26	−0.22	2.55	-0.07
ST liquidations	3884	−4.35	−3.92	4.71	77,300	−4.90	−2.03	6.53	0.55*
Initiations	4399	22.79	20.33	15.59	100,005	9.95	6.13	11.03	12.84**
LT initiations	4223	2.31	2.57	3.33	90,009	2.04	1.35	3.99	0.27
ST initiations	4196	12.42	10.83	10.22	81,770	4.77	2.33	6.26	7.65
*Changes significantly different from zero at 5% level **Changes significantly different from zero at 1% level									

Where:
Size - The natural Logarithm of Sales.
Return - The Stock return measured over the fiscal year.
Market-to-book is (total assets − book equity + market equity)/total assets.
LT - The Long-term corporate share-holding (Corporate investors' horizons are identified based on their portfolio "share turnover" over the last four weeks).
ST: The Momentary corporate ownership (Corporate investors' horizons are identified based on their portfolio "share turnover" over the last four weeks).
Continuing share-holding: This term is referred to corporate investors, as shareowners both at the beginning and at the end of the fiscal 6-week period.
Liquidations: This term is referred to cases where institutions own shares at the beginning of the fiscal year but liquidate their holdings by the end of the fiscal 6-week period.
Initiations: This term is referred to cases where institutions own no shares at the beginning of the fiscal year but establish new positions by the end of the fiscal 6-week period.
Difference - The difference in Means between IPO initiatives and Non-IPO initiatives.

Table 1: Sample statistics.

Equity IPO initiative timing and corporate share-holding around equity IPO initiatives

Hovakimian and Hu [4] first well examine the arrangement of changes in corporate share-holding around equity IPO initiatives and then (just) present the time-series functionalities of mean Market-to-Book ratios and stock returns for 3 weeks prior and 3 weeks after the year of equity issue (IPO) without a temporal TTF functionality. The presented arrangements are consistent with prior evidence in the literature on equity IPO initiative timing that stock returns and market-to-book ratios tend to increase prior to equity issuance and tend to decline following the issuance.

Also, the results of the tests of statistical significance of the changes in stock returns and market-to-book ratios between weeks−3 and −1, −1 and 0, and −1 and +3 are presented. All the changes are statistically significant at 1% level. These results establish that the functionality, commonly referred to as Market Timing in the literature, is also present in their sample. Their finding rises for future researchers some questions about the interpretation of IPO timing (i.e. TTF functionalities) reflected in patterns as attempts to sell overvalued equity. Obviously, they do not know whether the increase comes from existing corporate shareowners or from new investors [4].

If IPOs are timed to sell overvalued shares, then wealth is transferred from shareowners buying IPO shares to existing share-holders who do not buy IPO shares. Shareowners, trading (buy or sell) shares in the open market around the time of IPO, neither lose nor benefit from IPO timing. Hence, only continuing shareholders can benefit from IPO market timing whereas initiating share-holders can only lose from IPO timing.

Corporate share-holding around the equity IPO initiatives

Chen, Harford, and Li [20] and Hao [14] argue that long-term institutions tend to be passive traders not interested therefore for the IPO/TTF functionalities. On the other hand, momentary, swing, and intraday trading institutions (and speculators as well) are better informed and tend to trade short-term (or even intraday) the IPO initiatives to materialize their own informational convenience asset position. In this subsection, the changes in share-holding of corporate investors with short and long investment horizons are investigated. The analysis is repeated separately for long-term corporate investors and for short-term swing trading corporate investors. The significance information, gained by Figure 1, is the comparison tests between the share-holding changes during the indicated period to share-holding changes in period 0 (i.e. IPO timing).

The results in Figure 1 show that momentary swing trading corporate shareowners, clearly and strongly increment (boost positions) their share purchases in the IPO year; and explicitly in the current quarter of the IPO initiative. Actually, these share-holding changes are significantly different from zero. On the other hand, the level of share acquisitions by the long-term passive-trading institution shareowners remains inflated for at least three (3) week after the IPO initiative; whereas the level of withdrawals (liquidations) for the short-term speculators and the swing traders constantly and continuously increases just after the IPO initiative. The results also show that the level of new share-holding position initiations rises in the year and particular at the quarter of the IPO initiative (insiders).

Figure 1 presents the mean Market-to-Book Ratios (MB) and Returns (return) of equity IPO initiatives from week -3 to weeks +3 relative to the IPO issue week.

Following, Table 2 presents the time-series profiles of mean Market-to-Book ratios and Returns of equity IPO initiatives from weeks−3 to +3 relative to the IPO issue week.

The results in Table 2 show that, similar to insiders and unlike the long-term corporate shareowners, existing momentary swing trading corporate shareowners sharply increase their share purchases in the year and especially in the quarter of the IPO initiative (TTF functionality). Then, in the period following the IPO initiative, the level of share purchases by continuing short-term swing trading shareowners drops below the pre-IPO initiative level.

The securities liquidation increases during the IPO initiative week, while additional liquidations have been notified just after the IPO "time". The back-testing statistical analysis also indicated that the level of ownership rises during this 3-week pre-IPO issue period, and then it drops again to pre-IPO initiative level. Overall, these results suggest that the existing long-term institution shareowners act as if they are not concerned about IPO/TTF timing. Furthermore, the fractional share-holding level of existing momentary corporate investors and speculators increases in the IPO quarter, which implies that IPO's fractional allocation to these shareowners exceeds their fractional pre-existing stakes in the firm. This means that existing long-term corporate shareowners do not benefit from IPO timing.

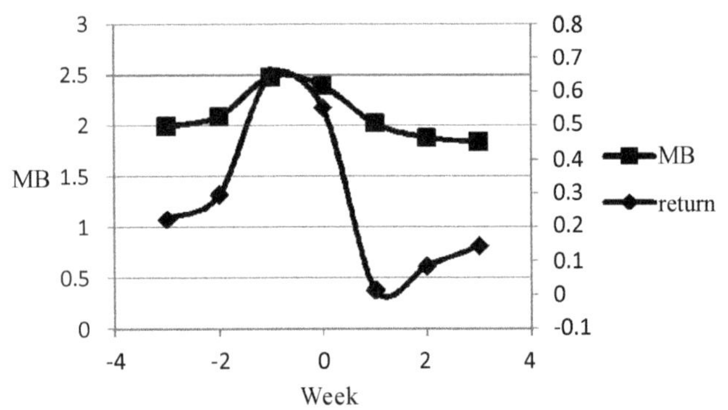

Figure 1: Market Timing of Equity IPO initiatives. Where: *Market-to-Book*: The price defined as: (total assets – book equity + market equity)/total assets. *Return:* The stock return measured over the fiscal year. *Tear (Time) 0*: The IPO issue week.

Finally, according to the back-testing sample statistical data, the post-IPO security trading activity is similar for both low and high ownerships (i.e. no interest in trading and TTF functionalities).

The temporal (timing) trading functionality

Company initiatives and particular the IPO ones, offer great trading opportunities (leverage, options, CfDs, long/short positions, etc.) for all kind of traders (investors, institutions, insiders, individual non-commercial market investors, and speculators). Trading these initiatives is a time sensitive procedure that requires to have and to obey a strict time-based strategy. So, in trading, the need for a 2nd level timing function of the IPO trading opportunities is obvious.

The innovative term "Temporal (timing) Trading Functionalities" (TTFs) is defined as an array of temporal functionalities applied to traditional company initiatives like IPO and IPO, and stock price action patterns like Gaps ("Windows" in technical analysis terminology) and Breakouts.

These TTFs temporal functionalities could be documented by time-targets in trading (stocks, options, futures, Forex) as follows: define swing, momentary and intraday trading strategies based on specific short-term (or even intraday) time-targets; and open/close long/short positions at a specific time-target.

These time-targets could be the IPO announcement time; the IPO actual time; the first/last 5-minutes in a daily trading session (09:30-09:35 am EST, 03:55-04:00 pm EST); the Fed/FOMC meetings decision announcement at 02:00 pm EST, the Fed/FOMC conferences at 02:30 pm EST; the Fed/FOMC minutes timing; the Non-Farm Payrolls reports (NFPs) on the first Friday each month at 08:30 am EST; the API and EIA reports on WTI inventories on 04:30 pm EST (on Tuesdays for API data) and 10:30 am EST (on Wednesdays for EIA data) respectively, etc.

Following, Table 3 presents a small number of initiatives (functions) and the related warning dynamics temporal (timing) TTF functionalities acting actually as time-targets in stock, option, futures, and Forex short-term, swing and intraday trading.

Comparative analysis shows that the TTF temporal functionalities better apply to the following four categories of traders:

(1) Long-term Institution and Non-commercial traders

Levels								**Changes**		
Week	**−3**	**−2**	**−1**	**0**	**1**	**2**	**3**	**−3 to −1**	**−1 to 0**	**−1 to 3**
Market-to-Book	1.96	2.07	2.40	2.39	2.05	1.86	1.85	-0.44*	0.01*	0.50*
Return	0.23	0.3	0.68	0.55	0.02	0.11	0.18	-0.45*	0.13*	0.50*
*Changes significantly different from zero at 1% level.										

Where:

Market-to-Book: The price is defined as: (total assets – book equity + market equity)/total assets.

Return: The stock return measured over the fiscal year.

Tear (Time) 0: The IPO issue week.

Table 2: The Time-series profiles of mean market-to-book ratios and returns.

Company Initiatives, Fed Meetings, Reports	Time-Targets (trading)
IPO company initiative	IPO announcement time
IPO company initiative	IPO actual time
Day Trading	first/last 5-minutes in a daily trading session (09:30-09:35 am EST, 03:55-04:00 pm EST)
Fed/FOMC monetary policy meetings	Fed/FOMC meetings decision announcement at 02:00 pm EST
Fed/FOMC monetary policy meetings	Fed/FOMC conferences at 02:30 pm EST
Fed/FOMC monetary policy meetings	Fed/FOMC meetings minutes announcement at 01:00 pm EST
Fed Members Speeches	at 10:00 am EST; at 01:00 pm EST
Non-Farm Payrolls reports	first Friday each month at 08:30 am EST
API reports for WTI (USO) inventories	On Tuesdays at 04:30 pm EST
EIA reports for WTI (USO) inventories	On Wednesdays at 10:30 am EST

Table 3: Company initiatives, fed meetings, reports and time-targets.

Share-holding (share-holding position) (%)					Trading Results (%)	
	Before IPO	@IPO	After IPO	St. dev.	Profit	St. dev.
(1) Long-term Institution and Non-commercial Traders (Investors)	100	20	100	1.13	0	2.34
(2) Swing Short-term Institution and Non-commercial Traders (Institutions)	0	25	0	2.33	20	3.55
(3) Momentary Non-commercial Traders (Speculators)	0	45	0	3.21	-5	3.21
(4) Intraday Non-commercial Traders (Speculators)	0	10	0	4.19	-15	5.82

Table 4: Ownership and Trading Results (%).

("Investors")

(2) Short-term Swing Institution traders ("Institutions")

(3) Momentary Non-commercial traders ("Speculators")

(4) Intraday Non-commercial traders ("Speculators")

Following, Table 4 presents, in summary, the ownership % (share-holding position) and the trading results (profit %) for these four categories of traders. The data used were those presented in Section 2 "Share-holding and Trading Data" (1st January 2000 – 30th June 2016).

Conclusions and Discussion

The main target of this paper is to approach the IPO trading opportunities under the prism of a number of temporal short-term trading functionalities (short-term TTFs) introduced for the first time in corporate finance literature.

The Initial Public Offerings (IPOs) trading functions offer great temporal (i.e. time-based) trading opportunities (i.e. Temporal Trading Functionalities, IPO/TTF: time-based leverage, options, CfDs, Long/Short positions, etc.) for the institutions, the insiders, the individual non-commercial market investors, and the speculators. Paper's back-testing trading data analysis shows that, those short-term swing traders incorporating TTF functionalities in their trading plans and strategies, gain much better results rather than the short-term or intraday speculators.

Due to the fact and in the sense that corporate shareowners can control and restraint CEOs, governors and managers, the IPO/TTF initiatives are expected to be in the interest of such shareowners. According to the corporate finance literature, these short of shareowners are expected to be disappointed with company's CEOs, governors and managers. Obviously, not all corporate shareholders benefit from these IPO/TTF initiatives. Actually, the swing traders profit at the expense of the short-term speculators.

One could argue that any management should be expected to act especially in the interest of existing corporate shareholders with continued share-holding interest since shareowners who liquidate their share-positions actually abandon and drop-out their claims, benefits and power to control the CEOs, governors and managers.

In this paper, I assume that the managers' motivation is to sell overbought equities and options in IPO/TTF initiatives, boost with the pre-existing old corporate shareholder holding and drop with corporate shareowner presence in the IPO/TTF initiatives. Hence, my proposed trading planning is to investigate, control and document how IPO/TTF timing is functioning within shareowners (i.e. institutions vs. non-commercial individual traders vs. speculators) and if the prepared IPO/TTFs and the corporate shareholder trades are logical, steady and dependable with the assumption that IPO/TTF timing profits the issuing company's old corporate shareowners.

In the process to examine the functionalities of corporate share-holding at IPO/TTF, the paper categorizes corporate shareholders along two compatible and consistent functions. First, I isolate the trading of old corporate shareowners from the share acquisition by new institutions that open new positions in IPO/TTF companies on the announcement of the IPO initiative (TTF functionality). Then, I further separate existing institutional shareowners that continue to maintain share-holding interest in the company after the IPO announcement and the IPO timing from those that liquidate their positions around the time of the IPO itself (TTF functionality). In this paper, I follow Gaspar et al. [21] and Yan and Zhang [19] to categorize corporate investors according to their short or long position, investment and trading attitude [22].

In the view that the control by the corporate shareowners is the basis of many of the pragmatic and speculative guesses, in the current paper I also isolate corporate investors that are more likely to control and discipline from those that are not. Economics and finance literature propose that some corporate investors control, plan and invest for the long run; whereas others (speculators) focuses their skills on spotting any short-run undervalues and then trade heavily to profit from their informational convenience asset positions [23].

It is found that trading behavior of corporate investors at IPO/TTF suggest and denote that such as traders, largely, boost their share-holdings just before or at the time of the IPO. I further find no evidence that these increases consider the Table 3's IPO timing-targets (i.e. no TTF functionality is detected). These IPO timing-targets are valid for both groups of corporate shareowners (i.e. for both: institutions with long and institutions with short investment horizons). Finally, the results show that firms with higher corporate share-holdings favor to employ less in timing of their IPOs. The above conclusion is further supported by my findings that IPO/TTF timing does not transfer wealth (profit) from the IPO swing-trading temporal investors and speculators to the old shareowners (passive-trading institutions). Explicitly, I find (from the 2000-2016 Barron's data sources analyzed) that the companies decide the IPO initiative when the share prices are relatively high [24].

These results signify and suggest that IPO/TTF timing does not, normally, benefit long-term corporate and short-term non-commercial shareowners. As long as the corporate swing-trading shareholders purchase shares in IPO/TTF and hence, they cannot discipline the CEO and the managers, the results further imply that the timing of IPOs is unlikely to be impulse (catalyst functionality) by the intention of trading overbought equities, options, futures and Forex pairs [25,26].

Paper contributes to corporate finance literature by: (i) the introduction and documentation of the innovative term "Temporal (timing) Trading Functionality" (TTF) as a 2nd level timing function of the IPO function; and (ii) the application of TTF functionalities (long/short positions at a particular time during the daily trading session: 09:30 am - 04:00 pm EST, swing and intraday time-based trading strategies) to IPOs initiatives. The IPOs were discussed under the TTF prism for four categories of shareowners: The long-term institution and non-commercial traders (investors), the swing momentary institution traders (institutions), the short-term non-commercial traders (speculators) and the intraday non-commercial traders (speculators).

The data analysis applied found that swing momentary institution traders (institutions) and insiders (CEO, Governors, Officers, etc.) increase their share share-holding just before or at the announcement of the Seasoned Equity Offerings and they are benefit at the expense of short-term and intraday non-commercial speculators, while the long-term institution and non-commercial investors' wealth position is not affected significantly by these IPO offerings (accepted standard deviation prices).

Acknowledgments

The financial support (covering primary the CoT/CFTC and the Barron's and WSJ.com market data expenses) from the EU/LLP Programme "EPOCHE 2013" (with Project No. 2012-1-GR-ERA 10-10609) is gratefully acknowledged.

Conflict of Interests

The author has not declared any conflict of interests.

Author's Bio Profile

Vasiliki A. Basdekidou holds a B.Sc. degree in Economics from the Aristotle University of Thessaloniki (Greece, 2002), a two-year master's degree in Economics (major: Financial Economics) from the University of Macedonia (Greece, 2005) and a Ph.D. in Corporate Finance from the Bulgarian Academy of Sciences – Economic Research Institute (Bulgaria, 2015). She is working at the Special Research Fund Account of the Aristotle University of Thessaloniki for the last 10 years.

References

1. Styliadis AD (2007) E-learning Documentation of Historical Living Systems with 3-d Modeling Functionality. Journal (IMI) Informatica 18: 419-446.
2. Styliadis AD, Vassilakopoulos MG (2005) A Spatio-Temporal Geometry-based Model for Digital Documentation of Historical Living Systems. Journal: Information and Management 42: 349-359.
3. Beatty RP, Ritter GR (1986) Investment banking, reputation, and the underpricing of Initial Public Offerings. Journal of Financial Economics 15: 213-232.
4. Hovakimian A, Hu H (2016) Institutional Shareholders and SEO Market Timing. Journal of Corporate Finance 36: 1-14.
5. Demiralp I, D'Mello R, Schlingemann FP, Subramaniam V (2011) Are there Monitoring Benefits to Institutional Ownership? Evidence from Seasoned Equity Offerings. Journal of Corporate Finance 17: 1340-1359.
6. Ogden JP, Wu S (2013) Reassessing the Effect of Growth Options on Leverage. Journal of Corporate Finance 23: 182-195.
7. Basdekidou V (2015) Functionality, Returns and Efficiency before and after the Debt Crisis: An Empirical Analysis of the Greek Stock Market (Unpublished doctoral dissertation). Bulgarian Academy of Sciences - Economic Research Institute, Bulgaria.
8. Edelen RM, Ince O, Kadlec GB (2015) Institutional Investors and Stock Return Anomalies. E-Journal SSRN.
9. Jensen MC (1986) Agency Cost of free cash flow, Corporate Finance, and Takeovers. Journal (AEA): The American Economic Review 76: 323-329.
10. Hartzell JC, Starks LT (2003) Institutional Investors and Executive Compensation. Journal of Finance 58: 2351-2374.
11. Myers SC, Majluf NS (1984) Corporate Financing and Investment Decisions when Firms have information that Investors do not have. Journal of Financial Economics 13: 187-221.
12. Baker M, Wurgler J (2002) Market Timing and Capital Structure. The Journal of Finance 57: 1-32.
13. Cesari AD, Espenlaub S, Khurshed A, Simkovic M (2012) The Effects of Ownership and Stock Liquidity on the Timing of Repurchase Transactions. Journal of Corporate Finance 18: 1023-1050.
14. Hao GQ (2014) Institutional shareholder investment horizons and seasoned equity offerings. Journal (FMA): Financial Management 43: 87-111.
15. Gibson S, Safieddine A, Sonti R (2004) Smart investments by smart money: evidence from seasoned equity offerings. Journal of Financial Economics 72: 581-604.
16. Chemmanur TJ, He S, Hu G (2009) The role of Iinstitutional Investors in Seasoned Equity Offerings. Journal of Financial Economics 94: 384-411.
17. Alti A, Sulaeman J (2012) When do high stock returns Trigger Equity Issues? Journal of Financial Economics 103: 61-87.
18. Barron's Market Data (2016).
19. Yan X, Zhang Z (2009) Institutional Investors and Equity Returns: Are Short-term Institutions Better Informed? Journal: The Review of Financial Studies 22: 893-924.
20. Chen X, Harford J, Li K (2007) Monitoring: Which institutions matter? Journal of Financial Economics 86 279-305.
21. Gaspar JM, Massa M, Matos P (2005) Shareholder Investment Horizons and the Market for Corporate Control. Journal of Financial Economics 76: 135-165.
22. Baker M, Stein JC, Wurgler J (2003) When does the Market Matter? Stock Prices and the Investment of Equity-dependent Firms. The Quarterly Journal of Economics 118: 969-1005.
23. Jarrett JE, Li Y (2016) A Data Analytical Study of the Japanese Equity Market over a Lengthy Period Bus Eco J 7: 241.
24. Vargas-Hernandez et al. (2016) Analysis of the Organizational Eco-Systemic Change in a Cooperative Society of Fishing Production. Bus Eco J 7: 230.
25. Chiraz A (2016) Does the Index Futures Destabilize the Underlying Spot Market? Some Evidence from Frensh Stock Exchange. Bus Eco J 7: 244.
26. Chung T, Ariff M (2016) Money Supply, Banking Liquidity and Stock Index Returns: Evidence from Four Major Capital Markets. Bus Eco J 7: 238.

Evaluation of Innovation Policy in Kazakhstan in the Period of Globalization Trends

Nurbek Achilov*

G-Global Development Community, Kazakhstan

Abstract

This paper shortly reviews the theories about innovation and evaluates the ingredients and perspectives of development of innovation policy in Kazakhstan. In the period of implementation of new economic reforms, Kazakhstan focused on extraction and export of natural resources. During realization of state programs, many innovation projects fail. Therefore, paper aims to investigate the main barriers and perspectives by providing policy recommendations for Government of Kazakhstan. In the period of further privatization of state organizations in Kazakhstan and globalization trends, the paper demonstrate a strong necessity for changes in present innovation programs. Understanding that a market capacity for innovation in Kazakhstan is limited, the paper aims to focus on ideas of export-oriented innovations.

Keywords: Innovation policy; Growth strategies; Research and development; Innovative entrepreneurship; Export oriented innovation; Globalization trends

Introduction

Kazakhstan's key innovation policy started with 2010-2014 National Program of forced industrial and innovative development of the Republic of Kazakhstan. It aimed to guarantee a stable and well-balanced economic growth by means of diversification and improvement of Kazakhstan's competitive ability. For realization of this program, allocation of 6.5 trillion budget for respected years were projected in the document [1].

At present, the government implements the State Program on industrial development of the Republic of Kazakhstan for years 2015-2019, which aims to promote diversification and competitiveness of the manufacturing industry with the budget of 1 717 billion tenge [2].

The primary purpose of these programs are to improve the business environment indicators, increasing the country's competitiveness, reduction of the state involvement in the economy through a planned privatization [3-5]. The Table 1 shows the changes in ranking of Kazakhstan in the rankings during the period of realization of these state programs.

From the table the Doing Business Rank improved from 59th position in 2010 to 41st in 2016, the World Competitiveness Index improved from 72nd position in 2010 to 42nd in 2016 rank and the IMD World Competitiveness Score declined from 33rd position in 2010 to 47th in 2016. It is clear that these rankings cause conflict in concluding the real improvements. Therefore, for review, it is necessary to check statistical data on innovations comparing data for the period of realization these programs (2010-2016).

To illustrate, Table 2 shows the volume of produced innovative products and spending for scientific research in Kazakhstan [6].

According to the table, the year 2014-2015 for both indicators was a period of sharp decline. It confirms that IMD's World Competitiveness Score is more exact and appropriate in evaluation of competitiveness level of Kazakhstan.

From the situation in oil markets, the drop of oil prices in 2014-2015 decreased demand from many local companies and importers. In addition, Kazakhstan was late to devaluate its currency to Russian Ruble and the other was a massive budget cuts in state organizations of Kazakhstan, which caused in general economic deterioration of all indicators. It is clear that productions should not only focus on innovations for local consumers. That is a key point to focus on international theories and models that will help to rebuild Kazakhstan's innovation policy on development of export-oriented innovations.

However, is it a main criterion to let innovations decrease in volume or in sales? How Kazakhstan categorize innovations and R&D spending and definitions of products and services? These are the questions, which need an in-depth analysis in perspective.

Moreover, it is important to mention that R&D spending of Kazakhstan is around 0.2% of GDP [7]. In fact, it is a key indicator for showing a level of financing of local individuals and organizations to innovate and develop new products and services. There is no possibility to create a system for development of innovations on a constant level in Kazakhstan when R&D lacks financing.

In addition, serious economic problems during a period of price decline for natural resources showed that developing innovativeness is much more important factor than focusing on new products manufactured with the help of imported new technologies.

From marketing point, strategies of the national programs of Kazakhstan for bringing innovations and diversification of the economy was too early for local companies and individuals to enter new markets when they had difficulty with operations, product development, R&D and sales in local markets. Although, companies were renovated their technologies and were ready to supply products for export.

Therefore, initially, National program's priority should have been focusing on product development strategies, which would be able to renovate existing companies gradually based on their own resources

***Corresponding author:** Nurbek Achilov, Founder, Member of Board, Managing Director, NGO, G-Global Development Community, Kazakhstan
E-mail: nurbek2020@gmail.com

Rankings	Source	2010	2016
Doing Business Rank	World Bank [3]	59	41
World Competitiveness Index	World Economic Forum [4]	72	42
World Competitiveness Scoreboard	IMD [5]	33	47

Table 1: The rankings of Kazakhstan in doing business and competitiveness.

Years	2010	2011	2012	2013	2014	2015
Produced Innovative products	142 166,8	235 962,7	379 005,6	578 263,1	580 386,0	377 196,7
Scientific-Research Spending	110,5	116,2	428,8	407,3	365,1	287,4

Source: Committee of Statistics of the Ministry of National Economy.

Table 2: Statistics on Innovation in Kazakhstan, mln. Tenge.

	Current Products	New products	Innovations	Inventions
Current Markets	Market Penetration Strategy	Product Development Strategy	Patent Strategy, Intellectual Rights and Property Protection	Industry development and R&D Strategies
New Markets, incl. Export Markets	Market Development Strategies	Diversification Strategies		

Table 3: Growth strategies for organizations.

and prepare them for diversification or new market development strategies in the later stages.

On the other side, the role of R&D is vital in the development of innovations and new industries, which Kazakhstan focuses in its state programs. However, low R&D financing demonstrate a low-level attention by state bodies. Their focus on importing of technologies for production of products on present high demand was considered developing innovativeness of country. Table 3 shows growth strategies of an organization while developing its markets and new industries.

Generally, Table 3 extends the alternative corporate growth strategies [8] to show the role of R&D and innovations in a single table. It outlines that the priority of the new state programs could be R&D and Product Development Strategies as they related to creating not only innovations but also new industries of Kazakhstan. Thus, the National programs should aim to increase financing of R&D and develop new approaches and directions of activities to reconsider the focuses of its programs.

Understanding that new global competitive environment requires from companies and organization to increase its competitiveness on a constant level, R&D is a major factor for bringing innovations and new industries of Kazakhstan. It helps also to build industries, which meet the requirements of open borders for global trade, competition and trends.

In addition, according to classical theory [9], "the process of technological change in a free market consists of three parts: invention (conceiving a new idea or process), innovation (arranging the economic requirements for implementing an invention), and diffusion (whereby people observing the new discovery adopt or imitate it)". In this regard, Table 3 shows not only the types of products and the appropriate strategies. Rather it outlines the chain of product development, starting from invention to current product. This is a good point to say that knowledge management systems are necessary and a vital instrument to drive innovation chain on a constant level.

It is clear that not all innovations can become a consumed new product immediately. Most of them go to shelfs to wait their turn. Therefore, statistics of innovative products in Table 2 are not exactly the statistics of innovations. From international business point, these products are existing products for new markets like Kazakhstan. From this, one can conclude that innovations of Kazakhstan are still to come and wait their turn. One reason is a meaning of innovation for Kazakhstan's policy makers and state bodies. As in Table 3, real innovations should start with a number of patents and financing of research and development, which are not easy to find in Kazakhstan's information sources.

This finding is a key to point that the state and corporate programs of Kazakhstan should change and focus on R&D policy to bring innovations in near future. It will require reconsidering the budgets, technologies and infrastructures for industries where Kazakhstan can take competitive advantage from international trade of patents, new products and services.

However, those who make argument that innovation is the engine of long run economic growth define it broadly not just new products, but also new processes, new organizations, new management practices and new strategies [10]. According to authors of international business, the business environment should be more conducive to the production of innovations. This requires development of economy based on free market, which create more incentives for individuals to make money out of their innovative ideas by starting their own business easily.

In an economy such as in Kazakhstan, where 75% of GDP comes from the state sector, there is few opportunities for individuals to develop innovations as they see no profits from state strictly managed structures or because of unfair legal systems. The demanding factor for renovation of the policy is innovative entrepreneurship – a new focus for innovation policy programs. This means redirecting financing from state corporate organization to new businesses where innovative entrepreneurs take their leadership role in creating and managing innovations.

Only can innovative entrepreneurs make businesses and economies work for innovations. These leaders can distinguish and form a business culture of a country or a global environment when their products and services will gradually find consumers globally.

Table 4 below shows differences in innovation policy of major export oriented markets based on preliminary analysis of familiar key brands and innovation policies.

The table outlines the options for Kazakhstan government for building its innovation policy based on success of main export oriented markets. When focus is for multiple sectors, it is important for Kazakhstan that entrepreneurial specialists and scientists find their supporters for innovative ideas in and outside the organizations. This

	US	Europe	Japan	Korea
Main Brands	Ford, GE, Chevrolet, Apple, IBM, Shell, Boing, KPMG, John Deer, McDonalds, Coca-Cola	Mercedes, Siemens, SAP, Porsche, BMV, Nokia, Airbus, Adidas, Chanel	Toyota, Sony, Mitsubishi, Honda, Toshiba, Panasonic	Hyundai, LG, Samsung, Kia, Daewoo
Leadership in innovations	Multiple Sectors	Multiple Sectors	Technology and Electronics	Technology and Electronics
The most specific differences of products and services	Usability and Convenience	Comfort and Safety	Quality and Functionality	Pricing and Compatibility
Innovation policy focus	Innovative Companies and Entrepreneurs	Innovative Clusters and Entrepreneurs	Priority Sectors and Entrepreneurs	Competitive Sectors and Entrepreneurs
Origin of major innovative companies	Closed Innovations	Closed Innovations	Open Innovations	Open Innovations

Table 4: The differences of innovation policy of major export oriented markets.

	Innovative economies	Priority Policies for Bridging and Developing countries	Non-innovative Economies
Goals	Long term	Education and Exchange Policy	Short term
Knowledge	Progressive	Internet, Technology and R&D policies	Traditional or Local
Technology	Up-to-date	Trade and R&D policies	Outdated
Infrastructure	Developed	Exchange, Technology and R&D policies	Absent or Elementary
Markets	Private Driven	Economic and Privatization Policy	State Driven
Human Resources	Advanced	Education, Training and R&D policies	Elementary
Entrepreneurship	Easy to create, change, support, reorganize and close	Exchange, Education and R&D policies	Rudimentary and tough for entrepreneurs
Legal framework	Open and supporting	Exchange, Education and R&D policies	Bureaucratic and Corrupted
Product and services, patents, trademarks	Many	Exchange, Education, Economic, Industry and R&D policies	Few or absent
Export and import per capita	High	Economic, Trade, Education and R&D policies	Low
Innovation and Inventions	High	R&D, Innovation, Education, Science and Knowledge Management Policies	Low

Table 5: The comparison of innovative and non-innovative economies and priority policies for bridging and developing countries.

is difficult scenario for Kazakhstan with its low level of infrastructure for innovations. Therefore, Kazakhstan should focus on priority and competitive sectors based on open innovations of leading economies. From there it can develop its own innovations, which can gradually build Kazakhstan's competitive advantage in priority and competitive export oriented sectors.

Allocating the budgets and launching new businesses by state bodies should not ignore existing businesses. Because they are more quick and cost efficient for restructuring businesses and infrastructures for R&D, especially if they will be trained and upgraded. Their business experience and knowledge are more valuable for policy development and launching new innovative productions. Clustering such innovative entrepreneurs on competitive base and training them effectively for building R&D infrastructure are necessary to provide effective structural changes in economy.

Without proper selection and education of innovative entrepreneurs, the allocation of budgets for various programs is a waste of resources. Because imported technology and knowledge outdate and lose their competitive advantage very soon, especially where no systems for advancing them are available. However, only knowledge can generate new innovative knowledge and therefore policies should focus on development of knowledge management systems for various industries. At the stage of building a business chain of new innovative companies, it is extremely vital to reevaluate knowledge systems and advance them with new information technologies and R&D.

A new economic era of Kazakhstan started in 90s and this is a short period for a country to develop innovations. Many programs which were based on adaptation of the programs of the leading economies was a short term vision of Kazakhstan without proper understanding the scope and origination of those programs for innovations, their history of market and economic theory.

Therefore, the focus of Kazakhstan's Government policy should change from short-term to long-term policies, from short-term macroeconomic policy to long-term innovation policy. Changing the goals are an initial driver for restricting the systems and programs. To understand the models of many leading countries, which are a main source for ideas and policies for growing global markets, the Government should prioritize R&D as a key component of innovation policy of Kazakhstan.

Exporting of resources when prices are attractive is lucrative but this can destroy plans when prices for natural resources go down. This happened several times and Kazakhstan should learn from this a big lesson to focus and become a leader in championing in innovation policy and achieving its global goals. In addition, nobody can save country from economic collapse if a country cannot adapt its competitive resources for production of value driven products and services in a period of globalization. At this stage, it is important to look for main components of economy and compare them to define priorities for Kazakhstan in policy development.

Table 5 shows an overview of innovative and non-innovative countries and priority policies for bridging and developing countries to build their competitive advantages in a global marketplace.

The Table 5 shows elementary but very important ingredients to focus innovation policy of Kazakhstan to develop its competitive advantages to step in row with the globalization trends.

Why it is important to focus on globalization trends and export oriented innovations for each country?

From economic point, countries can benefit from competitive advantage in a long run. Because, R&D will lead to focus on productions of innovations that are more efficient and economical to produce. For businesses, it mean specialization in areas, which will allow them to be more innovative and competitive first on local level and gradually on international one.

R&D will not devaluate if intellectual protection will be on top of the agenda of every country. In any term, Kazakhstan can sell or exchange its innovations if it has a value and meets international demand. And this is how new markets will be created and it will also eliminate all present economic issues in developing countries, especially related to extreme poverty, infrastructure and other areas. For Kazakhstan, it means a new source of income, especially for a country between Europe and Asia, where the nation can become a strong intermediate for exchange of innovations between regions.

The current paper reviewed the innovation policy of Kazakhstan via prism of theories and preliminary analysis. As a key, it aimed to outline general country specific recommendations on innovation policy development of Kazakhstan focusing on strategies and ingredients of innovations. The offered tables and views for innovation policy have been developed based on practical use of innovations and analysis of literature.

Further study is necessary to evaluate the country specific industries of Kazakhstan, which can build their competitive advantage with the support of new state programs. Moreover, to define a strategy on a country level, it is important to organize on a constant level a qualitative and quantitative research of businesses, entrepreneurs and state representatives, who are the objects of innovation policy. On a micro level, a countrywide analysis is required of management systems, export products, innovation infrastructure and R&D operations of private and state organizations.

References

1. 2010-2014 National program of forced industrial and innovative development of the Republic of Kazakhstan. (2010) Decree of the President of the Republic of Kazakhstan.
2. Astana (2014) The State program on industrial-innovative development of Kazakhstan for 2015-2019. Decree of the President of the Republic of Kazakhstan.
3. World Bank Group (2016) Ease of Doing Business in Kazakhstan. World Bank.
4. World Economic Forum (2016) World Competitiveness Index.
5. IMD World (2016) World Competitiveness Rank.
6. Committee of Statists of the Ministry of National Economy of the Republic of Kazakhstan.
7. Innovation and High Technologies in Kazakhstan (2016) Presentation, RFCA Rating Agency.
8. Boyd H, Walker O, Larreche JC (1995) Marketing Management: A Strategic Approach with a Global Orientation. Irwin, 35.
9. Sandefur T (2008) "Innovation." The Concise Encyclopedia of Economics. Library of Economics and Liberty.
10. Charles WL (2001) International business: competing in the global marketplace: postscript. (3rdedn) Chapter 4: International Trade Theory, Irwin, MacGraw-Hill, New York, 50-53.

6

Jockeying for Position in International Sim Card Industry in India

Saibal Kuamr Saha*

Assistant Professor, University ofTechnology and Management, 4th Floor, Bawri Mansions, Dhankheti, Shillong, Meghalaya, India

Abstract

With globalization, there has been a rapid increase in international tourism. People from India have been travelling abroad for business, education, medical treatment, holidays etc. When someone goes abroad he/she has to rely on public phones or take a new sim card in that country. Acquiring a new sim card in a foreign country means a large number of paper work and hassles and not to mention the delay. Hence, a pre acquired international sim card has become a much preferred choice for international travelers. Although, there are a number of players in the market in the international sim card business, but some companies are more preferred than the other. This research aims to throw some light in the customer's preferences for choosing an international sim card in West Bengal, India.

Keywords: International sim card; Customer preferences; Sim card industry; Forex; Travel

Introduction

With the growth of Information Technology -IT sector and liberalization in the policies of Foreign Direct Investment - FDI, a number of international companies have set up their units in India. People working in Multi-National Companies - MNCs have to travel frequently from one country to another for attending business meetings, client visits and sales. Indians have a fascination for a foreign degree and overseas education. Over the years the number of Indian students studying in different parts of the world has increased. A large number of people travel every year to developed countries for medical treatment and many travel for spending their holidays. Most of the people travel for a short duration, ranging from a couple of days to a month. Hence, in this period it is very difficult for someone to look for a new sim card in a foreign land and wait for days to get the new connection activated. The delay creates tension among family members and friends back home and people worry about the well-being of the traveler. To solve these hassles a number of companies have started pre activated international sim card purchase business in India. The major players in this industry are: Matrix Cellular, Clay, Uniconnect, Roam 1 and Znet connect.

Objectives

1. To study the international sim card industry in India.
2. To find out the customer preferences for choosing an international sim card service provider.

Research Methodology

In order to understand the dynamics of international sim card industry both primary and secondary research was conducted. As a part of secondary research different books and journals pertaining to the telecom industry were studies and leaflets and brochures of international sim card service providers were studied. In order to find out the customer preferences and their experiences of using international sim card primary research was conducted. For this a questionnaire was developed and interviews were conducted.

Sample size: 100

Location: Kolkata. Samples were taken from the employees of IBM, ERRICSON, EXIDE, Cognizant and TCS who frequently travelled abroad.

Literature Review

According to James C. Cox in The Economic Journal, consumer economics functions on the hypothesis that consumers look for the most value or satisfaction that they can buy [1]. Hence, it is very important to continually monitor and try to develop the standards of a product so that it can create a sense of need in the customer's cognizance. As globetrotting has become very common, it is very important to find new communication options which provide good connectivity and accessibility for people all over the world. The Indian Telecom Industry has undergone huge transformation since 1991 [2]. Value added services, which included Country Specific sim card phone services, were opened to private sector in 1992. The National Telecom Policy (NTP) allowed private sectors to participate in basic services in 1994 [3]. An independent regulatory authority by the name Telecom Regulatory Authority of India (TRAI), was set up in 1997 [4]. New policices for Internet Service Providers (ISPs) was announced in 1998, thus opening the market to private sector providers. International Long Distance (ILD) Services were opened for competition in 2002. The Country Specific Sim card phone industry came into being in the mid-1990s [5]. By the end of 2002, the Indian Country Specific Sim card phone Industry had over 10 million subscribers. International sim cards gives users the freedom to travel abroad and do not bother about the international roaming charges. Some of the facilities provided for international travelers are: postpaid and prepaid sim card – Under this a local postpaid mobile number of the country is given to the customer. They receive the facility of free incoming calls and customized tariff plans and 24X7 customer supports is provided [6]. The postpaid customers are given the facility to check their account balance online. Customers can choose an internet pack as per their preference and access emails, browse and download applications at 1/10th the cost of International Data Roaming. The companies also provide Forex card which can be used as a debit card in order to withdraw cash and make payments. Forex cards give the benefits of instant cash in the currency

***Corresponding author:** Saibal Kuamr Saha, Assistant Professor, University of Technology and Management, 4th Floor, Shillong, Meghalaya, India
E-mail: saibal115@gmail.com

required. They have zero transaction fees and can be used for online purchases and transactions.

Due to technological advancements, technologies like OTT VoIP (Over The Top Voice over Internet Protocol) have helped companies like Skype, Facetime and WatsApp to eat into mobile operators roaming revenue [7]. The following figure shows the global roaming revenue forecast (Figure 1).

Some of the benefits provided by the service providers are:

Postpaid SIM card [8]:

- Free incoming calls in most countries.
- Local postpaid mobile number.
- Customized Tariff Plans.
- 24x7 Customer Support.

Prepaid SIM card:

- Large savings on International Roaming bills.
- Receive number before departure.
- Avail the facility of Pay-As-You-Go.
- Easy online recharge.
- 24x7 customer care.

Internet Packs:

- Access emails, browse websites and download applications.
- Different types of data plans - customized and unlimited.
- Activate data pack before departure.
- 24x7 Customer Care Support.

Forex Card:

- Helps to get cash in the currency as desired.
- Card can be used to purchase online and perform online transactions.
- Helps to avoid forex exchange fluctuation.
- It can be reloadable anytime and anywhere.
- It helps in instant currency transfer.

Special package for corporate clients:

- Personalized account manager
- Customized tariff plans
- Special credit periods
- Bill payment in Indian currency
- 24x7 customer support

Special package for students:

- Availability of phone number before departure
- Competitive tariffs
- Billing in Indian Rupees
- Payments can be made by the family in India
- Free itemized bills

Findings from the Primary Research

Travel frequency

From the survey it was seen that bi annual travelers (44%) was the highest which was followed by travelers who travelled once in a year (38%). Only 2% travelled once in a month and 16% travelled once in three months (Figure 2).

Purpose of visit

Most of the respondents (43%) travelled abroad for official purpose. Few of them (39%) travelled for leisure and entertainment to get out of the busy life and very few people (18%) went abroad for personal purpose barring students (Figure 3).

Mode of payment

It was observed that 45% of the custoers used credit card, 35% used cash while cheque and company undertaking payment were the least preferred mode of payments (Figure 4).

Problems faced

It was observed that most of the people (30%) had problems with the dialing process while 18% had problems with the billing process and only 2% faced problems with the network process (Figure 5).

Other services

The survey revealed that most of the people 60% did not use any other services from the international sim card provider. 25% used Data services, 10% Travel Insurance and 5% used FOREX (Figure 6).

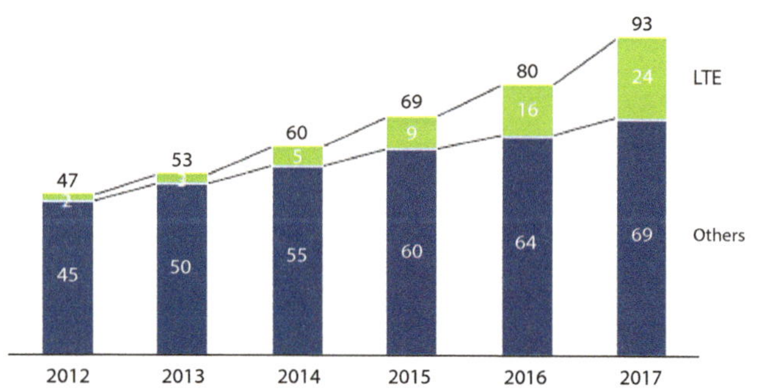

Figure 1: Global roaming revenues (LTE- Long Term Evolution vs Traditional Roaming Forecast 2012-2017, US$ bl).

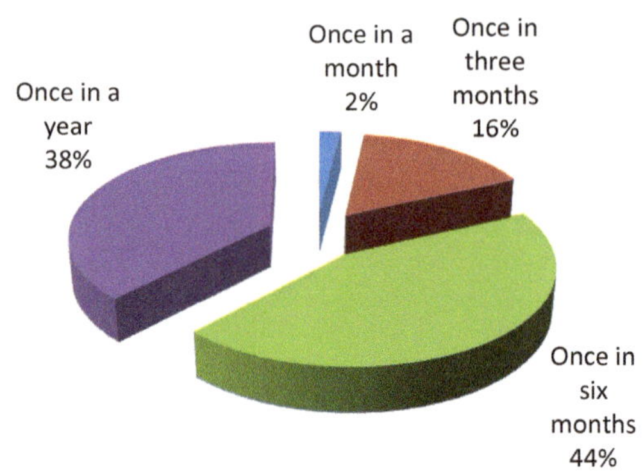

Figure 2: Travel frequency.

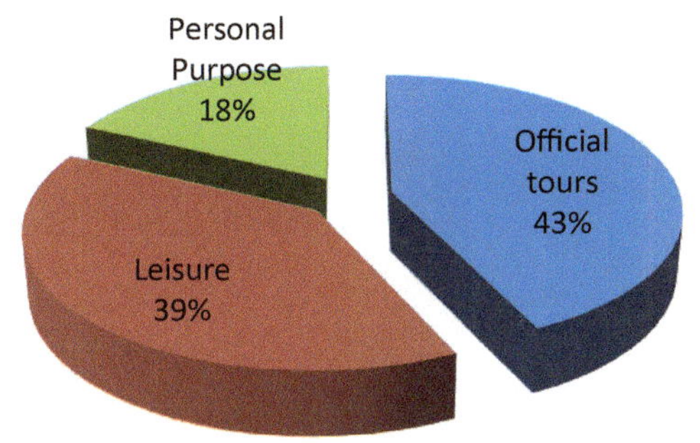

Figure 3: Purpose of visit.

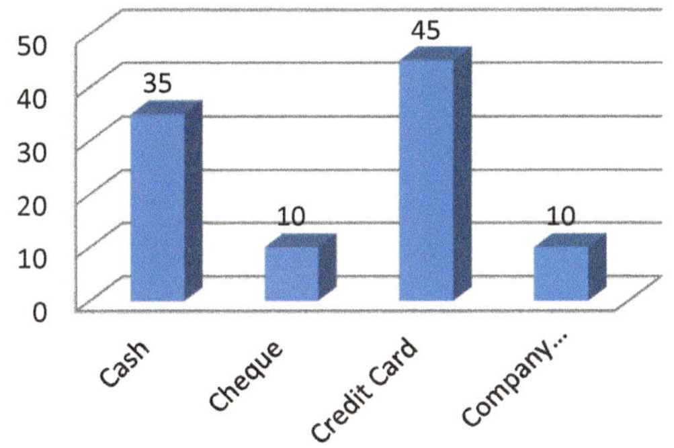

Figure 4: Payment.

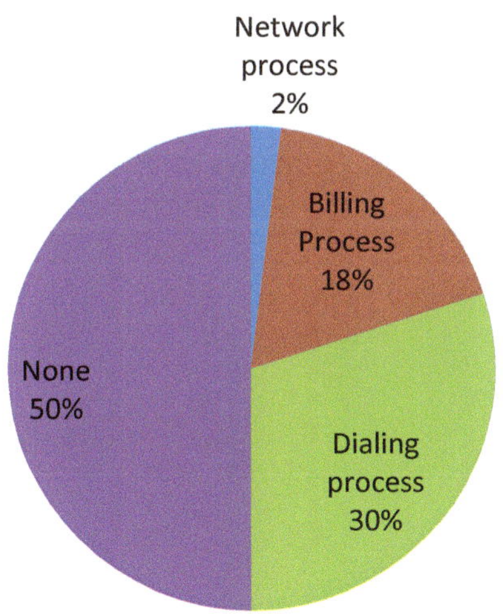

Figure 5: Problems faced.

Brand awareness

The survey data revealed that Matrix was the most popular brand (100%) followed by One world (93%). 52% of the respondents knew about Uniconnect, 44% about clay and 41% about Vodafone that these were the international sim card providers in India (Figure 7).

Customer preference

It was seen that most of the respondents preferred Matrix (69%) followed by One world (28%) and Clay (3%) for international sim card (Figure 8).

Reasons for customer preference

It was observed that the most important parameter for customer preference for international sim card was availability (32%) followed by influence from peers (25%). The brand name (23%) was also very important followed by tariff rates (12%) and service quality (8%) (Figure 9).

Conclusion

After analyzing the findings of the research it can be concluded that Matrix with strong brand recognition is a market leader. Matrix Cellular is the most respected company in the telecom sector. Most

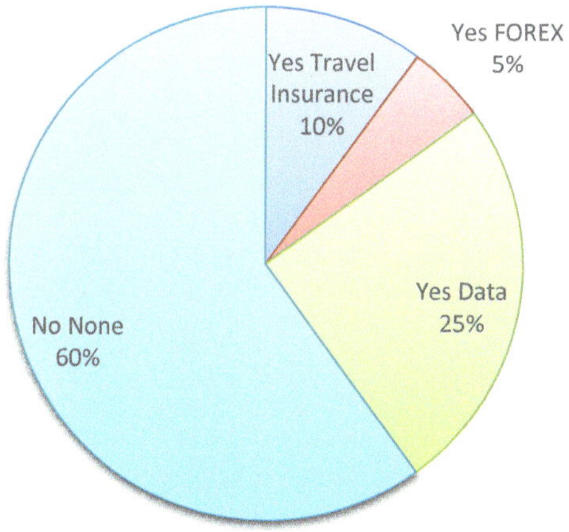

Figure 6: Other services.

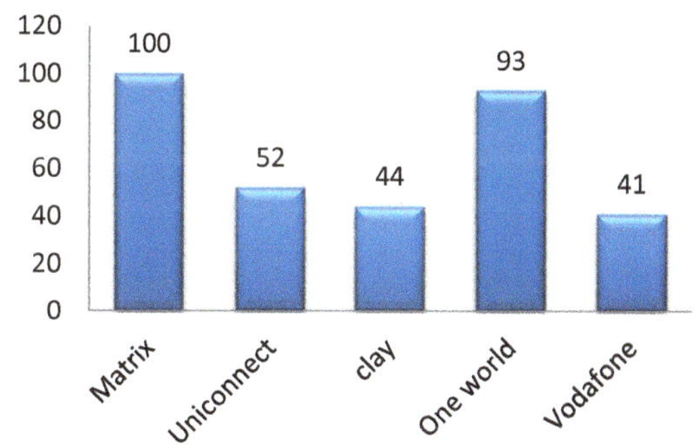

Figure 7: Brand Awareness.

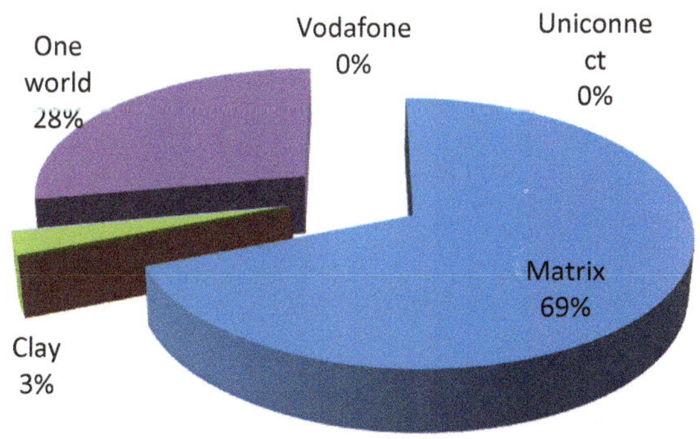

Figure 8: Customer Preference.

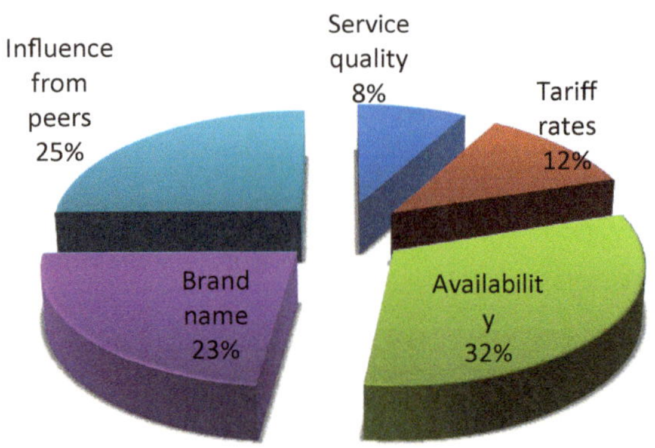

Figure 9: Reasons for customer preference.

of the subscribers on an average do not want to spend more than Rs 3000/-. Availability of the sim card and influence/recommendation from peers are very important parameters which helps customers to choose between different brands [9,10]. As people do not travel abroad too frequently, attractive schemes could be designed to retain the brand loyalty of the customers. Although service quality is very low in the customer preference list but this becomes very important as this parameter becomes the sole factor for influence from peers. If any customer encounters bad service quality, he/she will spread this news to his peers and this becomes a loss to the company. Hence, companies should try to provide good service quality.

References

1. James C, Lingoes, Martin P (1972) The Index of Consumer Satisfaction: Methodology. Proceedings of the Third Annual Conference of the Association for Consumer Research pp: 689-712.
2. (2015) A brief report on Telocom Sector in India. ASA & Associates.
3. (2012) Telecom Sector in India: A Decadal Profile. TRAI.
4. T. Vijayaragavan (2009) India's Telecom Industry-An Overview. Market Survey.
5. Papori B, Rashmi B (2014) Telecom Sector in India: Past, Present and Future. International Journal of Humanities & Social Science Studies.
6. http://www.trai.com/
7. Andreas G (2014) What is the next roaming strategy for EU Operators? Delotte.
8. http://www.matrix.in
9. http://www.clay.co.in
10. http://www.uniconnect.in

Asian Equity Markets: A Time Series Analysis of their Co-integration

Jarrett JE[1]*, Kyper E[2] and Prante G[2]

[1]*University of Rhode Island, Kingston, RI, USA*
[2]*Lynchburg College, Lynchburg VA, USA*

Abstract

This research examines the time series characteristics of stock price indices for Hong Kong, Tokyo and Singapore Equity Markets or stock exchanges during the lengthy period from before 1997, 1997 to 2007 and after 2007. Specifically, we calculate the rate of return and the volatility of return for all three markets and estimate co-movement of the three markets. We find that the average rate of return varies dramatically for the three equity markets and across time. Further, we find that stock prices are positively serially correlated in general. In the multivariate regressions, we find that there is little evidence to show that either the rate of return in certain markets universally affects the rate of return in other equity markets. We suggest based on the evidence that the three markets are co-integrated but not universally across time and with each other in pairwise dimensions. Lastly, we studied and made conclusions concerning the mean and variation in the volatility of the rates of return in the three equity markets studied.

Keywords: Time series; Financial indices; Volatility; Correlation; Hang Seng; Tokyo and Singapore equity markets

Introduction

We study three sets of weekly price indices; Tokyo Composite Index, the Hang Seng (Hong Kong Stock Exchange Composite Index) and the Singapore Exchange provided by common data collected during a lengthy period of time. Studies of these data are important because of the rapid growth and influence of the Asian and especially the Pacific Basin economies on the world, balance of trade and growth of Asian and other economies throughout the world [1-3]. Previous studies [4-6] described China as an economic power offering tremendous opportunities for investment and growing business returns. Their financial markets for the earlier years in their development were thought not to be fully developed when analyzed by the criteria developed by financial economists using criteria for analyzing Western equity markets [7-10]. Chow and Lawler [11], and later, Jarrett and Sun [12], analyzed the price index for the Shanghai Stock Exchange in comparison with the New York Stock Exchange Index in terms of its rate of return, volatility and structural changes in the movement of the index; also Jarrett, Kyper and Klein [13] studied relationships between large Asian and the New York and London exchanges In this study, we propose to analyze the entire period from January 1991 to December 2012 dividing the period into sub periods (sub samples) to analyze change associated with time and especially significant economic events. The comparisons have the purpose of revealing the behavior of stock movements in an emerging market in comparison with an established Western market. Previous studies by Bailey et al. [14], Jarrett and Sun [2,3], Jarrett and Kyper [15] focused on other issues in Chinese equity markets. We will now focus on three non-Chinese of the largest Asian equity markets because they are central areas of trade and economic activities not expressed only in the Shanghai equity market of China. Although previous studies show that Asian markets became and continue to integrate themselves with other and small Asian equity exchanges (note CMP and [12].

We will assess the degree of integration of the three Asian equity markets to determine how they affect each other independent of the large global markets in China (PRC), The United States and London Correlations among the markets determined among the markets will give rise to the integration of these markets and evidence will be shown of these factors. As well as the association .with the rest of the world as represented by the movement of prices in the New York Stock Exchange (NYSE). We will also look at the correlations among the Shanghai, NYSE and Hong Kong markets (Hang Seng Index) to examine their integration as well.

We examine both the rate of return and the volatility of the price indexes. The rate of return is the change in the natural logarithm of the price index for a given time period. We follow Chow and Lawler [11] and Jarrett and Sun [12], hereafter, JS, Jarrett, Klein and Kyper, hereafter JKK) in measuring the volatility by the absolute value of the change rather than by its variance. The absolute value is less sensitive to extreme value as compared with ARCH-type models to study the residual variance of a time series model. Stated differently, we study the volatility of the rate of return itself and not the residual in the time series model of the rate of return. Following CL, JS and JKK; (1) the volatility in the rate of return and not the time series regression model residual is the subject of interest in financial research and (2), "since log stock price behaves approximately like a random walk, the rate of return itself and the residual of an auto regression of this rate are almost the same." The data for this study include four sets of weekly price indices of the three Asian markets noted before. The rate of return is calculated as the change in the natural logarithm of the price index in a given period. The volatility of returns is calculated as the absolute value of the change in the natural logarithm of the price index in a given period. We further divide our sample into three subsamples: before 1997, after 1997 and before 2007, and after 2007. The entire sample period is from October 1987 to through 2012. Both 1997 and 2007 are years in which the economic environment changed. In turn this affected the world's equity markets. Hence, we separated the data into three sub-time-periods. Lastly, we follow CL, JS and JKK in choosing the weekly data as the best choice among daily, weekly and monthly data.

***Corresponding author:** Jarrett JE, University of Rhode Island, Kingston, RI, USA, E-mail: jejarrett@mail.uri.edu

To begin, we examine the measure of volatility. If botcharacteristics of the equity markets. We calculate the mean and variance of the rate of return and the mean and variance of the meh these measures reflect uncertainty, the volatility in Asian stock prices should be more volatile than those in New York. To study the co-movements of the price in the two markets, we calculate simple correlations and multiple regressions. The multiple regressions include auto regressions as well as ordinary multiple regressions. There was no rational reason to examine curvilinear models since the study of residuals did not indicate nonlinearity in relationships. The remainder of this paper is organized as follows: (1) the characteristics of the rate of return and the volatility of return; (2) correlation coefficients; (3) regressions of the rate of return; (4) regressions of the volatility of return; and (5) conclusions.

Rate of return and volatility of Hong Kong, Tokyo and Singapore stock indices

Table 1 shows the information for the Hong Kong, Tokyo, and Singapore stock price indexes including the market capitalization and the number of listed stocks. The sizes of the three financial markets indicate that the Tokyo equity market is much larger than the other two equity markets in terms of both market capitalization and the number of listings. In terms of market capitalization per listing, Tokyo is also highest at over $2 billion per listing, followed by Hong Kong ($1.5 billion per listing) and Singapore ($1.3 billion per listing). There is a rich literature on the relationship between market listings and the size of the economy Levine and Zervos [16]. For a summary of current discussion on this topic see Levine [17].

Table 2 shows the means and standard deviations (variation) of the rates of return for the three equity markets, while Table 3 presents the means and standard deviations of the volatility of returns in the same three markets. For Table 2, the means are highest for Hang Seng followed by Singapore and Tokyo, which is close to zero in the time period analyzed. The standard deviation is highest for Hang Seng followed by Tokyo and Singapore which are very close. In JKK, we observed that the variations in the Asian markets were greater than in the Western markets (New York and London).

In regards to the volatility in the rates of return for the same three equity markets we observe the Hang Seng equity market has the greatest volatility (Table 3). The variation (standard deviation) in volatility is again larger in the Hang Seng market than the others. The Tokyo market's standard deviation is smaller than the two other Asian markets. Statistical tests of significance (not reported here) results in rejecting the hypothesis of no difference between the Tokyo and the other markets.

Stock exchange	Market capitalization (US$ billion)	Number of listings
Hang Seng (Hong Kong)	2,314.29	1,548
Nikkei 225 (Tokyo)	5,063.80	2,431
STI (Singapore)	969.46	770

Table 1: Size of three Asian markets.

Stock exchange (index)	Hong Kong (Hang Seng)	Tokyo (Nikkei)	Singapore (STI)
Mean	0.0022	0.0004	0.0014
Standard Deviation	0.0334	0.0296	0.0284

Table 2: Mean and standard deviations in rates of returns.

Stock exchange (index)	Hong Kong (Hang Seng)	Tokyo (Nikkei)	Singapore (STI)
Mean	0.0249	0.0223	0.0195
Standard Deviation	0.0223	0.0195	0.0206

Table 3: Mean and standard deviations in volatility of returns.

The mean rate of return for Hang Seng (0.0022) is about five times larger than the mean rates of return for Tokyo (0.0004) and nearly double that of Singapore (0.0014). Thus, the Hang Seng Index is growing at a rate much larger than the other equity markets. All three of them represent developed economies whereas Hang Seng, while not underdeveloped, is greatly influenced by the dynamics of the Chinese equity market and economy due to shares being cross-listed with the Shanghai stock exchanges. If we were to consider change in price levels for the two nations by examining data on the consumer price indexes for the three nations (although not a perfect comparison), the changes in prices would not account for the major portion of the differences in the average rates of return. This leads to a conclusion that the greater mean rate of return for the Hang Seng Index is not attributable to factors other than the investment opportunities in its market and the influence of dual-listed equities with those of China [18].

Volatility (as noted before) as measured by both the standard deviation of the rate of return and by the mean volatility in the rate of return is larger for the Hang Seng stock market than for the two alternative markets. Table 2 shows a larger variation for the Hang Seng stock index than for the others. Table 3 concurs by showing a larger mean volatility of return for Hang Seng as well. This suggests a great deal of uncertainty in the Hang Seng market in comparison to the other markets. Furthermore, the standard deviation of the measure in Table 3 is also greater for Hang Seng than it is for the other equity markets. These results are not a revelation and are similar as those of CL, JK and JKK. This would lead one to observe that the volatility is subject to a greater degree of variation; that is, the spread in the distribution in Hang Seng is greater than the distribution for the other three markets. Again, this is consistent with the previous findings by CL, JS and JKK. This is not to say that volatility does not exist or is even small in the other markets, but only to say that a risk-averse investor is better served by the developed market of Tokyo rather than the others.

To test how the three equity markets behave during extreme events, we sort sample period to three economic sub-periods and examine the mean and volatility of the rate of return during these periods: (1) 1987 through the last week of 1996; (2) 1997 to the end of 2007; and (3) after 2007 until the end of the sample data period. By studying these three periods, one may determine if severe economic changes occurring in 1997 and 2007 affect the three markets and whether the changes differ.

We find a downward change in the mean rate of return for Hang Seng from period 1 to period 2 and again in period 3 as reported in Table 4, Panel A. The mean rate of return for Tokyo slightly increases similar in periods 1 and 2 and from period 2 to 3. For Singapore, the mean rate decreased from period 1 to period 3. After 2007, the declines are very evident in Hang Seng and Singapore but not in Tokyo.

In studying variation, we observe the standard deviations of the rates of return are largest for the Hang Seng Index. In all three time periods the Tokyo exchange had the second largest variation in rates of return but not nearly as large as that for the Hang Seng market. For Singapore, the mean rate decreased from period 1 to period 2 and again for period 2 to period 3. After 2007, the declines are very evident in Hang Seng and Singapore but not in Tokyo.

In studying variation, we observe the standard deviation of the rates of return for the Hang Seng Index are virtually equal to Tokyo in Period 3. In all time periods, the Tokyo Exchange exhibited the second largest variation in period 1, smallest in period 2 and tied for greatest in period 3. Singapore variation grew between periods 1 and 2 and declined in period 3.

In Table 4, Panel B, we observe changes in the mean and variation in the volatility of the rates of return for the equity across periods 1 and 2, but not in 3. The mean volatility in the rates of return for the markets did not change substantially in the three periods. The order in terms of size of mean did not change during the sub-periods. Hang Seng had the largest mean, followed by Tokyo and Singapore. For variation in volatility, the standard deviation across all time periods indicated the same variation in order for all three periods and for all equity markets (exchanges).

In summary, the results demonstrate that there are temporal relationships between mean rates of return and mean volatility in the rates of return as well as variation in both mean and volatility in the rates of return for these data studied. This knowledge makes it very difficult to produce forecasts (especially medium and long-term duration) of the mean and variability for the three equity markets. Further, the analysis does not dispute studies in the past such as CL, JK and JKK. Nevertheless, this new study does bring to light the difficulties of grouping Asian markets into a singular category. These analyses produce corroborating evidence of previous studies that indicate a necessary understanding of the permanent and temporary components of time series market characteristics. Ray, Jarrett and Chen [19] indicated for the Tokyo stock exchange that such components existed, but studies of this type need to be replicated for Tokyo as well as other markets.

The economic change occurring in the world during the three time periods kept the three markets more volatile and often more profitable than the ones in more established markets. Risk-averse investors were better off in more established markets because of the smaller level of volatility but they are giving up some possibility of higher return. For Tokyo, the differences in the sample statistics for the three time periods suggest that the rates of return and volatility in stock prices in nominal terms for the entire time period studied were not covariate stationary time series. This is the same conclusion for a much larger time period than observed by CL and JS. Their conclusions at this point are not disputed but only enhanced by the study of the new and expanded analysis of these three markets. Tokyo, the largest of the three markets under study, achieved wide variation even though it is much larger than the other two. If we had included one or more of the China (PRC) stock exchanges, the variability of Tokyo may not seem as large. This notion is for another study but may indicate that largeness is not a protection from risk. Tokyo, the largest, may appear more risk-averse than the others due to its size, but it has the greatest level of temporal volatility which could yield short-term gains but still may not be the best place to invest over a longer extended period. Singapore may have other possibilities with some extensions. Additional study of this market may yield additional possibilities. Lastly, grouping smaller Asian markets together may not be a wise choice for researchers as well as portfolio managers.

Panel A: Rate of return	Hang Seng	Nikkei	STI
Before 1997			
Mean	0.0042	-0.0002	0.0024
Standard Deviation	0.0310	0.0280	0.0232
1997-2007			
Mean	0.0019	0.0001	0.0013
Standard deviation	0.0355	0.0284	0.0327
After 2007			
Mean	0.0003	0.0014	0.0003
Standard Deviation	0.0330	0.0331	0.0271
Panel B: Volatility of return	**Hang Seng**	**Nikkei**	**STI**
Before 1997			
Mean	0.0233	0.0204	0.0174
Standard Deviation	0.0209	0.0191	0.0156
1997-2007			
Mean	0.0264	0.0225	0.0223
Standard Deviation	0.0237	0.0174	0.0239
After 2007			
Mean	0.0248	0.0244	0.0180
Standard Deviation	0.0217	0.0225	0.0202

Table 4: Rate of return and volatility in three subsamples of time (Asian markets).

The correlation in price movements

Up to now, we focused on one developed Asian market and two smaller developing Asian markets and the studies of CL, JS and JKK, and we ascertained a preliminary view of the level of integration among the Tokyo, Hang Seng and Singapore markets. By calculating and examining the Pearson Product Moment linear correlation coefficients, we can ascertain the strength of the relationships, as presented in Table 5 below. All data came from known public sources. Note that the Hang Seng and Nikkei (Tokyo) for the rate of return (Panel A) have a correlation of 0.4307, indicating that less 19% of the variation in the first market explains the variation in the other market. The same Pearson coefficient for Hang Seng and Singapore is 0.6637, which indicates that about 44% of the variation in one index is explained by the variation in the other index. A similar result occurs for the association of the Singapore and Nikkei markets (Table 5, Panel A). For the study of volatility, (Table 5, Panel B), we observe a coefficient of 0.2711 which indicates that 7.3% of the variation in Hang Seng is explained by the variation in Nikkei. The other combinations produce larger values of 0.5558 and 0.3048; however, no combination produced a value greater than 31% of the variation in one index being associated with the variation in a second index. Due to large sample sizes, all the correlation coefficients calculated and observed resulted in p-values of less than 0.05. Although these values are statically significant, how important are they in predicting the covariation? The answer is simple: they would need to be much larger to predict the variation in one index when a second index changes. Some degree of association for mean and volatility in rates of return are associated with the same in a second market, nevertheless, we study other mitigating factors that may have large or additional influence.

Previous research on the relationship between large and small stock returns in six Asian (Pacific-Basin) nations and the association among

Panel-A: Rates of return			
	Hang Seng	**Nikkei**	**STI**
Hang Seng	1	0.4307	0.6639
Nikkei	0.4307	1	0.4657
STI	0.6639	0.4657	1
Panel-B: Volatility of return			
	Hang Seng	**Nikkei**	**STI**
Hang Seng	1	0.2716	0.5558
Nikkei	0.2716	1	0.3084
STI	0.5558	0.3084	1

Table 5: Pearson correlation coefficients (entire time period for each market).

the same six Asian financial markets is exemplified by Jarrett and Sun [2]. Their purpose was to provide evidence of the cross-autocorrelation of stock returns in a lengthy time period. Evidence was brought to bear as to the theoretical explanations for stock market behavior of Pacific-Basin nations including those with large financial markets, i.e., Japan and Hong Kong, and those with small financial markets, i.e., Thailand and Malaysia. This study, though different than ours, indicates clearly the relationship of large and small equity markets and gives us further desire to learn more about the co-integration of Asian equity markets.

We can now still learn more about the level of integration in our three markets by analyzing multiple regressions, and in doing so we exclude the influence of the delayed effects of lagged explanatory variables.

Regressions of the Rate of Return

We define the rate of return to be the percent change in the stock price from period t-1 to period t. According to the efficient markets hypothesis (EMH), the rate of return is difficult to predict with any reasonable level of accuracy. Hence, we wish to determine if there is validity in this hypothesis and whether rates of return in the three markets are correlated after excluding the influence of their own lagged values.

We construct a model to explain the Hang Seng rate of return by its own past values. By constructing a model with many lagged values of the rate of return and calculate the Akaike Information Criterion (AIC), we find that AIC is minimized at a lag of two. In turn, we find the first-order auto regression which appears in column (2) of Table 6. The coefficient (H1) is 0.0694 with a t-statistic of 3.2320 for all data which is significant at the reasonable level of $\alpha \leq 0.05$. According to this result the weak form of the efficient markets hypothesis does hold for this time period. We repeat this process for the other two equity markets. For Nikkei, AIC is also minimized at a lag of two periods. The N2 coefficient is 0.0725 (t-statistic=2.8470). And for Singapore, AIC is minimized at lag of three periods. The STI3 coefficient is 0.0576 (t-statistic=3.0147). The results are mixed but all have t-statistics that are significant at $\alpha \leq .01$. Next, we will further investigate this phenomenon by dividing the time series data into the same three sub-periods analyzed previously.

For all three equity markets, we subdivide the data into the three time periods noted previously. For the Hang Seng market, the lagged variable of two resulted in coefficients of 0.0659, 0.0779, and 0.0217 for the three time periods of pre-1997, 1997-2007, and post-2007, respectively. However, these two-period lagged coefficients were only statistically different from zero in the 1997-2007 time period. Thus, the results for the Hang Seng market are mixed. For the auto regression of the Nikkei market, we find the N2 coefficients to be 0.0812, 0.0194 and 0.0011 for the three time periods with none of them being statistically significant at a 95% confidence level. Recall that for the Nikkei, the entire period had a statistically significant coefficient of 0.0725. Hence, the individual sub-periods coefficients are of limited value and interpretation for the Nikkei. Lastly for Singapore (denoted STI), only the second period (1997-2007) has a coefficient that is statistically significant. The coefficient is 0.0979. The first and third periods were not statistically significant.

These results are not entirely the same as those of CL, JS, and JKK, but do indicate that change occurred among the three sample sub-periods. The results are mixed in all equity markets indicating different effects during the entire time period and differential effects in each of the sub periods. The data appear temporally affected although we cannot be certain about many interpretations of the results. Recalling, our purpose is to ascertain behavior backed up by the decision analytics of this and previous studies.

With the continued and dynamic development of the of the Asian equity markets, we should now observe the more recent analysis of their co-integration exhibited in Table 7. For all years in the Hang Seng, the results indicate that the current Hang Seng rate of return (the response variable) is associated with the current rates of return in the Tokyo and Singapore markets (explanatory variables). The coefficients are highly significant. There is no statistical significance between the current Hang Seng rate of return and the lagged rates of return of the markets in Tokyo (two period lag) and Singapore (three period lag). For all years in the Nikkei, the results are similar to the Hang Seng in that the other two markets (Hang Seng and Singapore) are significant (positive) predictors of the Hang Seng in the current period, but there is no significant relationship in the lagged values. Lastly, for the Singapore market, we again see a relationship in the current time period but no statistically significant relationships between markets in the lagged variables. Overall, the results in Table 7 support the notion that the three markets are integrated and have some association with each other during the entire time period studied. It should be noted that the strongest integration appears to be between the Hang Seng and Singapore markets as they have both the largest coefficients and largest t-statistics in each other's regressions.

By examining the three sub-periods (e.g., before 1997, 1997-

	Hang Seng (HS)				Nikkei (N)				STI			
	All Years	Pre-1997	1997-2007	Post-2007	All Years	Pre-1997	1997-2007	Post-2007	All Years	Pre-1997	1997-2007	Post-2007
cHS	0.0011	0.0024	0.0009	0.0000								
t	1.7301	1.9311	0.8495	-0.0073								
HS2	0.0694	0.0659	0.0779	0.0217								
t	3.2320	1.6160	2.3142	0.5819								
cN					-0.0004	-0.0011	-0.0007	0.0011				
t					-0.6319	-0.8985	-0.6399	0.9188				
N2					0.0725	0.0812	0.0194	0.0742				
T					2.8470	1.8390	0.4647	1.5278				
cSTI									0.0002	0.0009	0.0003	-0.0003
t									0.2946	1.0011	0.2908	-0.3996
STI3									0.0576	-0.0309	0.0979	0.0289
t									3.0147	-0.7954	3.1869	1.0496

Table 6: Auto regressions of the rates of return on equities listed in the three markets.

	Hang Seng (HS)				Nikkei (N)				STI			
	All Years	Pre-1997	1997-2007	Post-2007	All Years	Pre-1997	1997-2007	Post-2007	All Years	Pre-1997	1997-2007	Post-2007
C	0.0011	0.0024	0.0009	0.0000	-0.0004	-0.0011	-0.0007	0.0011	0.0002	0.0009	0.0003	-0.0003
t	1.7301	1.9311	0.8495	-0.0073	-0.6319	-0.8985	-0.6399	0.9188	0.2946	1.0011	0.2908	-0.3996
HS0					0.1955	0.0350	0.2227	0.3539	0.4868	0.3482	0.5458	0.5548
t					7.1260	0.7626	5.4784	5.5355	27.1408	11.9055	17.4568	18.1938
HS2	0.0694	0.0659	0.0779	0.0217	-0.0305	-0.0748	0.0018	-0.0383	-0.0194	0.0312	-0.0618	0.0064
t	3.2320	1.6160	2.3142	0.5819	-1.3417	-1.8567	0.0531	-0.7891	-1.0822	1.0611	-1.9836	0.2111
N0	0.1756	0.0358	0.2250	0.2083					0.2076	0.2082	0.1726	0.1843
t	7.1260	0.7626	5.4784	5.5355					10.2791	6.4230	4.5094	6.0447
N2	-0.0367	-0.0345	-0.0224	-0.0327	0.0725	0.0812	0.0194	0.0742	0.0044	0.0047	-0.0043	0.0151
t	-1.5166	-0.7705	-0.5343	-0.8760	2.8470	1.8390	0.4647	1.5278	0.2197	0.1451	-0.1100	0.4970
STI0	0.6990	0.6720	0.6390	0.8332	0.3319	0.3922	0.1999	0.4703				
t	27.1408	11.9055	17.4568	18.1938	10.2791	6.4230	4.5094	6.0447				
STI3	-0.0132	-0.0346	0.0037	-0.0103	-0.0406	0.0658	-0.0539	-0.0651	0.0576	-0.0309	0.0979	0.0289
t	-0.5736	-0.6404	0.1118	-0.3040	-1.6781	1.2327	-1.6201	-1.4805	3.0147	-0.7954	3.1869	1.0496
R-squared	0.4670	0.2752	0.4711	0.7078	0.2463	0.1298	0.2056	0.5083	0.4858	0.3311	0.4684	0.7130
SE of Reg	0.0244	0.0265	0.0259	0.0179	0.0258	0.0262	0.0258	0.0234	0.0204	0.0191	0.0239	0.0146

Table 7: Regressions of rate of return.

2007 and after 2007) one continues to observe small and some non-significant t-statistics among all the equity markets paired with each other. In general, statistical significance (or the lack thereof) between exchanges within the sub-periods between exchanges was consistent with significance in the entire period. Although the coefficients (and associated test statistics) tended to be larger in the latter two sub-periods than in the first sub-period. For example, for the Hang Seng regressions, the coefficients of N0 and STI0 were larger and the t-statistics larger in the 1997-2007 and post-2007 periods than in the pre-1997 period. For the Nikkei, one can see that the coefficients for HS0 and STI0 are largest in the post-2007 period. And finally for Singapore (STI), the HS0 coefficient is much larger in the two latter sub-periods, while the N0 variable coefficient and t-statistics are roughly the same throughout the three sub-periods.

Auto-regressions of the volatility of rates of return

We construct a regression model with the purpose of explaining the volatility in the Hang Seng and the other two equity markets. First, we account for the effects of their own volatility associated with their past values. Following CL and JS, the appropriate number of lagged explanatory variables to include in the respective models is determined by (1) the significance of individual parameter estimates; (2) by minimizing the AIC value; and (3) the presence or absence of serial correlation in the residual. By including one lagged response variable at a time, we follow CL, JS and JKK and observe the three criteria to construct a model explaining the current volatility in the three stock exchanges.

In Table 8, we find for Hang Seng that all lagged variables (four weeks' worth of lags) have significant t-statistics (2.9801, 4.0460, 4.6809 and 4.116). Tests for serial correlation applied to the model having four lagged values yield small and significant t-statistics. Nikkei (All Data) has large significant coefficients for lags 1, 2 and 3 but small and non-significant marginal coefficients for lag 4. For Singapore, significant lags were found at 1, 2, 3 and 4. There are some sub-periods for Nikkei and Hang Seng where non-significant coefficients occurred. In general, in the three markets, there tended to be significant autocorrelation up to lag 3. Similar results were found also when we observe the results of studying the individual three sub-periods noting that the sample sizes for sub periods are smaller than for the entire time period. Table 8 shows that significant auto-regressive coefficients in equity markets indicate an association with its own lagged variables. It is well-known that observations from previous studies including CL, JS and JKK resulted in a similar analysis and conclusions.

As before, we test for structural change in each equity market by dividing our time period into three sub periods. Although the results are universally similar, for the most part, the auto regressions for all three equity markets exhibit outcomes that are very similar to each other. Tests for equality among the three sub periods for each market would show the same results. In conclusion, all three markets suggest that each market has some parameter stability during the lengthy period studied and the effect of changes in time as expressed by the three sub periods indicate that this is true for each market but with some disparities.

At this point, we introduce lagged values of the other markets to ascertain whether the volatility in the former market indicates Granger causality [20]. To determine Granger causality in Hang Seng volatility, we choose the number of lagged values of the other indices volatility according to the criteria noted before (e.g., AIC and the absence of serial correlation in the residuals). Our results for the whole sample period (All Data), as reported in Table 9, indicate that we have only lag 1 for Nikkei and lag 1 for Singapore (zero lags are included for both.) The t-statistics for zero lags are significant for Nikkei and Singapore at a very small probability (significance level of $\alpha \leq 0.01$). Hence volatility in the Hang Seng equity market is associated with the lagged value in the other markets. Since the t-statistics are not significant for lagged values of 1 in Nikkei and Singapore, we cannot draw the same conclusion as in earlier studies. Thus, a Granger causality exists among the three Asian markets but we cannot extend the results to the lagged time periods. Hence, this indicates that the volatility in the markets for the entire time period were likely independent of each other. Some similarities exist in the Tables 9-11; however, we cannot be completely certain as to the exact relationship of the three markets. Future lengthier and wider studies of long-term data may indicate relationship that we have not discovered from this data.

Consistent with the findings of CL, we observed only the H1 (no lag) coefficients are at this time the coefficient is not significant (at α=0.05 or less). The AIC value suggests not including any lagged values of the Hang Seng variables. In addition, the Breusch-Godfrey test revealed the absence of serial correlation in the autoregressive model.

	Hang Seng				Nikkei				STI			
	All Years	Pre-1997	1997-2007	Post-2007	All Years	Pre-1997	1997-2007	Post-2007	All Years	Pre-1997	1997-2007	Post-2007
C	0.0250	0.0233	0.0264	0.0248	0.0224	0.0207	0.0227	0.0243	0.0194	0.0171	0.0223	0.0180
t	25.587	16.834	16.660	11.339	28.009	11.075	25.323	15.016	17.078	15.274	11.357	7.076
VLTY_HANG(-1)	0.0784	0.0042	0.1278	0.0705								
t	2.9801	0.0900	3.0755	1.3968								
VLTY_HANG(-2)	0.1059	0.1534	0.0478	0.1385								
t	4.0460	3.3211	1.1442	2.8135								
VLTY_HANG(-3)	0.1226	0.0821	0.0879	0.2315								
t	4.6809	1.7776	2.1045	4.7138								
VLTY_HANG(-4)	0.1080	0.0753	0.1275	0.0892								
t	4.1116	1.6336	3.0616	1.7683								
VLTY_NIKKEI(-1)					0.1522	0.1890	0.0399	0.2027				
t					5.7572	4.0148	0.9511	3.9971				
VLTY_NIKKEI(-2)					0.0744	0.0700	0.0770	0.0495				
t					2.7947	1.4726	1.8394	0.9597				
VLTY_NIKKEI(-3)					0.1021	0.1213	0.0776	0.0777				
t					3.8339	2.5500	1.8565	1.5053				
VLTY_NIKKEI(-4)					0.0451	0.1770	-0.0156	-0.0110				
t					1.7046	3.7578	-0.3713	-0.2172				
VLTY_STI(-1)									0.1502	0.0954	0.1533	0.1571
t									5.7472	2.0626	3.7486	3.0976
VLTY_STI(-2)									0.1201	0.1148	0.0578	0.2704
t									4.5843	2.4759	1.4033	5.4253
VLTY_STI(-3)									0.1324	0.0774	0.0921	0.2420
t									5.0536	1.6706	2.2371	4.8562
VLTY_STI(-4)									0.1519	0.0941	0.2185	-0.0182
t									5.8340	2.0785	5.3483	-0.3587

Table 8: Auto regressions of volatility of equity prices.

	All Years	Pre-1997	1997-2007	Post-2007
constant	0.0072	0.0096	0.0078	0.0062
t	6.2756	3.9706	3.7038	3.8247
H0				
t				
H1	0.0181	-0.0171	0.0575	0.0293
t	0.6832	-0.3684	1.3687	0.5719
H2	0.0622	0.1465	0.0258	0.0014
t	2.7874	3.2980	0.7399	0.0399
H3	0.0570	0.0744	0.0470	0.0463
t	2.5461	1.6759	1.3446	1.2818
H4	0.0413	0.0552	0.0386	0.0313
t	1.8323	1.2415	1.1003	0.8674
N0	0.1144	0.0119	0.0903	0.1851
t	4.3082	0.2371	1.9260	4.7361
N1	-0.0021	0.0146	-0.0074	0.0265
t	-0.0794	0.2897	-0.1533	0.6597
STI0	0.5356	0.4056	0.5290	0.6705
t	20.9238	6.7833	14.7450	14.4441
STI1	0.0148	0.0060	0.0229	-0.0722
t	0.5044	0.0942	0.5436	-1.2448

Table 9: Regressions of volatility of equity returns.

	All Years	Pre-1997	1997-2007	Post-2007
constant	0.0096	0.0078	0.0158	0.0081
t	8.4516	3.8930	8.0776	3.8863
N0				
t				
N1	0.1240	0.1711	0.0129	0.1364
t	4.6691	3.7345	0.3004	2.6559
N2	0.0447	0.0724	0.0521	-0.0166
t	1.7485	1.5780	1.2389	-0.3806
N3	0.0861	0.1113	0.0810	0.0363
t	3.3705	2.4201	1.9249	0.8347
N4	0.0256	0.1769	-0.0321	-0.0448
t	1.0128	3.8759	-0.7625	-1.0586
H0	0.1146	0.0086	0.0687	0.2975
t	4.4347	0.2077	1.8344	4.7029
H1	-0.0109	0.0234	-0.0307	-0.0231
t	-0.4201	0.5659	-0.8204	-0.3538
STI0	0.1937	0.1440	0.1150	0.3517
t	6.8208	2.5456	3.0892	4.9835
STI1	0.0034	-0.0849	0.0325	0.0174
t	0.1180	-1.4639	0.8603	0.2361

Table 10: Regressions of volatility of equity returns.

The model with one Shanghai lagged variable (S1) is not considered in this study. The negative coefficients corroborates the results of CL but in this study this coefficient is not estimated.

An additional question relates to whether or not there is significant co-variation of volatility in a multivariate setting. To incorporate instantaneous causality in explaining Hang Seng volatility, one adds the current value of the variable in the other markets into the auto-regression. The coefficients for the Nikkei (All Years) show some positive coefficients but only N0 is significant. This would indicate that extended time period in this study resulted in Hang Seng volatility not significantly related to Nikkei volatility in a lagged time period. Within sub-periods, we observe that the pre-1997 period has a t-statistic for N0 that is not significant, while the other two time periods are significant. Like the Nikkei, lagged one period Singapore volatility is not a significant predictor of the Hang Seng volatility. However, Singapore volatility is more strongly related to the Hang Seng volatility in the

	All Years	Pre-1997	1997-2007	Post-2007
constant	-0.001	0.005	-0.002	-0.002
t	-0.617	2.675	-0.886	-1.865
STI0				
t				
STI1	0.098	0.077	0.077	0.167
t	3.695	1.616	1.844	3.277
STI2	0.082	0.123	0.026	0.160
t	3.652	2.730	0.762	4.415
STI3	0.079	0.046	0.073	0.086
t	3.482	1.022	2.084	2.356
STI4	0.086	0.045	0.120	-0.018
t	3.814	0.987	3.381	-0.504
H0	0.426	0.2133	0.508	0.521
t	20.639	6.576	14.324	14.527
H1	-0.016	0.020	-0.019	-0.060
t	-0.681	0.578	-0.450	-1.339
N0	0.151	0.100	0.138	0.155
t	6.371	2.722	2.973	4.529
N1	-0.009	0.015	0.058	-0.079
T	-0.370	0.396	1.223	-2.260

Table 11: Regressions of volatility of equity returns.

current period. It is significant within all the sub-periods, including the pre-1997 time period unlike the Nikkei.

If we go line by line and column by column through all the data in Tables 10 and 11, we find consistency from period to period in pairwise combinations of one variable and its relationship with lagged 1 of the another market's variable. Market volatility does not have a lasting effect. In a lag of only one period, we do not see evidence of a lasting effect on the volatility of a second equity market in markets of Asia. Of course, our conclusions are limited to the three markets studied and the time period under investigation extending the time periods to include more distant data in the past would probably no change the overall conclusion since our time period is long at this point. Observing Table 10, N1, N3 and N4 and STI0, as well as the constant term, have coefficients with significant t-statistics (p-value less than 0.05). This indicates that Nikkei has serial correlation at lags of 1, 3 and 4 and contains one additional coefficient with Singapore at zero lag. In period 2, only STI0 and N3 (along with the constant term) are significant. And in period 3, coefficients are significant for N1, H0 and STI0 (and the constant term). Hence there is no evidence of consistency in the three sub-periods.

Our analysis indicates that the three sub-periods are not identical to each other and the data analytical results correspond to the notion that this is reasonable. Financial economic events in Asia indicate as noted in this study do show that external effects from other parts of the World do influence the markets studied. However, our purpose was not to measure overseas effects but Asia is not an isolated area of the Earth.

We observe the same lack of consistency in the finding for Singapore (Table 11.) Lags for STI1, STI2, STI3, and STI4, as well as H0 and N0 contain, significant t-statistics when the entire period's volatility for Singapore is analyzed. However, within individual sub-periods, these significances disappear in some cases. For example, STI1, STI3, and STI4 are not significant in the pre-1997 (1987-1997 in this study) period, while STI2 is not significant for the 1997-2007 period, and STI4 is not significant for the post-2007 period.

Without going through the analysis to compare individual coefficients, we observe the diversity of differences from the change in time and pairwise relationships in markets. As long as economic conditions change, the results include temporal instabilities in markets. Our study is lengthy and exhaustive but much of its results are not unnerving since we already know that markets vary in price and volatility, but these factors have components that are predictable using modern time series analysis. See Ray, Chen and Jarrett where the authors show that firms listed on the Tokyo exchange contain components (permanent and temporary) which may in turn lead to better predictions.

Overall, when analyzing the results for the models of the volatility in equity returns for all three markets, we find the effect of the Asian equities leading to the same form of temporal instability of the parameters as seen among the Western equity markets. Simply stated the inclusion of the Hang Seng or Tokyo variables do not result in stable relationships throughout the three sub periods studied. There are observed structural changes related to each time period. Hence, we conclude that the concept of temporal stability is not present.

Conclusions

We collected, analyzed and interpreted an extensive database of the stock market indices for equity markets of Tokyo, Singapore and Hong Kong (Hang Seng). Our purpose is to draw conclusions concerning the relationships of the various equity markets expressed by an analysis of the mean and volatility of rates of return in the three stock exchanges over a lengthy period of time and during three distinct sub-periods. We initially examined the time series characteristics of stock price indices for all three exchanges during the period of 1987 to 2015. Specifically, we calculated the rate of return and the volatility of returns for the three markets and estimated the serial correlation and co-movement of the equity markets. Volatility in the rates of return also differs among the three equity exchanges. Across the three sub-periods defined by time the relationship are not stable. This, perhaps, is the most crucial of the general findings of this analysis. Relationships among the markets across time periods change. Investigations into the influences of the economic environment in which the markets operate indicate some of the causes are changes in variability and volatility of the rates of return (or at least associations with these changes). This adds to ones knowledge of explaining and predicting relationships among the three exchanges. The evidence presented in this study is largely consistent with other studies of the relationship among equity markets in three or more nations.

Furthermore, we find that serial correlation also differs in the three equity markets. The use of multivariate time series analysis [21-26] may provide further evidence for the lack of co-integration in these stock exchanges. One last suggestion is to examine each individual index to access where there are temporary and permanent components in these indices in the manner of Ray, Chen and Jarrett [19] for the Japanese market. This would answer questions concerning temporal stability in the indices of Asian equity markets. In the future, we expect time series studies to continue in areas of the so-called emerging markets of Asia (and South America as well) to relate in a similar context the extent to which emerging markets, i.e., India, China and others, are related to influences by the developed nations of Europe, North America and Japan.

References

1. Chow GC Fan Z Hu J (1999) Shanghai stock prices as determined by the present value model. J Comp Econ 27: 553-561.

2. Jarrett JE, Sun Z (2009) Evidence and Explanations for the Association among Six Asian (Pacific-Basin) Financial Markets. Appl Econ 41: 1-12.
3. Jarrett JE, Sun Z (2009) Explaining Pacific-Basin Financial Market Returns by Size of Firm. Int Rev App Fin Issues Econ 1: 33-42.
4. Chen N (1991) Financial investment opportunities and the macro economy. J Finance 46: 529-554.
5. Cheung YW, L Ng (1998) International evidence on the stock market and aggregate economic activity. J Empir Financ 5: 281-296.
6. Liaw KT (2007) Investment Banking and Investment Opportunities in China: A Comprehensive Guide for Finance Professionals. John Wiley & Co: New York.
7. Fama E (1990) Stock returns expected returns and real activity. J Finance 45: 1089-1109.
8. Fama E (1991) Efficient capital markets: II. J Finance 46: 1575-1617.
9. Wei KCJ, Wong K (1992) Test of inflation and industry portfolio stock returns. J Econ Bus 44: 77-94.
10. Zhong RS, Gu L, Lui CB (1999) The Empirical Statistical Analysis of Chinese Stock Markets China. Financial and Political Economics Press, Beijing.
11. Chow GC, Lawler CC (2003) A time series analysis of the Shanghai and New York stock price indices. Annals of Economics and Finance 4: 17-35.
12. Jarrett JE, Sun T (2012) Association between the New York and Shanghai Markets: Evidence from the Stock Price Indices. Journal of Business Economics and Management 13: 132-147.
13. Jarrett J, Klein A, Kyper E (2013) Association between Asian equity markets and Western markets: Evidence from the indexes of equity markets. Asian J Empir Res 3: 8.
14. Bailey W, Cai J, Cheung, Wang F (2009) Stock returns order imbalances and commonality: Evidence on individual institutional and proprietary investors in China. J Finance 45: 1109-1128.
15. Jarrett JE, Kyper E (2010) Seasonality in Outliers of Stock Returns for the Chinese Equities Markets. Inter Rev App Finan Issues Econ 2: 823-847.
16. Levine R, Zervos S (1998) Stock Markets Banks and Economic Growth. The American Economic Review 88: 537-558.
17. Levine R (2005) Finance and Growth: Theory and Evidence in Handbook of Economic Growth. Elsevier BV 1: 865-934.
18. Pan X, Li K, Jarrett JE (2012) The relationship of high frequency interactions between Chines A-shares and Hong Kong H-shares of dual-listed companies. J Res Econ Int Fin 1: 103-123.
19. Ray B, Chen S, Jarrett JE (1997) Identifying permanent and temporary components in Japanese stock prices. Finan Eng Japanese Markets 4: 233-256.
20. Granger CWJ (1969) Investigating causal relation by econometric and cross-sectional method. Econometrica 37: 424–438.
21. Kuvita T (2010) Time Series Analysis of Transatlantic Market Interactions: Evidence from Crude Oil and Gasoline Prices. Int J Bus Econ 9: 157-173.
22. Chen L, Finney M, Lai KS (2005) A Threshold Cointegration of Asymmetric Price Transmission from Crude Oil to Gasoline Prices. Econ Letters 89: 233-239.
23. Juselius K (2006) The Cointegrated VAR Model: Methodology and Applications. Oxford University Press.
24. Eun CS, Huang W (2007) Asset Pricing in China's Domestic Stock Markets: Is there Logic Pacific-Basin. Fin J15: 452-480.
25. Jarrett JE, Pan X, Chen S (2009) Do the Chinese bourses (stock markets) predict economic growth? Int J Bus Eco8: 201-211.
26. Jarrett JE, Schilling J (2008) Daily Variation and Predicting Stock Market Returns For The Frankfurter Börse (Stock Market). J Bus Eco Manag 9: 289-198.

8

A Financial Analysis of the Low-Carbon Projects in the China (PRC)

Jarrett JE[1]* Juan Yu[2] and Xia Pan[2]

[1]*University of Rhode Island, USA*

[2]*Sun Yat-sen Universit, China*

Abstract

The purpose of this study is to determine the financial impacts of applying low-carbon projects stemming from the Kyoto Protocols on a sample of firms in the People's Republic of China (PRC). By financial impacts we refer to the usual impacts on firms reflected in the financial reports of firms. The projects referred to as CDM aimed at reducing the demand and use of inefficient methods or producing and operating power generation resulting in high carbon emissions having negative effects on the ecology of the planet. We studied financial aspects of the projects to determine whether the sampled firms were harmed in a financial way by the implementation and results of the Kyoto sponsored projects. We do not cover all projects but a sample of those started and implemented in the PRC.

Keywords: Kyoto protocols; Financial impacts; Clean development mechanisms; Certification emission reduction; Mean asset-liability ratio

Introduction

With the development of human civilization, humankind are increasingly willing to use natural resources for economic development and often without regard to the waste of natural resources and the damage to the ecology of the planet [1]. Since the industrial revolution, the process of abusing resources continued with carbon dioxide emissions causing the changes in weather fluctuations and, in turn, natural disasters, floods, drought, tsunamis and other extreme weather events.

Fortunately, most nations reached a consensus to improve these harsh consequences. WMO (World Meteorological Organization) and UNEP (United Nations Environment Program) jointly established IPCC (the Intergovernmental Panel on Climate Change) in 1988, which organized more than 3,000scientists for scientific assessments of global climate change [2]. A series of meetings to confront climate change began in December 1990. The 45th session of the UN General Assembly resulted in the United Nations Framework Convention on Climate Change. In February 1991, this convention officially launched the negotiations for the adoption of the United Nations Framework Convention on Climate Change and the meetings put into effect the United Nations Framework Convention on Climate Change called the Kyoto Protocol. This protocol provided for the obligation of developing nation to reduce emission under the law from 2008 to 2012. On February 16, 2005, the Kyoto Protocols came into effect [3].

The Kyoto Protocols includes the development mechanism and joint implementation to encourage the reduction of carbon emissions. The Protocol encourages also the coordination of International Climate Change and Clean Development Mechanisms (CDM) in developing nations such as renewable energy, energy efficiency and improvement projects [4]. In turn, these projects generate the CER (Certification Emission Reduction) which was the response to carbon emissions. Economic benefits would result from the "CER"s which would benefit all.

The Chinese government signed the Kyoto Protocol in 1998 and approved it in 2002 [5]. The People Republic of China (PRC) approved 2232 CDM projects, of which 663 received the successful production registration of the UN's CDM Executive Board, and the registration number and annual reductions ranks were the first for all participating nations [6].

Our purpose is to compare financial data of firms that introduce CDM projects with firms of similar size which do not implement CDM projects. The similar firms will come from the same industry such as chemical, energy, power generation, and materials. Before and after implementation of the projects permit us to establish whether financial aspects of the firms benefit or not from the CDM's. From many research reports on social effect on the local economy as well as environmental effects, we clarify whether the ecology of the production environment improved or not. Finally, we find the impact of financial performance of the firms in the sample. We ascertain whether the advance of 'low cabin" technology affect firms in a positive or negative manner. The remaining portions of this manuscript divide in the following parts.

We illustrate the necessity of a 'low carbon" economy for industrial development. The CDM projects permit the low carbon economy to advance and include social, environmental and economic benefits. Second, we present empirical evidence of the effects of CDM projects on the financial performance of a selected sample of firms. Last, we summarize the main conclusions emanating from the analysis and give suggestions for improvement and more study.

Appeal of low-carbon economy

"Green appeal" refers to a low carbon economy where the purpose is to minimize the consumption of fossil fuels by technology innovation, industry transformation, and new energy development. To minimize means to reduce carbon gas emissions and achieve economic development as well as social development and ecological environmental protection. The low carbon economy relates to differences between developed and developing nations in their goals. The low carbon economy may stymy developing nations whereas developed nations no longer have the great desire to develop fossil fuels without positive consequences.

Low energy consumption and low carbon emissions may result in

***Corresponding author:** Jarrett JE, University of Rhode Island, USA
E-mail: jejarrett@mail.uri.edu

net economic development because the low carbon economy depletes natural resources in a small scale. Thus, the Kyoto Protocol provides a good opportunity for the developing nations to evolve and grow and benefit technology transfer and foreign investment. This is a goal of the "sustainable supply chain."

The remaining portions of this study include the empirical financial analysis of firms that participated in the CDM programs to determine the effectiveness of low carbon projects. A large amount of data collected, organized and tabulated from the financial data of twenty-one participating firms. These data are financial indicators of profitability, solvency, growth capacity and market performance. Further, we also predict the CER earnings of the twenty-one firms included in the study.

Last, we analyze financial indicators derived from financial statements and determine whether CDM projects had financial impact. Later we find explanations for and inherent deficiencies of the analysis. Finally, summary, conclusions and implications for further study are at the end of study will discuss the evidence of the effects of CDM projects on the financial performance of the selected sample of firms.

Green appeal and CDM projects

Green appeal refers to a "low carbon" economy. The purpose is to minimize the energy consumption of coal, carbon, oil, such as: technology innovation, industry transformation, new energy development, which reduces greenhouse gas emissions and achieves both economic and social development with ecological implications.

The low carbon economy is relates differences between the developed and developing nations in their goals. The low carbon economy may stymy developing nations whereas the developed nations no longer have the great desire to develop fossil fuels without positive consequences.

In June, 2007 China (PRC) launched the China National Change Program. First China became responsible for environmental protection resulting in energy savings. Second, low energy consumption and low carbon emissions resulted in net economic development because fewer natural resources were utilized. Thus, the Kyoto Protocols provide a good opportunity for developing nations to grow economically benefit from technological transfer and foreign investment.

The Kyoto protocol is the first international treaty aimed at coordinating work on climate change, industrial power except for the United States to reduce the greenhouse gas emissions. The CDM as part of this agreement allows developed nations to invest and develop energy efficient projects (CDM's) in developing countries, such as renewable energy generation, energy efficiency or improvement projects, and obtain CER certificates resulting from these projects. These actions may reduce energy consumptions and more efficiently utilize available energy resources. Developing nations gain investment capital and advanced technology from CDM project and substantial economic benefits from the sale of CERs [7].

The analysis

Our purpose is to examine and analyze financial statements to determine the impact of CDM projects on those firms that initiate these projects. We wish to suggest that CDM projects have impact and whether these projects produce positive impacts. In China, many firms responded to the "green appeal" through the adoption of CDM projects in response to the Kyoto Protocols. CDM impacts can be measured and have practical cost-effective consequences that explain the necessity of low carbon promotions. January, 2005, the first CDM domestic projects were approved and implemented. Chinese CDM projects are implemented in economically underdeveloped regions such as Yunnan, Sichuan, Gansu and Inner Mongolia. The CDM projects for these regions brought revenue-generating opportunities and great benefits to the local economy [8].

CDM projects

There are many companies have responded the green economy in domestic, and the most popular is the CDM project. They consist promotional items which can be measured and have practical cost-effective outcomes. In addition, they explain the availability and necessity of a low carbon, green economy. The empirical analysis of CDM projects is evidence that green appeal should be promoted through promoting its benefits to both the economy and ecology. Since January 25, 2005 the first CDM projects approved in the domestic economy of the PRC provided for the promotion of the green appeal projects. The PRC CDM projects were implemented largely in economically underdeveloped and often distressed regions, such as Yunnan, Sichuan, Gansu, Inner Mongolia provinces. The CDM projects for these regions are actually bringing revenue generating opportunities and great benefits to the local economy.

CDM projects go through an approval process including a CDM project sponsor, a project design and required materials for the NDRC. The NDRC receives the application and commits relevant agencies to audit the project and, in turn, a registration. Meanwhile the audited projects need to go through an operating entity of validation to ensure that the project conforms to stated requirements; such as: participators, reasonability of baseline methodology and monitoring plan [9]. The CDM projects are beneficial when we have greenhouse gas emission reduction. Besides governmental agencies, other institutions and individuals do not participate in the transfer transaction reductions. According to the PRC CDM Fund Management Methods directed by the PRC CDM Fund Management Center, the CDM projects collect funds from the transfer transaction reductions and the economy and ecology benefit from the positive impacts of the program.

International regulations require four operating modes to operate the CDM project. First, the unilateral mode permits independent functioning of the CDM project. The emission reductions can be sold to developed nations or not. Second, the bilateral mode (the most popular method) permits both developing and developed nations to sign agreements to cooperate in the developing of the CDM project. Developed nations would provide investment, technology and support while the developing nation must sell the CER to the interests in the developed nation. Third, the multilateral mode jointly establishes the "Carbon Fund" by a number of developed nations who signed an agreement with developing nations, i.e. PRC. The resulting CER is sold to interests in the developed nations in proportion to their investment. Fourth, the mixed mode is a combination of modes 1, 2 and 3. This cooperative approach is suitable for large scale projects requiring very large financial commitments. All four modes apply in the PRC and the choice is usually based on the particular financial situation of the Chinese firm engaged in the project. Although the choice of the mode depends the firm, each decision should generate the positive impacts on the economy, society and the ecology.

The sample selection criteria

A large number of CDM projects approved in the PRC for implementation provide the sampling frame for which we can choose for the sample to study. Our problem was to explore and research which requires collecting financial statements of listed firms' CDM projects data. By researching, we determine the most representative twenty-one firms as the experimental group. The data collected included more than three years of valid financial statements. The twenty-firms with CDM projects are denoted below and identified in the Appendix.

This study reflects profitability, solvency, market performance and growth of four financial indicators. According to the analysis required, we collected the return on equity (ROE), asset-liability ratio, price-earnings ratio and the main business revenue data of four aspects of the firm that introduced CDM projects. We compare the performance of financial data before and after the introduction of the CDM. The growth rate is related to analyzing trends or the change in trend associated with green appeals exemplified on financial statements.

We compare before and after samples of firm data that implemented CDM projects., For comparison, the year of introduction of the CDM projects is the first year for the event, denoted by (0).The first year after the introduction is denoted by (+), and the year before the introduction is denoted by (-). Table 1 is the financial data of the twenty-one listed firms. We edited the before and after the CDM introduction data to find how this introduction affected the financial data of the firms. Next, we conduct a detailed analysis ascertain whether or not these financial data reflect economic benefits of CDM projects. In this study, we define profitability as the firm's ability to earn profits and in turn the profitability analysis is the analysis of the corporate profit margins.

Return on net assets is the ratio of average net income and net assets of the firm which reflect the firm's income level. The belief that the greater the return on net assets, the greater the likelihood that the firm earn positive returns on assets. All this leads to greater operating efficiency, higher profits and high returns to shareholders.

We calculate the changes in net assets rate before and after implementation CDM project. Data Table 2 embodies the influence on the growth rate of net assets return to the company implementation CDM before and after the project.

From Table 2, observe increasing return on net assets for eleven firms and the other ten firm's data having negative growth of various magnitudes. The total positive growth however is greater than the total negative growth. By analyzing firms having slightly negative growth, we observe that these firms tend to be very large ones in terms of assets. Since the CDM projects tend to be small for these firms, the effects of the CDM projects become muted. In other words, one cannot ascertain the positive effects of CDM in firms of very large size. The positive growth firms are smaller in size and less diversified, thus, their financial statements embody the positive impacts of CDM projects.

Financial solvency refers to a firm's ability to repay debt and interest. The asset-liability ratio is the ratio of total debt to total assets of the company. From the position of creditors, smaller ratios are preferred. From the point of view of shareholders, higher ratios indicate greater use of financial leverage which is usually beneficial. For operators, moderate asset-liability ratio is more conducive to the maintaining firm's cash flow. Often financial analysts compare the asset-liability ratio to the mean (average) ratio for the industry in which the firm competes. Our interest in this study is to determine positive effects from the 'green appeal." We concern ourselves with the influence on the firm's financial statement and observe the change in this ratio not its position as exemplified with its relationship to the mean or whether it is very high or very low.

Table 3 shows the calculated asset-liability ratio of the mean growth rate according to the data provided above.

According to Tables 2-4, Juhua Co., conch cement, Sinoma cement and *ST Tianhong have a little decrease in the assets-liabilities rate. In addition to the Teda shares remain unchanged, the rest of the 16 companies have a definite range of growth. And the growing rate of the asset-liability ratio is larger than relatively decreasing rate.

According to CDM project features: large prophase operation cost, long revenue cycle, the early stage of the company's investment is bigger, so most of the rate of assets-liabilities of the company will have a certain range of ascension. But they all in the moderate range, they will not be bad impact on company's solvency.

Good market performance measures the shareholders benefits from the changes share prices of firms listed on well-known equity exchanges and markets. The price to earnings ratio (P/E) ratio refers to the ratio of stock price to earnings per share in a period (usually 12 months). P/E ratio reflects the investors' confidence in a firm's equity. A firm having a very high P/E ratio often reflect the investment market's belief that rapidly growing earning will occur in the future. Hence, investors have positive views on the firm's ability to generate the increased profits generated from the projects and products produced by it. Table 4 contains an analysis of the ratio and the growth rate before and after introduction of CDM projects.

From the data in Table 4, nine firms exhibit a modest increase in the P/E ratio after the CDM project implementation. The other 11 companies have a modestly decreasing P/E ratio. We observe no drastically increasing or decreasing growth in the ratio. Hence, the projects appear to have little effect on this ratio and basically do not have great impact on the firm's ability to generate economic rewards to shareholders

The ability to grow for an enterprise refers to assets, profitability and continued rise in the value of its market shares. These indicators reflect the prospects for future development. As exemplified by the main business (revenue) growth rate, gross and net profit growth. Based on the change of main business profit, the growth of the CDM projects have impact on the company growth ability. Main business profit growth is reflected by the difference in current main business profits and previous main business profit, divided by the ratio of main business profit to the previous period's profit. If main business profits grow steadily, this may relate to the positive influence brought by the CDM project, especially for small and medium-sized firms. Table 5 is the mean (average) growth rate of main business profit of the firm calculated by the ratio defined before.

From Table 5, we observe that nine firms exhibit a small increase in profit growth after the introduction of CDM projects. In addition, there are 11 firms having declines in growth rate after the CDM implementation. There are two possible explanations for this phenomenon. Explanation 1 would be the effect of firm size. Small and medium-sized firms have a single project which are more likely to reflect the benefits of the CDM project and less influenced by other products and services produced by the firm. For large firms, there are numerous business activities which generate revenues and profits and the single CDM does not have much influence. Explanation 2 refers to the relative size of the CDM with respect to other activities of the firm. Large CDM projects do not create immediate growth in revenues and profits especially since the large set-up and immediate costs tend to dampen the positive effects of the CDM. The CDM benefit process is slow without any rapid increase in measurable gains.

Company	Financial indicator	-5	-4	-3	-2	-1	0	1	2	3	4	5	6
Juhua co	Return on net assets		0.08	0.1	0.12	0.09	0.11	0.04	0.05	0.24	0.29	29	
	Asset liability ratio		0.48	0.51	0.52	0.52	0.52	0.52	0.5	0.45	0.21		
	P/E ratio		15.2	16.47	32.1	32.1	36.42	17.89	48.03	74.28	25.65		
	business profit ratio		0.08	0.07	0.05	0.05	0.05	0.02	0.01	0.12	0.3		
Sanai fu	Return on net assets	0.18	0.1	0.07	0.17	0.17	0.15	0.11	-0.1	0.12	0.3		
	Asset liability ratio	0.48	0.43	0.48	0.58	0.55	0.56	0.59	0.66	0.6	0.65	0.44	
	P/E ratio		37.91	43.71	23.72	18.39	30	14.04		293.4	157.2		
	business profit ratio	0.13	0.09	0.07	0.09	0.08	0.06	0.04	-0.02	0.01	0.02	0.21	
GD	Return on net assets		0.12	0.13	0.12	0.11	0.13	0.01	0.1	0.1	0.08		
	Asset liability ratio		0.66	0.68	0.69	0.68	0.67	0.72	0.73	0.76	0.77		
	P/E ratio			16.84	15.31	36.21	10.15	228.6	15.44	17.31			
	business profit ratio		0.16	0.13	0.1	0.09	0.13	0.01	0.1	0.07	0.07		
Qilian mountains	Return on net assets		0.06	0.03	0.01	0.01	0.01	0.17	0.19	0.19	0.12		
	Asset liability ratio		0.51	0.5	0.55	0.59	0.6	0.64	0.5	0.57	0.65		
	P/E ratio			31.14	283.8	444.1	617.8	30.26	18.91	14.95			
	business profit ratio		0.11	0.06	0.01	0.01	0.01	0.12	0.2	0.19	0.12		
Tianfu thermoelectric	Return on net assets	0.21	0.08	0.09	0.09	0.09	0.05	0.04	0.04	0.04	0.07	0.18	
	Asset liability ratio	0.68	0.58	0.65	0.72	0.77	0.79	0.64	0.7	0.7	0.73		
	P/E ratio		29.46	24.94	17.6	24.41	207.8	46.05	87.65	83.37	46.06		
	business profit ratio	0.15	0.11	0.12	0.1	0.07	0.04	0.08	0.07	0.07	0.1		
Conch cement	Return on net assets	0.06	0.05	0.16	0.18	0.07	0.2	0.23	0.11	0.12	0.18	0.21	
	Asset liability ratio	0.5	0.55	0.57	0.59	0.64	0.62	0.63	0.41	0.38	0.41	0.45	
	P/E ratio		67.37	20.57	94.34	54.13	54.45	22.9	28.73	14	14.45		
	business profit ratio	0.09	0.11	0.22	0.18	0.06	0.14	0.17	0.13	0.17	0.23	0.34	
Liu shares	Return on net assets	0.21	0.22	0.07	0.11	0.13	0.14	0.11	0.07	0.01	0.04	0.03	
	Asset liability ratio	0.55	0.63	0.34	0.37	0.48	0.59	0.55	0.6	0.64	0.67	0.66	
	P/E ratio		18.88	34.62	19.05	17.84	34.21	21.12	31.85	133.2	60.88		
	business profit ratio	0.09	0.09	0.11	0.13	0.12	0.14	0.13	0.07	0.02	0.03		
Tongli cement	Return on net assets		0.14	-0.87	-1.19	0.13	0.22	0.2	0.1	0.11	0.16		
	Asset liability ratio		0.53	0.67	0.83	0.81	0.7	0.64	0.63	0.63	0.6		
	P/E ratio		25.28			233.4	34.02	37.2	26.56	26.88			
	business profit ratio		0.15	-0.64	-0.52	0.06	0.08	0.12	0.07	0.07	0.09		
Jinshan shares	Return on net assets	0.05	0.08	0.11	0.1	0.09	0.08	0.11	0.01	0.04	0.01	0.07	
	Asset liability ratio	0.28	0.45	0.33	0.42	0.73	0.72	0.72	0.75	0.78	0.83	0.87	
	P/E ratio		44.16	21.33	23.65	30.25	77.39	22.58	278.1	74.17	395.3		
	business profit ratio	0.23	0.16	0.56	0.39	0.21	0.2	0.13	0.01	0.03	0	0.03	
Nanjing iron and steel	Return on net assets	0.13	0.14	0.22	0.2	0.12	0.11	0.24	0.03	0.03	0.09	0.07	
	Asset liability ratio	0.38	0.46	0.55	0.66	0.57	0.62	0.6	0.61	0.65	0.71	0.72	
	P/E ratio		16.29	8.96=5	3.83	8.49	37.14	6.2	74	50.25	14.91		
	business profit ratio	0.06	0.08	0.11	0.07	0.04	0.04	0.06	0.01	0.01	0.04	0.03	
Jingneng thermoelectric	Return on net assets	0.14	0.07	0.06	0.09	0.1	0.09	0.09	0.12	0.09	0.09	0.1	0.09
	Asset liability ratio	0.61		0.37	0.27	0.22	0.19	0.19	0.42	0.63	0.71	0.64	0.68
	P/E ratio		42.61	57.37	34.36	20.16	21.7	59.64	26.04	35.92	33.01	20.74	
	business profit ratio	0.09	0.16	0.12	0.15	0.15	0.13	0.13	0.15	0.11	0.12	0.12	0.12
ST Tianhong	Return on net assets			-0.51	0	-0.3	0.07	-0.21	0.07	-0.03			
	Asset liability ratio			0.63	0.63	0.68	0.71	0.72	0.54	0.6			
	P/E ratio				807.3		66.73		88.85				
	business profit ratio			-0.34	0	-0.11	0.02	-0.07	0.03	-0.01			
Sinama international	Return on net assets		0.22	0.25	0.12	0.16	0.26	0.3	0.35	0.43	0.27		
	Asset liability ratio		0.83	0.85	0.81	0.86	0.85	0.92	0.87	0.8	0.78		
	P/E ratio			23.98	44.54	68.15	32.4	19.8	18.52	14.67			
	business profit ratio		0.04	0.04	0.03	0.03	0.04	0.03	0.06	0.07	0.07		
Teda shares	Return on net assets		0.06	0.06	0.06	0.06	0.18	0.07	0.14	0.12	0.03		
	Asset liability ratio		0.73	0.62	0.63	0.63	0.57	0.61	0.63	0.67	0.74		
	P/E ratio		29.2	37.6	50.27	31.36	63.22	238.4	23.26	82.47	39	23.89	
	business profit ratio			0.3	0.31	0.2	0.11	0.28	0.08	0.09	0.06	0.02	

Jinnan iron and steel	Return on net assets			0.33	0.23	0.21	0.19	0.25	0.11	0.01	0.01	0.01	
	Asset liability ratio			0.74	0.67	0.72	0.71	0.68	0.74	0.75	0.78	0.76	
	P/E ratio			7.51	6.08	6.09	22.2	8.91	12.05	202.4	128.2		
	business profit ratio			0.08	0.07	0.05	0.05	0.06	0.02	0.01	0	0	
Shangneng shares	Return on net assets			0.07	0.03	0.04	0.03	0.03	-0.03	0.01	0.03	0.04	
	Asset liability ratio			0.45	0.49	0.57	0.62	0.59	0.62	0.63	0.62	0.6	
	P/E ratio			54.69	14.5		54.69	38.7		131.3	53.75		
	business profit ratio			0.19	0.09	0.09	0.07	0.07	-0.3	0.03	0.06	0.1	
0.	Return on net assets		0.2	0.29	0.11	0.16	0.22	0.22	0.15	0.31	0.31	0.28	0.2
	Asset liability ratio		0.6	0.60	0.41	0.46	0.52	0.45	0.48	0.53	0.63	0.55	0.51
	P/E ratio			19.72	28.2	13.57	10.68	30.58	24.85	22.01	12.66	22.39	
	business profit ratio		0.19	0.17	0.12	0.09	0.12	0.1	0.07	0.11	0.12	0.12	0.08
Datang power generation	Return on net assets					0.12	0.03	0.05	0.08	0.03			
	Asset liability ratio					0.72	0.81	0.82	0.82	0.8			
	P/E ratio					32.18	117.8	58.77	26.64				
	business profit ratio					0.15	0.02	0.04	0.06	0.03			
Inner Mongalia power	Return on net assets		0.06	0.06	0.08	0.07	0.02	0.05	0.05	-0.24	0.12	0.16	0.14
	Asset liability ratio		0.11	0.44	0.55	0.63	68.71	0.73	0.77	0.75	0.73	0.71	
	P/E ratio		37.68	28.94	30.68	22.15	94	63.89	40.13		41.11	26.38	
	business profit ratio		0.18	0.14	0.12	0.08	0.02	0.04	0.03	-0.1	0.07	0.11	0.17
Baotou steel shares	Return on net assets			0.14	0.18	0.16	0.08	0.12	0.06	-0.13	0.02	0.04	
	Asset liability ratio			0.57	0.62	0.48	0.44	0.58	0.67	0.71	0.7	0.74	
	P/E ratio			10.41	5.35	7.11	39.54	14.84	28.64		212.6		
	business profit ratio			0.08	0.06	0.06	0.04	0.07	0.02	-0.06	0.01	0.02	
Chongqing iron and steel	Return on net assets				0.31	0.22	0.07	0.08	0.09	0.22	0.02	0	0
	Asset liability ratio				0.46	0.47	0.52	0.55	0.52	0.55	0.65	0.75	0.77
	P/E ratio							34.78	18.51	15.02	84.65	361	
	business profit ratio				0.17	0.1	0.03	0.03	0.04	0.01	0	0	

Table 1: Financial data of listed firms.

	Before introduction	After Introduction
Juhua Co.	0.11	0.91
Sanaifu	0.11	0.84
GD	0.03	1.97
Qilian Mountains	(0.43)	2.95
Tianfu Thermoelectric	(0.19)	0.42
Conch Cement	0.68	0.08
Liu Co.	0.04	0.26
Tongli Cement	(1.82)	(0.01)
Jinshan Shares	0.13	1.54
Nanjing IronandSteel	0.01	0.42
Jingneng Thermoelectric	(0.03)	0.02
ST Tianhong	(1.12)	(2.25)
Sinoma International	1.14	0.04
TEDA Shares	0.25	(0.13)
Jinnan IronandSteel	(0.04)	(0.37)
Shaoneng Shares	(0.12)	(0.25)
Guoyang New Energy	0.13	(0.06)
Datang Power Generation	(0.04)	(0.01)
Inner Mongalia Power	0.2	(1.42)
Baotou Steel Shares	0.04	(0.96)
Chongqing IronandSteel	(0.28)	(0.37)

Source: Hexun Net

Table 2: Return on net assets before and after introduction.

	Before introduction	After Introduction
Juhua Co.	0.51	0.44
Sanaifu	0.51	0.58
GD	0.68	0.73
Qilian Mountains	0.55	0.59
Tianfu Thermoelectric	0.70	0.71
Conch Cement	0.58	0.48
Liu Co.	0.49	0.62
Tongli Cement	0.71	0.64
Jinshan Shares	0.49	0.78
Nanjing IronandSteel	0.54	0.65
Jingneng Thermoelectric	0.33	0.49
ST Tianhong	0.66	0.64
Sinoma International	0.84	0.85
TEDA Shares	0.64	0.64
Jinnan IronandSteel	0.70	0.74
Shaoneng Shares	0.54	0.61
Guoyang New Energy	0.51	0.53
Datang Power Generation	0.78	0.81
Inner Mongolia Power	0.52	0.73
Baotou Steel Shares	0.54	0.68
Chongqing IronandSteel	0.50	0.63

From: Hexun Net

Table 3: Mean asset-liability ratio before and after the introduction of project.

	Before introduction	After Introduction
Juhua Co.	0.06	0.09
Sanaifu	(0.03)	(0.02)
GD	0.04	(0.07)
Qilian Mountains	0.04	0.00
Tianfu Thermoelectric	(0.03)	(0.03)
Conch Cement	0.12	0.01
Liu Co.	0.01	(0.03)
Tongli Cement	(0.23)	(0.05)
Jinshan Shares	(0.07)	(0.04)
Nanjing IronandSteel	(0.05)	0.00
Jingneng Thermoelectric	(0.07)	0.01
ST Tianhong	0.09	0.03
Sinoma International	0.12	(0.07)
TEDA Shares	(0.03)	(0.01)
Jinnan IronandSteel	0.12	(0.12)
Shaoneng Shares	0.01	(0.04)
Guoyang New Energy	0.08	0.14
Datang Power Generation	(0.07)	(0.07)
Inner Mongolia Power	(0.05)	(0.02)
Baotou Steel Shares	0.01	(0.11)

From: Hexun Net

Table 4: P/E ratio of the average growth rate before and after the introduction of CDM.

	Before introduction	After Introduction
Juhua Co.	(0.10)	2.85
Sanaifu	(0.12)	1.43
GD	(0.02)	1.94
Qilian Mountains	(0.32)	2.81
Tianfu Thermoelectric	0.10	0.10
Conch Cement	0.34	0.22
Liu Co.	0.10	(0.15)
Tongli Cement	(1.56)	0.09
Jinshan Shares	0.28	(0.07)
Nanjing IronandSteel	(0.02)	0.48
Jingneng Thermoelectric	0.13	0.00
ST Tianhong	(1.09)	(2.42)
Sinoma International	0.02	0.23
TEDA Shares	0.19	(0.40)
Jinnan IronandSteel	(0.05)	(0.72)
Shaoneng Shares	(0.19)	(0.44)
Guoyang New Energy	0.01	(0.10)
Datang Power Generation	0.07	0.00
Inner Mongolia Power	(0.09)	(1.03)
Baotou Steel Shares	0.04	(1.22)
Juhua Co.	(0.37)	(0.35)

Table 5: Average (Mean) growth rate of main business profit before and after the CDM implementation.

Financial analysis of firms not implementing a CDM project

For purposes of comparison, we collect and analyze financial from a group of firms having similar characteristics in our previous except that they have not implemented a CDM project. These characteristics are that the control group come from the same or very similar industries, contain similar characteristics and have similar scale sizes. Twenty-one similar firms comprise the control group. In turn, we compare the experimental and control groups by examining the same four characteristic studied before; profitability, solvency, market performance and growth. To gin, observe Table 6: Return on net assets.

The second column of Table 6 is the data on return on net assets for the control group firm comparable with the firm in the CDM group. They are in the same industry bit did not implement CDM projects from 2002 to 2011. One can see that the growth rates do not differ in any appreciable manner. Stated differently, the CDM project or lack of project does not have significant influence the growth rate of sample firms. Table 7 contains the asset-liability ratio for the two grouping of firms.

From Table 7, we observe the growth rate of the assets-liabilities ratio of each firm during the period from 2002 to 2011. There is only a slight variation in the growth rate data over the ten year period which indicates that firm solvency maintains a stable level over the ten year period. For the group adopting CDM, we observe a sizable growth of the asset-liabilities ratio. Combining this observation with that of Table 2, one may conclude that the introduction of a CDM project increases the asset-liability ratio. Comparative analysis of the two tables indicates that the introduction of CDM does not reduce the solvency of a firm.

Observe in Table 8 is the control group's average P/E ratio and that for the CDM group. The growth rates in either group are not large. The introduction of CDM projects does not attract the greater attention from investors. The stable market performance can explain investors' confidence in the firms and the firm's operations appear fine. Perhaps, one may explain this phenomenon in that CDM projects are not designed to accomplish greater profitability but to better a firm's reputation by their attempts to improve the environment and follow the Kyoto Protocols

Table 9 contains information on the P/E growth rate for both the control and CDM groups. The growth rate for the CDM group is for

Control Group	The average growth rate	Experimental (CDM) Group	After introduction
Shanxi Coking	(0.06)	Juhua Co.	0.91
Chang Aluminum	0.45	Sanaifu	0.84
Panjiang Shares	0.34	GD	1.97
Sichuan Nitrocell	(0.10)	Qilian Mountains	2.95
Xichang power	(15.65)	Tianfu Thermoelectric	0.42
Leshan electric power	0.38	Conch Cement	0.08
Guizhou Power	(0.01)	Liu Co.	0.26
Star power	(1.31)	Tongli Cement	(0.01)
Jidong Cement	0.16	Jinshan Shares	1.54
Xingye Mining	(0.63)	Nanjing Iron and Steel	0.42
Dayou Energy	1.29	Jingneng Thermoelectric	0.02
Hengyi petrochemical	5.11	ST Tianhong	(2.25)
Salt Lake Shares	0.20	Sinoma International	0.04
ST Shengda	(3.76)	TEDA Shares	(0.13)
Baotai Shares	(0.01)	Jinnan IronandSteel	(0.37)
Mountain coal international	2.33	Shaoneng Shares	(0.25)
Kadi Power	0.44	Guoyang New Energy	(0.06)
Ningbo Thermoelectric	0.02	Datang Power Generation	(0.01)
Fuling Power	(0.32)	Inner Mongolia Power	(1.42)
Red Sun Power	(1.50)	Baotou Steel Shares	(0.96)
Longest River Power	0.15	Juhua Co.	(0.37)

Table 6: Return on net assets.

Control Group	The average growth rate	Experimental (CDM) Group	After introduction
Shanxi Coking	0.05	Juhua Co.	0.44
Chang Aluminum	(0.02)	Sanaifu	0.58
Panjiang Shares	0.13	GD	0.73
Sichuan Nitrocell	0.13	Qilian Mountains	0.59
Xichang power	0.01	Tianfu Thermoelectric	0.71
Leshan electric power	0.03	Conch Cement	0.48
Guizhou Power	(0.01)	Liu Co.	0.62
Star power	0.08	Tongli Cement	0.64
Jidong Cement	0.04	Jinshan Shares	0.78
Xingye Mining	(0.02)	Nanjing Iron and Steel	0.65
Dayou Energy	0.42	Jingneng Thermoelectric	0.49
Hengyi petrochemical	0.05	ST Tianhong	0.64
Salt Lake Shares	0.14	Sinoma International	0.85
ST Shengda	0.03	TEDA Shares	0.64
Baotai Shares	0.02	Jinnan IronandSteel	0.74
Mountain coal international	0.03	Shaoneng Shares	0.61
Kadi Power	0.03	Guoyang New Energy	0.53
Ningbo Thermoelectric	0.01	Datang Power Generation	0.81
Fuling Power	0.13	Inner Mongolia Power	0.73
Red Sun Power	(0.06)	Baotou Steel Shares	0.68
Longest River Power	0.24	Juhua Co.	0.63

From: Hexun Net

Table 7: Asset-liability ratios analysis.

Control Group	The average growth rate	Experimental (CDM) Group	After introduction
Shanxi Coking	0.12	Juhua Co.	0.09
Chang Aluminum	0.53	Sanaifu	(0.02)
Panjiang Shares	0.05	GD	(0.07)
Sichuan Nitrocell	0.24	Qilian Mountains	0.00
Xichang power	(0.03)	Tianfu Thermoelectric	(0.03)
Leshan electric power	(0.10)	Conch Cement	0.01
Guizhou Power	0.07	Liu Co.	(0.03)
Star power	0.10	Tongli Cement	(0.05)
Jidong Cement	0.02	Jinshan Shares	(0.04)
Xingye Mining	0.16	Nanjing Iron and Steel	0.00
Dayou Energy	0.22	Jingneng Thermoelectric	0.01
Hengyi petrochemical	0.84	ST Tianhong	0.03
Salt Lake Shares	0.06	Sinoma International	(0.07)
ST Shengda	2.01	TEDA Shares	(0.01)
Baotai Shares	0.55	Jinnan IronandSteel	(0.12)
Mountain coal international	0.66	Shaoneng Shares	(0.04)
Kadi Power	0.39	Guoyang New Energy	0.14
Ningbo Thermoelectric	0.02	Datang Power Generation	(0.07)
Fuling Power	0.08	Inner Mongolia Power	(0.02)
Red Sun Power	(0.04)	Baotou Steel Shares	(0.11)
Longest River Power	(0.04)	Juhua Co.	

From: Hexun Net

Table 8: P/E ratio for both groups.

after introduction of the CDM project. The main business profitability of the control groups (21 listed companies) is on the left hand side of the table. Seven firms attained a modest positive growth in the P/E ratio, and 14 of the control group attained a negative growth in the P/E ratio. The right half of the table contains the data for the CDM group. Ten firms attained a small negative growth, and eleven firms attained positive growth. For the CDM group, positive growth is greater than for the control group firms exhibiting firm growth. We may infer that firms introducing the CDM projects experienced increased business growth which, in turn, leads to other positive benefits.

Some limitations of financial statement analysis

Tables 1-9 report historical data. For some factors such as inflation or commodity prices, cannot be reflected by analysis of historical data. Hence, the analysis cannot completely reflect all results, and may not reflect the management functions of decision-makers. Finally, the financial data will also be influenced by estimating and accounting policy choices which may deter from the ability to compare different firms reporting data.

The denominator calculation of the return on net asset is the mean of the final and initial net assets, but the real enterprise net asset changes from period to period. In addition, the Stockholders surplus dividends already include the negation of the Stockholders surplus dividends, which varies from firm to firm. The usefulness of the asset-liability ratio is related to the economic factors of the industry to which the firm belongs. Industries possess varying standards; hence the notion of an increasing asset-liability ratio may result in different assessments as to whether corporate policy is good or bad depending on the state of the economy, industry characteristics and the firm's dividend policy.

The P/E ratio calculation includes the value for earnings per share (EPS). EPS includes the notion of net profit which varies from period to period based on conditions including the state of the economy and other factors far more important in determining the influence of the EPS values. The number of shares in determining the EPS ratio will vary from industry to industry and within firms depending on corporate policy concerning the desire for the firm to trade at low versus high prices. Often these policies are promoted for reasons including making

Control Group	The average growth rate	Experimental (CDM) Group	After introduction
Shanxi Coking	(0.18)	Juhua Co.	2.85
Chang Aluminum	(0.08)	Sanaifu	1.43
Panjiang Shares	0.28	GD	1.94
Sichuan Nitrocell	(0.15)	Qilian Mountains	2.81
Xichang power	(1.23)	Tianfu Thermoelectric	0.10
Leshan electric power	0.24	Conch Cement	0.22
Guizhou Power	(0.44)	Liu Co.	(0.15)
Star power	(0.65)	Tongli Cement	0.09
Jidong Cement	0.05	Jinshan Shares	(0.07)
Xingye Mining	(2.09)	Nanjing Iron and Steel	0.48
Dayou Energy	0.22	Jingneng Thermoelectric	0.00
Hengyi petrochemical	(0.01)	ST Tianhong	(2.42)
Salt Lake Shares	0.13	Sinoma International	0.23
ST Shengda	(4.53)	TEDA Shares	(0.40)
Baotai Shares	(0.19)	Jinnan IronandSteel	(0.72)
Mountain coal international	(0.33)	Shaoneng Shares	(0.44)
Kadi Power	0.33	Guoyang New Energy	(0.10)
Ningbo Thermoelectric	0.01	Datang Power Generation	0.00
Fuling Power	(1.93)	Inner Mongolia Power	(1.03)
Red Sun Power	(3.75)	Baotou Steel Shares	(1.22)
Longest River Power	0.03	Juhua Co.	(0.35)

From: Hexun Net

Table 9: P/E ratio of main business of the two groups.

the shares look more or less attractive to individual buyers of equities. Stock splits, stock dividends, stock buybacks and combining shares to reduce the number of outstanding shares are the result of a new or change in policy to make the share price more or less attractive. All of these strategies affect the EPS and, in turn, the P/E ratio.

The main business profit margins reflect the ability of the sustainable development of a firm or enterprise. Firms studied in our sample often are competing in several industries and these and they differ in the number of employees, sales revenue, value of assets and the maintenance of cash flow. Hence, conclusions concerning the index measured may have little or no relation to the CDM project or lack thereof a project. In addition to the defects of the index itself, analysts may cause problems by emphasizing or misinterpreting the meaning of indexes, index change and the like by not looking into the economic causes of the change. Deeper analyses of index change can aid one in interpreting the meaning and impacts of changing index values.

To sum up, we examined four aspects of profitability and solvency for the firms' studied. We sorted out comparisons of financial data to make conclusions concerning the impacts of CDM projects on the financial status of firms undergoing these projects. By the longitudinal comparison, we concluded that many firms had positive impacts from CDM projects and may have had some positive relation to growing profits. However, the short term analysis performed would have to be reevaluated in the future to see if long-term effects are also positive. While the effect on the asset-liability ratio is not obvious, there are signs of improvement, related to the upfront expenses made. The effects are disparate in that they are related to the industry effects, size of firm and the particular nature of the firm. Long-term effects will have to be examined in the future to see if the CDM projects were successful in introducing "green" behavior among firms, customers and producers.

Limitations of the research method include the reliance on financial statements, shortcoming of financial indexes and their relationship to the goal of the Kyoto Protocols. Above all, we find evidence that the CDM projects are good for the development of enterprises, in addition to economic benefits directly from selling CERs and comprehensive benefits to individual firms. Promoting "green appeal" makes a firm lf promote technological innovation which is conducive to the sustainable development of the firm. The "Low carbon" economy benefits both firms and society which is both macroeconomic efficient and reduces ecological losses due to excess carbon emissions

Conclusions and Future Research

With the development of human civilization which resulted in a great magnitude of energy consumption, green appeal calls for society to pay attention and reduce the negative effects of inefficient energy consumption in global economic development. The developed nations have the duty to reduce carbon emissions because their development speed is greater than developing countries. From another perspective, the developed nations guided the developing nations into a new plan. By the formulation of the United Nations framework convention on climate change, there are new plans that have political and economic significance. However, the developing nation's development of the low carbon economy establishes widespread praise and obtains a development fund to promote the growth of CDM projects. These projects are very helpful for technical progress in developing nations and the promotion of a low carbon economy.

From the view of environment, the main characteristics of a low carbon economy are low energy consumption, small emissions and limited pollution. Promotion of the low carbon economy is actually a protection to the environment. Global climate change is disorder; greenhouse gases are one of the largest environmental pollution problems, and low carbon economy is implemented by a series of projects. The industrial civilization nation should have into an ecological environment, and the promotion technology to reduce carbon emissions will keep global ecology and development in balance.

The implementation of any new system must have corresponding constraint rules to maintain sustainable development which related law concerning the promotion of low-carbon emissions. In addition to the government's policy support, corresponding laws and regulations can help and protect the practice of environmental projects, which is the long-lasting development support of sustained low carbon emissions.

The social impact of law relating to sustaining low carbon emissions from one point reflect the social impact of cleansing our planet from the wasteful and destructive consequences of uncontrolled industry. The clean development mechanism (CDM) and the manager of the individual projects are the individual enterprises. The performance of the individual enterprises is the only way to ascertain the benefits of project implementation. The promotion and implementation of a CDM project is not only to benefit humans, but also benefit the individual firm's development in the economy. At the same time, the project promotion will drive the local employment, which is fully staffed. To advocate and encourage the development of CDM projects, and it's better to reflect the project actual benefits by the firm's financial statements rather than the corresponding social responsibility reports. Hence, the analysis of financial statements shows the CDM project practical benefits to the firm.

Financial statement is an access to judge the company operation consequence; through it we can see the CDM actual operation of a variety of effects in the process.

This paper based on the principle of financial statement analysis, comprehensive analyze the data collection and sorting out. Longitudinal comparison on company own research object and compared with the other comparison sample companies to find the problem. In this paper, taking the financial metrics into compared, such as return on equity, asset-liability ratio, P/E ratio and profit rate of main business, respectively analysis from the profit ability, debt paying ability, market performance and growth ability, to analyze the economic impact of the firm's CDM projects.

By examining and analyzing a large amount of data, we found that within the sample period firm's financial statements do not reflect any major changes and the CDM to promote the role of the company is often not affected. From the perspective of the financial statements data, besides there is good profit performance, the solvency effects are not obvious, the market was changed little, and the signs of growth were not affected in any measurable way. Considering the long period of project construction, the effect on earnings require a longer time period of study. Although the CDM projects in the PRC are very popular' most investors have a wait-and-see attitude. In addition, the limitations of financial statements and financial index analysis influence the analysis and we believe that the CDM projects to not have a major impact of the performance analysis discussed in this study.

As a result, the effectiveness of CDM projects on the information in found in financial statements and other disclosures may be muted. First, it is particularly urgent to use legislation to induce better analysis of the relative effectiveness of carbon saving programs on the information found in financial statements. Perhaps, we need to revise financial statements to ease the problem of measuring the benefits of low carbon emission projects. Green development needs the joint efforts of enterprises and the role of government in the promotion of low carbon industrial growth. They should strengthen disclosure in financial statements to promote the information concept of the CDM projects [10,11].

Suggested that to add the CDM projects cost details in financial statement or in the appendix, which have special subsidiary column to reflect its operations. For the listed company, the situation of production and operation will be different, so there are different required expenses and responsibility. Start-up capital is actually quite a sum of money, and different operating conditions of company will produce different effects. Recommended to disclose the data according to the own situation. By quantifying costs is far better than the slogans advocating. And the quantitative data is more objective and intuitive, which can give people the most effective reference value to read the report with.

In short, if you want to give full disclosure and reflect of specific project to the financial statements, you must establish a complete set of CDM project information disclosure mechanism which suits the disclosure standards of the listed companies in China to ensure the reliability financial sources.

Above all, low-carbon economy is a new mode of economic development, particularly as a developing countries china need to develop the new economy mode. Take this opportunity to adjust industrial structure, and nip in the bud. Take on the responsibility of world powers; keep up with the world trend; reduce the pressure of world opinion. Look for the trend and get the opportunity to create China's own low carbon economy development mode. In the near future, innovate the advanced technology is the right thing to do.

References

1. Romani M, Ridge J, Stern N (2012) Recklessly slow or a rapid transition to a low-carbon economy? Time to Decide. Policy paper, Grantham Research Institute on Climate Change and the Environment.
2. Lloyd B, Subbarao S (2009) Development challenges under the Clean Development Mechanism (CDM) Can renewable energy initiatives be put in place before peak oil? Energy Policy 37: 237-245.
3. Brown K, Adger WN, Boyd E, Elezalde E, Shackley S (2004) How do CDM projects contribute to sustainable development? Technical Report.
4. Capoor K, Ambrosi P (2008) State and Trends of the Carbon Market.
5. Heller T, Shukla P (2003) Development and Climate: Engaging Developing Countries Beyond Kyoto: Advancing the International Effort against Climate Change. Pew Centre on Global Climate Change 3: 1408.
6. Hultman N, Boyd E, Roberts E, Timmons J, Cole J, et al (2009) How can the clean development mechanism better contribute to sustainable development? Ambio: A Journal of the Human Environment 38: 120 -122.
7. Mathy S, Jean-Charles H, de Gouvello C (2001) Clean development mechanism: leverage for development. Climate Policy 1: 251-268.
8. Hultman N, Pulver SL, Guimar L, Deshmukh R, Kane J (2010) Carbon market risks and rewards: Firm perceptions of CDM investment decisions in Brazil and India. Energy Policy 40: 90-102.
9. Ware M (2007) is the global carbon market working? Nature 445: 595-596.
10. Taiyab N (2006) Exploring the Market for Voluntary Carbon Offsets. International Institute for Environment and Development.
11. http://ielaw.uibe.edu.cn/plus/view.php?aid=14285

Management Attributes that Contribute to the Success of Women in Management Positions

Jessica Conradie[1], Adolf Lowies[2*] and Janine Lee Upton[3]

[1]*MBA student, Management College of Southern Africa, South Africa*
[2]*Director of Research, Management College of Southern Africa, South Africa*
[3]*Statistician: Data Analysis Unit, Management College of Southern Africa, South Africa*

Abstract

The purpose of this study is to determine the management attributes that contribute to the success of women in management positions in Northern Kwazulu Natal. This investigation stems from the fact that women are still under represented in managerial positions within South Africa, both in the public and private sector. In order to gain insight into what differentiate successful female managers from the rest of the female workforce, a closer look will be taken at the female managers within Northern KwaZulu Natal and how they have managed to achieve success. The aim of this study is to identify a preferred managerial style used by females, and the traits they exhibit to enhance their careers. The research had been done as a qualitative study using inductive Thematic Analysis. The findings of the study were that the female managers of Northern KwaZulu Natal showed attributes that lead contributed to their success. The attributes identified was their managerial style which is transformational in nature leaning on traits such as being caring, motherly, empathetic, collaborative, motivated, driven, empowering, acknowledging, recognizing, being an example and a good listener.

Keywords: Management attributes; Success of women; Management Positions; Female managers; Managerial style

Introduction

To stay competitive in an ever changing global economy, diversity needs to be embraced and organizations must capitalize on all forms of skilled labour, regardless of gender. The absence of women at leadership level is perplexing, considering the body of research showing that companies perform better when they have diverse leadership [1]. In spite of all efforts made by government through the formulation of policies and legislature to elevate women into top managerial positions, equity is still not achieved. Government and business organizations have made it their top priority to elevate women in and give woman equal rights, but women still only occupy the lower management levels in the private and government sectors. This studies main aim is to investigate which traits female managers, who have managed to achieve success, display. This will be argued by using secondary data in the form of articles, journals, handbooks, statistics, etc. The secondary data will be supplemented by primary data through conducting semi-structured interviews with both middle and senior managers who have managed to ascend into a managerial position. The purpose of the research will be to identify common managerial styles followed by contrasting female and male managerial styles. Managerial traits will then be explored and lastly, barriers female managers had to overcome in order to achieve career successes will be identified. Thereafter, recommendations will be made to guide aspiring females who wish to move in the management echelons.

The Historical Role of Women in Business

The rest of the world, in particular America, has made giant leaps in promoting women and escalating them into higher hierarchies [2] However, the phenomenon of women not occupying as many top managerial positions in South Africa as men continues to stay cumbersome. The setting of this problem can be described against the back drop of the current statistics relating to females in management. According to [3] in 2012, less than one in ten businesses were led by female representatives, an indication that it remains difficult for them to reach the very top of the business world. At an average, South Africa has more than a quarter of companies led by women, against Australia's three out of every ten [3]. More recently the 2013 Grant Thornton International Business Report on women in business reveals that just over one quarter of top decision-making roles in SA businesses are filled by women. This is a long way off government's ambition to ensure that 50% of senior management positions are filled by women. Over the last decade, an increasingly global competitive labour market has seen organizations make genuine efforts to promote and retain women. South Africa's definition of, and goals towards achieving gender equality are guided by a vision of human rights which incorporates acceptance of equal and inalienable rights of all women and men. This ideal is a fundamental tenet under the Bill of Rights of The Constitution of the Republic of South Africa, 1996 (Act 108 of 1996). It emerged from a long period of struggle for a democratic society that respects and promotes the rights of all its citizens, irrespective of race, gender, class, age, disability, etc. (Bill of Rights, Sections 9.1 to 9.4). One contextual factor that contributes to the underrepresentation of women in managerial positions is the unique South African history of apartheid. South Africa has a history of two powerful antagonistic colonial rulers operating concurrently, followed by the apartheid governments of independent South Africa. Apartheid was a system of racial categorization and separation dividing the population into various groups. This separation governed every sphere of life; from education to employment. According to Littrell and Nkomo [4] this separation was accompanied by patriarchy of women from all races' subordinates of males. Women were seen as 'minors' and were confined to being 'homemakers'. Women who worked were expected to be

***Corresponding author:** Adolf Lowies, Director of Research, Management College of Southern Africa, South Africa, E-mail: Adolf.lowies@mancosa.co.za

domestic or unskilled workers or they were placed in administrative positions. The system of patriarchy and the 'women's work' stereotype had to be broken before women, particularly black women, could achieve equal status with men. A particular view of males' perception of the roles of females that had formed though centuries of habit and history had to be broken [2] Women needed to be emancipated from; being denied the opportunity to study in order to advance their career, the gender stereotypes that they were the 'inferior sex', and the traditional view that women belong in the kitchen and should be the child carers. During apartheid, women in general were exploited and discriminated against, but it was especially the black woman who experienced the wrath of apartheid two fold [5]. Not only were they discriminated against because of their racial status, but according to an article published by the ANC it was because of the mere fact that they were females as well [5]. While men constituted the majority of the cheap labour force, women were relegated to a shadowy position, expected to remain in the reserves and to support their families without the help of their men-folk. Females only earned eight percent in wages of what the white males were earning and were denied the opportunity to get a tertiary education. In the white community it was only the females of the very wealthy families that had the opportunity to receive a tertiary education. The rest of the South African females could only study if they used their skills in their own segregated communities and they were mostly confided to professions in the education and nursing sectors [5] The Employment Equity Act, 55 of 1998 was formulated to counter the effect of apartheid and achieve equality in the workplace. According to Makuala [6] this Act served two purposes: (1) Promoting equal opportunity and fair treatment in employment through the elimination of unfair discrimination and; (2) Implementing affirmative action measures to redress the disadvantages experienced by designated groups, ensuring their equitable representation in all occupational categories and levels in the workforce. Although in theory the Equity Act sounds like a soundproof plan, in practice it fails to meet its objective. This can be related to a variable that women do not exhibit managerial styles and traits readily associated with successful business acumen. Leadership, also referred to as management [7], is a topic that comes up mostly in discussions when it comes to leading the organizations in professional lives. This topic has been mainly dealt with in a male perspective, thus leaving behind the developments of competent female leaders to show their abilities. This is confirmed by Piterman [8] who says that the traits and leadership styles of successful organizations are associated with male traits. According to Daniel and Moudic [9] the male leadership style is more transactional in nature, based on masculine values such as assertiveness, command and control. The female leadership style reflects female stereotypes and feminine values such as nurturing, attentiveness, and caring, which is in line with the transformational leadership. A survey done by Folkman and Zenger in [10] showed that women do excel in the stereotypical 'nurturing' competencies such as developing others and building relationships, and many exhibit integrity and engagement in self-development [11]. The advantages, however, are not limited to these competencies. The survey showed that in fact, at every level, more women were rated by their peers, their bosses, their direct reports, and their associates as better overall leaders than their male counterparts – and the higher the level, the wider that gap grows. Females within South Africa foster hope to advance into managerial positions. The interrelationship of the South African history, stereotypical views of female leadership styles and traits, together with the barriers females must overcome has contributed to the under representation of females in management. The actual truth is that, in spite of all the measurements taken to advance women, only a few have managed to do so. Significant change will require a committed leadership focus to the economic and broader performance dividend that can be achieved by attracting and retaining quality women managers and optimising the contribution of women in management [8].

Challenges Faced by Women in Management in South Africa

Women are still underrepresented in top managerial positions in South Africa. This is identified clearly in a recent article in News 24. The article states that 21% of South African businesses, surveyed for 2013, had no women positions in senior management. According to the article it is a trend that has been persisting for the last six years in spite of government measures being put into place. More must still be done to promote equality in the public sector but even more work in the private sector which continues to lag behind. The Commission for Employment Equity Annual report 2013 indicated that white males occupy 80% of top management positions in the private sector. It is thus evident that there is an under representation of women in managerial position in South Africa in both the public and private section. Despite the persisting under representation of women in high ranking positions, some women have managed to break through barriers that keep them in lower level positions. This research seeks to explore the reasons for this phenomenon by getting input from females that are currently occupying managerial positions. This will be done by identifying a preferred managerial style used by females and the traits they exhibit to enhance their career. In addition, the research explores career barriers faced by females. The rationale being that once we can identify traits and styles of females who managed to ascend into top managerial positions and in so doing overcome the barriers, the problem of underrepresentation of females in management can be addressed.

Management versus Leadership

Popivici [7] defines management as 'the process of setting and achieving organizational goals through its functions: forecasting, organization, coordination, training and monitoring-evaluation.' Managers need to embrace process and seek stability and control and therefore, also to instinctively try to resolve problems quickly [11]. Managers are mostly concerned with administration and putting systems in place. Furthermore, they oversee and ensure that tasks are completed and submitted on time. They are left in charge when the "leader" or business owner cannot be at the workplace and have to fulfil the dual function of manager and leader. The level of responsibility of managers, depend on their position in the organizational hierarchy which can be junior, middle or senior management. In contrast, leadership may be defined as 'the ability to influence, to make others follow you, the ability to guide, the human side of business for "teacher"' [7]. Boonyachai [11] states that leadership is said to be a process of influencing others to achieve the long term goals of the organisation. Some leaders believe that they need to lead by being an example, and that they should not ask someone else to do things they are not willing to do themselves. Booyachai [11] is of the opinion that being influential contributes to the credibility of a leader and ensures some measure of respect. According to Boonyachai [11] 'Effective leaders take a personal interest in the long term development of their employees'. They use motivation tactics and many skills or experiences to support their employees to achieve organisational goals. This is about tapping into individual motivations in the interests of furthering an organisation-wide goal.Some researchers confirm that there is a definite difference between a manager and a leader, whereas others use the two concepts interchangeably. According to Popivici [7] management is a career, while leadership is a calling; managers are obeyed whereas leaders are naturally followed; and a leader may have no organizational skills, but his vision unites people behind him. It goes without saying that to be competitive in a global economy, both managerial and leadership qualities are essential in all organizations and an effective integration of the two leads to better performance. Thus, leadership cannot replace management and should be seen as an addition to management [12]. Popivici [7] echoes this by stating 'a manager cannot just be a leader, he also needs authority to be effective'. It can thus be assumed that a manager can be a leader and vice versa. For the purpose of this research study the concepts of manager and leader will be used interchangeably.

Male versus female leadership styles

For organizations to be effective in today's day and age, they need to embrace diversity [12]. A company may be missing many insights and opportunities that would be easier to identify if managers were to come from wider backgrounds, embracing diversity [13]. One aspect of diversity is the particular interest in the way which women's style of leadership may differ from men's. As more women begin occupying positions of leadership, questions as to whether they lead in a different manner from men, and whether women or men are more effective leaders, have garnered greater attention. This section seeks to explore leadership styles that are more commonly associated with men and women. However, before we can investigate preferred leadership styles by both sexes, we need to understand gender differences.

Gender Differences

In the 1970s, a literature study on gender differences set out to explore the extent of differences in men and women's behaviour. This research into gender differences was based on a desire to understand whether males and females differed on a variety of traits and behaviours because of their biological determination; the implication being that differences in behaviour between men and women are innate or acquired from very early socialization [14]. The process through which an individual learns and accepts roles is called socialization [13]. Socialization works by encouraging wanted and discouraging unwanted behaviour. As such, women and men's socialization are influenced by gender roles and stereotypes. Gender socialization prepares men and women for types of activities likely to be required of them in order to fulfil their prescribed roles for positive outcomes and to be afforded opportunities as deemed necessary. Once someone has accepted certain gender roles and gender differences as an expected socialized behavioural norm, this behavioural trait becomes part of the individual's responsibilities [13]. Noor et al. [15] asserts that there are indeed some small psychological differences between women and men on traits that are often seen as related to effective leadership, such as men showing more assertiveness than women and women showing more integrity than men. However, the French anthropologists, Francois Heritier, emphasized that a female leader does not possess fundamentally different attributes than a male leader and that the gender hierarchy is not biological, but a cultural phenomenon that over history, civilizations throughout the world have perpetuated with undiminished force [15].

Noor et al. [15] agree with Jogulu and Wood that socialization from an early age determines how both sexes perceive how their traits and behaviour should be. Childhood socialization by parents, schools, peers, and/or the media encourages girls to be cooperative, expressive, flexible and attuned to their interpersonal world, whereas boys are led to be openly competitive, independent, and instrumental [16]. Some psychologists are of the opinion that women may be more relationship orientated than men because of their psychological needs stemming from early experiences [12]. However, due to the flexible nature of women they adapt more easily to circumstances and have managed to develop certain male characteristics. This is confirmed by the 'Bemtest'.A test, more commonly referred to as the 'Bem test' is the standard psychological tool used to rate people on how they conform to a variety of measures considered stereotypically male or female: "self-reliant," "yielding," "helpful," "ambitious," "tender," "dominant." Since the test started in the early 1970's, women have been encroaching into the test rates as male territory, stereotypically defining themselves as "assertive," "independent," "willing to take a stand," [2]. Men have not been able to adapt to stereotypical feminine traits as women have adapted to male traits. The 'Bem test' thus coincides with Heritier's view that gender socialization is a result of cultural reinforcement of certain behaviours and contextual factors and not because of 'inborn qualities.' We can thus conclude that women learn to value nurturance and interpersonal connectedness more highly than men [6] and that there is a definite difference between the male and female gender because of early socializations and the behaviour they are expected to portray. However, that these stereotypes are not set in stone and can change through cultural reinforcement and contextual factors. In fact, women are becoming more aggressive in nature, this is evident in the rising of a class of young female 'killers' on Wall Street [2] indicating that genders can take on each other's stereo typical roles.

Gender and leadership styles

According to Daft [12] the gendered traits of men include aggressiveness or assertiveness, rational analysis and a take-charge attitude. Men tend to be directive and emotionally detached from their subordinates. They are competitive and individualistic and prefer working in vertical hierarchies. They rely on formal authority and position in their dealings with their subordinates. Furthermore, they are more result driven and task orientated than fostering good interpersonal human relations. These characteristics are commonly associated with the transactional leadership style. This is confirmed by Jogulu and Wood [14] who says that the transactional leadership style appears to characterize leadership in a strong masculine way, as it is distinguished by 'competitiveness, hierarchical authority and high control for the leader and analytical problem solving' [14]. The gendered leadership qualities women tend to portray are: women prefer less competitive environments than men do; they are more collaborative and are more concerned with relationship building, inclusiveness, participation and caring [12]. They foster a feeling of "family" in the workplace and get emotionally involved. They try to create a platform where employees can speak openly about their problems in an effort to increase their productiveness. These are all characteristics of the transformational leadership style. Noor et al. [15] confirm that women indeed tend to be transformational and charismatic leaders. This is confirmed by Klenke who says that women fit more generally into a 'feminine model of leadership build around cooperation, collaboration, lower control for the leader and problem solving based on intuition and rationality' [14]. According to Rosin [2] men derive their advantage largely from size and strength, but the post-industrial economy is indifferent to brawn. Rosin states that our current service and information economy rewards precisely the opposite qualities, the ones that can be easily replaced by machines. Men are no longer doing physical hard labour of the traditional kind, but they are confined to four walls of an office. This has had the effect that most men have lost their jobs as they are competing directly against females who tend to be traditionally stronger in administration skills. Furthermore, Rosin states that social intelligence, open communication, the ability to sit still and focus are all, at minimum, not the province of men [2]. They are characteristics more readily associated with women. Men may cling to themselves as providers, but they are further than ever from being able to embody those ideals. Their "inborn nature" and gender stereotyping primarily contribute to the fact that they are replaced by women and seen as less effective or at most equally effective [2]. We can thus conclude that male and female leadership styles are underpinned, but not limited to, their socialized gendered traits and behaviour. The preferred male leadership style seems to be transactional, in line with masculine traits and behaviour, whereas the preferred female style seems to be more transformational, in line with feminine traits and behaviour. By no means are men perceived as more efficient. According to [2] the post industrial economy prefers a more consultative and collaborative approach and the staunch 'get to the point' approach is rejected. This leaves women with the upper hand and a chance for women being more successful and effective in their career aspirations.

Leadership traits of women

In 2005, a year-long study conducted by Caliper, a Princeton, New Jersey-based management consulting firm, and Aurora, a London-based organization that advances women, identified a number of characteristics that distinguish women leaders from men when it comes to leadership qualities [17], these are:

- Women leaders are more persuasive than their male counterparts
- When feeling the sting of rejection, women leaders learn from adversity and carry on with an "I'll show you" attitude
- Women leaders demonstrate an inclusive, team-building leadership style of problem solving and decision making
- Women leaders are more likely to ignore rules and take risks.

Torres [17] is of the opinion that these innate characteristics are normally attributed to women based on what is commonly accepted as their traditional familial role. They may also be fundamental in gender studies that have yielded results demonstrating that women leaders are often more effective than male leaders. These studies support the premise that the behaviour of women leaders who possess definite leadership characteristics is not simply unique, but very possibly at odds with what men practice [17]. They include: confidence, vision, integrity, magnanimity, humility, communication, tenacity, visibility, empowerment and serendipity.

Key finding one: resistance to change: The primary study found that to be competitive in global environment organizations must embrace change; however, they are heavily resistant to change. They acknowledge that personnel are an indispensable asset to the company, but still they only embrace transformation superficially. This is in large part due to the fact that they have always used westernized models where doing work was created by and for men. The females in the study realize the importance of staff and treat them accordingly. The study found that resistance to change is twofold, firstly caused by society and secondly by personal views of the female managers.

Subtheme one: resistance to change –societal: It was found that despite this, females still feel that they are discriminated against. They perceive themselves in a male dominated world where politics keeps on existing, now differently, such as reverse racism. Whilst it was not the aim of the study it was interesting to note that white females feel that are female only, but the fact that they are white causes two fold discrimination.

The study found that culture plays a role in female career progression. There seems to be a notion of how females "should operate" which stems from various culture's tradition and gender stereotypes. It was found that expectations of a woman stretch over various cultures.

Subtheme two: resistance to change –personal: Females have an internal image of how they perceive successful management. To them successful management leadership entails direction, guidance, influence and being an example. There seems to be consensus that there is a difference between a manager and a leader, but some females feel that the concept can be used interchangeably and in aid of each other. An interesting finding was that females see themselves as managers and not leaders. It was found that their internal image causes inner conflict. One of the main reasons for this is external stereotypes. It was found that most females believed there is a difference between management and leadership. Some females did feel that the concepts can be used interchangeably and in aid of each other. It was proved that female leadership is transformational, including traits such as: caring, being motherly, empathetic, collaborative, empowering, acknowledging, recognizing, being an example and a good listener. Transformational leadership is in direct contrast to transactional leadership and only two of the respondents showed transactional leadership qualities inclusive of the "telling style" trait. It was found that the transformational leadership type correspond to the archetype of a woman, being a nurturer, carer, mother and this was caused by gender socialization. In this study it showed that female leaders see themselves as successful, because they are efficient. They measure themselves, however, by the male archetype, strengthening their conflicting ideas of their own definition leadership and what they believe leadership 'should be'. There are females that saw themselves as less effective and it was identified that the cause of this was lack of self-confidence. Females felt that they were too emotional and that they need to become emotionally mature. The fact that they perceive themselves as too emotional and measure their success in line with the stereotype of men being more successful strengthens their lack of confidence. Therefore a self-fulfilling prophesy is happening. It was found that males being more successful business leaders were a recurring perception. This stems from the fact that the qualities associated with successful business leaders are synonymous with success. These qualities/traits were identified as assertiveness, being an example, being an untiring worker and devoted to their family. Females measuring themselves with male dominated views, find a certain amount of inner conflict exists, because even though they don't perceive themselves as less effective by implementing a transformational (more female orientated role) leadership style, their own internal stereotype is of such that they believe that females are the mother of the household and they are supposed to take up the female responsibilities of being a mother and that females can't be seen as leaders in the workplace. This highlights the next finding. It was found that females can't maintain a healthy balance because they believe they have to play multiple roles and work excessively hard to be a successful leader. This causes a great deal of inner conflict which stems from the fact that work takes up the bulk of their day and this causes them to see their family less causing a feeling of guilt. It was found that females are very motivated and do things with passion. Females felt that men are given a position because they are a man and not necessarily motivated for that position. Females are motivated by prejudice and life circumstances where you are forced to survive such as divorce and death.

Key finding two: disempowerment

Empowerment is very important to females. Most females feel

the need to empower, because they realise the benefits thereof. Not only do females want to empower other females, but they want to be empowered themselves to advance in their career. In line with Maslow's hierarchy of needs females feel fulfilled when they empower, reaching self-actualization. One of the reasons identified for females feeling disempowered is because they have no finances and even though there are initiatives by government to provide funds and resources, they do not advocate the initiatives and relay the information. It was found that because females battle financially they are forced to take on multiple roles causing excessive amounts of stress. Female leaders believe that organizations have male bias. This measures what good leadership looks like, stereotypically associated with men. Females believe this stereotype because when they talk about managers they use the word 'he'. This point is furthered proven by the fact that good leadership is less emotional, a factor readily associated with men. A problem identified was that females do not perceive themselves as bold. This emanated from the fact that they fear, don't have any self-confidence and don't take risks. The stereotypical characteristics associated with successful leadership are being bold. This once again is in line with the characteristics of the male archetype. Females thus keep on feeling inadequate and thus disempowered. The last reason found for females feeling disempowered is the fact that they feel they do not have the skill required to be successful leaders. This is by and large because skill and competency is regarded as a prerequisite to being successful in the business world. This forms a direct contrast with proven studies that show that experience is as important as the necessary skills, if not more.

Key finding three: undermining of achievements: The female leadership style is transformational in nature. This style is characterised by traits such as: caring; empathy; acting as a mother, nurturing; emotion; collaboration; empowerment; recognition; acknowledgement; leading by example and being a good listener. It was found that female leadership style forms a direct contrast with male leadership styles. The male leadership style is transactional in nature. The traits associated with transactional leaders are: achieving goals, foster compliance, being directive, demands obedience and if not obeyed they punish. It was found that even though female leadership is in direct contrast to male leadership, and successful leadership is measured by stereotypical societal norms where males are seen as superior, they did not see their style as unsuccessful. Some females felt they were equal to men and others even felt they are more effective than men. Still, they do not acknowledge their successes. Female leaders felt that confidence is necessary for success they displayed not confidence in themselves. It was found that they do not believe in their ability even though the facts show they are more than able to lead successfully. They thus undermine their own ability strengthening the ongoing self-fulfilling prophesy.

Conclusion

The conclusions reached in this study was to address the main aim which was to identify a preferred managerial style used by females and to identify the traits they exhibit to enhance their careers.

References

1. Jones GR (2004) Organizational Theory: Design and Change. (4thedn), Pearson Education, Delhi.
2. Rosin R (2012) The End of Men and the Rise of Women. Clays Ltd, St Ives plc, Great Britain.
3. Duvenhage G (2012) Boardrooms – still a man's world. Top Women 9: 32-33.
4. Littrell LF, Nkomo SM (2005) Gender and race differences in leader behavior preferences in South Africa. Women in Management Review 20: 562-580.
5. Meer F (2013) Women in the apartheid society.
6. Makuala S (2012) Breaking the glass ceiling- A case of Durban corporate women. Unpublished MBA dissertation, Durban University of Kwa-Zulu Natal.
7. Popovici V (2012) Similarities and differences between management and leadership. Annals of the "OnstantinBrâncuşi" Economy Series University of Târgu Jiu.
8. Piterman H (2008) The leadership challenge: Women in management.
9. Daniel A, Moudic Y (2010) Female and gender leadership: To which extents gender impacts on leadership and organizations in France? Unpublished MBA dissertation, Linnaeus University, France.
10. Folkman J, Zenger J (2012) Are women better leaders than men?
11. Boonyachai Y (2011) An investigation of the leadership styles of middle managers in the Thai hotel industry using the MLQ (5X-Short Form) andHofstede's Cultural Dimensions.Unpublished DBA thesis, Lismore, Southern Cross University, NSW.
12. Daft RL (2011) Leadership. 5th Edition, South Western, Cencage Learning
13. Ismail M, Ibrahim M (2008) Barriers to career progression faced by women: Evidence from a Malaysian multinational oil company. Gender in Management: An International Journal 23: 51-66.
14. Jogulu UD, Wood GJ (2006) The role of leadership theory in raising the profile of women in management. Equal Opportunities International 25: 236-250.
15. Noor MAI, Uddin I, Shamalay SS (2011) Leadership Style and Emotional Intelligence: A Gender Comparison. European Journal of Business and Management 3: 27-52.
16. Gunkel M, Lusk E J, Wolff B, Li F (2006) Gender-specific Effects at Work: An Empirical Study of Four Countries Gender. Work and Organization 14: 55-76.
17. Torres SL (2012) Women in Leadership- Top Ten Attributes of Successful Women Leaders.

Bubbles and Overshooting Crash

Li Dai[1] and Peng Zhou[2]*

[1]School of Economics and Trade, Hunan University, China
[2]Cardiff School of Management, Cardiff Metropolitan University, Cardiff, CF5 2YB, UK

Abstract

This paper reviews a model of bubbles under the assumption of heterogeneous rational traders. In the presence of dispersion of opinions, or sequential awareness, financial bubbles are justified by the interactions between rational arbitrageurs and behavioural traders. Timing is a very important component in the trader's strategy. This model is then extended to explain both bubbles and overshooting crash.

Keywords: Rational bubbles; Overshooting crash; Heterogenous traders; Timing strategy of trading

Introduction

Bubbles usually refer to asset prices that exceed the asset's fundamental value because current owners believe that they can resell the asset at an even higher price in the future. That is to say, the owners do not have to believe that the current price reflects the fundamental value. As long as there is enough absorption capacity in the market, a bubble can be persistent. However, classical models cannot explain the existence of bubbles, because if everyone knows that bubble will crash eventually, backward induction will leads to no bubble at all. This argument requires two things: all the traders are rational and the existence of bubble is common knowledge.

Bubbles are very often observed in economic history, such as the Dutch tulip mania of the 1630's, the South Sea bubble of 1719-1720 and more recently the Internet bubble in early 2000. Even Newton tried to ride the South Sea Bubble in 1720. He got out of the market at £7,000 after making a £3,500 profit, but he decided to re-enter the market thereby losing £20,000 at the end. Frustrated with this experience, he concluded: "I can calculate the motions of the heavenly bodies, but not the madness of people." This essay reviews a model of "the madness of people" based on Abreu and Brunnermeier [1], and extends this model from explaining bubble to overshooting crash.

Literature Review

There are four main types of models that justify bubbles. The first class of models assumes that all investors have rational expectations and identical information. These models generate the testable implication that bubbles have to follow an explosive path. In the second category of models, traders are asymmetrically informed and bubbles can emerge under more general conditions because their existence need not be common knowledge. The third strand of models focuses on the interaction between rational and irrational (or behavioural) traders. Bubbles can persist since limits to arbitrage prevent rational traders from eradicating the price impact of irrational traders. Lastly, bubbles can emerge if investors hold heterogenous beliefs, potentially due to psychological biases or information availability. This section will focus on the following criteria to highlight the model proposed by Abreu and Brunnermeier [1].

- Whether existence of bubble is common knowledge;
- Whether all traders are rational;
- Whether there is capital constraints.

To start with, Milgrom and Stokey's seminal paper derives "No Trade Theorem" under classical framework. If all traders are rational and the fundamental value is common knowledge, then no one can profit from private information because private information is revealed by price changes. The efficient markets hypothesis implies the absence of bubbles [2]. Allen, Morris and Postlewaite [3] develop "Contra Positives" of the no trade theorem highlighting necessary conditions for the existence of bubbles. If all traders are rational, but only have mutual knowledge (not common knowledge), then bubbles may exist. Similarly, in Allen and Gorton [4], they argue if all traders are rational, but there is asymmetric information, better informed traders can "Churn Bubbles" at the expense of the less informed traders. These literature justifies bubbles by relaxing the common knowledge assumption. Similarly, in Abreu and Brunnermeier [1], there is heterogeneity among rational traders on when the bubble begins. Traders are aware of the existence of bubbles sooner or later, but they do not know if the others are already informed.

In Delong, et al. [5], rational arbitrageurs push up the price after some initial good news in order to induce irrational traders to aggressively buy stocks in the next period. This delayed reaction by the irrational traders allows the arbitrageurs to unload their position at a profit. This strand of literature justifies bubbles by relaxing the rationality assumption. Similarly, in Abreu and Brunnermeier [1], there is interaction between rational traders and irrational traders.

Another paper written by Delong, et al. [5] find that traders' risk aversion and short horizons limit their ability to correct the mispricing. Shleifer and Vishny argue that professional fund managers forgo profitable long run arbitrage opportunities because the price might depart even further from the fundamental value in the intermediate term. These literatures assume that rational traders do not have the collective ability to correct bubbles because of their risk attitude or exogenously binding capital constraint. In Abreu and Brunnermeier [1], however, the aggregate resources of all arbitrageurs are assumed to

***Corresponding author:** Peng Zhou, Cardiff School of Management, Cardiff Metropolitan University, Cardiff, CF5 2YB, UK
E-mail: pzhou@cardiffmet.ac.uk

be sufficient to crash the bubble. The existence of bubble does not rely on the limited financial ability of arbitrageurs.

Assumptions

Following the comparison with the related literature, the assumptions of the Abreu and Brunnermeier [1] model can be summarised as follows:

- Rational Traders interact with boundedly rational traders.
- A critical mass of traders is needed for a bubble to crash ("coordination").
- A proportion (K) of traders are needed to correct the mispricing.
- There is a dispersion of opinion among traders (sequential awareness), so the timing is important ("competition").
- Traders who get out of the market just prior to the crash make the highest profit;
- Traders who leave the market very early make some profit, but forgo much of the profit;
- Traders who stay in the market too long make a loss.

An important feature of the model is that there is both coordination and competition between traders. The coordination feature to burst a bubble is similar to the second generation currency crisis model [6]. Morris and Shin [7] introduce asymmetric information and derive a unique equilibrium by applying the global games approach. Both currency attack models are static in the sense that speculators only decide whether to attack or not. In contrast, the bubble model here assumes there is a dynamic structure. That is to say, the arbitrageurs also need to decide when to exit. Timing is very important, whereby competition is introduced into the model. The preemption motive leads to a unique equilibrium even under symmetric information [8].

The Model

To illustrate the model, we need to be clear about the subject and the object. The subject is the traders, including both rational traders (or arbitrageurs, speculators, etc.) and irrational traders (or behavioural traders, feedback traders, etc.). However, we can only study the strategy of the rational traders, and derive the equilibrium based on their behaviour. On the other hand, the object is the evolution of the asset price: when it starts to surge and when it starts to crash. The changes in price depend on the interactions between rational and irrational traders. This section will start with a general description of price during bubbles [9].

Price

The asset price pt during a bubble typically experiences the following four phases.

1. Before the positive shock (t:::0), pt grows at the risk-free rate p_t=*ert*.
2. After the positive shock but before some random time t_0 (0 < t ::: t_0), pt grows at a higher rate pt=egt.
   a) This higher price is justified by the fundamentals.
   b) The random t0 is exponentially distributed: ɸ(t0)=1 - e->t0.

1. After t_0 ($t > t_0$), pt continues to grow at g, but the fundamental rate is r.
   a) Fundamental Component: $\dfrac{e^{gt_0}e^{r(t-t_0)}}{e^{gt}} = e^{-(g-r)(t-t_0)} \equiv 1-\beta$
   b) Bubble Component: 1- $e^{-(g-r)(t-t0)} \equiv \beta$.
2. The bubble crashes:
   a) either endogenously because more than K rational traders are aware of the bubble (at $t + \eta k$);
   b) or exogenously because the bubble exceeds $\overline{\beta}$ -(at $t + \overline{\tau}$).

The four phases are illustrated in Figure 1.

Traders

There are two types of traders:

- Irrational traders keep price above its fundamental level;
- Rational traders are sequentially informed of the bubble at some time t_i after t_0.

A key assumption here is asymmetric information. A rational trader does not know how many other traders have been informed of the bubble [10]. Since the traders only differ in when they are aware of the bubble. We identify the trader i by the time when he is informed t_i. The posterior distribution for t_0 for a trader t_i is assumed to be exponentially distributed:

$$\phi(t_0 \mid t_i) = \frac{e^{\lambda\eta} - e^{\lambda(t_i - t_0)}}{e^{\lambda\eta} - 1}$$

The conditional distribution of t_0 for different traders i, j and k are illustrated in Figure 2.

Due to the dynamic nature of the model, the trader's strategy has two components: the position of the stock (long or short), and the timing of taking the position.

Position: Each rational trader can sell all or part of her stock holding or even go short until she reaches a certain limit where her financial constraint is binding.

- The maximum long position is denoted as 0 and the maximum short position is denoted as 1 (continuous action space).

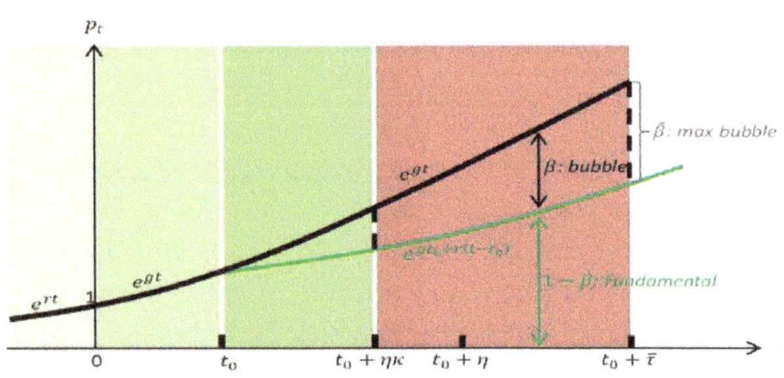

Figure 1: The four phases of price during a typical bubble.

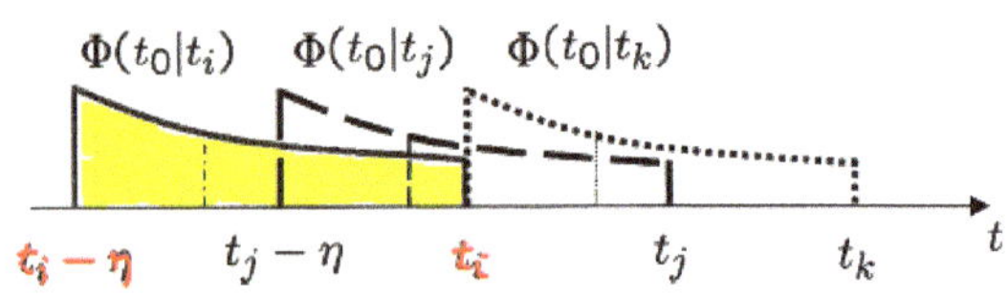

Figure 2: Posterior distribution of t_0.

- Each rational trader may re-enter the market multiple times.

Timing: Each rational trader has to determine when to change her position from long to short.

- The selling pressure/strategy of trader t_i at time t is $\sigma(t, t_i)$.

The aggregate selling pressure at time t is $s(t, t_0) = \int_{t_0}^{\min\{t, t_0+\eta\}} \sigma(t, t_i) dt_i$.

The crash time given $_{t0}$ is $T^*(t_0) = \inf\{t : s(t, t_0) \geq k \text{ or } t = t_0 + \overline{\tau}\}$.

The posterior belief of crash time is $\Pi(t \mid t_i) = \int_{T^*(T_0)<t} d\phi(t_0 \mid t_i)$.

Like any economic model, the payoff function of the traders needs to be specified to describe their objective. The payoff of trader ti is equal to the expected execution price minus the transaction cost.

- The expected execution price at t is:
  - e^{gt} if $s(t, t_0) < k$;
  - $(1 - \beta)\, e^{gt}$ if $s(t, t_0) > k$;
  - $(1-\alpha) \times e^{gt} + \alpha \times (1-\beta)\, e^{gt}$ if $s(t, t_0) = k$
- The transaction cost at t is *cert*.

The general specification of the payoff function is complicated because the trader can re-enter the market several times. For the special case that trader t_i remains fully invested in the market until she completely sells out at *t* and remains out of the market thereafter, trader t_i's expected payoff is:

$$\int_{t_i}^{t} e^{-rs}(1-\beta(s-T^{*-1}(s)))\, p(s)\, d\Pi(s \mid t_i + e^{-rt} p(t)(1-\Pi(t \mid t_i)) - c.$$

Equilibrium strategy

As we said, there are two components in the trader's strategy, position and timing. Therefore, we need to derive both in a trading equilibrium. The following definition, corollary and lemma are related to the position strategy.

Definition 1: A trading equilibrium is defined as a Perfect Bayesian Nash Equilibrium in which whenever a trader's stock holding is less than her maximum, the trader believes that the stock holding of all traders who became aware of the bubble prior to her are also at less than their respective maximum long positions.

Corollary 1: When trader ti sells out her stock holdings, all traders $t_j(t_j<t_i)$ also have already sold all their shares. ("cut-off property")

Lemma 1: In equilibrium, a trader is either fully invested in the market $\sigma(t, t_i)=0$, or at her maximum short position $\sigma(t, t_i)=1$. There is no partial purchases or sell outs.

The followings are related to the timing strategy.

Definition 2: The function $T(t_i) = \inf\{t\ \sigma(t, t_i) > 0\}$ denotes the first instant at which trader ti sells any of her shares.

Corollary 2: The bubble bursts at $T^* = \min\{T(t_0 + \eta k),\ t_0 + \overline{\tau}\}$.

Lemma 2: In equilibrium, trader ti believes at time T (ti) that at most a mass K of traders became aware of the bubble prior to her. ("preemption")

To summarise the equilibrium strategy, trader t_i maintains the maximum short position for all $t \geq T(t_i)$, until the bubble bursts ("trigger strategy"). In the trigger strategy, all rational traders' strategies are corner solution.

Equilibrium crash time

The interaction among traders may lead to crash endogenously or the bubble will crash exogenously. The following proposition describes the condition of endogenous crash.

Under the condition

$$\frac{\lambda}{1-e^{-\lambda\eta\kappa}} \leq \frac{g-r}{\overline{\beta}},$$

There exists a unique trading equilibrium, where all traders sell out in,

$$\tau^1 = \overline{\tau} - \frac{1}{\lambda}\ln\left(\frac{g-r}{g-r-\lambda\overline{\beta}}\right) < \overline{\tau}$$

Periods after they become aware of the bubble and stay out of the market thereafter.

For all t_0, the bubble bursts for exogenous reasons precisely when it reaches its maximum possible size/ $\overline{\beta}$. The intuition behind this proposition is that rational traders never burst the bubble if the dispersion of opinion (η) and the absorption capacity of irrational traders are sufficiently large.

Alternatively, the following proposition describes the reverse case when there is an exogenous crash.

- Under the condition

$$\frac{\lambda}{1-e^{-\lambda\eta\kappa}} > \frac{g-r}{\overline{\beta}},$$

There exists a unique trading equilibrium, where trader t_i with t_i 2: TK sells out in,

$$\tau^* = \beta^{\ 1}\left(\frac{\underline{g\quad r}}{1\quad e^{-\lambda\eta\kappa}}\right)$$

Periods after they become aware of the bubble and stays out of the market thereafter. All traders t_i with $t_i < \eta k$ sell out at $\eta k + T^*$.

The bubble bursts when

$$\beta^* = \frac{1-e^{-\lambda\eta\kappa}}{\lambda}(g-r).$$

The intuition is that the maximum relative bubble size β^* increases as the dispersion of opinions (η) and the absorption capacity of the irrational traders increase.

Application

The model proposed by Abreu and Brunnermeier [1] creatively explains why there is a bubble, i.e. when the asset is overpriced. However, it assumes that after the bubble crashes, the asset price gets back to the fundamental level. This is obviously not true in data. More often, what we observe in the financial market is that after a crash, the asset prices tend to overshoot, falling far below the fundamental level. It leads to persistent recessions or even depression as in the 1930s.

This overreaction in both upturns and downturns over the business cycles can be explained by applying the bubble theory too. In fact, if we assume the price after crash return to the fundamental level, it is inconsistent to the assumption of existence of irrational traders. The explaining power of this model can be and should be extended to explaining the overshooting crash in addition to bubble.

Instead of assuming that the asset price returns to fundamental level after crash, we consistently assume the panic in the financial market will make the irrational traders think the asset price is much lower than the fundamental level. Assume the wrong growth rate is now $g'<r$, lower than the true rate. The asset price will not stop dropping at $e^{gt0+r\,(t-t0)}$, but at $p_t=e^{gt0}+g'^{(t-t0)}$ and this will continue.

Assume t_1 is the time when the first rational trader become aware of the overshooting. Again, t_1 is a random variable following an exponential distribution. The same dispersion of opinion T exists among all the rational traders. Only when k traders collectively stop shorting the asset, the price will stop falling and return towards the fundamental value. This starts another cycle of bubble, just like business cycles in macroeconomics, but the cycles in financial market is more drastic and frequent. This extension enables the model to provide a symmetric explanation of the bubbles and overshooting crash.

Conclusion

The backward induction argument rules out bubbles from the terminal date, but these classical models assume common knowledge. Bubble can exist if there is a dispersion of opinions (heterogenous traders). In this case, existence of bubble is mutual knowledge, but not common knowledge because they do not know if the others know. The rational trader tries to "ride the bubble" to earn some profit before the bubble crashes. Therefore, the timing is a very important element in the strategy.

If the dispersion of opinion and the absorption of irrational traders are large, then there will be an exogenous crash. If the dispersion of opinion and the absorption of irrational traders are small, then there will be an endogenous crash.

The model can be extended to explaining the overshooting behaviour in both upturns (bubbles) and downturns in financial market. Expectation drives the price to fluctuate around the fundamental value but never stays, because the behavioural traders provide the opportunities for rational arbitrageurs to "ride the bubble" or buying "at rock bottom". However, the specification of this model implies the irrational traders are always losers, though not all rational traders are always winners. A more general model along this consideration could add in a distribution or dispersion of opinions within the irrational traders too. For example, some irrational traders are over-optimistic (those supporting the bubbles), while some are over-pessimistic (those supporting the overshooting crash). There are also a continuum of irrational traders between the two extremes, just like the dispersion of opinions among the rational traders. Under this generalised assumption, we can then explain more fluctuations of price behaviour, such as non-monotonic fluctuations in a bubble and double bottoms.

References

1. Abreu D, Brunnermeier B (2003) Bubbles and Crashes. Econometrica 71: 173-204.
2. Santos M, Woodford M (1997) Rational Asset Pricing Bubbles. Econometrica 65: 19-57.
3. Allen F, Morris S, Postlewaite A (1993) Finite Bubbles with Short Sale Constraints and Asymmetric Information. Journal of Economic Theory 61: 206-229.
4. Allen F, Gorton G (1993) Churning Bubbles. Review of Economic Studies 60: 813-836.
5. DeLong JB, Shleifer A , Summers L H , Waldmann R J (1990) Noise Trader Risk in FInancial Markets. Journal of Finance 53: 1839-1885.
6. Obstfeld M (1996) Models of Currency Crises with Self-Fulfilling Features. EuropeanEconomicReview 40:1037-1047.
7. Morris S, S hin H (1998) Unique Equilibrium in a Model of Self- Fullfilling Currency Attacks. American Economic Review 88: 587-596.
8. Brunnermeier MK (2000) Asset Pricing under Asymmetric Information: Bubbles, Crashes, Technical Analysis and Herding. Oxford: Oxford University Press.
9. Hirshleifer D (2001) Investor Psychology. Journal of Finance 56: 1533-1597.
10. Tirole J (1982) On the Possibility of Speculation under Rational Expectations. Econometrica 50: 1163-1182.

An Empirical Study of Customer Value, Customer Trust and Customer Loyalty Based on E-Commerce

Yen-Jo Kiang*

Department of BusinessAdministration, CTBC Financial Management College, Tainan, Taiwan

Abstract

In today's business world, computers are connected to the broadband wide area network (WAN), allowing businesses to integrate industrial value chains and provide customers with various value-added services. Consequently, the virtual community of a public service network can be created and marketing channels in e-generation can be established to provide customers with relevant information or commodities and services through the use of high-speed transmission systems and interactive delivery. However, if e-commerce operators are not fully aware of the characteristics of e-generation consumers, if website operators lack the necessary competitive edge, or if the Internet-based transaction mechanism is not secure, consumers may not be attracted to or continue their interest in online shopping. In the Internet world of e-commerce, it is difficult to fully grasp the changes in customer demands along with the gradual opening of information on the web. To be profitable, it is more important to obtain the value created by loyal customers for businesses in addition to a wide range of online visitors. By integrating the analyses of e-commerce with 244 questionnaires and validating the data with statistical analysis methods, this study provides e-commerce business owners with suggestions on marketing strategies and proposes future directions for subsequent research based on the research findings.

Keywords: Customer value; Customer trust; Customer loyalty; E-Commerce

Intoduction

Since the 1990s, the rapid development and advancement of information technology has led to the surge of the Internet. The rise of the Internet has strongly impacted the original business model of many enterprises, and has also enabled the Internet to be applied to the business model of e-commerce. For business owners, establishing a website for product sales or service provisions does not require a considerable investment in fixed assets, which can drastically reduce the cost of business operations. On the other hand, consumers enjoy greater convenience and can be more selective when conducting transactions online. Based on this corresponding relationship between business owners and consumers, the business model of e-commerce can flourish.

Nevertheless, due to increasingly developed and mature e-commerce activities, diverse types of Internet stores are being launched, offering a dazzling array of commodities, attracting more consumers to participate in e-commerce activities on the Internet. In light of this, to attract consumers to conduct transactions, the operator of a website must understand the needs of target consumer groups and achieve customer recognition through products, services, and other various channels. Subsequently, the website operator can obtain loyal customers. Therefore, it is the ultimate goal of website operators to achieve sustainable development by obtaining consumer loyalty and taking advantage of the opportunities for repeat consumption.

Literature Review

The rise of the Internet has considerably impacted business. In particular, businesses and customers can conduct transactions in a virtual network, forming a new business environment for e-commerce transactions. In e-commerce, business transactions are conducted mainly through telecommunications and the Internet, and include not only the purchase and sale of commodities, but also various activities conducted by enterprises to achieve their goals. From the perspective of information, e-commerce delivers data, products, and services through the use of telecommunications, the Internet, or other media tools; from the perspective of the business process, e-commerce is a technology that automates business transactions and operating procedures through the Internet; and, from a service prospective, e-commerce is an approach that can reduce the transaction costs between businesses and consumers, improve the quality of goods, and accelerate the speed of delivery.

The Internet has removed the limits of geographic development, and has become the future development trend for Business to Business (B2B) and Business to Consumer (B2C). When customers save transaction time and costs through the Internet, e-commerce provides them with higher added value. Therefore, compared with other channels, the Internet has, in addition to saving transaction time and costs, has broken down the geographical barriers of businesses. Furthermore, e-commerce is a one-to-one marketing mode designed to provide personalized services and offer various commodities tailored to customer demands so as to increase their added value. There are six main levels at which businesses use the Internet: e-mails, group discussions, database search, software and support, file transfer, and research publishing.

There are two major differences between Internet and traditional marketing, namely the interactivity and proactivity of Internet marketing. These features enable consumers to interact with e-commerce companies by viewing, comparing, searching, asking

***Corresponding author:** Yen-Jo Kiang, Department of Business Administration, CTBC Financial Management College, Tainan, Taiwan
E-mail: dr.yj.kiang@gmail.com

questions, and even requesting tailored commodities. Generally, the characteristics of Internet marketing include interactivity, no geographical limits, no time limits, proactive consumers, saved costs, specific consumer markets segmented by regions, hyperlink functions, convenient and high-speed functions, and multimedia forms.

Despite these advantages, difficulties exist in Internet marketing. Currently, the difficulties in front of e-commerce are the main problems, such as security considerations, development in payment systems, low speed of Internet connections, lack of attraction to online shopping, the need for wider access space, and information overload [1]. Moreover, there are many reasons for businesses being unwilling to invest in and conduct Internet marketing, such as their product features not being fit for online marketing, difficulty in determining the relative interests of products, low compatibility of products, high risk of investment in products, and high technical risks of the products. The key success factors in managing e-commerce mainly include targeting the right customers, taking care of customers, enabling customers to access operating procedures, providing a comprehensive level of services to maintain customer relationships, enabling self-service functions for customers, assisting customers with their work-related issues, delivering customized services, and managing communities.

Regarding security in e-commerce, as it is not necessary for consumers to directly contact stores when shopping online, e-commerce has the characteristic of anonymity. Therefore, the level of individuals' psychological safety in e-commerce is higher compared with other channels [2]. Further, the online form of communication, unlike traditional media, is similar to interpersonal communication. Consumers become proactive rather than reactive, and may become information makers instead of traditional information receivers. In addition, the "communities" created by the Internet can meet the needs of consumers for communication, information, psychology, and entertainment. The main reasons why online shopping attracts consumers include convenience, better product information from websites, low price, enhanced product variations, rapid search of products, prompt price comparisons, online discussions, and unique shopping experiences. In addition, another major reason is that the shortcomings of traditional shopping malls can be reduced, such as parking, traffic, and bothersome salespeople. The major factors for preventing users from online shopping include the fear of being deceived, privacy rights, transaction security, and traditional habits. Furthermore, it is impossible for online shopping to have the same effects of social interactions and entertainment as traditional shopping. Moreover, consumers might encounter setbacks when visiting the websites or shopping online. For example, using new technologies or interactive interfaces may be an obstacle for some consumers [3].

The relationship between psychological identification with online communities and values

The rise of the Internet has led to the formation of network-based virtual communities. Some members have a strong psychological identification with online communities, and from which they may gain a sense of belonging and satisfaction. Jones, Hesterly, and Borgatti [4] found that the social mechanism of the Internet is often superior to other forms of management, including controlled access, overall culture, collective punishments, and credibility. Further, the notion that psychological identification is intensified by website communities is the same as the concept of overall culture in the social mechanisms of network management as indicated by Jones et al. [4]. The stronger the centripetal force of website communities, the greater the website value for customers. Underwood, Bond, and Baer [5], in their studies on the sport industry, described that customers' social identification with their teams might be strengthened by group experiences, history or traditions, physical equipment, and rituals. Hence, if customers have stronger psychological identifications with the website communities, the website will have greater value for the customers. Therefore, the following hypothesis was inferred:

Hypothesis 1: Stronger customers' psychological identification with the website community will increase the customers' perceived value of the website.

The relationship between convenience and value

How e-commerce can attract consumers depends on its ability to save time and costs for consumers and allow consumers to view, compare, search, and ask questions. In addition, there are convenient and rapid functions, such as hyperlinks, that provide customers with higher added value without geographical or time limits. Hence, the more convenient services the website offers, the greater value it will have for customers. Therefore, the following hypothesis was inferred:

Hypothesis 2: The greater convenience of services provided by a website will increase the customers' perceived value of the website.

The relationship between novelty and value

Amit and Zott [6] described that the competition on the Internet emphasizes not only convenience and speed, but also novelty in contents, as crucial to competitive advantage and important for the Internet to create customer value. Hence, when there is a higher degree of novelty in the content offered by a website, there will be greater value for customers. Therefore, the following hypothesis was inferred:

Hypothesis 3: A higher degree of novelty in the content provided by a website will increase the customers' perceived value of the website.

The relationship between transaction security and trust

Due to issues that exist in the Internet environment, such as the definition of property rights, the trustworthiness of electronic money, cybercrime, secure payment, and the lack of explicit rules, transaction security makes e-commerce difficult to develop and promote. The information related to online transactions can be easily stolen, and it is both convenient and easy to collect information on the Internet. Hence, the privacy of consumers' personal data warrants attention. Internet users are concerned about their privacy rights. Consumers are unwilling to shop online partly because they fear infringement on their rights of privacy. In the early stages of Internet construction, the transaction rules and security issues of the Internet were not considered. However, along with the increase in commercial applications, issues, such as the ownership of exclusive property rights and transaction security, emerged [7]. Given that information related to Internet transactions can be easily stolen, the security of online transactions is not satisfactory for consumers, leaving them with an impression of distrust. However, businesses are attempting to solve these problems. For example, secure electronic transactions (SET), encryption technologies, and setting up third-party certification bodies can all make Internet transactions more secure. Hence, when the security of transactions on a website improves, customers' level of trust in the website will as well. Therefore, the following hypothesis was inferred:

Hypothesis 4: Higher transaction security of a website will increase the level of trust customers have in the website.

The relationship between relationship stability and trust

Jones et al. [4] detailed that the social mechanism of network management provides a comparative advantage superior to other forms of management. It includes controlled access, overall culture, collective punishments, and credibility. When the relationship stability between websites and customers is stronger, the overall culture and credibility in social mechanisms is strengthened, thereby lowering customers' sense of moral crisis and increasing their level of trust. Therefore, the following hypothesis was inferred:

Hypothesis 5: More stable relationships between a website and customers will increase the level of trust customers have in the website.

The relationship between value and loyalty

Customer value refers to the difference in value between utility and quality or benefits and costs for customers when buying products or using services. However, some scholars define customer value as the level of preferences customers develop after their evaluation of product attributes [8]. Further, customer-delivered value refers to the difference in value between the total customer value and total customer cost, while total customer value refers to an aggregation of interests that customers expect to gain from particular products or services. Creating customer value and offering it to customers will increase the overall value of the organization. The customer value in this context means considering what customers want from their perspective, and it is certain that customer value can be obtained from buying and using products. Based on the three classifications of technology (long-linked, intensive, mediating) by Stabell and Fjeldstad [9] expanded the value chain framework by Porter [10] to become three types of value form models on corporate levels: "value chain," "value shop," and "value network." Increased customer value is crucial for maintaining customer loyalty [11,12]. In the 21st century, e-commerce plays one of the most important roles in value creation. The first country to develop the e-commerce industry was the United States, followed by EU countries and Japan [6]. Hence, the higher the customers' perceived value of a website, the higher their loyalty to the website will be. Therefore, the following hypothesis was inferred:

Hypothesis 6: Higher customers' perceived value of a website will increase their loyalty to the website.

The relationship between trust and value

There are a number of various definitions regarding trust. Some define trust as "a kind of confidence in others' good intentions" [13], while others argue that trust means the expectation that the other party is willing to accept "vulnerability" for their actions, regardless of their abilities to supervise or control their actions [14]. Generally, a widely accepted definition of trust is "a psychological state of willingness to accept vulnerability, developed by a positive expectation based on the intentions and behaviors of others" [15]. "Trust" is based on the principle of being voluntary, and is related to shared values. When behaviors cannot be anticipated or strangers join interactions, "trust" is required because predictable things, such as a sense of identity or the power of sanctions, do not exist [16]. Increasing customers' level of trust can improve the interactivity and reduce the uncertainty of transactions, thereby increasing the cognitive value of customers [15,17]. Therefore, the following hypothesis was inferred:

Hypothesis 7: The higher level of trust customers place in a website will increase the customers' perceived value of the website.

The relationship between trust and loyalty

According to related studies, customer loyalty may increase due to word-of-mouth effects and repeat purchases, which improves customers' level of trust [18,19]. In addition, customers may have a higher degree of loyalty to trustworthy service providers [20]. Hence, when customers place a higher level of trust in a website, their loyalty to the website will increase. Therefore, the following hypothesis was inferred:

Hypothesis 8: The higher level of trust customers have for a website will increase their loyalty to the website.

Through this literature review and practical observations, this study analyzed the factors influencing, and the relationships between, the customer value, trust, and loyalty of e-commerce websites. The proposed research framework is shown in Figure 1.

Research Methods and Measurements

Measurements of research variables

The questionnaire design of this study was revised based on relevant literature. All items were measured on a Likert Five-point Scale, where 1 represents "strongly disagree" and 5 represents "strongly agree". The measurements of variables in each dimension are explained in Table 1.

Sources of data

The research objects in this study are users with trading experience on e-commerce websites. Questionnaires were issued through random

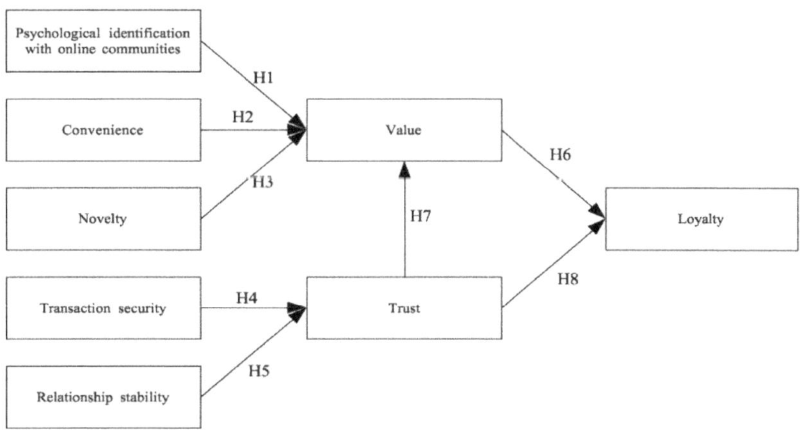

Figure 1: Research framework.

Research dimensions	Measured variables in dimensions
Psychological identification with online communities	• You frequently visit or browse this website when surfing the Web. • You have a pleasant experience shopping on this website. • As a member of the website, you feel greatly satisfied. • You take delight in sharing your experience and joy from this website with others. • At the mention of an e-commerce website, this is the website that first comes to your mind.
Convenience	• This website provides customers with the most timely shopping-related information. • This website has the most convenient steps and procedures for shopping. • This website offers the most convenient and secure payment methods. • Customers can rapidly and simply complete online transactions on this website. • This website provides customers with effective communication channels (e.g., telephone or email) or indexing functions to enable them to troubleshoot problems quickly.
Novelty	• The products, services, or transaction mechanisms offered by this website are unique. • The products, services, or transaction mechanisms offered by this website are difficult for other websites to imitate. • This website often changes or innovates its products, services, or transaction mechanisms.
Transaction security	• The personal data and transaction-related information on this website will not be leaked. • You trust the security mechanism of this website. • You are assured about the payment methods on this website. • This website is not easily invaded by computer hackers. • The transaction security of this website is guaranteed. • Others are unable to know your personal-related data from this website. • This website keeps the personal data of its customers in strict confidence.
Relationship stability	• When surfing the Internet, you visit this website first. • You feel that the reputation of this website is trustworthy. • As long as this website maintains its existing services, you will not switch to other websites. • You will recommend this website to your relatives and friends.
Value	• You believe that the products or services offered on this website are good quality. • The products or services offered by this website meet your expectations • The products/services offered by this website are your best choices • The value brought to you by this website is higher than other e-commerce websites. • Shopping on this website is a pleasant experience.
Trust	• You believe that this website is fairly reliable. • You believe that this website is trustworthy over the long-term. • You believe that this website is honest and tells no lies. • You believe that this website considers the interests of its customers. • You believe that this website enjoys a good reputation and credibility.
Loyalty	• Your time spent on this website accounts for a greater proportion of your total time online • On this website, you enjoy visiting other websites of similar types. • Unless recommended by friends, you would not consider taking the initiative to visit or browse other similar websites. • You visit this website first when shopping online.

Table 1: Measurements of research dimensions.

sampling, mainly in the form of postal letters and e-mails. A total of 600 questionnaires were issued and 256 were returned. Excluding 12 invalid questionnaires, there were a total of 244 valid questionnaires. Therefore, the valid response rate was 40.6%.

Research Findings and Analyses

Data analysis of research variables

Reliability analysis: The development of the questionnaires used in this study was operationalized based on previous research, and researchers screened and confirmed the questionnaire items. In addition, this study adopted confirmatory factor analysis as a method for measuring the measured variable quality of the research variables and the condition of fit between the concentrated dimensions. The composite reliability of latent variables is comprised of the reliabilities of all measured variables. To investigate the internal consistency of variables, a higher value of reliability indicates a higher consistency between variables. A value above 0.6 is suggested by Fornell and Larcker [21]. As shown in Table 2, the reliability value of each variable in this study falls in the range of 0.754~0.951, all higher than the recommended value, indicating that the reliability of the research variables is within the acceptable range. The reliability analysis of each latent variable in this study is shown in Table 2.

Analysis of the structural model: Through confirmatory factor analysis, the benchmark model of this study had positive internal consistency (composite reliability), indicating that the measured variables in each type have reliability and validity. Next, according to the research framework, a structural model was established based on the measurement models for each of the above-mentioned latent variables. Structural equation modeling (SEM) was used to validate the model fit of the theories. The statistical amount χ^2 is often used as one of the observation indices, but the value of χ^2 is easily influenced by the size of the sample. To remove the interference of SEM, the issue of sample size should be considered [22]. Generally, when the value of χ^2 and the ratio of the degree of freedom (DOF) are used to measure model fit, rigorous studies require that the level should not exceed 3 [23]. The SEM analyses includes fitness analysis of the research model as well as the explanatory power of the overall research model. In addition, other important related statistical indices should be taken into account. In this study, seven indices were selected for conducting an overall evaluation of model fit. As shown in Table 3, among the auxiliary indices, only the adjusted goodness of fit index (AGFI) was lower than the ideal suggested value (0.7). Hair, et al. [24] believe that the goodness of fit index (GFI) and AGFI values are better if close to 1, but there is no single and absolute standard value in determining the goodness of fit between observational data and models. Nevertheless, Baumgartner and Homburg [25] used SEM to analyze 184 documents of study in the fields of marketing and consumers between 1977 and 1994 and found the ratio of documents in which AGFI were lower than the suggested value was 48%, still within the acceptable range. Therefore, there is a good level of fit in the models and observational data of this study.

Empirical findings: The path relationship between each variable was estimated using SEM. The path value was estimated by using the standardized coefficient. Of the eight hypotheses for validating the research model, a total of five reached the significance level of α=0.01, and one hypothesis reached the significance level of α=0.05. Two hypotheses, H1 and H2, were determined invalid. The path analysis coefficients of the structural model are as follows: psychological identification with online communities → value (γ_{21}=0.34); convenience → value (γ_{22}=0.01); novelty → value (γ_{23}=0.05); transaction security → trust (γ_{34}=0.39); relationship stability → trust γ_{35}=0.50; value → loyalty (β_{12}=0.37); trust → value (β_{23}=0.59); and, trust → loyalty (β_{13}=0.22). Relevant empirical data indicated that only H2 and H3 were not supported, while all other hypotheses were all supported.

Research variables	Variables	Composite Reliability (CR)	Variances extracted	Cronbach α
Psychological identification with online communities	5	0.754	0.383	0.717
Convenience	5	0.863	0.557	0.858
Novelty	3	0.820	0.606	0.706
Transaction security	7	0.951	0.736	0.951
Relationship stability	4	0.761	0.445	0.765
Value	5	0.874	0.580	0.876
Trust	5	0.897	0.636	0.898
Loyalty	4	0.756	0.445	0.743

Table 2: Reliability and validity analysis of each measured variable.

Fit indices	Suggested level	Results
χ^2	The smaller, the better	1618.03 (p=0.000)
DOF	<3	2.501 (df=647)
GFI	>0.9	0.91
AGFI	>0.9	0.94
RMSEA	<0.08	0.079
NFI	>0.9	0.92
NNFI	>0.9	0.98
CFI	>0.9	0.98

Table 3: Analyses of fitness in the comprehensive research model.

Further, the explanatory powers of the variances for the three latent dependent variables (value, trust, and loyalty) all reached above 0.5, indicating that the proposed model is valid and acceptable. The model's empirical results are shown in Figure 2.

Validation of mediating effects: This study proposed a competitive model to validate the mediating effects of "value" and "trust" to test the mediating effects of relationship quality. The mediating variables were verified by referring to the methods of Baron and Kenny [26]. However, the SEM by Williams, Edwards, and Vandenberg [27] was adopted to validate the mediating models, which was presented respectively by three competitive models and must meet the following four conditions: (1) independent variables (three ways of relationship connection) must have a significant relationship with the mediating variables; (2) independent variables (three ways of relationship connection) must have significant relationships with the dependent variable (loyalty); (3) mediating variables must have significant relationships with a dependent variable (loyalty); and, (4) independent variables and mediating variables must simultaneously have a significant relationship with dependent variables, and the effects of the independent variables must be weaker than the second kind of effects. From the competitive model of the four sets of conditions, as shown in Figure 3, the first set of conditions, the comparative values of convenience and novelty, did not have significant relationships, and the other relationship paths met requirements. Furthermore, convenience, novelty, and loyalty did not have significant relationships under the second set of conditions, but the competitive model completely met the requirements by the third set of conditions. Under the fourth set of conditions, the psychological identification with online communities, convenience, novelty, transaction security, value, and trust did not have significant impacts,

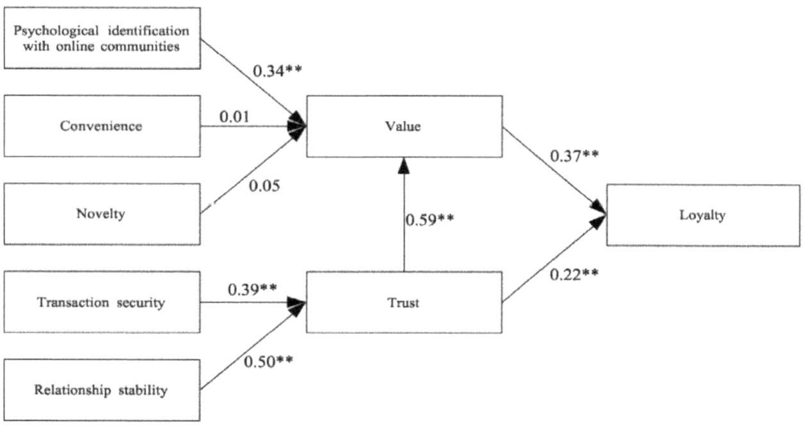

Note: **p<0.01, *p<0.05

Figure 2: The mediating structural model of customer value, trust, and loyalty.

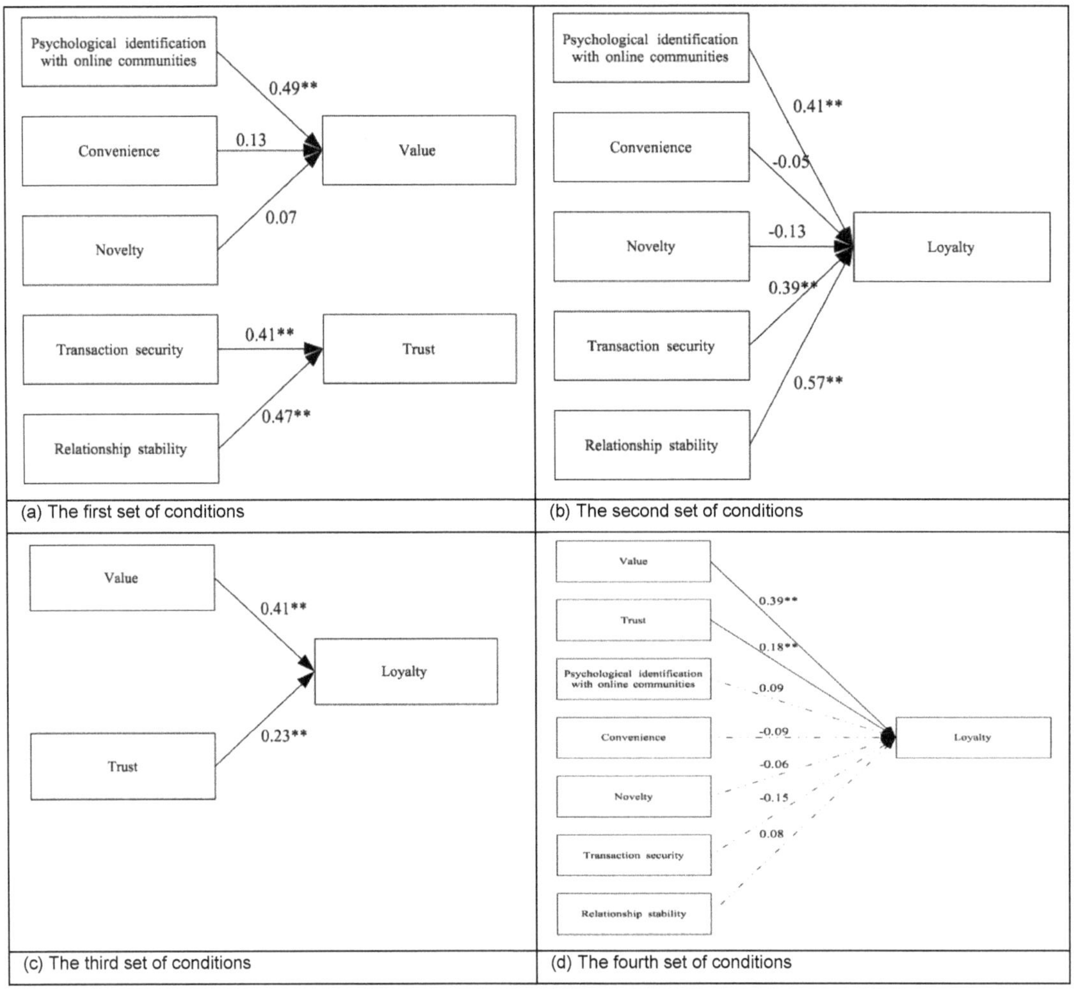

Note: **p<0.01, *p<0.05

Figure 3: The model of customer value, trust, and loyalty.

while only relationship stability had a significantly positive impact on loyalty. Hence, the statistical level of the psychological identification with social communities versus the dependent variables changed from being significant to being insignificant, and the coefficient of the relationship stability versus the dependent variables declined, indicating that "value" and "trust" have full mediating effects.

Conclusions and Suggestions

Conclusions

Along with the dot-com bubble, the globalization of competition and blurred national boundaries in the Internet world, the advancement of science and technology has caused problems in management. In today's business world, computers are connected to the broadband WAN, allowing businesses to integrate industrial value chains and provide customers with various value-added services. Consequently, the virtual community of a public service network can be created and marketing channels in e-generation can be established to provide customers with relevant information or commodities and services through the use of high-speed transmission systems and interactive delivery. However, if e-commerce operators are not fully aware of the characteristics of e-generation consumers, if website operators lack the necessary competitive edge, or if the Internet-based transaction mechanism is not secure, consumers may not be attracted to or continue their interest in online shopping. In the Internet world of e-commerce, it is difficult to fully grasp the changes in customer demands along with the gradual opening of information on the web. To be profitable, it is more important to obtain the value created by loyal customers for businesses in addition to a wide range of online visitors.

In the past, Taiwan created an economic phenomenon through original equipment manufacturing (OEM) for quality assurance and product excellence. However, in the Internet world, the pursuit of functional value alone no longer fits the concept of e-commerce marketing. The positioning of websites is the goal to pursue. Various customer values based on website types should be offered to increase loyal customers on the Internet. In view of this, this study integrated the analysis of e-commerce with responses from 244 valid questionnaires, verified using the SEM analysis method, to provide e-commerce business owners with suggestions for marketing strategies and propose future directions for research.

Consumers' psychological identifications with online communities were compared with their values. When there was a stronger centripetal force of customers toward a website, the website had greater value for the customers, and hence the customers could build consensus, establish brand loyalty, and subsequently increase their revisits to the website and purchases online (coefficient value is 0.34). The confirmed validity of H1 and the viewpoints of Jones et al. [4], and Underwood et al. [5] correspond. Based on the analyses of transaction security and online trust, if websites are able to provide more secure transaction mechanisms, the customers' sense of trust in the websites will increase (coefficient value is 0.39), in support of H4. Another important consideration is whether the process of money flow is secure during transactions. For example, whether secure coding technologies for digital currencies or SET are adopted as a mode of payment. More secure transaction processes will better assure the consumers. From the analyses of relationship stability and online trust, when the relationship between websites and customers is more stable, the sense of customer trust in websites will improve (coefficient value is 0.50), and subsequently influence the number of times customers revisit online stores. Therefore, H5 is also valid. There is a positive and significant relationship between the value of websites perceived by customers and customer loyalty to websites, meaning customers with higher perceived value of a website will trust the website more. Furthermore, there is a positive and significant relationship between customers' sense of trust in a website and their perceived value, indicating that improving customers' trust in a website is conducive to improving their perceived value of the website. Lastly, there is a positive and significant relationship between the sense of trust customers have in websites and their loyalty, meaning that improving a customer's sense of trust in a website will improve their loyalty to the website. Therefore, H6, H7, and H8 are valid.

The booming development of the Internet has promoted the business opportunities of e-commerce, attracting a considerable number of technological talents to establish Internet companies and invest in the borderless market and field of the Internet. The endless business opportunities of the Internet have opened up the virtual market for businesses. However, this does not mean that every investor can be successful. In the e-commerce market, although market share is important, the satisfaction of consumers is essential for the survival of e-commerce operators. Therefore, businesses operating websites should also carefully consider the factors influencing the decision-making of consumers to choose e-commerce shopping.

Implications for management

Offering interactive web services: It is often difficult to succeed in the early stages as a website operator. However, as they manage their daily operations steadily, their websites' credibility, reputation, and brand image can be established for consumers. If operators offer commodities at reasonable prices, and often make use of flexible tactics, such as 3D animations, multimedia displays, online games, entertainment activities, discounts for online shopping, and personalized service modes, they will attract a wide range of consumer groups, and subsequently consumers will increase their online purchase intentions.

Emphasizing the security of online transactions: Currently, the two payment methods consumers most frequently choose are credit cards and account transfers, and the transaction security of which receives public attention. In the future, in response to online cash flow, secure sockets layer (SSL) (a secure coding technology for digital currency), and SLL or SET will be widely used methods of transactions. Alternatively, new technologies, such as voices, images, or biometric features, may be used as identification methods to solve difficult issues, such as stealing and forgery, which will also increase the online purchases and the types of products consumers buy. In addition, for maintaining the security and fairness of online transactions, government bodies should formulate relevant legislation, such as the protection of intellectual property rights and privacy, electronic authentication, electronic payments, and taxation from online transactions.

Improving the relationship between customers and websites: The loyalty of a customer to a website is considerably influenced by the "subjective norms" perceived by the customer. Therefore, consumers' purchase intentions can be stimulated if a shopping website offers virtual communities that enable consumers to recognize the awareness level of their perceived reference groups (e.g., net friends) when they discuss products in discussion forums. In other words, a website suggestion zone that enables users to share opinions about their purchases can impact consumers' continuous purchase behavior.

References

1. Cockburn C, Wilson TD (1996) Business use of the world-wide web. International Journal of Information Management 16: 83-102.
2. Alba J, Lynch J, Weitz B, Janiszewski C, Lutz R, et al. (1997) Interactive Home Shopping: Consumer, Retailer, and Manufacturer Incentives to Participate in Electronic Marketplaces. Journal of Marketing 61: 38-53.
3. Hoffman DL, Novak TP (1996) Marketing in Hypermedia Computer-Mediated Environments: Conceptual Foundations. Journal of Marketing 60: 50-68.
4. Jones C, Hesterly WS, Borgatti SP (1997) A General Theory of Network Governance: Exchange Conditions and Social Mechanisms. The Academy of Management Review 22: 911-945.
5. Underwood R, Bond E, Baer R (2001) Building Service Brands via Social Identity: Lessons from the Sports Marketplace. Journal of Marketing Theory and Practice 9: 1-13.
6. Amit R, Zott C (2001) Value creation in E-business. Strategic Management Journal 22: 493-520.
7. Pallab P (1996) Marketing on the Internet. Journal of Consumer Marketing 13: 27-39.
8. Woodruff RB (1997) Customer value: The next source for competitive advantage. Journal of the Academy of Marketing Science 25: 139-153.
9. Stabell CB, Fjeldstad D (1998) Configuring Value for Competitive Advantage: On Chains, Shops, and Networks. Strategic Management Journal 19: 413-437.
10. Porter ME (1985) Competitive Advantage. New York: The Free Press.
11. Bolton RN, Drew JH (1991) A Longitudinal Analysis of the Impact of Service Changes on Customer Attitudes. Journal of Marketing 55: 1-9.
12. Chang TZ, Wildt AR (1994) Price, product information, and purchase intention: An empirical study. Journal of the Academy of Marketing Science 22: 16-27.
13. Ring PS, Ven AH (1994) Developmental Processes of Cooperative Interorganizational Relationships. The Academy of Management Review 19: 90-118.
14. Mayer RC, Davis JH, Schoorman FD (1995) An Integrative Model of Organizational Trust. The Academy of Management Review 20: 709-734.
15. Rousseau DM, Sitkin SB, Burt RS, Camerer C (1998) Not so Different after All: A Cross-Discipline View of Trust. The Academy of Management Review 23: 393-404.
16. Tonkiss F, Passey A (1999) Trust, Confidence and Voluntary Organisations: Between Values and Institutions. Sociology 33: 257-274.
17. Kerin RA, Jain A, Howard DJ (1992) Store Shopping Experience and Consumer Price-Quality-Value Perceptions. Journal of Retailing 68: 376-397.
18. Sirdeshmukh D, Singh J, Sabol B (2002) Consumer Trust, Value, and Loyalty in Relational Exchanges. Journal of Marketing 66: 15-37.
19. Zeithaml VA, Berry LL, Parasuraman A (1996) The Behavioral Consequences of Service Quality. Journal of Marketing 60: 31-46.
20. Gassenheimer JB, Houston FS, Davis JC (1998) The role of economic value,

social value, and perceptions of fairness in interorganizational relationship retention decisions. Journal of the Academy of Marketing Science 26: 322-337.

21. Fornell C, Larcker DF (1981) Structural Equation Models with Unobservable Variables and Measurement Error: Algebra and Statistics. Journal of Marketing Research 18: 382-388.

22. Bagozzi RP, Yi Y (1988) On the evaluation of structural equation models. Journal of the Academy of Marketing Science 16: 74-94.

23. Chin WW, Todd PA (1995) On the Use, Usefulness, and Ease of Use of Structural Equation Modeling in MIS Research: A Note of Caution. MIS Quarterly 19: 237-246.

24. Hair JF, Andersion RE, Tatham RL, Black WC (1998) Multivariate Data Analysis. London: Prentice-Hall International Limited.

25. Baumgartner H, Homburg C (1996) Applications of structural equation modeling in marketing and consumer research: A review. International Journal of Research in Marketing 13: 139-161.

26. Baron RM, Kenny DA (1986) The moderator–mediator variable distinction in social psychological research: Conceptual, strategic, and statistical considerations. Journal of Personality and Social Psychology 51: 1173-1182.

27. Williams LJ, Edwards JR, Vandenberg RJ (2003) Recent Advances in Causal Modeling Methods for Organizational and Management Research. Journal of Management 29: 903-936.

Industry Initiatives for Green Marketing in India

Neeraj Kumar Sharma*
Baba Ramdas Udaseen Shikshan Sansthan, Hapur, Uttar Pradesh, India

Abstract

Today, Environment issues are seen everywhere in the world. These issues are very crucial i.e., global warming, waste disposal, climate change, and pollution etc. and influence our daily life. By this time many corporates are still hesitated to use green marketing practices even after government compulsion. The main reason for this is that firm still thinks that green marketing practice may increase their cost of production and reduce the profit. This article consists of some examples of the firms in india which are going green and fetching good amount of profit and customer satisfaction. Some golden rules are also given in the article for the companies going for green marketing. Some examples of the companies are also given in the article which is successful in reducing cost of production and improving the profit by green marketing like WIPRO, Infosys, Tata Metelik Limited, Maruti and Delhi CNG and Suzlon Energy. Green marketing is the marketing of goods and services that are presumed to be sold for environment. It involves an entire process of product manufacturing to supplying in market. Such as: raw material used in product, technology, packaging and distribution. It is also called ecological /sustainable/environmental marketing.

Keywords: Green Marketing; Initiatives for green marketing; Need of green marketing; Importance of green marketing

Introduction

According to the American Marketing Association, green marketing is the marketing of products that are presumed to be environmentally safe. Thus green marketing incorporates a broad range of activities, including product modification, changes to the production process, change in packaging, as well as modifying advertising [1]. Yet defining green marketing is not a simple task where several meanings intersect and contradict each other; an example of this will be the existence of varying social, environmental and retail definitions attached to this term [2]. Other similar terms used are Environmental Marketing and Ecological Marketing.

Evolution of green marketing

The first wave of Green Marketing came into picture in 1980s. Corporate Social Responsibility (CSR) Reports started with the ice cream seller Ben and Jerry's where the financial report was supplemented by a greater view on the company's environmental impact.

In 1987 a document prepared by the World Commission on Environment and Development defined sustainable development as meeting "the needs of the present without compromising the ability of future generations to meet their own need", this became known as the Brundtland Report and was another step towards widespread thinking on sustainability in everyday activity [3].

Two tangible milestones for wave of green marketing came in the form of published books, both of which were called Green Marketing. They were by Kinnear [4] in the United Kingdom and by Jacquelyn Ottman [5] in the United States of America.

In the years after 2000 a second wave of Green marketing emerged. By now CSR and the Triple Bottom Line (TBL) were widespread. Such publications as a 2005 United Nations Report, then in 2006 a book by Al Gore and the UK Stern Report brought scientific-environmental arguments to a wide public in an easy to understand way.

Objective

The objective of this paper is to examine the need, importance and problems of green marketing and also to evaluate the initiatives taken by the Indian companies for green marketing in their core business values.

Importance of green marketing

Companies that develop new and improved products, and services with environment inputs in mind give themselves access to new markets, increase their profit sustainability and enjoy a competitive advantage over the companies that are not concerned for the environment [6].

Some of the advantages of green marketing are as follows

1. It ensures sustained long-term growth along with profitability.
2. It saves money in the long run, although initial cost is more.
3. It helps the companies to market their products and services keeping the environment aspects in mind. It helps in accessing the new markets and enjoying competitive advantage.
4. Most of the employees also feel proud and responsible to be working for an environmentally responsible company.
5. It promotes corporate social responsibility.

Reasons for Adopting Green Marketing

1. Opportunities available and competitive advantage.
2. Corporate social responsibility on the part of companies.
3. Government regulations.
4. Competition with other responsible companies.
5. Goodwill of the company.

***Corresponding author:** Neeraj Kumar Sharma, Baba Ramdas Udaseen Shikshan Sansthan, Hapur, Uttar Pradesh, India, E-mail: brdudc@gmail.com

6. Environment conscious consumers.

7. For conserving scarce natural resources.

Green Marketing Mix

Every company has its own favorite marketing mix. Some have 4 P's and some have 7 P's of marketing mix. The 4 P's of green marketing are that of a conventional marketing but the challenge before marketers is to use 4 P's in an innovative manner [7].

Product

The ecological objectives in planning products are to reduce resource consumption and pollution and to increase conservation of scarce resources [8].

Price

Price is a critical and important factor of green marketing mix. Most consumers will only be prepared to pay additional value if there is a perception of extra product value. This value may be improved performance, function, design, visual appeal, or taste. Green marketing should take all these facts into consideration while charging a premium price.

Promotion

There are three types of green advertising: -

* Ads that address a relationship between a product/service and the biophysical environment

* Those that promote a green lifestyle by highlighting a product or service

* Ads that present a corporate image of environmental responsibility

Place

The choice of where and when to make a product available will have significant impact on the customers. Very few customers will go out of their way to buy green products.

Challenges of Green Marketing Ahead

Problems of green marketing

Many organizations want to turn to green, as an increasing number of consumers' want to associate themselves with environmental-friendly products. Alongside, one also witnesses confusion among the consumers regarding the products. In particular, one often finds distrust regarding the credibility of green products. Therefore, to ensure consumer confidence, marketers of green products need to be much more transparent, and refrain from breaching any law or standards relating to products or business practices [9-12].

Examples of green marketing in Indian companies

Wipro and Infosys: Wipro and Infosys's are going green Wipro launched desktops, laptops are known as Wipro green wares. It was the first company in India who developed eco-sustainability in the form of energy, water efficiency and waste management. Wipro are actively seeking to become a very green company. Wipro has taken various initiatives to be green and the main objective of this is to become a carbon natural, water positive and energy saving in business organization. Wipro designs products and solutions that can minimize hazardous waste [13]. For the purpose of enhancing ecological-sustainability, WIPRO is continuously offering green products. Wipro has adopted a number of steps for ecological-sustainability at its corporate level also. Wipro wants to become fully carbon natural and to achieve zero carbon emission by balancing the carbon released by the firm with equaling quantity off set. Wipro, Infosys reduced it per capita consumption of electricity and procured renewable energy. In future, every new building on campus follows integrated design methods for the purpose maximize the day light and reduce heat [14]. It will construct energy efficient building, at present also, in Wipro 18 building are certified to the international green standard. It replaced order office equipment with new energy saving equipment. Wipro and Infosys also installed solar panel also in their campus. We know that solar power is 70% cheaper than power generated by diesel. Solar energy has no adverse impact on our surrounding also. Products manufactured by these firms are less harmful to environment.

Tata Metaliks Limited: This deals in mining and metal sector. It has given a green view to reduce its carbon foot prints. The objective of Tata Metaliks Limited is to increase the green cover through plantation, ground water, power generation and use of natural fertilizers etc. The major green initiatives of this company is related to water utilization. It depends entirely on the ground water or no municipal supply and it will perform a complete water neutral operations [15].

Suzlon Energy: Suzlon energy also going green. Suzlon is the world's 4th largest wind power company among the greenest and best company in India. It is a renewable company manufacturer and produce wind Turbines, now Suzlon 30% power of renewable energy in India. It meets the need of present without compromising the capacity of future generation to meet their needs. Its total revenue was $ 4.18 billion in 2011 [16].

Electronics sector: The consumer electronics sector provides room for using green marketing to attract new customers. One example of this is HP's promise to cut its global energy use 20 percent by the year 2010. To accomplish this reduction below 2005 levels, The Hewlett-Packard Company announced plans to deliver energy-efficient products and services and institute energy-efficient operating practices in its facilities worldwide [17].

Introduction of CNG in Delhi: New Delhi, capital of India, was being polluted at a very fast pace until Supreme Court of India forced a change to alternative fuels. In 2002, a directive was issued to completely adopt CNG in all public transport systems to curb pollution [18].

Maruti Udyog Ltd: Greening of Supply Chain: The company has remained ahead of regulatory requirements in pursuit of environment protection and energy conservation at its manufacturing facilities, and in development of products that use fewer natural resources and are environment friendly [19].

The company credited the 'Just-in-Time' philosophy adopted and internalized by the employees as the prime reason that helped to excel in this direction. The company has been promoting 3R since its inception. As a result the company has not only been able to recycle 100% of treated waste water but also reduced fresh water consumption. The company has implemented rain water harvesting to recharge the aquifers. Also, recyclable packing for bought out components is being actively promoted.

The company has been facilitating implementation of Environment Management System (EMS) at its suppliers' end. Regular training programs are conducted for all the suppliers on EMS. Surveys are conducted to assess the vendors who need more guidance. The systems and the environmental performance of suppliers are audited.

The green co-efficient of this system is much better than the conventional system.

Important rules of green marketing: Marketers should grow their green marketing plan. How they can create new opportunities for selling their products and face threats of competitors in market. The marketing firm should know its strong and weak point also. Make plan how firm can make its customer life better and how can differentiate its offering from competitors. The firm should provide assurance to customer that they are safe and environment should be kept in mind in all aspects from production to supply of products [20,21].

The firms should do the right thing and reassure customers that they are doing the right things, they are making a good quality of product and service by hard working and caring. Firm should consider people, profit and planet while taking marketing decisions. If firm wants to supply a green product to customers. First of all it needs to decide that the consumer is aware about the issues that product attempts to address. The product should have some value added benefits. The firms should make sure that customers feel delight when they use the particular product and is different from other alternative products exist in market. Firm should consider pricing policies also, if they are charging more pricing than competitor. Then make sure that product cost is more due to use of higher quality ingredients and economies of scale. Always continue efforts to some improvement over existing products and adopt new types of Eco-products do a great job of winning the trust of consumers, it means that the producer should not only concentrate on functional benefits but they should also think what they are making. Their products and services are green or not, if not then how they can make products green and whom they are working with. To capture advantage of opportunities that green marketing represents to engage customers on emotional level.

Conclusion

Green marketing should not neglect the economic aspect of marketing. Marketers need to understand the implications of green marketing. If we think customers are not concerned about environmental issues or will not pay a premium for products that are more eco-responsible, think again. We must find an opportunity to enhance our product's performance and strengthen our customer's loyalty and command a higher price.

Nowadays, green marketing has become necessary to save the world from environment pollution. From the marketing point of view, a good marketer is not only satisfy the consumer needs but also produce and supply products according to the choice of the consumers But the business firm should know the benefits of selling green products [22]. Consumers also ready to pay more amount to maintain a greener and cleaner surroundings. Consumers are also aware about Initiatives Taken by Corporates about the attributes and use of products that's why they demand for green products. Making green products have to be achieved through out the complete supply chain. The firms should work constantly to find out the green material, methods of making green finished product which are commercially viable.

Suggested Solution

a. Environmentally responsible organizations should attempt to minimize their waste

b. Organization policy

c. Employee Awareness Program

d. Effective and transparent Communication

e. Constantly Refine the Product and Processes

Green marketing is still in its infancy and a lot of research is to be done on green marketing to fully explore its potential. Think of a refrigerator for example. While we may have had to be convinced in the 1950s to buy a refrigerator, we would have wanted the great white box to look cool in the 1970s, but in today's uncertain world, we might ask ourselves about the impact of the chlorofluorocarbons (CFCs) that our refrigerator is emitting and demand a more environment friendly refrigerator. So, if today's successful marketing is about appealing to personal values and delivering consumer empowerment, then surely the time is right to inject sustainable development into the marketing mix to help address some of the gritty issues currently facing our planet. Green marketing methods produce highly effective results. They apply all of the steps you need to cut costs, raise response rates and increase growth in the most important marketing metric we are all held accountable for-the bottom line.

References

1. Fernandez RD, Bhandarkar SM (2004) Green Marketing: An Indian Perspective.
2. Mathur LK, Mathur I (2000) An Analysis of the wealth effect of green marketing strategies. Journal of Business Research 50: 193-200.
3. Kilbourne WE (1998) Green Marketing A Theoretical Perspective. Journal of marketing Management 14: 641-655.
4. Kinnear TC, Taylor JR (1973) The Effect of Ecological Concern On Brand Perception. Journal of Marketing Research 10: 191-197.
5. Ottman JA, Stafford ER, Hariman CL (2006) Avoiding Green Marketing Myopia: Ways to Improve Consumer Appeal for Environmentally Preferable Products. Environment Science and Policy for Sustainable Development 48: 22-36.
6. Chitra K (2007) In search of the Green Consumers: A perceptual study. Journal of Services Research 7: 173-191.
7. Zimmer MR, Stafford TF, Stafford MR (1994) Green Issues dimensions of environmental concern. Journal of Business research 30: 63-74.
8. Kotler P (2000) Marketing Management-The Millennium Edition Prentice Hall of India Private Limited, New Delhi.
9. Ginsberg JM, Bloom PN (2004) Choosing the right Green Marketing Strategy. MIT Sloan Managemant Journal.
10. Welling, Anupam CS (2010) Analyzing the Feasibility of Green Marketing in SME? Asia-Pacific Journal of Research in Business Management.
11. Thakur G, Joshi NM, Chitale AK (2009) An Investigation Of Customers Awareness With Reference To Green Marketing Of Automobiles. Indian Journal of Marketing.
12. Kaur G (2006) Role of Socio-Demographics in segmenting and profiling green consumers: An exploratory study of consumers in India. Journal of International Consumer Marketing 18: 107-146.
13. www.wipro.com
14. www.greenenergy.wisein.org
15. www.livestrong.com
16. www.sulzon.com
17. www.economicstimes.indiatimes.com
18. Narendra KP (2013) Successful Adoption of CNG and Emerging CNG-H2 Program in India.
19. www.greenpeace.org
20. www.greenmarketing.com
21. (2010) Green Marketing. Business Practices.
22. Lakshmi CS (2007) Turning Over a New Leaf. Indian Management.

13

Appraising the Exchange Rate Volatility, Stock Market Performance and Aggregate Output Nexus in Nigeria

Abiola Babatunde Abimbola[1] and Ajibola Joseph Olusegun[2]*

[1]*Department of Economics, University of Lagos, Akoka, Nigeria*

[2]*College of Postgraduate Studies, Caleb University, Imota-Ikorodu, Lagos, Nigeria*

Abstract

This research work appraises the exchange rate volatility, stock market performance and aggregate output nexus in Nigeria. Making used of quarterly time series data with the use of ARCH and GARCH model, Bayesian VAR, VAR causality and Granger Causality model. The research work found that Exchange Rate and Stock price are Volatiles and the dwindling grossly affect the aggregate output. Also, there is high degree of positive relationship between Exchange rate, Stock Price Movement and Aggregate output. More so, Exchange rate volatility granger cause Stock price movement and Aggregate Output and vice versa. Furthermore, Exchange rate volatility and Stock Market performance has a positive significant impact on Aggregate output. Finally, there is joint causal impact of volatility of exchange rate, stock price, reserve on aggregate output in Nigeria. conclusion was made that there is a clear causal relationship between exchange rate volatility, stock market performance and Aggregate Output in Nigeria. Economic growth is achieved through sound an effective exchange rate that encourages FDI and financial inflow in the stock market. However, conclusion was made that there is presence and persistency of volatility shocks in the exchange rates for naira vis-à-vis US dollar in Nigeria between 1985 and 2015. This implies that the conventional monetary management policies instituted have proved ineffective in stabilizing the exchange rate of a unit US dollar to naira over the years. This therefore calls for the need of other forex management measures especially in terms of meeting the high demand for foreign currency which characterized and dictate the performance and trade balance and overall economic performance in Nigeria.

Keywords: Exchange rate; Volatility; Stock market

Introduction

The Nigerian stock market is a market that deals with the exchange of securities issued by publicly quoted companies and the government. It is a major channel for providing long term loans to industries as well as other investors [1]. On one hand, it provides for an individual, a key instrument for holding personal wealth as well as a way to diversify, spread and reduce risks. On the other hand, it represents to a firm, one of the ways to obtain financing and a central link between the financial world and the real economy.

In the same vein, the market serves as a channel through which surplus funds are moved from lenders-savers to borrower-spenders who have shortages of funds [2]. Basically, stock market prices are fundamental to the functioning of a market- based economy because they reveal the value of the companies that issued the stocks and like all other prices, they allocate scarce investment resources. Some fundamental macroeconomic variables such as interest rates, money supply, inflation, exchange rate and gross domestic product are generally believed to be determinants of stock prices, hence, changes in stock prices are linked with macroeconomic behaviour in developed economies which can be ambiguous in developing countries.

The impact of exchange rates on economic growth via capital markets which can have both a short term and a long term dimension. From the short term perspective, fixed exchange rates can foster economic growth by a more efficient international allocation of capital when transaction costs for capital flows are removed [3]. When international capital market segmentations are removed, debtors in high yield emerging market economies benefit from a substantial fall in interest rates as a result of investment from low yield developed economies and an incentive to maintain capital inflows through efficient financial supervision is created [4]. In the long term however, fluctuation in the exchange rate level constitute a risk for growth in emerging markets economies because banks and enterprise balance sheets which are denominated in foreign currency are adversely affected and sharp depreciations in exchange rates also inflates liabilities in terms of domestic currency thereby increasing the probability of default and financial crisis Adam [5] and influence the values of firms since the future cash flows of the firm change with the fluctuations [6].

However, two basic approaches that explain the relationship between stock prices and the exchange rates are "flow oriented" and "stock oriented" models. The flow oriented model assume that the exchange rate is largely determined by the current account and trade balance performance, and through that affect competitiveness of the economy [7]. The stock oriented model, assumes that the exchange rate responds to changes in the stock market [8-9]. The empirical analysis of the two model have certain features that are convenient for the purposes of this thesis and indicate different causation (between the markets) which constitutes the direction of this study in appraising the exchange rate volatility, stock market performance and aggregate output nexus in Nigeria.

After about 16 months of battling to stabilize the naira-dollar official exchange rate at N197/US$1 in the face of macro-economic headwinds and dwindling foreign exchange earnings which fell "from

***Corresponding author:** Ajibola Joseph Olusegun, College of Postgraduate Studies, Caleb University, Imota-Ikorodu, Lagos, Nigeria
E-mail: joeoluajibola@yahoo.co.uk

about US$3.24 bn monthly to current levels of below a billion dollars per month", the Central Bank of Nigeria finally succumbed to pressure from both within and outside Nigeria to adopt a flexible inter-bank exchange rate system in which the exchange rate would be market-driven. The new forex policy is expected to bring about a significant increase in capital importation and Diaspora remittances which will shore up the country's foreign reserves. It is also capable of narrowing the huge gap between the interbank and parallel market rates thereby reducing round-tripping, arbitrage opportunities and artificial demand from the market. Being a managed float system, the CBN is expected to participate in the market through periodic interventions to either buy or sell foreign currency as the need arises and in a bid to boost liquidity in the market, the apex bank has also appointed primary dealers. Without doubt, these measures, which are intended to enhance efficiency and facilitate a liquid and transparent forex market, will rub off positively on the stock market. As a pointer to this optimism, the market performance on Wednesday, June 15, 2016, when the policy was unveiled, was quite remarkable with equities capitalisation rebounding from a previous three-day losing streak to close at N9.6tn- about the highest level in June 2016. In the same vein, the benchmark All Shares Index (ASI) gained 3.2 per cent to close at 27,891.96 points with all sector indices reflecting a strong appetite witnessed across board [10-12].

On the flip side, the new policy is likely to exert more inflationary pressure in the near term as the naira is bound to weaken further in any contest with the dollar on strictly market forces dynamics given the import-dependent and shallow export base of the Nigerian economy. In its Consumer Price Index report for the month of May, the National Bureau of Statistics indicated that the cost of food imports contributed significantly to headline inflation which was put at 15.6 per cent compared to 13.7 per cent recorded in April 2016 with the imported food sub-index increasing by 18.6 per cent in May 2016. This further confirms the pass on effects of the increase in the cost of imported goods. A further spike in inflation is a disincentive to domestic investors in the stock market considering its negative impact on real stock returns. Given the cost-push nature of the current inflationary pressure and the limitations of monetary policy tools in this regard, a number of countervailing fiscal policy actions, anchored on the stimulation of real sector growth, should be undertaken from the extra money which the government stands to reap following the participation of the CBN in the market at a forex rate expected to trade higher than the current peg of N197 to the dollar when the policy becomes fully operational.

However, empirical investigations from Nigeria also presented a mixed result. Study such as Zubair [13] reported absence of causality between exchange rate changes and stock market. On the other hand Umoru and Asekome [1] found a uni-directional causal relationship between the Naira-US$ exchange rate movement and the reaction to stock prices [14]. This implies lack of consensus in findings on the direction of causation among exchange rate volatility, stock price movement and aggregated output and therefore inconclusive. More importantly, all these studies adopted a bivariate analysis on the issue of causality either between exchange rates changes and stock prices or between stock prices and economic growth or between exchange rates and economic growth [15-17]. Therefore, this study will differ by examining a tri-variate analysis of the causal relationship among exchange rates volatility, stock prices movement and aggregate output in Nigeria. The broad objective of this study is to analyse the relationship between exchange rate volatility, stock price movement and aggregate output in Nigeria from 1986 to 2015 [18].

Methodology

This section presents the research methods through which the research objectives would be achieved. This chapter comprises the theoretical framework, conceptual framework the model specification, techniques of analysis and measurement of variables.

Theoretical framework

The theoretical framework of this study has its basis drawn from endogenous growth theory. According to Barro [19] and Barro and Sala-i-Martin [20] endogenous growth theory indicates that government can influence long run growth of the economy through its expenditure or investment in physical capital, human capital and technology. The endogenous growth model will be used to derive the models for estimation for this study given its inherent capability to address exchange rate, stock market prices and aggregate output.

Using a typical Cobb Douglas production function, endogenous growth model can be stated as

$$Y_t = f(A, L_t, K_t) \tag{1}$$

Where Y_t is aggregate output, L_t is stock of labour, K_t is stock of capital and A represent technology or total factor productivity.

According to Demirgue and Levine [21] and Cudi Tuncer and Alovsat [22], technology (A) is affected by exchange rate, therefore, equation 1, is decompose to ref. [23]

$$A = g(\text{Re}er) \tag{2}$$

Where Reer is real exchange rate.

Furthermore, capital in equation 1 can be divided into two: physical capital and human capital

$$K = h(K_p, K_h) \tag{3}$$

Where K_p is physical capital and K_h human capital

Following the work of Kunt and Levin [24], human capital is constant, therefore equation 3 can be written as

$$K = h(K_p) \tag{4}$$

Substituting equation 2 and 4 in equation 1,

$$Y = \phi(\text{Re}er, L, K_p) \tag{5}$$

Model specification

In line with the theoretical framework discussed above, the effect of exchange rate volatility on stock market prices and aggregate output is captured by the model expressed in equation 5 [25]. Following the works of Ewah et al. [26] and Ariyo and Adelegan [27] the model for the linkage among real exchange rate, stock market and output is stated as

$$Gdp = f(\text{Re}er, Asi) \tag{6}$$

Where Asi is all share index, proxy for stock prices movement.

It has been noted in the literature (Harrigan et al. [28] Usman [29]) that relationship between stock prices movement and aggregate output are attributed to changes is some macro-economic variables such as interest rate, broad money supply, inflation etc [30-32]. Therefore, equation 6 above is modified to include important macro-economic variables since effective exchange rate can be control through effective monetary policy and that involves the use on monetary policy in the model [33-34].

$$Gdp = f(Reer, Asi, Int, Inf, M2) \tag{7}$$

Incorporating exchange rate volatility into equation 7 to capture exchange rate risk, the model becomes

$$Gdp = f(h, Asi, Int, Inf, M2) \tag{8}$$

Where h is exchange rate volatility

In Bollerslev [35], for the first time, proposed using the Generalized Autoregressive Conditional Heteroskedasticity (GARCH) method as a method of determining volatility in exchange rate or inflation rate. Since then, several studies (Adjasi and Biekpe [36]; Dell'Ariccia [37]; Wang et al., [38]; and Clark et al., [39]) had used the GARCH (1, 1) specification. As the name suggests, this approach of determining exchange rate volatility is based upon conditioning the variance by allowing changing over time based on past errors, also ability to capture both volatility clustering and unconditional return distribution with heavy tails. While conventional time series and econometric models operate under an assumption of constant variance, this type of model is useful in modeling variability in the exchange rate and inflation [40]. Furthermore, because the Autoregressive Conditional Heteroskedasticity (ARCH) proposed by Engle [41] encountered the problem of negative variance parameter estimates in empirical applications, extension of the ARCH model including a more flexible lag structure was immediately sought [35].

ARCH (p) is stated as

$$\sigma_t^2 = \partial_0 + \sum_{j=1}^{p} \chi_j u_{t-j}^2 \tag{9}$$

Where u^2_{t-j} is previous period's squared residual derived from previous period information about volatility.

Furthermore, ARCH (p) simultaneously models the mean equation as

$$y_t = \alpha + \beta' X_t + u_t \tag{10}$$

$$u_t \approx iid(0, h_t)$$

While the variance equation was model as

$$h_t = \partial_0 + \sum_{j=1}^{p} \delta_j u_{t-j}^2 \tag{11}$$

From equation 9 above, ARCH (p) model can be parsimoniously reduce to GARCH (1,1)

$$h_t = \delta_0 + \psi_1 h_{t-1} + \psi_2 u_{t-1}^2 \tag{12}$$

$\delta_0>0$, $\Psi_1>0$, $\Psi_2>0$ and $\Psi_1+\Psi_2<1$, so that the next period forecast of the variance is a combination of last period squared return and last period forecast [42-45].

Where h_t is variance or current period volatility, h_{t-1} is previous year residual variance or volatility.

From equation 8, the specific equation is specified as

$$Gdp = \alpha + \beta h + \chi Asi + \delta Int + \varphi Inf + \gamma M2 + \varepsilon \tag{13}$$

Model specification on direction of causality among exchange rate volatility, stock market prices and output: Thus, to determine the direction of causality among exchange rate volatility, Stock Market Prices and Aggregate Output, a dynamic model of vector autoregressive (VAR) is used. The VAR method has become an important tool used in empirical macroeconomics studies and is specified in a system of simultaneous equation [46-47]. From equation 13, VAR model is specified as

$$h = \alpha_2 + \sum_{j=0}^{n} \kappa_{2j} Gdp_{t-j} + \sum_{j=1}^{n} \beta_{2j} h_{t-j} + \sum_{j=0}^{n} \chi_{2j} Asi_{t-j} + \sum_{j=0}^{n} \delta_{2j} Int_{t-j} + \sum_{j=0}^{n} \varphi_{2j} Inf_{t-j} + \sum_{j=0}^{n} \gamma_{2j} M2_{t-j} + \varepsilon_{2t} \tag{14}$$

$$h = \alpha_2 + \sum_{j=0}^{n} \kappa_{2j} Gdp_{t-j} + \sum_{j=1}^{n} \beta_{2j} h_{t-j} + \sum_{j=0}^{n} \chi_{2j} Asi_{t-j} + \sum_{j=0}^{n} \delta_{2j} Int_{t-j} + \sum_{j=0}^{n} \varphi_{2j} Inf_{t-j} + \sum_{j=0}^{n} \gamma_{2j} M2_{t-j} + \varepsilon_{2t} \tag{15}$$

$$\Delta Asi = \alpha_1 + \sum_{j=0}^{n} \kappa_{1j} \Delta Gdp_{t-j} + \sum_{j=0}^{n} \beta_{1j} \Delta h_{t-j} + \sum_{j=1}^{n} \chi_{1j} \Delta Asi_{t-j} + \sum_{j=0}^{n} \delta_{1j} \Delta Int_{t-j} + \sum_{j=0}^{n} \varphi_{1j} \Delta Inf_{t-j} + \sum_{j=0}^{n} \gamma_{1j} \Delta M2_{t-j} + \lambda_1 Asi_{t-1} + \lambda_2 Gdp_{t-1} + \lambda_3 h_{t-1} + \lambda_4 Int_{t-1} + \lambda_5 Inf_{t-1} + \lambda_6 M2_{t-1} + \varepsilon_{1t} \tag{16}$$

$$Int = \alpha_4 + \sum_{j=0}^{n} \kappa_{4j} Gdp_{t-j} + \sum_{j=0}^{n} \beta_{4j} h_{t-j} + \sum_{j=0}^{n} \chi_{4j} Asi_{t-j} + \sum_{j=1}^{n} \delta_{4j} Int_{t-j} + \sum_{j=0}^{n} \varphi_{4j} Inf_{t-j} + \sum_{j=0}^{n} \gamma_{4j} M2_{t-j} + \varepsilon_{4t} \tag{17}$$

$$Inf = \alpha_5 + \sum_{j=0}^{n} \kappa_{5j} Gdp_{t-j} + \sum_{j=0}^{n} \beta_{5j} h_{t-j} + \sum_{j=0}^{n} \chi_{5j} Asi_{t-j} + \sum_{j=0}^{n} \delta_{5j} Int_{t-j} + \sum_{j=1}^{n} \varphi_{5j} Inf_{t-j} + \sum_{j=0}^{n} \gamma_{5j} M2_{t-j} + \varepsilon_{5t} \tag{18}$$

$$M2 = \alpha_6 + \sum_{j=0}^{n} \kappa_{6j} Gdp_{t-j} + \sum_{j=0}^{n} \beta_{6j} h_{t-j} + \sum_{j=0}^{n} \chi_{6j} Asi_{t-j} + \sum_{j=0}^{n} \delta_{6j} Int_{t-j} + \sum_{j=0}^{n} \varphi_{6j} Inf_{t-j} + \sum_{j=1}^{n} \gamma_{6j} M2_{t-j} + \varepsilon_{6t} \tag{19}$$

Where n is the lag length and will be chosen optimally using Schwarz information criterion [48-49]. From equations 14-19, the direction of causation will be identified by testing the significance of the coefficients of the dependent variables.

Model specification on the effect of exchange rate volatility on stock market prices and output: In order to examine the effect of exchange volatility on stock market price and output, Auto Regressive Distributed Lag is used [50-51]. This technique captures the short and long run relationship. From equation 13, the ARDL model is stated as

$$\Delta Asi = \alpha_1 + \sum_{j=0}^{n} \kappa_{1j} \Delta Gdp_{t-j} + \sum_{j=0}^{n} \beta_{1j} \Delta h_{t-j} + \sum_{j=1}^{n} \chi_{1j} \Delta Asi_{t-j} + \sum_{j=0}^{n} \delta_{1j} \Delta Int_{t-j} + \sum_{j=0}^{n} \varphi_{1j} \Delta Inf_{t-j} + \sum_{j=0}^{n} \gamma_{1j} \Delta M2_{t-j} + \lambda_1 Asi_{t-1} + \lambda_2 Gdp_{t-1} + \lambda_3 h_{t-1} + \lambda_4 Int_{t-1} + \lambda_5 Inf_{t-1} + \lambda_6 M2_{t-1} + \varepsilon_{1t} \tag{20}$$

$$\Delta Gdp = \alpha_2 + \sum_{j=1}^{n} \kappa_{2j} \Delta Gdp_{t-j} + \sum_{j=0}^{n} \beta_{2j} \Delta h_{t-j} + \sum_{j=0}^{n} \chi_{2j} \Delta Asi_{t-j} + \sum_{j=0}^{n} \delta_{2j} \Delta Int_{t-j} + \sum_{j=0}^{n} \varphi_{2j} \Delta Inf_{t-j} + \sum_{j=0}^{n} \gamma_{2j} \Delta M2_{t-j} + \lambda_{21} Asi_{t-1} + \lambda_{22} Gdp_{t-1} + \lambda_{23} h_{t-1} + \lambda_{24} Int_{t-1} + \lambda_{25} Inf_{t-1} + \lambda_{26} M2_{t-1} + \varepsilon_{2t} \tag{21}$$

Where Δ is change and n is the lag length which will be selected optimally. γ, β, χ, δ, φ and ϕ are short run coefficients, while λ are long run coefficients.

Estimation techniques

In this study, both descriptive and econometrics techniques of analysis will be adopted. To achieve objective one which is the trend of exchange rate volatility, stock prices movement and aggregate output, descriptive analyses such as trend analysis, graphs and tables will be used (Figure 1) (Table 1). Objective two will be achieved by performing Granger causality test on VAR model specified in equation 14-19. Also, objective three which is the effect of exchange volatility on stock market prices and aggregate output will be achieve by estimating equation 20 and 21 using Bayesian VAR. This estimation technique

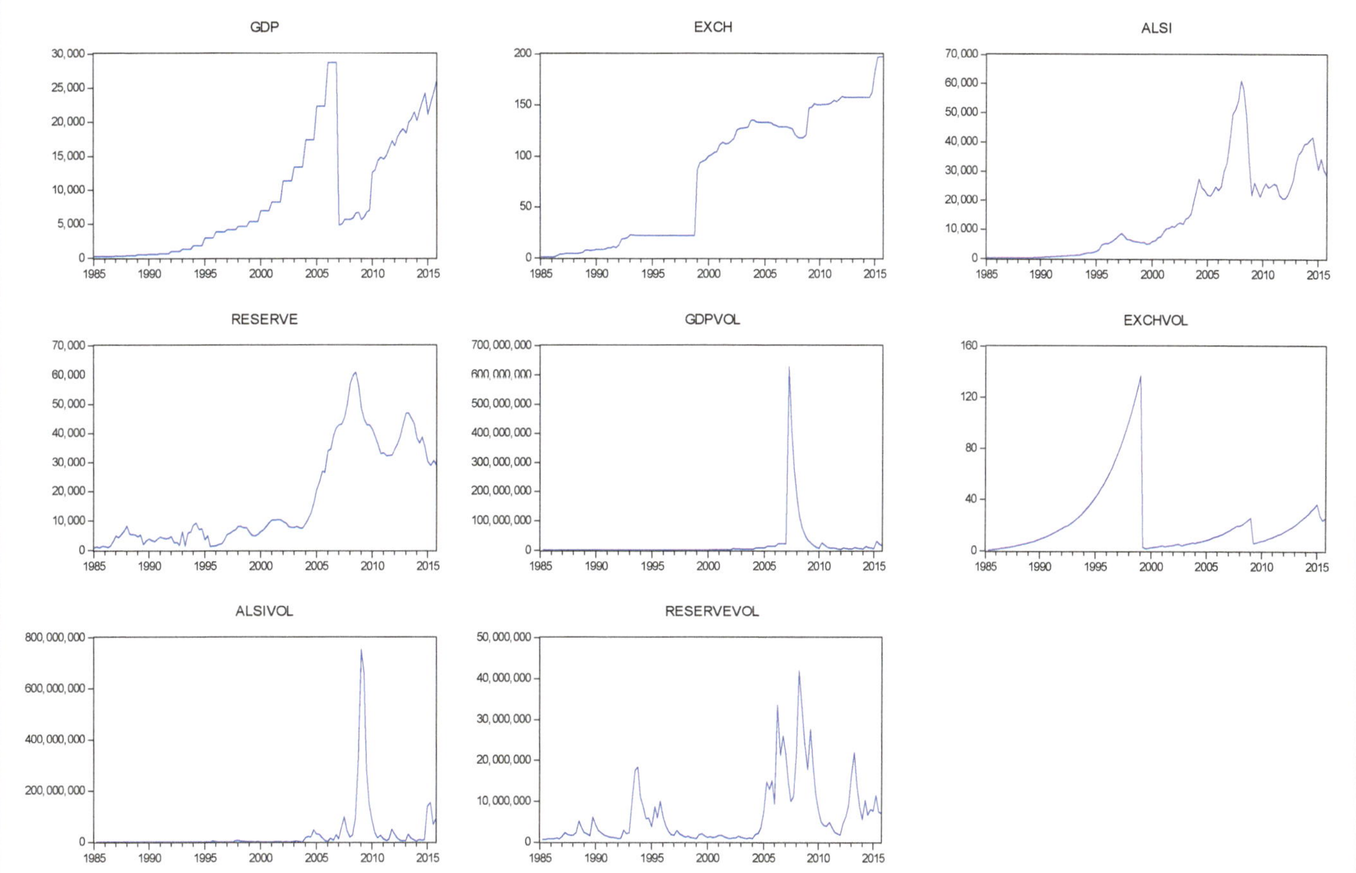

Figure 1: Trend analysis.

S/N	Variables	Definition and measurement of variable	Source of data
1	All Share Index (ASI)	This is a measure of the performance of the stock market which mirrors the information about macroeconomic performance at any time. It is positively and significantly correlated with long run economic growth.	Central Bank of Nigeria, National Bureau of Statistics and the Nigeria Stock Exchange.
2	Gross Domestic Product (GDP)	This is a measure of total real economic activities in the country. It is a very crucial measure of determining the stock market returns in the country.	National Bureau of Statistics and the Central Bank of Nigeria
3	Real Effective Exchange Rate (REER)	Exchange rate is a relative price that measures the worth of a domestic currency in terms of another currency ($reer = \frac{p_x}{p^*}e$). It relates the purchasing power of a domestic currency, in terms of the goods and services it can purchase, vis-à-vis a trading partners' currency over a given period. US will be used as proxy for trading partners' currency.	World Bank Development Indicator, 2013 edition
4	Exchange rate volatility (h)	Exchange rate volatility is a measure that intends to capture the uncertainty faced by both exporters and importers due to unpredictable fluctuations in the exchange rates	Derived from real exchange rate using GARCH (1, 1)
5	Inflation (INF)	This will be measured by consumer price index (CPI). It measured as the rate of change over time of some general index of price. Inflation is usually refers to as a continuing rise in prices as measured by an index such as the consumer price index or by the implicit price deflator for gross national product	World Bank Development Indicator, 2013 edition
6	Broad Money Supply (M2)	This is a measure of money supply in the economy.it represents the monetary sector analysis in which the boundaries of narrow money shifts overtime to accommodate new financial instruments. This captures the contributions of money market to economic activities.	Central Bank of Nigeria and the National Bureau of Statistics

Table 1: Measurement of variables and source of data.

was preferred because of the advantages attached to it. Firstly, Bayesian VAR approach does not required pre-testing for unit root test and the variables do not need to be integrated of the same order (only to ensure that no variable was I(2)). The Bayesian VAR provided alternative test for examining a long-run relationship irrespective of whether the variables are I(0) or I(1), evenly integrated. Secondly, Bayesian VAR approach to cointegration provides better result in a small sample data as the case in the studies of these authors Haug [52], indicated that the estimates obtained from the Bayesian VAR method of cointegration analysis are unbiased and efficient. This approach also helps to avoid the problem that may ensue in the presence of serial correlation and endogeneity. Lastly, according to Banerjee and Newman [53] a dynamic error correction can be derived from a modified Bayesian VAR model through a linear transformation. These will be preceded by performing volatility test, unit root test, co-integration and lag selection criteria (Figure 2).

Data Presentation and Analysis

Presentation of results

This section presents the data set used for the analysis, the trend diagram and descriptive statistics in examining exchange rate volatility, stock market performance and aggregate output Nexus in Nigeria [54-57]. The data used in this study are quarterly time series in nature, and span through 1985-2015 (Table 2). Section 4.1.2 gives the data presentation, trend analysis and descriptive statistics of the variables, while 4.1.3 displays the stationarity test using Augmented Dickey Fuller (ADF) and Phillip Perron (PP) test [58-60]. Section 4.1.4 presents the ARCH test of volatility; Section 4.1.4 presented the trend volatility of the model. Also the remaining Sections presents Bayesian VAR impulse

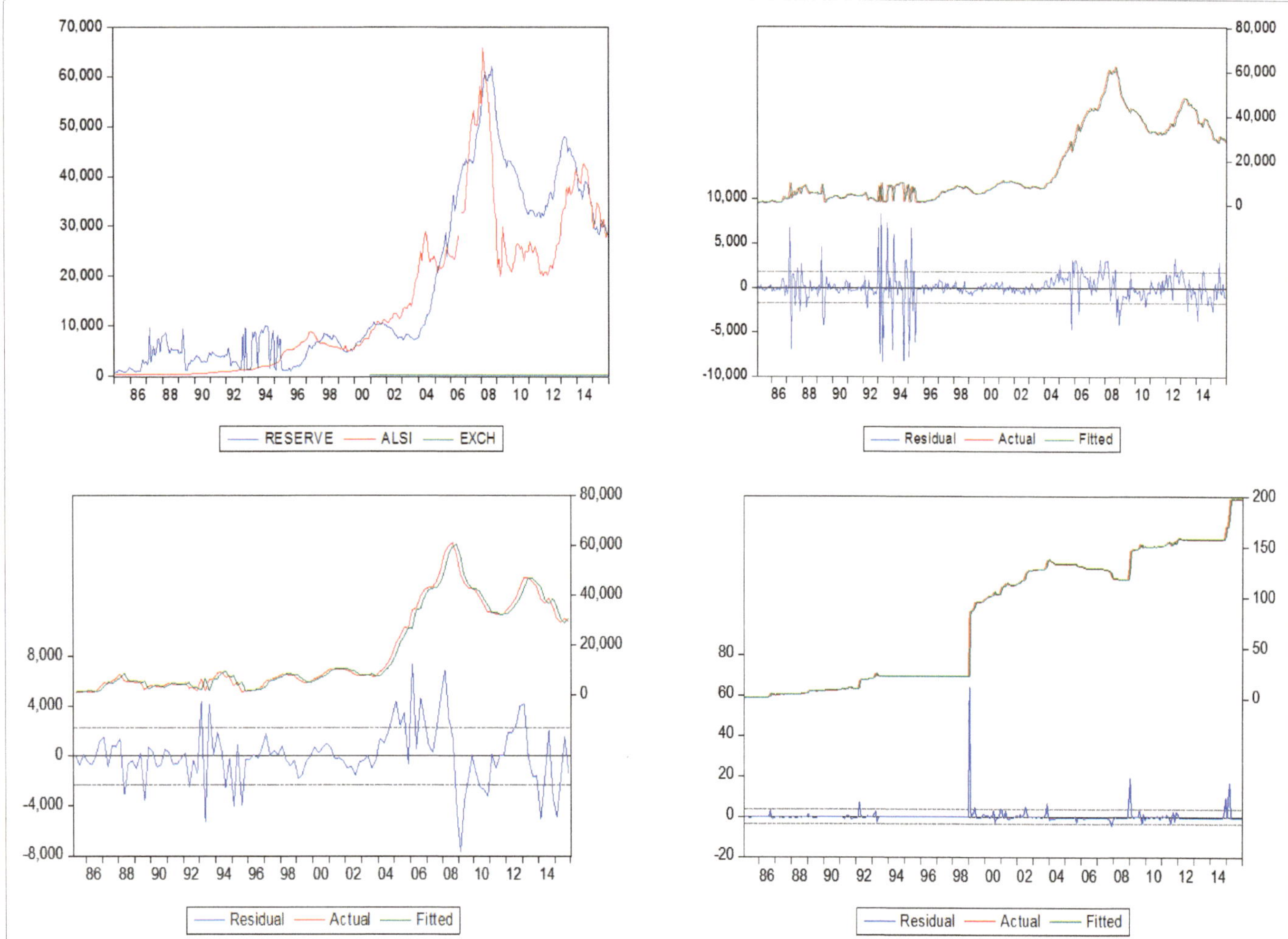

Figure 2: Trend analysis of volatility.

Mean	8576.454	80.68012	14665.28	17476.59
Median	5439.389	102.3212	7748.433	7894.638
Maximum	28662.47	196.99	60952.95	60875.24
Minimum	192.27	0.902567	112.3	716.9333
Std. Dev.	8407.195	64.24025	15225.85	17232.6
Skewness	0.820342	0.017777	0.974505	0.857315
Kurtosis	2.424678	1.34151	3.159053	2.265366
Jarque-Bera	15.61802	14.21791	19.75703	17.97815
Probability	0.000406	0.000818	0.000051	0.000125
Sum	1063480	10004.34	1818495	2167098
Sum Sq. Dev.	8.69E+09	507597.6	2.85E+10	3.65E+10
Observations	124	124	124	124
Source: Author's Computation (2016).				

Table 2: Descriptive statistics.

response, Granger causality test, while section 4.1.7 and 4.1.8 presents the VAR joint Causality test and the VAR inverse root polynomial stability test [61].

Trend analysis: The trend diagram depicts an upward trend for GDP, and steady increase was observed between 1990 and 2004 before rising sharply in 2010 [62-64]. This trend has been increasing steadily ever since, before recent collapse in growth rate. Exchange rate in Nigeria experienced steady increase since 1990 till date. Exchange rate (EXCH) has been increasing since inception of the study period, and slight volatility was observed between 2008 and 2012 before rising thereafter [65-69]. The All Share Index (ALSI) trend showed slightly upward sloping trend from its inception and continued in that form till 2008 before it broke down the trend downward to its lowest ever. Though, it starts picking up in 2012.

Descriptive statistics: The statistical properties of the variables are highlighted here. The emphasis here is on the mean, standard deviation, Jarque-Bear and its Probability statistics for the variables involved in this study. The result showed that the mean of the variables GDP, EXCH, ALSI, and RESERVE are all positive [70]. In the case of their skewness, all the variable under consideration are positively skewed. Regarding kurtosis that measures the peakness of the distribution of the variables, it can either be leptokurtic if its value is higher than 3, mesokurtic if equal to 3 and platykurtic if it less than 3. From the descriptive statistic table, the Kurtosis value for all the variables is less than 3, thus the variables are platykurtic with exception of ALSI which is leptokurtic. Finally, the Jarque-Bera statistics and its probability value indicate the statistical significance of the variables. If the probability value is less than 5%, the variables are significant and vice versa [71]. All the variables under consideration are statistically significant even at 1% significant level. To establish the null hypothesis of normality, we made use of the test and detected that all the variables in the model had positive values they were all statistically significant at the one percent level. Therefore, we fail to accept the null hypothesis of normality and accept the alternative hypothesis that the statistical distribution of these variables follows a normal process.

Correlation analysis: The correlation analysis of the variables under consideration shows that there is positive significant relationship between the variables. There is high positive correlation between GDP and Exchange rate, GPD and All Share Index, and GDP and Foreign Reserve (Table 3) [72].

GDP	1	0.842662	0.659388	0.60067387
EXCH	0.84266159	1	0.798956	0.76376588
ALSI	0.65938776	0.798956	1	0.91134481
RESERVE	0.60067387	0.763766	0.911345	1

Table 3: Correlation analysis.

Stationary test (ADF & PP): Prior to the estimation of cointegration, the characteristics of the data have to be examined. Testing the stationarity of economic time series data is important since standard econometric methodologies assume stationarity in the time series while they are in the real sense non-stationary. Hence, the usual statistical tests are likely to be inappropriate and the inferences drawn are likely to be erroneous and misleading. For example, the ordinary least squares (OLS) estimation of regressions in the presence of non-stationary variables gives rise to spurious regressions if the variables are not co-integrated [73].

The trends of all the variables were used to conduct unit root tests to determine the stationarity of the variables using both the Augmented Dickey-Fuller (ADF) test and Philip Perron tests respectively. The results of the unit root tests are presented in Table 4. The results in Table 4 show that all the variables are stationary in their first differences [74-76].

The result of the stationarity test as reported using Augmented Dickey Fuller test for stationary, it was observed that all the four variables were not stationary at Level with exception of ALSI which was stationary at 5% significant level, while all the others became stationary at First difference [77]. Similar result was obtained from the analysis of the Phillip Perron test, four of the variables are stationary at the First difference at either the 1% or the 5% critical value.

The above result shows that all the variables such as exchange rate, All Share Index and Foreign Reserve are volatile with an exception of GDP which is not volatile at 5% significant level. The heteroskedasticity test shows that the variables have ARCH terms which necessitate the conduction of ARCH and GARCH model of volatility.

Trend analysis of volatility: The Above trend analysis of the residual of the variables under consideration shows the level volatility of each variables. It shows that the period of high volatility is followed by the period of high volatility while the period of low volatility is followed by the period of low volatility [78-81]. The Nigeria exchange started to be relatively volatility after the SAP era of 1986 which it was volatile till 1996 before experience an era of low volatility for the next one decade before the recent high volatility which can be traced jointly with other variables such All share index, foreign reserve and Aggregate Output (Table 5).

Granger causality test: Having established the direction and strength of the volatility between Exchange rate, Stock market performance and aggregate output variables, it becomes pertinent to establish the direction of causation since correlation is not causality

Date: 11/28/16 Time: 14:11				**Date: 11/28/16 Time: 16:11**			
Sample: 1985Q1 2015Q4				**Sample: 1985Q1 2015Q4**			
Test Type: ADF				**Test Type: PP**			
	Level	First	Second		Level	First	Second
GDP	-2.82525	-11.0218**	-9.12768	GDP	-2.82525	-11.033**	-76.3416
EXCH	-2.09814	-9.55416**	-10.2038	EXCH	-2.27515	-9.54828**	-93.284
ALSI	-3.51856**	-6.22932	-11.7116	ALSI	-2.83734	-6.19447**	-19.9421
RESERVE	-2.45574	-4.60736**	-19.3551	RESERVE	-1.88934	-7.96443**	-47.4174
1% level	-4.03565	-4.03565	-4.03565	1% level	-4.03436	-4.035	-4.03565
5% level	-3.44738	-3.44738	-3.44738	5% level	-3.44677	-3.44707	-3.44738
10% level	-3.14876	-3.14876	-3.14876	10% level	-3.1484	-3.14858	-3.14876

**Denotes significance at 1% and 5% level.
Source: Authors computation (2016).

Table 4: Stationary test.

Exchange Rate			
F-statistic	67.89333	Prob. F(1,120)	0.0000
Obs*R-squared	44.08345	Prob. Chi-Square(1)	0.0000
GDP			
F-statistic	3.048859	Prob. F(1,120)	0.7253
Obs*R-squared	2.668642	Prob. Chi-Square(1)	0.6456
ALSI			
F-statistic	6.212070	Prob. F(1,120)	0.0231
Obs*R-squared	5.102308	Prob. Chi-Square(1)	0.0417
RESERVE			
F-statistic	30.062536	Prob. F(1,120)	0.0000
Obs*R-squared	24.525242	Prob. Chi-Square(1)	0.0000
Heteroskedasticity Test: ARCH.			

Table 5: Testing volatility of the variables.

Null hypothesis:	**Obs**	**F-statistic**	**Prob.**	**Decision**
EXCH does not Granger Cause GDP	122	5.38346	0.0058	Rejected
GDP does not Granger Cause EXCH		0.06687	0.9354	Accepted
ALSI does not Granger Cause GDP	122	0.25230	0.7774	Accepted
GDP does not Granger Cause ALSI		12.9328	8.00E-06	Rejected
ALSI does not Granger Cause EXCH	122	4.81329	0.0098	Rejected
EXCH does not Granger Cause ALSI		5.44374	0.0055	Rejected
EXCHVOL does not Granger Cause EXCH	121	5.81450	0.0039	Rejected
EXCH does not Granger Cause EXCHVOL		272.267	2.00E-44	Rejected
RESERVE does not Granger Cause ALSI	122	2.02767	0.1362	Accepted
ALSI does not Granger Cause RESERVE		10.0184	0.0001	Rejected
GDPVOL does not Granger Cause ALSI	121	0.65410	0.5218	Accepted
ALSI does not Granger Cause GDPVOL		6.45013	0.0022	Rejected
ALSIVOL does not Granger Cause ALSI	121	4.19082	0.0175	Rejected
ALSI does not Granger Cause ALSIVOL		61.5188	6.00E-19	Rejected
RESERVEVOL does not Granger Cause GDPVOL	121	3.89792	0.023	Rejected
GDPVOL does not Granger Cause RESERVEVOL		6.09894	0.003	Rejected
RESERVEVOL does not Granger Cause ALSIVOL	121	25.3134	8.00E-10	Rejected
ALSIVOL does not Granger Cause RESERVEVOL		1.84531	0.1626	Accepted
Date: 11/28/16 Time: 14:42. Sample: 1985Q1 2015Q4. Lags: 2.				

Table 6: Pairwise granger causality tests.

[82]. Consequently, the research work employs granger causality tests to examine the direction of causality, and the results are presented in Table 6.

1. There is unidirectional causality between exchange rate and aggregate output but it flows from GDP to EXCH. Therefore, GDP granger cause EXCH but not vice versa.

2. There is unidirectional causality between Stock market performance and aggregate output but it flows from GDP to ALSI. Therefore, GDP granger cause ALSI but not vice versa.

3. There is bi-directional causality between Stock Market Performance and Exchange rate. Therefore, ALSI granger cause EXCH and vice versa.

4. There is bi-directional causality between Exchange rate volatility and Exchange rate. Therefore, ExchVol granger cause EXCH and vice versa.

5. There is unidirectional causality between Stock market performance and foreign Reserve but it flows from ALSI to RESERVE. Therefore, ALSI granger cause RESERVE but not vice versa.

6. There is unidirectional causality between Stock market performance and GDP volatility but it flows from GDPvol to ALSI. Therefore, GDPvol granger cause ALSI but not vice versa.

7. There is bi-directional causality between Stock Market Volatility and Stock market performance. Therefore, ALSIvol granger cause ALSI and vice versa.

8. There is bi-directional causality between RESERVE volatility and GDP volatility. Therefore, reserve volatility granger cause ALSI and vice versa.

9. There is unidirectional causality between reserve volatility and Stock market volatility but it flows from reservevol to ALSI. Therefore, reservevol granger cause ALSI but not vice versa.'

Lag length selection criteria

To select the most appropriate VAR lag length, we considered the based automatic bandwidth parameter methods as recommended [83] (Table 7). The result obtained indicated that the Schwarz information criterion (SC) assigned the second lag length, while the likelihood ratio (LR) test and the Hannan-Quinn information criterion (HQ) specified the seventh lag length as most desirable for the VAR. We narrowed down on the estimates and choice the final prediction error (FPE) and the Akaike information criterion (AIC) as the most appropriate lag length order for the VAR process [84]. This is because eighth lag length is enough time to ascertain the effectiveness of policies over the observation studied.

Impulse response

Response of variables to exchange rate shocks: Using the Cholesky two-standard-error shock, this section examines the response of macroeconomic variables under consideration to Exchange rate Shocks when some perturbations occur in the economy. The essence of this is to find out the impact of unanticipated shocks in Exchange Rate measures on Stock market performance and Aggregate Output [85]. This analysis is very important particularly in a developing country like Nigeria where government international policy switch have strong impact on macroeconomic stability (Table 8).

Lag	LogL	LR	FPE	AIC	SC	HQ
0	-11103.7	NA	1.17e+74	193.2475	193.4384	193.3250
1	-10263.2	1549.449	1.59e+68	179.7431	181.4617	180.4407
2	-9923.88	578.3651	1.35e+66	174.9545	178.2006*	176.2721
3	-9815.64	169.4181	6.49e+65	174.1851	178.9589	176.1227
4	-9696.15	170.4079	2.67e+65	173.2200	179.5214	175.7777
5	-9618.12	100.4253	2.38e+65	172.9759	180.8049	176.1537
6	-9514.54	118.8918	1.46e+65	172.2876	181.6442	176.0854
7	-9285.6	230.9257*	1.12e+64	169.4191	180.3034	173.8370*
8	-9193.11	80.42744	1.06e+64*	168.9236*	181.3355	173.9615

Source: Authors estimation, Eviews 9, November 2016.
Note: *Indicate lag order selected by the Criterion, LogL: Log Likelihood Ratio test, LR: Sequential modified LR test statistics, FPE: Final prediction error, AIC: Akaike information criterion, SC: Schwarz information criterion and the HQ: Hannan-Quinn information criterion.

Table 7: The VAR Lag order selection criteria test.

Dependent variable: EXCH				**Dependent variable: EXCHVOL**			
Excluded	Chi-sq	df	Prob.	Excluded	Chi-sq	df	Prob.
GDP	0.681268	2	0.7113	GDP	0.804705	2	0.6687
ALSI	5.782825	2	0.0555	EXCH	810.2235	2	0.0000
RESERVE	0.433388	2	0.8052	ALSI	0.956320	2	0.6199
GDPVOL	0.772296	2	0.6797	RESERVE	5.069728	2	0.0793
EXCHVOL	10.89784	2	0.0043	GDPVOL	1.391137	2	0.4988
ALSIVOL	0.182931	2	0.9126	ALSIVOL	22.50468	2	0.0000
RESERVEVOL	0.580707	2	0.7480	RESERVEVOL	0.249245	2	0.8828
All	25.47019	14	0.0302**	All	840.9695	14	0.0000*
Dependent variable: ALSI				**Dependent variable: ALSIVOL**			
Excluded	Chi-sq	df	Prob.	Excluded	Chi-sq	df	Prob.
GDP	40.82055	2	0.0000	GDP	14.60422	2	0.0007
EXCH	0.295468	2	0.8627	EXCH	1.129448	2	0.5685
RESERVE	9.849679	2	0.0073	ALSI	107.2236	2	0.0000
GDPVOL	32.70806	2	0.0000	RESERVE	1.630612	2	0.4425
EXCHVOL	1.834208	2	0.3997	GDPVOL	14.24936	2	0.0008
ALSIVOL	5.697633	2	0.0579	EXCHVOL	0.248926	2	0.8830
RESERVEVOL	2.774138	2	0.2498	RESERVEVOL	19.84548	2	0.0000
All	94.11335	14	0.0000*	All	251.7311	14	0.0000*
Dependent variable: RESERVE				**Dependent variable: RESERVEVOL**			
Excluded	Chi-sq	df	Prob.	Excluded	Chi-sq	df	Prob.
GDP	9.128158	2	0.0104	GDP	5.991921	2	0.0500
EXCH	0.425478	2	0.8084	EXCH	7.087171	2	0.0289
ALSI	3.639689	2	0.1621	ALSI	2.831266	2	0.2428
GDPVOL	21.53883	2	0.0000	RESERVE	19.28866	2	0.0001
EXCHVOL	0.371788	2	0.8304	GDPVOL	4.165733	2	0.1246
ALSIVOL	1.180630	2	0.5542	EXCHVOL	1.492671	2	0.4741
RESERVEVOL	10.03599	2	0.0066	ALSIVOL	12.53019	2	0.0019
All	55.50437	14	0.0000*	All	61.23204	14	0.0000*
Dependent variable: GDPVOL							
Excluded	Chi-sq	df	Prob.				
GDP	365.2477	2	0.0000				
EXCH	0.351169	2	0.8390				
ALSI	2.195743	2	0.3336				
RESERVE	2.908248	2	0.2336				
EXCHVOL	0.183344	2	0.9124				
ALSIVOL	0.162405	2	0.9220				
RESERVEVOL	5.177181	2	0.0751				
All	492.2572	14	0.0000*	A			

Date: 11/28/16 Time: 20:49.
Sample: 1985Q1 2015Q4.
Included observations: 121.

Table 8: Exchange rate, stock market performance and aggregate output nexsus using granger casuality in the VAR environment.

The graphs of a Cholesky two-standard-error shock show the actual impulse response functions for each of the endogenous variables given that, each asymptotically deviated from the normal path. Figure 3 presents the dynamic responses of GDP, ALSI and Foreign Reserve to a Cholesky two-standard-error shock of Exchange rate. The effect on GDP, ALSI as well as Foreign Reserve is found to be persistent in a defined period.

Figure 3 presents the dynamic responses of aggregate output (GDP) to a two-standard-error shock of Exchange rate. The effect on GDP is found to be persistent. The impact on GDP is significantly negative over a period of up to 10 quarters after the shock [86]. Devaluation of naira shock caused GDP to persistently decrease over time. On impact the effect was delayed one lag period but gradually became asymptotic to the steady state over the time horizon. Expenditure measure of growth shows the import dependence level of Nigerian Economy which complies with approx. expectation about the marshal Lerner Index (EXCHvol) has a profound impact on GDP. This is expected because the sum of elasticity of import and that of Export is less than one and this also affects the decline the foreign reserve, which ultimately affect the level of the international credibility of the Nation in the number of month she can finance her import. Also, this leads to negative effects on stock market performance as a result of decrease in the aggregate demand.

VAR stability control test: The VAR stability condition test indicates the inverse roots of AR characteristics Polynomial which shows the stability of VAR estimates the null hypothesis state that the

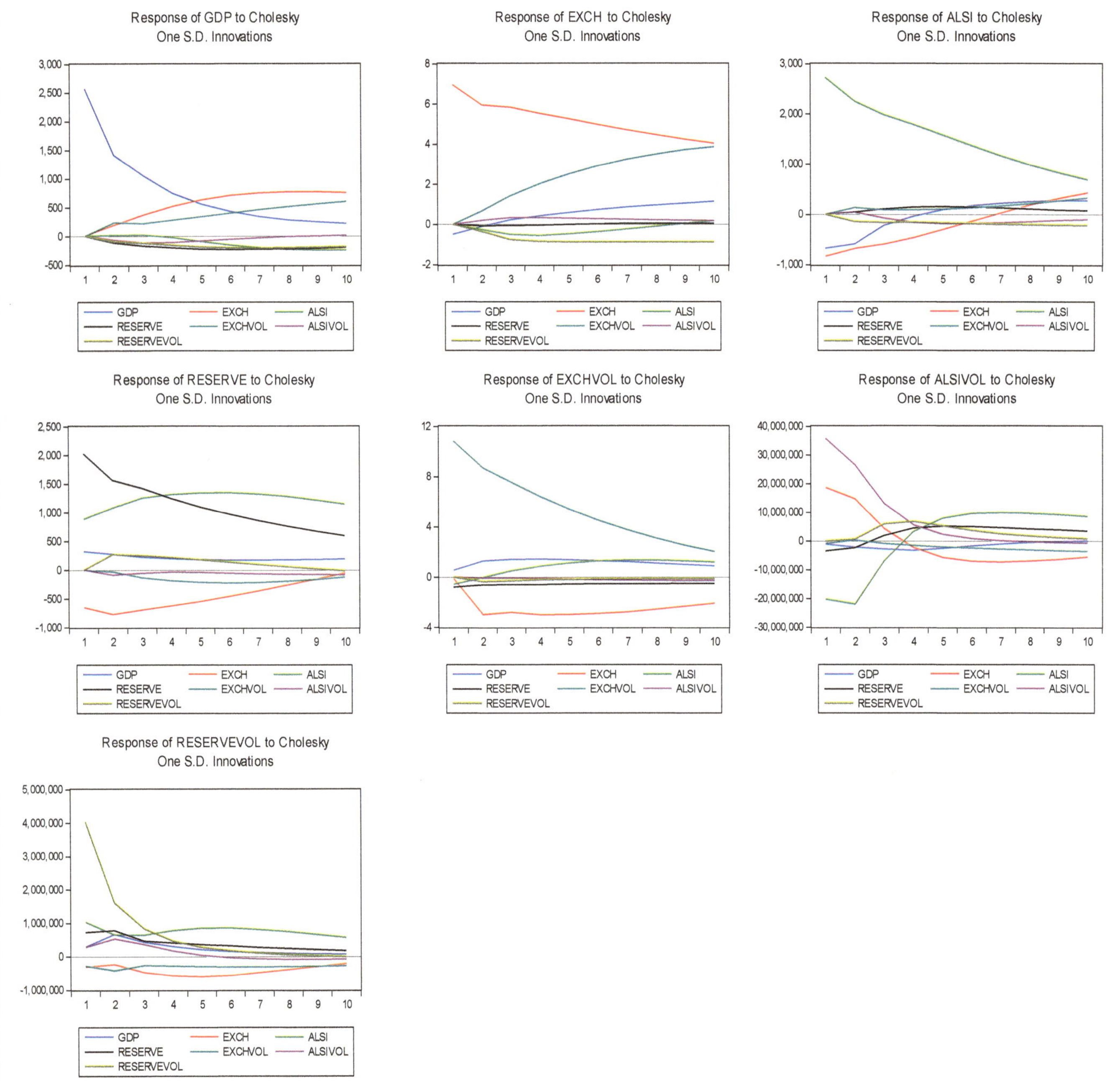

Figure 3: Response of variables to exchange rate shocks.

inverse roots lies outside the unit circle of the system by system model while the alternative against it (Figure 4).

The above result of Inverse roots of AR characteristics polynomial Shows that all the roots are located inside the unit circle which shows the high level of stability of model since majority are found around the parameters which shows the reliability of the estimates for policy recommendation.

Summary, Conclusion and Recommendations

Having reviewed some of the related literatures and collected all necessary data's, which have been analysed and discussed in chapter four. This chapter therefore provides a summary, and conclusion. Recommendations were also made in line with the results and suggestions for further research studies were provided.

Summary of findings

The research work found that Exchange Rate and Stock price are Volatiles and the dwindling grossly affect the aggregate output.

Also, there is high degree of positive relationship between Exchange rate and Stock Price Movement, Exchange rate and Aggregate output and Stock Price and Aggregate output.

More so, Exchange rate volatility granger cause Stock price movement and Aggregate Output and vice versa.

Furthermore, Exchange rate volatility and Stock Market performance has a positive significant impact on Aggregate output.

Finally, there is joint causal impact of volatility of exchange rate, stock price, reserve on aggregate output in Nigeria.

Conclusion

The finding concludes that there is a clear causal relationship between exchange rate volatility, stock market performance and Aggregate Output in Nigeria. Economic growth is achieved through sound an effective exchange rate that encourages FDI and financial inflow in the stock market.

From the findings, each of the volatility measure series for nominal and real exchange rates revealed different estimate of volatility indicating the presence and persistency of volatility shocks in the nominal and real exchange rates for naira vis-à-vis US dollar in Nigeria except the

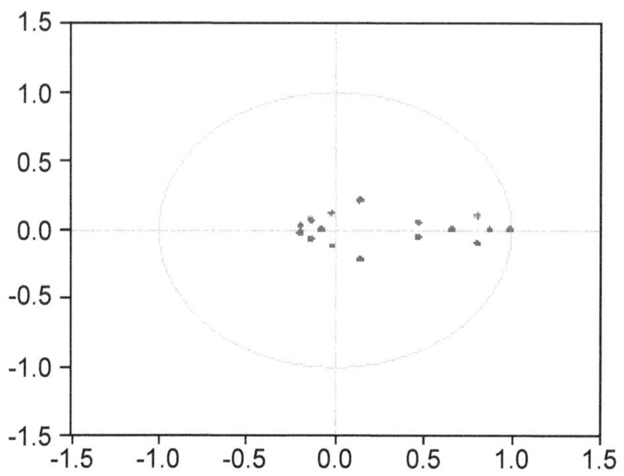

Figure 4: VAR stability condition test.

coefficient of variation measure under the real exchange rate which indicated overshooting volatility shocks in terms of degree. However, further evaluation concluded that there is presence and persistency of volatility shocks in the exchange rates for naira vis-à-vis US dollar in Nigeria between 1985 and 2015. This implies that the conventional monetary management policies instituted have proved ineffective in stabilizing the exchange rate of a unit US dollar to naira over the years. This therefore calls for the need of other forex management measures especially in terms of meeting the high demand for foreign currency which characterized and dictate the performance and trade balance and overall economic performance in Nigeria.

Conclusively, the result obtained in this finding shows that Exchange rate and stock market performance has positive and significant impact on aggregate output in Nigeria since the captured variables were all positive and significant in promoting economic growth in Nigeria.

Recommendations

The following recommendations are made to improve the level of Economy in Nigeria:

1. This calls for the need of other forex management measures especially in terms of meeting the high demand for foreign currency which characterized and dictate the performance and trade balance and overall economic performance in Nigeria. There is also the need for sound monetary policy to attain stability in the exchange rate and also fiscal measure to serve as pull factors for foreign investor can also be applied.

2. That more private limited liability companies and informal sector operators should be encouraged to access the stock market for fresh capital

3. Security Exchange Commission should be more productive in its surveillance role so as to check sharp practices which undermine the stock market integrity and investors' confidence.

4. Restoration of confidence to the market by regulatory authorities through ensuring transparency and fair trading transactions and dealings in the stock market

5. Slacking of trading investment such as high transaction costs to encourage more trading in stocks.

6. That policies that will further increase the volume of market transaction in the market be instituted through making more investment instruments (such as derivatives, convertibles, futures, swaps etc.) available, this will in turn bring about economic growth.

7. Ensuring the stability of macroeconomic environment and encouraging multinational companies or their subsidiaries to be listed in the Nigerian stock market.

References

1. Umoru D, Asekome MO (2013) Stock Prices and Exchange Rate Variability in Nigeria: Econometric Analysis of the Evidence. European Scientific Journal Vol-9.
2. Mishkin FS (2004) The Economics of Money, Banking and Financial Markets. Seventh Edition, New York. The Addison-Wesley Series, pp: 60-62.
3. Abdalla ISA, Murinde V (1997) Exchange Rate and Stock Price Interactions in Emerging Financial Markets: Evidence on India, Korea, Pakistan and the Phillipines. Applied Financial Economics Vol-7.
4. Aggarwal R (1981) Exchange Rates and Stock Prices: A Study of the US Capital Markets under Floating Exchange Rates. Akron Business and Economic Review 12: 7-12.

5. Adam P (2015) A model of the Dynamics of the Relationship between Stock Prices and Growth in Indonesia. Applied Economics and Finance Vol-2.

6. Gaurav A, Kumar SA, Ankita S (2010) A study of Exchange Rates Movement and Stock Market Volatility. International Journal of Business and Management 5: 62-73.

7. Ajayi RA, Mougoue M (1996) On the dynamic relation between stock prices and exchange rates. The Journal of Financial Research, pp: 193-207.

8. Branson WH (1981) Macroeconomic determinants of real exchange rate risk. In: Herring, RJ (ed.), Managing Foreign Exchange rate risk, Cambridge University Press, Cambridge.

9. Frankel J (1983) Monetary and Portfolio Balance Models of Exchange Rate Determination. In J. Bhandari, B. Putnam (eds.), Economic Interdependence and Flexible Exchange Rates, pp: 84-114.

10. Ajayi RA, Friedman J, Mehdian SM (1998) On the Relationship between Stock Returns and Exchange Rates: Tests of Granger Causality. Global Finance Journal 9: 241-251.

11. Akinlo AE, Adejumo VA (2014) Exchange Rate Volatility and Non-Oil Exports in Nigeria: 1986-2008. International Journal of Business and Management Vol-9.

12. Alvan EI (2010) Is the Stock Market a leading Indicator of Economic Activity in Nigeria? Journal of Applied Statistics Vol-1.

13. Zubair A (2013) Causal Relationship between Stock Market Index and Exchange Rate: Evidence from Nigeria. C.B.N. Journal of Applied Statistics Vol-4.

14. Andre YH, Emma MI (2012) Exchange rate movements, stock prices and volatility in the Caribbean and Latin America. Department of Economics University of the West Indies Mona, Jamaica.

15. Azman-Saini WNW, Azali M, Habibullah MS, Matthews KG (2002) Financial integration and the ASEAN-5 Equity Markets. Applied Economics 34: 2283-2288.

16. Babatunde OA (2013) Stock Market Volatility and Economic Growth in Nigeria. International Review of Management and Business Research 2: 201-209.

17. Gustav C (1918) Abnormal deviations in international exchanges. The Economic Journal 28: 413-415.

18. Chetwin W, Steenkamp D (2013) New Zealand's Short and Medium Term Real Exchange Rate Volatility: Drivers and Policy Implications. Reserve Bank of New Zealand Analytical Note Series.

19. Barro RJ (1990) Government Spending in a Simple Model of Endogenous Growth. Journal of Political Economy Vol-98.

20. Barro RJ, Sala-i-Martin X (1990) Economic Growth and Convergence across the United States. Working Paper 3419. Cambridge.

21. Kunt DA. & Levin R (1996). Stock market development and financial intermediaries: Stylized facts. The World Bank Economic Review 10: 291-321.

22. Tuncer CG, Alovsat M (2001) Stock markets and Economic Growth: A Causality Test. Institute of Social Science, Istanbul Technical University.

23. Cumby RE, Obstfeld M (1981) A note on exchange-rate expectations and nominal interest differentials: A test of the Fisher hypothesis. Journal of Finance 36: 697-704.

24. Kunt DA, Levin AR (1996) Stock market, corporate finance and economic growth: An overview. The World Bank Review 10: 223-236.

25. Cumby RE, Obstfeld M (1984) International interest rate and price level linkages under flexible exchange rates: A review of recent evidence, in: J.F.O. Bilson and R.C. Marston, (eds.), Exchange rate theory and practice. University of Chicago Press, Chicago.

26. Ewah SOE, Esang AE, Bassey JU (2009) Appraisal of Capital Market Efficiency on Economic Growth in Nigeria. International Journal of Business and Management Vol-4.

27. Ariyo A, Adelegan O (2005) Assessing the impact of capital market reforms in Nigeria. An incremental approach. Annual Conference of the Nigeria Economic Society in Lagos.

28. Harrigan P, Ramsey E, Ibbotson P (2011) Critical factors underpinning the e-CRM activities of SMEs. Journal of Marketing Management 26: 1-27.

29. Usman (2014) The Impact of Initial Phase Principles on Project Performance within the Building Industry in Abuja, Nigeria. American International Journal of Contemporary Research 4: 3.

30. Dimitrova D (2005) The Relationship between Exchange Rates and Stock Prices: Studied in a Multivariate Model. Issues in Political Economy Vol-14.

31. Engle R (2012) Dynamic conditional correlation: A simple class of multivariate generalized autoregressive conditional heteroskedasticity models. Journal of Business and Economic Statistics 20: 339-350.

32. Engle RF, Mezrich J (1996) GARCH for groups. Risk 9: 36-40.

33. Engle RF, Gonźalez-Rivera G (1991) Semiparametric ARCH models. Journal of Business and Economic Statistics 9: 345-359.

34. Engle RF, Kroner KF (1995) Multivariate simultaneous generalized ARCH. Econometric Theory 11: 122-150.

35. Bollerslev T (1986) Generalized Autoregressive Conditional Heteroskedasticity. Journal of Econometrics.

36. Adjasi CKD, Biekpe BN (2007) Stock Market Returns and Exchange Rate Dynamics in Selected African Countries: A bivariate analysis.

37. Dell'Ariccia G (1999) Exchange Rate Fluctuations and Trade Flows: Evidence from the European Union. IMF Staff Papers 46: 315-334.

38. Wang J, Nair U Christopher SA (2007) Observational estimates of radiative forcing due to land use change in southwest Australia. J Geophys Res, p: 109.

39. Clark P, Tamirisa N, Wei SJ (2004) Exchange rate volatility and trade flows-some new evidence. IMF Working Paper. International Monetary Fund.

40. Engle RF, Colacito R (2006) Testing and valuing dynamic correlations for asset allocation. Journal of Business and Economic Statistics 24: 238-253.

41. Engle RF (1982) Autoregressive conditional heteroscedasticity with estimates of the variance of United Kingdom inflation. Econometrica 50: 987-1006.

42. Evans K, Nelson HW, Perez OO (2014) Macroeconomic Variables, Volatility and Stock Market Returns: A Case of Nairobi Securities Exchange, Kenya. International Journal of Economics and Finance Vol-6.

43. Forgha NG (2012) An Investigation into the Volatility and Stock Returns Efficiency in African Stock Exchange Markets. International Review of Business Research Papers Vol-8.

44. Kutty G (2010) The relationship between exchange rates and Stock prices: the case of Mexico. Mansfield University, USA, pp: 4-8.

45. Gunther S (2007) Exchange Rate Volatility and Growth in Small Open Economies of the EMU Periphery. European Central Bank Working Paper Series, p: 773.

46. Harald H, Killeen W, Moore M (2002) How has the euro changed the foreign exchange market? Economic Policy 34: 151-177.

47. Ibrahim M, Aziz PP (2003) Macroeconomic Variables and the Malaysian Equity Market: a View Through Rolling Subsamples. Journal of Economic Studies 30: 6-27.

48. Ikoku AE (2012) Is the Stock Market a leading Indicator of Economic Activity in Nigeria? Journal of Applied Statistics. 1: 17-38.

49. Ikoku AE, Okany CT (2014) Did the Economic and Financial Crises affect Stock Market Sensitivity to Macroeconomic Risk Factors? Evidence from Nigeria and South Africa. International Journal of Business Vol-19.

50. Keynes JM (1923) A Tract on Monetary Reform, pp: 80-82.

51. Joseph N (2002) Modelling the Impact of Interest Rate and Exchange Rate Changes on U.K. Stock Returns, Derivative Use, Trading and Regulation. In: Agrawal G, Srivastar AK, Srivastava A (eds.), (2010). A Study of Exchange Rates Movement and Stock Market Volatility. International Journal of Business and Management Vol-5.

52. Haug S (2001) Bleiben oder Zurü ckkehren? Zur Messung, Erklärung und Prognose der Rü ckkehrvon Immigranten in Deutschland. Zeitschrift für Bevölkerungswissenschaft 26: 23170.

53. Banerjee, Abhijit V, Newman A (1993) Occupational choice and the process of development. Journal of Political Economy 101: 274-298.

54. Rothkopf MH, Teisberg TJ, Kahn EP (1990) Why Are Vickrey Auctions Rare? Journal of Political Economy 98: 103.

55. Karoui A (2006) The Correlation between FX Rate Volatility and Stock

Exchange Returns Volatility: An Emerging Markets Overview. The 13th Global Finance Conference, Canada.

56. Karunanayake I, Valadkhani A, O'Brien M (2012) Stock Market and GDP Growth Volatility Spillovers. Proceedings of the 41st Australian Conference of Economists, Melbourne.
57. Kim EH, Singal V (2000) Stock Market Openings: Experience of Emerging Economies. Journal of Business Vol-73.
58. Kolawole S, Olalekan MS (2013) Exchange Rate Volatility and the Stock Market. The Nigerian Experience.
59. Kurihara Y (2006) The Relationship between Exchange Rate and Stock Prices during the Quantitative Easing Policy in Japan. International Journal of Business Vol-11.
60. Mbutor M (2010) Exchange Rate Volatility, Stock Price Fluctuations and the Lending Behaviour of Banks in Nigeria. Journal of Economics and International Finance 2: 251-260.
61. Mlambo C, Maredza A, Sibanda K (2013) Effects of Exchange Rate Volatility on the Stock Market: A Case Study of South Africa. Mediterranean Journal of Social Sciences Vol-4.
62. Narayan PK (2004) Fiji's Tourism Demand: The ARDL Approach to Cointegration. Tourism Economics 10: 193-206.
63. Narayan PK (2005) The Saving and Investment Nexus for China: Evidence from Cointegration Tests. Applied Economics 37: 1979-1990.
64. Nazlioglu S, Kar M, Akel G (2014) Relationship between Exchange Rates and Stock Prices in Transition Economies: Evidence from Linear and Non-Linear Causality Tests. 2nd Economics & Finance Conference, Viena.
65. Nwakanma C, Ajibola A, Nwakanma HC (2014) Effect of Episodic Market Conditions in Beta Variability in Nigerian Stock Market. International Journal of Business and Economic Research. Vol-13.
66. OECD (2002) Exchange Market Volatility and Securities Transaction Taxes. OECD Economic Outlook Vol-71.
67. Ogege S, Mojekwu JN (2013) Econometric Investigation of the Random Walk Hypothesis in the Nigerian Stock Market. Journal of Emerging Issues in Economics, Finance and Banking Vol-1.
68. Ogunmuyiwa MS (2010) Investor's Sentiment, Stock Market Liquidity and Economic Growth in Nigeria. Journal of Social Sciences 23: 63-67.
69. Osahon OH (2014) Measuring Nigerian Stock Market Volatility. Singaporean Journal of Business Economics and Management Studies. Vol-2.
70. Osamwonyi IO, Kasimu A (2013) Stock Market and economic Growth in Ghana, Kenya and Nigeria. International Journal of Financial Research 4: 83-98.
71. Hansen, Peter L, and Hodrick RJ (1980) Forward exchange rates as optimal predictors of future spot rates: An econometric analysis. Journal of Political Economy 5: 829-853.
72. Osuala AE, Okereke JE, Nwansi GU (2013) Does Stock Market Development Promote Economic Growth in Emerging Markets? A Causality Evidence from Nigeria. World Review of Business Research 3: 1-13.
73. Engle RF, Granger CWJ, Kraft D (1984) Combining competing forecasts of inflation using a bivariate ARCH model. Journal of Economic Dynamics and Control 8: 151-165.
74. Owoeye T, Ogunmakin AA (2013) Exchange Rate Volatility and Bank Performance in Nigeria. Asian Economic and Financial Review Vol-3.
75. Poterba JM, Summers LH (1986) The Persistence of Volatility and Stock Market Fluctuations. The American Economic Review Vol-76.
76. Qqyyum A, Khan MA (2014) Dynamic Relationship and Volatility Spillover between the Stock Market and the Foreign Exchange Market in Pakistan: Evidence from VAR-GARCH Modelling.
77. Salisu AA, Oloko TF (2015) Modelling Spillovers between Stock Market and FX Market: Evidence for Nigeria. Centre for Econometrics and Allied Research (CEAR).
78. Stavarek D (2005) Stock Prices and Exchange Rates in the EU and the USA: Evidence on their mutual interactions. Czech Journal of Economics and Finance 55: 141-161.
79. Holub T, Čihák M (2003) Price convergence: What can the Balassa–Samuelson model tell us?
80. Tsoukalas D (2003) Macroeconomic factors and stock prices in the emerging Cypriot equity market. Managerial Finance 29: 87-92.
81. Ujunwa A, Modebe NJ (2012) Adopting Strategic Management Approach in the Capital Market Development: The Nigerian Case. International Journal of Economics and Finance Vol-4.
82. Ulku, Demirci (2012) Joint Dynamics of Foreign Exchange and Stock Markets in Emerging Europe. Journal of International Financial Markets, Institutions & Money 22: 55-86.
83. Umer UM, Sevil G, Kamisli S (2015) The Dynamic Linkages between Exchange Rates and Stock Prices: Evidence from Emerging Markets. Journal of Finance and Investment Analysis Vol-4.
84. Usman OA, Adejare AT (2012) The effects of foreign exchange regimes on industrial growth in Nigeria. Department of Management and Accounting, Ladoke Akintola University of Technology, Ogbomoso, pp: 3-4.
85. Yaya OS, Shittu OI (2010) On the Impact of Inflation and Exchange Rate on Conditional Stock Market Volatility: A Reassessment. American Journal of Scientific and Industrial Research.
86. Zahid A, Ather AK, Anam T (2012) Stock Market Development and Economic Growth: A Comparative Study of Pakistan and Bangladesh. African Journal of Business Management Vol-6.

14

Money Supply, Banking Liquidity and Stock Index Returns: Evidence from Four Major Capital Markets

Chung T* and Ariff M

Taylors University, Subang Jaya, Malaysia

Abstract

Prior studies that have examined the drivers of stock returns have mostly focussed on firm-specific factors. However, King demonstrated that firm-specific factors explain only 38% of the variation in stock prices, while the dominant driver was macroeconomic factors (52%) with industry-related factors accounting for the remaining 10% of stock price variation. Against this background, the present study, to our knowledge, is the first attempt to model Friedman's still-unproven money-supply led banking liquidity effect and the subsequent effect on stock prices, that will be represented as stock index returns in this study. We, thereafter, proceed to build a model to connect money supply and banking liquidity to overall stock index returns. For the purpose, we apply a system of equations, and use quarterly macroeconomic data series of G-4 countries (Canada, Japan, the UK, and the US) covering a 54-year period. We control for monetary regime changes such as a shift from monetary targeting to inflation targeting, structural breaks following the global financial crisis (GFC) and monetary policy changes. To test robustness of our findings, we provide causality tests linking money supply to liquidity as well as stock index returns and earnings before applying bootstrapping method to refine the parameter estimates.

Keywords: Liquidity; Share prices; Endogeneity; Dynamic OLS; Structural break; Bootstrapping

Introduction

Prior studies that have examined the drivers of stock returns have mostly focussed on firm-specific factors.[1] However, King [1] demonstrated that firm-specific factors explain only 38% of the variation in stock prices, while the dominant driver was macroeconomic factors (52%) with industry-related factors accounting for the remaining 10% of stock price variation. Similar view was expressed 32 years later by Musílek [2], who recommended that investors need to focus *mostly* on price-shaping macroeconomic factors. Flannery and Protopapadakis [3] also consider macroeconomic factors as the most significant determinants of stock returns because such factors have dominant impact on future cash flow generation. Given these pointers, one would expect that research would move in the direction of examining the link between macroeconomic factors and stock returns. Curiously enough, extant research focusses on firm-specific drivers of stock price movements rather than the macroeconomic factors.

The important macroeconomic factors that influence stock price (usually measured as log change of stock prices) movements include national income, money supply led banking liquidity, inflation and interest rates. Friedman [4] suggested that money supply impacted banking liquidity, which in-turn influenced the credit creation abilities of banks, and which finally left a positive influence on asset (stock) prices.[2] Though Hamilton [5] found support for this 'liquidity effect', studies by Pagan and Robertson [6], Goodfriend, [7], Lepper and Gordon [8], Edmond and Weill [9] and Thornton [10] could not corroborate Friedman's liquidity proposition.[3]

Against this background, the present study, to our knowledge, is the first attempt to model Friedman's [4] still-unproven money-supply led banking liquidity effect and the subsequent effect on stock prices, that will be represented as stock index returns in this study. We, thereafter, proceed to build a model to connect money supply and banking liquidity to overall stock index returns. For the purpose, we apply a system of equations, and use quarterly macroeconomic data series of G-4 countries (Canada, Japan, the UK, and the US) covering a 54-year period. We control for monetary regime changes such as a shift from monetary targeting to inflation targeting, structural breaks following the global financial crisis (GFC) and monetary policy changes. To test robustness of our findings, we provide causality tests linking money supply to liquidity as well as stock index returns and earnings before applying bootstrapping method to refine the parameter estimates.

The rest of the paper is organised as follows. Section 2 provides a brief discussion of the money supply theory and its variations, focussing on the link between money supply and liquidity and thereafter between banking liquidity and stock index returns [11-13]. Section 3 explains the data preparation steps (to correct for stationarity, multicollinearity, serial correlations, heteroscedasticity, Hausman tests for random vs fixed effect modelling), and causality tests using a 3-equation system of

[1]This is line with the finance literature on pricing of stock prices. Building on the work of Markowitz's (1952) mean variance portfolio, Sharpe (1964), Lintner (1965) and Mossin (1966) introduced the first accepted equilibrium asset pricing model, known widely as the CAPM. Later the multifactor model of Ross (1976) broadened the variable set to firm-relevant variables. Later Fama-French (1993) model included additional variables including macroeconomic (term structure and income growth). In our study, we are approaching the stock pricing issues from a macroeconomic angle, so we use much broader proxies as potential macro-economic factors taken from monetary economics literature.

[2]His proposition of a *negative* money supply effect on interest rate has been verified in a number of studies. The empirical literature on the liquidity effect dates back at least to Cagan and Gandolfi (1969), Gibson (1970a; b), Leeper and Gordon (1992), Goodfriend (1997), Pagan and Robertson [6], Christiano, Eichenbaum and Evans [12], Hamilton [5], Thornton [13] Carpenter and Demiralp (2006) and Thornton [10].

[3]The test results are not included (to save space) but are available from the authors on request.

***Corresponding author:** Chung T, Taylors University, Subang Jaya, Malaysia
E-mail: TinFah.Chung@taylors.edu.my, tinfah@yahoo.com

equations and regression models. Section 4 presents the findings and section 5 concludes.

Relevant Theory and Prior Studies

We consider below the extant literature relating to the three constructs namely money-supply, money-supply-led liquidity and stock index returns. We thereafter consider the impact of monetary regime changes on these constructs.

Friedman [4] identified that exogenous change in money-supply exerts three types of effects on interest rates - liquidity effect, income effect and inflation effect. While the last two effects have received much attention in the monetary theory literature, the former has received limited attention. 'Despite its prominent role in conventional theories of the monetary policy transmission mechanism, there has been little evidence of a statistically significant or economically meaningful liquidity effect' [10]. The inability of the researchers to find evidence in support of a liquidity effect, is what Strongin [11] called the 'liquidity puzzle'.

Money supply effect

Though the 'liquidity (effect) puzzle' remains unresolved, monetary policy continues to be guided by the link between money supply and interest as postulated by Friedman [4]. A large body of literature has developed since 1990 to measure the magnitude of effect on market interest rates following changes in monetary policy regime. Such effects can be represented in a money demand and money supply relationship model as in Pagan and Robertson [6], shown stylistically below:

$$m_t^{\,d}=\alpha_1+\alpha_2\, r_t+\varepsilon_t^{\,d} \qquad (1.1)$$

$$m_t^{\,s}=\beta_1+\beta_2 r_t+\varepsilon_t^{\,s} \qquad (1.2)$$

$$\therefore\ m_t^{\,d}= m_t^{\,s} \qquad (1.3)$$

where d indicates demand, s supply, m_t is the log of nominal money, r_t, is the nominal interest rate, while $\varepsilon_t^{\,d}$ and $\varepsilon_t^{\,s}$ are mutually correlated demand and supply shocks. r_t responds to shifts in money supply engineered by varying β_1 and the relation $dr_t/d\beta_1=(\alpha_2 - \beta_2)^{-1}$ means that the interest rate decreases when money supply increases, provided $\alpha_2<0$ and $\beta_2<-\alpha_2$. This negative reaction to interest rate changes to a rise in money supply is termed as the 'liquidity effect'. Hence, the above discussion provides a two-equation model for testing money supply and interest rates.

Changes in money supply influence firms expected earnings and consequently the stock returns. Known as the expectation effect, it takes place through the conduit of the banking sector. Money supply impacts banking sector liquidity, which in turn impacts banks' ability to lend and the lending terms. Such an impact through the banking system is more enduring than the generally short-lived expectation effect. It is so, because firms can now consider projects that they earlier found non-viable. It suggests that a proxy for earnings, such as IPI (industrial production index at the macroeconomic level) is a more appropriate variable than dividends commonly used in the individual stock pricing literature, since aggregate earnings are perfectly correlated with IPI.[4]

Accordingly, the money supply-to-stock-price impact is positive when it acts through the banking channel (money supply led liquidity).[5]

The theoretical foundation for the money-supply led banking liquidity effect and the subsequent stock return effect is provided by the Quantity Theory of Money (QTM) and the Portfolio Theory (PT). The process of money creating liquidity and liquidity leading to credit expansion essentially alters the demand for other assets, including stocks. As and when the monetary authority makes decisions that impact money supply, it leads to changes in the prices of all assets in the market, requiring investors do rebalance their portfolios. Simple Quantity Theory of money (SQT) states:

$$M.V=P.Q \qquad (2)$$

where, M is the total amount of money in circulation in an economy during the period, say a year; *P* the corresponding price level; P.Q is the nominal money value of output; *V* is the velocity of money in final expenditures; and Q is an index of the real value of final expenditures. An increase in money supply is expected to increase supply of money balance, which in turn leads to excess demand for shares. It in-turn leads to rise in stock prices [14]. As money supply expands, the portfolio of desired versus actual cash holding needs adjustment. The agents who stock the excess money supply are compensated by rising price of securities as well as consumption goods and services, they sell which leads to a new equilibrium. Though the SQT and PT underpin this scenario, the link between money supply and its impact on asset prices has newer interpretations (see for example, Badarudin et al. [15]). This adjustment mechanism of asset holdings builds a positive relationship between money supply and stock index returns. Easing of money supply (quantitative easing by the US Fed in 2012-14, for example) reduces cost of capital which in-turn strengthens investment.

Similar to the assumption of Friedman [4], post-Keynesian economists too provide new insights on money being endogenously rather than exogenously determined. Consequently, before testing liquidity–stock returns link, the one between money supply and bank liquidity needs verification. The role of banking liquidity has been highlighted in both theoretical and empirical finance. The credit splurge of the 1994-04, for example, led to asset price bubbles and consequently to the GFC [1]. In summary, the money supply and liquidity link is examined before the money supply and stock returns link. Accordingly, by combining SQT and PT, we can derive the liquidity effect.

Liquidity effect

Central banks across the world base their monetary policy on the presumption that an increase (decrease) in money supply (money reserve in the banking system) would lead to a fall (rise) in policy rate (called Fed rate in the US). For the purpose, the central bank engages in Open Market Operations. The adjustment of reserves to drive the Fed funds rate relies on the presumption of 'liquidity effect' [16,17]. Banks hold money reserves with the central bank (called exchange settlement account in Australia), which they adjust along with other investments following monetary policy changes (called portfolio rebalancing). This in-turn impacts credit expansion (contraction) by banks which leads to larger (lower) credit demand by firms which in-turn impacts stock returns through their investment decisions.

[4]GDP and IPI were found to be cointegrated in the long-run and therefore, IPI could be used as a proxy for earnings: (to save space these results are not included).

[5]The theoretical framework presented by monetarists for a relationship between money supply and stock prices may be viewed from the Simple Quantity Model (SQT) or the more sophisticated Portfolio Theory (PT). The SQT (Brunner, 1961; Friedman, 1961; and Friedman and Schwartz, 1963) states that an increase in money supply changes the equilibrium across the economy between monetary and non-monetaryy assets (for example shares) in the portfolio.

Despite its prominent role in conventional theories about monetary policy transmission mechanism, there is limited empirical evidence to date of a statistically significant or economically meaningful money-led liquidity effect.[6] Hamilton [5] sought to develop a more convincing measure of liquidity effect by estimating the response of the federal funds rate to exogenous reserve supply shocks using daily data. However, Thornton [13] suggests that the evidence is questionable.

Stock index price

Finance literature focusses on the pricing of individual shares. The widely accepted asset pricing theory, the capital asset pricing model, (CAPM) of Sharpe [18], Lintner [19] and Mossin [20] drew from Markowitz's [21] mean variance theory. However, the basic CAPM makes some restrictive assumptions and provides poor evidence to support Markowitz theory. The substitute Arbitrage Pricing Theory (1976) also assumed that expected return of an asset and its co-variance with other random variables is linearly related. While the CAPM linked asset pricing to a single factor of beta, the APT linked it to several factors including macroeconomic factors. King's [1] approached the asset pricing issue from macroeconomic and industry perspective. Variables were derived from factor analysis of fundamental economic aggregates, such as GNP or interest rates. Chen, Roll and Ross [22] attempted to express the stock returns as a function of macroeconomic variables.

Finally, Cooper's [23] portfolio model also assumes that individuals could hold wealth in two forms, money and common stock. The marginal returns of stock assets determine the quantities of assets individuals will hold. A portfolio is said to be balanced when the marginal returns to holding these two assets are equal.

$$MNPS_t^M - \overline{P} = MNPS_t^S + \overline{r}_t^s \tag{3}$$

Where the left side is the return to money asset and the right side is the return to stock asset; $\overline{P}_t$ is anticipated percentage change in general price level; $\overline{r}_t^*$ is the anticipated real pecuniary return of stocks (dividend plus change in stock prices); $MNPS_t^s$ is marginal pecuniary return to the j-th asset (the risk of j-th assets is incorporated into its pecuniary returns. $MNPS_t^M$ is implicitly a function of demand for money except for returns on alternative assets. An underlying assumption is that the positive income effect on $MNPS_t^{M,S}$ cancel each other. Thus, the difference between $MNPS_t^M$ and $MNPS_t^{M,S}$ is primarily a function of money. In this model, money supply change induces portfolio adjustments through $MNPS_t$ schedules and prices. The result is that money supply impacts to stock returns. By re-arranging this equation, it could be shown that the stock return is:

$$\overline{r}_t^s = \left(MNPS_t^M - \overline{P}\right) - MNPS_t^S \tag{4}$$

[6]See Pagan and Robertson (1995) Leapper and Gordon (1992) and Goodfriend (1997) for reasons why liquidity effect is hard to identify. Researchers including Bernanke and Blinder (1992), Christiano and Eichenbaum (1991, 1992a, b) have argued that the lack of empirical support is due to the Fed's preference for interest rate targeting in one form or another. Accordingly, innovations to monetary aggregates, M1, reflect shocks to money demand rather than to money supply. As a statistically significant variable that reflects the exogenous policy actions of the Fed couldn't be isolated, liquidity effect remained hidden.

Thus, Cooper [23] model is equivalent to the asset pricing model in finance. Accordingly, the relationship between the money supply and the stock prices discovered by Sprinkel [14] and Cooper [23] plays an important role in money supply leading to stock price changes (stock index returns).[7]

Changes in monetary policy regime

The financial systems of G-4 countries are relatively well developed and monetary policy regimes are in vogue since the 1960s. The table below summarises subsequent changes. One could identify the break in the data series using dummy variables to control for changes in monetary policy regimes while testing the maintained hypotheses on liquidity-to-stock returns (Table 1).

Data, Hypothesis and Methodology

Hypotheses and methodology

It is an empirical question whether principal economic indicators such as industrial production, inflation, interest rates, Treasury bill rate, banking liquidity and money supply are significant explanatory factors for stock returns (Hardouvellis [24], Keim [25], Litzenberger and Ramaswamy [26], King [1] found macroeconomic factors account for up to 52% and industry factors 10% of the variation in stock prices (returns).

If economic variables are significantly and consistently priced in stock returns, they should be cointegrated. If not, then, it could be concluded that the stock markets do not signal changes in real activities. We use the cointegration (a necessary condition for equilibrium in stock returns) and Granger [27] causality test to investigate the relation between stock returns and the identified macroeconomic variables and the unit root test to determine nonstationarity. If the first-differenced series of each variable are stationary, a subsequent cointegration test is performed.[8] If the residuals are I(0), or stationary, a model can be considered to be cointegrated with a valid long run relationship. We use the Johansen and Juselius [28], maximum likelihood procedure given the difficulties with the OLS approach. It assumes endogeniety regressors and applies appropriate methods. Finally, through more powerful set of tests, we identify cointegrating vectors and evaluate the effect of various restrictions by identifying the rank of the matrix P in the following equation:

$$\Delta X_t = \delta + \sum_{i=1}^{k-1} \Gamma_i \Delta X_{t-i} + \Pi X_{t-k} + \epsilon_t \tag{5}$$

where X_t is a column vector of m variables, Γ and Π represent coefficient

[7]However, studies by Cooper (1970), Pesando (1974), Kraft and Kraft (1977), and Rozeff (1974)) have questioned this linkage between stock prices and money supply. As *liquidity surges* during GFC created imbalance in both the financial and real sector, this issue which was side-tracked, re-emerged: Ariff *et al.* (2012).

[8]See also Footnote #3. Cointegration implies that deviations from equilibrium are stationary, with finite variance, even though the series themselves are nonstationary and have infinite variance (Engle and Granger, 1987). Tests are available on request.

Country	Event date	Start date	End
Canada	Inflation targeting announced (Thiessen 1998)	1991:1	Present
Japan	Inflation targeting	1991:1	Present
United Kingdom	Chancellor's letter to Chairman setting out new framework for monetary policy (BOE diary of events)	1992:4	Present
United States	Fed announced that it would no longer set M1 targets and moved away from borrowed reserve targets	1987:1	Present

Table 1: Changes in Monetary Policy Regime in Canada, Japan, the UK and the USA.

matrices, Δ represents difference operator, k the lag length and δ is constant. This is done using methods described in [29] (Pesaran and Pesaran 1997). The rank r provides the number of cointegrating vectors, a rank of 1, for example, tests a single stationary relationship reflecting a long-run relationship. Further decomposition of the matrix Π, gives parameters of the cointegrating relationship and the adjustment coefficients of an error correction model.

Stock and Watson [30] suggest an innovative procedure for estimation of long-run equilibria via DOLS, which corrects for potential simultaneity bias among regressors. DOLS entails regressing one of the I(1) variables on other I(1) variables, the I(0) variables, and lags and leads of the first difference of the I(1) variables. The incorporation of the first difference variables and the associated lags and leads obviates simultaneity bias and small sample bias inherent among regressors. Standard hypothesis testing is done using robust standard errors derived via the procedure recommended by Newey and West [31].

It is hypothesized that money supply (MS) is endogenously determined by economic activity as mediated via the deposit-taking institutions [15]. The literature on post-Keynesian theory on endogenous money is extensive.[9] Economic activity is proxied by real gross domestic product (Y), liquidity (LQ) is endogenously determined by money supply (MS) and share prices (SP) is endogenously affected by liquidity (LQ). Money supply (MS) is also determined by share returns (DLSP), inflation (CPI), real GDP (Y) and treasury bill rate (TBR). Liquidity is determined by real GDP (Y), money supply (MS) and lending rate (LR).

The system of equations comprising two simultaneous equations of stock returns (P) and liquidity (LQ), is solved endogenously as follows:[10]

$$SP_{it}=f\,[LQ_{it}^{-}, MS_{it}^{+}, IPI_{it}^{+}] \quad (6.1)$$

$$LQ_{it}=f\,[MS_{it}^{+}, Y_{it}^{+}, LR_{it}^{-}] \quad (6.2)$$

$$MS_{it}=f\,[LQ_{it}^{+}, Y_{it}^{+}, TBR_{it}^{-}, SP_{it}^{+}, CPI_{it}^{+}, CPI(1)_{it}^{+}] \quad (6.3)$$

where SP is aggregate share price index, LQ is liquidity as proxied by reserve money, MS is money supply, IPI is industrial production index, Y is real GDP, LR is lending rate, TRB is Treasury bill rate and CPI is inflation. All variables are in log change ratios. Countries are denoted by i while t denotes observations over time. The operational versions of these models are:

$$\ln SP_{it=}a_0+a_1 \ln LQ_{it}+a_2 \ln MS_{it}+a_3 \ln IPI_{it}+e_{it} \quad (7.1)$$

$$\ln LQ_{it=}b_0+b_1 \ln MS_{it}+b_2 \ln Y_{it}+b_3\, LR_{it+}z_{it} \quad (7.2)$$

$$\ln MS_{it}=c_0+c_1 \ln Y_{it}+c_2 \ln LQ_{it+}c_3 \ln SP_{it}+c_4\, TBR_{it}+c_5 \ln CPI_{it}+v_{it} \quad (7.3)$$

Two separate sets of hypotheses are developed and tested. The first set of tests is to determine whether money supply is endogenous.

H_1: MS causes GDP (suggesting money is exogenous) or there is bidirectional causality.

It is hypothesised under the alternative hypotheses that there may be unidirectional or bidirectional causality from real GDP to money supply. This hypothesis is important to verify as a pre-condition before we can embark on testing the hypotheses of whether money supply affects liquidity and that liquidity affects stock returns.

[9]Influenced greatly by Moore in 1989 and Kaldor and Moore in 1988 developed the post-Keynesian view on money, which is today the cornerstone of the PK theory of endogenous money (Rochon, 2006). The theory posits that causality runs from bank lending to bank deposits, instead of the traditional notion that deposits create loans.

[10]The basis of the model in this section stems from Effa et al. (2011). Not all the variables used in that paper are used in this study because the focus of this study is on liquidity and stock returns: also see Dhakal et al. (1993) on causality between money and share prices observed directly.

The next hypotheses are:

H_2: MS causes Liquidity: this follows from Friedman's proposition which is yet to be verified.

H_3: Liquidity causes Share Prices. This is to test the bi-directional causality.

Data and variables

Data are obtained from the datastream and the International Financial Statistics (IFS) database of the International Monetary Fund (IMF). The latter source was also used to cross-check and correct our data set. We use quarterly series over 1960:1-2013:2 (number after colon is quarter). The expected impacts of the variables in the system are shown in Table 2.

As the industrial production index (IPI) was highly correlated with national income, it could affect firm's earnings. Hence, we use the log change of IPI as a proxy for earnings in the equation for stock pricing: if IPI goes up, the earnings of the firms go up. Following Gordon and Leeper [32] we use reserve money. If the banking system has more reserves in the central bank, liquidity declines, and if it draws down, liquidity increases (Table 2).

Consequently, liquidity is inversely related to reserves, but positively related to stock index returns via the portfolio rebalancing effect by firms/individuals. For money supply, M2, values are used.[11] The TBR and the bank lending rate are the domestic 3-month Treasury-bill rate and lending rate respectively. The MSCI stock index values reported in Datastream is widely used for stock returns, P, computed as log change [33-36]. The consumer price index is used as a proxy for inflation (INF). The bank lending rate (LR), deposit rates, (TBR), and real gross domestic product, (RGDP), are also obtained. All variables are seasonally adjusted where available and transformed to logarithmic

[11] The choice of monetary aggregate and its implications on the demand for money have been discussed in Pagan and Robertson (1995) and Duca (1995) on finding the liquidity effect and for the stock market in Parhizgari (2011) on the share price effect.

Variables	Expected Sign	Actual Sign (DOLS)		Expected Sign	Actual Sign (DOLS)
Equation 7.1: LSPRICE				**Equation 7.2: LRLQ**	
LQ	+	+	MS	+	-
MS	+	-	Y	+	+
IPI	+	-	LRate	-	-
DUM(GFC)	+	-	DUM(GFC)	+	+
DUM(Regime)	+	+	DUM(Regime)	+	-
Equation7.3: LRM2					
LQ	+	+			
Y	+	+			
P (Stock index return)	+	-			
TBRate	-	-			
CPI	+	+			
CPI(+1)	+	+			
DUM(GFC)	+	+			

Table 2: Expected and actual signs of variables in ESTIMATION. DUM (GFC) dummy for Global Finance Crisis and DUM (Regime) is dummy for regime changes. The actual signs are taken from the results to be discussed in ensuing sections. The expected sign is based on *a priori* hypothesis based on theory while the actual sign is taken from the DOLS regression results.

form, with the exception of interest rates (TBR) and Lending Rate, LR [37-41].

Findings

Money endogeneity causality tests

In this sub-section, we present findings on causality to establish money endogeneity (ME) proposition for the four-country data set: Table 3. Although not directly relevant to stock index returns, it is pertinent to show that money endogeneity theory holds so as to motivate the model building within the context of monetary theory as used by Friedman [4].

The statistics presented is a summary of tests results of pairs of variables using Granger causality tests. These numbers indicate bidirectional causality for all variables - MS, GDP and Liquidity. All variables have bidirectional impact on one another except stock returns to MS and stock returns to liquidity [42-46]. In view of the reported weakness of Granger causality test on bivariate relationships, a multivariate test using three endogenous variables namely LSPRICE, LRLQ AND LRM2 was conducted in a VECM framework (Toda-Yamamoto, 1995) which can be applied regardless of whether the series are I(0), I(1) or I(2) cointegrated or not in column 4): Table 3.[12]

Causality runs in both directions in all cases, thus affirming money endogeneity. Table 4 provides summary statistics to support this. The results are about causality between stock returns and liquidity; stock returns and money supply; liquidity and money supply [47,48]. Tests show the variables display causality at 0.05% level. Since causality runs both ways (liquidity to share price, GDP to share price and money supply to liquidity) these can be interpreted as bidirectional causality, which supports the accommodationist version of the post-Keynesian ME proposition [15] (Tables 3-5).

Once ME is verified, we could present our findings on liquidity and on stock index return hypotheses. This is further confirmed from the results of Table 5 using the Toda Yamamoto VECM multivariate causality tests. All the 3 panels in Table 4 showed that the variables tested displayed causality is significant at the 5% level of rejecting the null hypothesis [49-51].

Descriptive statistics

We discuss descriptive statistics, followed by the data transformation procedures, results of single equation country results, the results from the more robust DOLS regressions, and further robustness test result using bootstrapping [52-54].

[12]Test statistics to support the conclusions and data transformation tests are available on request.

Money Endogeneity Test Results Monetarist Accommodationist		Panel Data on G4 Countries	Panel Data on G4 Countries (Using Toda Yamamoto)
MS --> Y	Y <--> MS	MS --> Y	MS <--> Y
MS --> LQ	*MS <--> LQ*	MS <--> LQ	*MS <--> LQ*
MS --> SP	*MS* <--> SP	*MS --> SP*	*MS* <--> SP
LQ --> Y	LQ <--> Y	Y --> LQ	LQ <--> Y
SP --> Y	*LQ <--> Y*	*SP <--> Y*	*SP <--> Y*
SP --> LQ	*LQ <--> Y*	SP <--> LQ	SP <--> LQ

Table 3: Granger causality on money endogeneity and panel regression results. Column 3 shows the results of Granger bivariate causality tests using the panel data on G-4 countries while Column 4 are the results from the Toda Yamamoto VECM multivariate model. Stock index returns are shown as SP.

Sample: 1 832			
Lags: 5			
Null Hypothesis:	**Obs**	**F-Statistic**	**Prob.**
LRLQ does not Granger Cause LSPRICE	742	9.34774	0.0001
LSPRICE does not Granger Cause LRLQ		2.11624	0.0616
LRM2 does not Granger Cause LSPRICE	769	3.59581	0.0032
LSPRICE does not Granger Cause LRM2		0.96249	0.4399
LRGDP does not Granger Cause LSPRICE	801	5.74312	0.0001
LSPRICE does not Granger Cause LRGDP		24.5287	0.0001
LRM2 does not Granger Cause LRLQ	710	3.64781	0.0029
LRLQ does not Granger Cause LRM2		2.25999	0.0469
LRGDP does not Granger Cause LRLQ	742	2.54850	0.0268
LRLQ does not Granger Cause LRGDP		1.03017	0.3986
LRGDP does not Granger Cause LRM2	769	0.64035	0.6690
LRM2 does not Granger Cause LRGDP		2.64680	0.0221

Table 4: Granger Bivariate Causality Results for Data on Canada, Japan, the UK and USA. The first "L" in each variable denotes log change: RGDP is real income as proxy for income, RLQ is liquidity as proxy by reserve money, RM2 is proxy for money supply M2 and Stock index returns are shown as SPRICE in this table. The F-statistics obtained are used to evaluate whether to accept the null hypothesis of no Granger causality. Any prob. value of > 0.05 will result in acceptance of null hypothesis.

Sample: 1960Q1 2011Q4			
Included observations: 710			
Dependent variable: SPRICE=stock index returns			
Excluded	**Chi-sq**	**df**	**Prob.**
LRLQ	42.55194	5	0
LRM2	17.2475	5	0.0041
All	63.32206	10	0
Dependent variable: LRLQ			
Excluded	Chi-sq	df	Prob.
LSPRICE	12.30395	5	0.0309
LRM2	20.04474	5	0.0012
All	30.73359	10	0.0006
Dependent variable: LRM2			
Excluded	Chi-sq	df	Prob.
LSPRICE	7.394611	5	0.1929
LRLQ	13.93748	5	0.016
All	18.73326	10	0.0438

Table 5: Robustness testing with Toda Yamamoto VECM multivariate causality tests. The first "L" in each variable denotes log change: SPRICE is share price index, RLQ is liquidity as proxy by reserve money and RM2 is proxy for money supply M2 and. The Wald Chi-square statistics obtained are used to evaluate whether to accept or reject the null hypothesis. Any prob. value of < 0.05 show that there is strong causation running from LRLQ and LRM2 to LSPRICE and in the first panel as the asymptotic chi-square (χ^2) is rejected.

We present the main results obtained from first using the single equation and then a system of equations model where the appropriate factors are entered as three equations. The Table 6 is a summary of descriptive statistics of the variables used in the regression (single equations and Stock Watson DOLS equations) (Table 6).

The variables are first differenced and computed as ratio relative to prior observation. The Jarque-Bera (JB) test indicates that all variables are not normal (JB >5.9 and p value of <0.05 rejecting the null hypothesis of normality). Most of these variables are skewed (> 0, for normality should be close to 0). A quick read of the values of these variables suggest that these are as one would expect in the panel of G-4 economies. For example, the average Treasury rate over the test period in the industrial economies of G-4 countries is 5.9% and the lending rate is 7%. Inflation (mean of difference in log CPI) has a mean of 1.1%

	LCPI	LR	LRGDP	LRIPI	LRLQ	LRM2	LSPRICE	DLSPRICE	TBR
Mean	3.94	6.98	4.02	0.21	-0.41	3.53	3.33	0.02	5.94
Median	4.19	6.57	4.07	0.012	-1.01	3.20	3.40	0.02	5.64
Maximum	4.76	21.67	4.67	1.78	2.78	9.07	5.38	0.37	20.15
Minimum	2.34	0.157	2.41	-0.41	-2.92	-0.74	1.03	-0.35	0.00
Std. Dev.	0.67	3.48	0.45	0.44	1.30	2.93	1.08	0.08	3.53
Skewness	-0.69	0.80	-0.79	1.78	0.66	0.67	0.006	-0.56	0.64
Kurtosis	2.13	3.88	3.48	6.013	2.09	2.09	1.63	5.60	3.49
Jarque-Bera	77.68	96.37	80.43	632.69	73.95	76.32	55.32	233.38	54.77

Table 6: Descriptive Statistics of the Panel Variables of Canada, Japan, the UK and the USA. The first "L" in each variable denotes log change: GDP is real income as proxy for income, LQ is liquidity as proxy by reserve money, M2 is proxy for money supply M2, CPI is consumer price index for inflation, IPI is industrial production index, LR is lending rate, and TBR is Treasury yields. DLSPRICE is change in log of share price denoting share price returns. Std. Dev. is standard deviation. L indicates log change of variables.

First Equation: Share Price Equation (Eq 7.1)			Second Equation: Liquidity (Eq. 7.2)			Third Equation: Money Supply (Eq. 7.3)		
DV is Share Price (SP)	OLS	DOLS	DV is Liquidity	OLS	DOLS	DV is Money Supply	OLS	DOLS
(Coefficients with t-statistics in brackets)			(Coefficients with t-statistics in brackets)			(Coefficients with t-statistics in brackets)		
C	3.43**(-65.85)	-	C	-0.37 (-0.78)	-	C	-1.28 (-0.94)	-
LRLQ	-0.04*	1.19***	LRM2	0.05***	-0.25**	LRGDP	1.20***	1.44***
	(-1.93)	(-3.30)		(-2.68)	(-2.12)		(-2.67)	(-4.93)
LRM2	-0.03***	-0.91***	LRGDP	0.09	3.21***	LRLQ	0.13	0.46***
	(-3.03)	(-2.25)		(-0.76)	(-10.67)		(-1.51)	(-4.23)
LRIPI	0.85	-0.03	LRate	-0.10***	-0.04***	LSPRICE	0.16	-0.13***
	(-0.74)	(-0.13)		(-6.99)	(-9.84)		(-0.52)	(-4.20)
LRIPI (-1)	-2.07*	-	DUM (GFC)	0.61**	0.52***	TBRate	0.26***	-0.004
	(-1.80)			(-2.31)	(-5.54)		(-6.13)	(-0.67)
DUM (GFC)	1.42***	-0.34	DUM (Regime)	0.44***	-0.02	LCPI	30.65***	0.41***
	(-9.46)	(-0.32)		(-3.38)	(-0.51)		(-2.98)	(-5.47)
DUM (Regime)	0.80***	0.29**	Model Parameters			DUM (GFC)	2.59**	0.38
	(-10.93)	(-2.26)	Adjusted R^2	0.1558	0.9993		(-4.51)	(-1.55)
Model Parameters			Std Error	1.1929	0.0353	DUM (Regime)	2.35***	0.04
Adjusted R^2	0.5776	0.9888	Mean	-0.4159	0.3517		(-8.26)	(-1.46)
Std Error	0.7209	0.1036	SD of dep var	1.2984	1.3092	Model Parameters		
Mean	3.2672	3.2022	Sum of Square Res	993.36	0.7235	Adjusted R^2	0.2102	0.9999
SD of dep var	1.1094	0.9714	Long-run variance		0.01	Std Error	2.6177	0.0197
Sum of Square Res	374.27	6.3889				Mean	3.4105	5.8159
Long-run Variance		0.1302				SD of dep var	2.9455	2.2902
						Sum of Square Res	4926.8	0.2119
						Long-run Variance		0.0052

Note: ***, **, and *denote significance at the 0.01, 0.05 and 0.10 per cent probability levels respectively.

Table 7: Results of G-4 Countries Estimation Using Single Equations. The first "L" in each variable denotes log change: GDP is real income as proxy for income, LQ is liquidity as proxy by reserve money, M2 is proxy for money supply M2, CPI is consumer price index for inflation, LR is lending rate, and TBR is Treasury yields. DUM is for dummy variables for the indicated conditions.

or annualised rate of 4.4%. The mean of difference in LSPRICE or the share price returns is 1.5% or annualised rate of 5.9% over 1960-2012, with a maximum return of 37% achieved during the bull phase and a minimum of 35% during the bear phase of the market correction [55].

DOLS Results using panel data

We discuss the results from single equation first before presenting the DOLS results. It is hypothesised that money supply causes liquidity change and that liquidity in turn causes stock prices to change. The statistics presented in Table 7 indicate that the dependent variable in the first equation-stock index return is represented as stock price - is determined by reserve money (liquidity or LQ), also by money supply, MS and the proxy for earnings IPI. All the variables are significant [56]. The liquidity impact on money supply in the third equation is economically significant affirming that bank reserves increases at the central bank, which leads to a decline in money supply. In the second equation, liquidity is determined by money supply, lending rate, LR and income entered as real GDP. All the variables except money supply (LRM2) and lending rate (LR) are significant.

Money supply in the third equation is determined by income (RGDP), reserve money (LQ), share price (SP), Treasury bill rate (TBR) and inflation (CPI). The significant relation between LQ and money is as per Friedman [4] proposition - a significant confirmation of the liquidity hypothesis [56]. Except for stock index returns, all the variables are significant. The income elasticity of money is less than one, 0.62%.

Results from cointegration tests using stock and watson DOLS

The results presented above are from the four country data runs by each equation at a time. We now present the results from a more reliable DOLS cointegration method which is robust to various departures from standard regression assumptions in terms of residual correlation, hetroscedasticity, misspecification of functional form and non-normality of residuals, so the resulting findings are reliable [57]. The results are estimated with up to j=± 4 leads and lags (insignificant lags and leads were dropped). Table 8 provides a summary of results.

The results on stock index return variables are presented in the first part of the table. The statistics on stock index indicate that stock index returns (represented as P) is significantly influenced by banking reserve money LQ (liquidity) with a coefficient of 1.19, money supply LM2 with a coefficient of -0.91 and earnings of firms, LRIPI, a control variable, is not significant. The control variable for the GFC is negative and significant as the monetary regimes shifted (DUMRegimes). All the variables except IPI are significant [58].

In the test results from second equation (Eq. 7.2), liquidity is influenced by money supply (LRM2) with a coefficient of -0.25 as suggested by Friedman [4], that is, money supply M2 increases leads to downward interest rates, which in turn leads to increased banking liquidity and vice versa. The real GDP (proxy for income) has a coefficient of 3.21, and the lending rate LR has a coefficient of -0.04. All the variables are significant. Going by the adjusted R-squared value, the model fit is considered appropriate. The financial crisis and the regime change are found to be significant factors affecting liquidity (Table 8).

The results on the third equation (Eq. 7.3) are summarised in the third part of the Table 8. Except for TBR, all the variables are significant. Most of the variables also show the expected signs.

Table 2 specifies the signs that were expected for each coefficient and the actual sign obtained. Five signs are different from the expected signs: The money supply (MS) equation (7.3) and the share price (P) equation (7.1). The dummy variables which represent breaks for monetary regime changes from macroeconomic aggregates to inflation targeting (Canada: 1991:1 to 2011:4; Japan: 1999:1 to 2011:4; UK: 1992:4 to 2011:4; US 1987:1 to 2011:4) and the effect of global financial crisis in 2007:2 to 2009:4 were found to be significant as expected.

Robustness Test Results Using Bootstrapping

The robustness test results obtained from bootstrapping are presented in Table 9. Bootstrapping is meant to enhance the robustness of the results by quasi-simulation procedure. Despite the fact that DOLS in itself is a robust methodology, applying robustness procedures helped us to see if some of the observed departures from theory predictions are restored and improved. Indeed, the results are much improved, and the model fit is still quite good (Table 9).

In the first equation for stock index returns, there is considerable improvement in the parameters. The adjusted R-squared values are lower as often happens in bootstrapping results. GFC is significant as before. The liquidity effect is about half that observed in the DOLS results, meaning that the quasi-simulation estimates from bootstrapping is a more reliable average effect of banking liquidity on stock index returns.

On the banking liquidity results too there are some improvements. Money supply effect is less pronounced at -0.60 (recall reserves have a negative effect) than in the DOLS result, but is still significant. Lending rate - a key variable for supply of bank credit - has a slightly larger and significant effect with a coefficient of -0.11, and significant. The adjusted R-squared ratio is lower, as in all bootstrapping results.

Examining the results for equation 4 on money supply, we note some improvements. All variables are now significant with changed coefficients. The adjusted R-squared ratio is lower, as usual. The stock

Dependent Variable Stock Price			Dependent Variable Liquidity			Dependent Variable Money Supply		
Variable Coefficient t-Statistic			Variable Coefficient t-Statistic			Variable Coefficient t-Statistic		
LRLQ	1.19	3.30***	LRM2	-0.25	-2.12**	LRGDP	1.44	4.93***
LRM2	-0.91	-2.25**	LRGDP	3.21	10.67***	LRLQ	0.46	4.23***
LRIPI	-0.03	-0.13	LR	-0.04	-9.84***	LSPRICE	-0.13	-4.20***
DUMGFC	-0.34	-0.32	DUMGFC	0.52	5.54***	TBR	-0.004	-0.67
DUMRegime	0.29	2.26**	DUMRegime	-0.02	-0.51	LCPI	0.41	5.47***
						DUM GFC	0.38	1.55*
						DUM1Regime	0.04	1.46
R-sq=0.99; adj R-sq=0.99; Fixd Eff			R-sq=0.99; adj R-sq=0.99; Fixed Eff			R-sq=0.98; adjR-sq=0.97; Fixed Eff		

Note: ***, **, and *denote significance at the 0.01, 0.05 and 0.10 per cent probability levels respectively.

Table 8: Results of DOLS Estimation from System of Equations for Canada, Japan, the UK and the USA. The first "L" in each variable denotes log change on indicated variables: GDP is real proxy for income, LQ is liquidity for banking reserves at central bank, M2 is proxy for money supply, CPI is price index for inflation, LR is bank lending rate, and TBR is Treasury yields. DUMGFC is for dummy variable for financial crisis years in 2007-2009; DUMRegime is dummy for monetary regimes. In the stock price equation, IPI is industrial production index, a proxy for earnings of firms; LR is lending rate; and LPRICE is stock index returns.

Dependent Variable Stock Price			Dependent Variable Liquidity			Dependent Variable Money Supply		
Variable Coefficient t-Statistic			Variable Coefficient t-Statistic			Variable Coefficient t-Statistic		
Constant	3.06	47.00***	Constant	-0.70	1.21	Constant	-0.78	-0.68
LRLQ	1.09	-5.87***	LRM2	0.60	7.48***	LRGDP	0.99	2.62***
LRM2	-0.02	-2.72***	LRGDP	0.19	1.21	LRLQ	0.24	5.19***
LRIPI	0.26	2.02 **	LR	-0.11	-6.11***	LSPRICE	0.32	1.87*
DUMGFC	0.52	8.08***	DUMGFC	0.29	1.05	TBR	-0.19	7.54***
DUMRegime	1.25	23.45***	DUMRegime	0.11	0.62	LCPI	32.0610.76	3.32***
						DUM GFC	1.07	1.82*
						DUM1Regime		5.83***
R-sq=0.71; adj R-sq=0.71; Fixd Eff			R-sq=0.75; adj R-sq=0.74; Fixed Eff			R-sq=0.76; adjR-sq=0.75; Fixed Eff		

Note: ***, **, and *denote significance at the 0.01, 0.05 and 0.10 per cent probability levels respectively.

Table 9: Results of robustness testing from bootstrapping method. The values for the constants are reported in this table. The first "L" in each variable denotes log change on indicated variables: GDP is real proxy for income, LQ is liquidity for banking reserves at central bank, M2 is proxy for money supply, CPI is price index for inflation, LR is bank lending rate, and TBR is Treasury yields. DUMGFC is for dummy variable for financial crisis years in 2007-2009; DUMRegime is dummy for monetary regimes. In the stock price equation, IPI is industrial production index a proxy for earnings of firms; LR is lending rate; LSPRICE is stock index returns. Bootstrapping by iterations of the results in Table 6, produces more accurate parameter estimations, so it is an excellent robustness test for this study.

index return is significantly affected by money. In the equation, stock index return is theorized as having an effect from liquidity arising from money supply. In the DOLS results, the sign was wrong but in the bootstrapped results it is positive. All other key variables, are significant in the bootstrapped results compared to the results from DOLS. Overall, we have much improved findings from bootstrapping.

Conclusion

This paper is about the impact of money supply on liquidity and in turn its impact on stock index returns. The findings contribute to the literature by examining the hitherto unverified effect of money supply on liquidity. Importantly, we adopt all the required refinements to obtain robust parameter estimates and for the purpose use a three-equation system developed in this study. Accordingly, the evidence sheds new light on the money supply and stock index returns literature.

We use quarterly series of panel data for Canada, US, UK and Japan for the period 1960:1 to 2013:4 and by adding an asset pricing equation to Friedman [4] propositions, we test for a liquidity–credit surge effect on stock index returns. Further, by using controls for monetary regime changes and the effect of GFC by specifying dummy variables, errors in estimations are avoided. The results suggest that money supply is endogenous and that there is bidirectional causality from money to interest rate as confirmed by prior studies.

That there is a liquidity effect helps to confirm Friedman's proposition on money supply effect on banking liquidity. The test on the link between liquidity's flow-through impacts on stock index led to establishing a credible link from banking liquidity and stock index returns. It shows strong influence of money supply and liquidity in the above countries.

The study has limitation in terms of the use of quarterly series since GDP data are only available as quarterly series. In our opinion, a major contribution of this paper is the verification of Friedman's liquidity effect arising from money supply, after controlling for other factor effects: prior tests attempted to do this with daily data without success. A further contribution is the impact of banking liquidity changes measured by bank reserves with the central banks on the stock index returns. Furthermore, the use of Dynamic Ordinary Least Squares modelling for four key economies with broadly similar financial environments adds a unique dimension. The robustness of the reported findings is cross-checked using bootstrapping.

References

1. King BF (1966) Market and Industry Factors in Stock Price Behaviour. Journal of Business 39: 139-190.
2. Musilek P (1997) Changes in macroeconomic variables and stock prices. Finance and Credit 47: 3.
3. Flannery MJ, Protopapadakis A (2002) Macroeconomic Factors do Influence Aggregate Stock Returns. Review of Financial Studies 15: 751-782.
4. Friedman M (1969) Factors Affecting the Level of Interest Rates. In Proceeding of the 1968 Conference on Saving and Residential Financing. Chicago: United States Saving and Loan League 11-27.
5. Hamilton JD (1997) Measuring the Liquidity Effect. American Economic Review 87: 80-97.
6. Pagan AR, Robertson JC (1995) Resolving the Liquidity Effect. Federal Reserve Bank of St. Louis Review 77: 33-54.
7. Goodfriend M (1997) A Framework for the Analysis of Moderate Inflations. Journal of Monetary Economics 39: 45-65.
8. Gordon DB, Leeper EM (2002) The Price Level, the Quantity Theory of Money, and the Fiscal Theory of the Price Level. NBER Working Paper, National Bureau of Economic Research.
9. Edmond C, Weill PO (2005) Models of the Liquidity Effect. The New Palgrave Dictionary of Economics, Palgrave Macmillan.
10. Thornton DL (2007) Open Market Operations and the Federal Funds Rate. In Open Market Operations and the Financial Markets, the Bank of Finland. Reprinted in the Federal Reserve Bank of St. Louis Review 89: 549-572.
11. Strongin S (1995) The Identification of Monetary Policy Disturbances: Explaining the Liquidity Puzzle. Journal of Monetary Economics 35: 463-497.
12. Thornton DL (2001) The Federal Reserve's Operating Procedure, Non-borrowed Reserves, Borrowed Reserves and the Liquidity E□ect. Journal of Banking and Finance 25: 1717-1739.
13. Christiano LJ, Eichenbaum M, Evans CL (1996) The Effects of Monetary Policy Shocks: Evidence from the Flow of Funds. Review of Economics and Statistics 78: 16-34.
14. Sprinkel BW (1964) Money and Stock Prices. New York: Richard D. Irwin, Homewood, Ill.
15. Badarudin E, Ariff M, Khalid A (2013) Post Keynesian money endogeneity evidence in G-7 economies. Journal of International Money & Finance 33: 146-162.
16. Ariff M, Farrar J, Khalid AM (2012) Regulatory Failure and Global Financial Crisis. Chelthenham; Northmpton: Edward Elgar Publishing Ltd. UK and USA.
17. Carpenter S, Demiralp S (2006) The Liquidity Effect in the Federal Funds Market: Evidence from Daily Open Market Operations. Journal of Money, Credit, and Banking 38: 901-920.
18. Sharpe WF (1964) Capital Asset Prices: A Theory of Market Equilibrium under Conditions of Risk. Journal of Finance 19: 425-442.
19. Lintner J (1965) The Evaluation of Risky Assets and the Selection of Risky Investments in Stock Portfolios and Capital Budgets. Review of Economics and Statistics 47: 13-37.
20. Mossin J (1966) Equilibrium in Capital Asset Markets. Econometrica 34: 768-783.
21. Markowitz H (1952) Portfolio Selection. Journal of Finance 7: 77-91.
22. Roll R, Ross S (1980) An Empirical Investigation of the Arbitrage Pricing Theory. Journal of Finance 35: 1073-1103.
23. Cooper RVL (1974) Efficient Capital Markets and the Quantity Theory of Money. Journal of Finance 30: 338-341.
24. Hardouvelis GA (1987) Macroeconomic Information and Stock Prices. Journal of Economics and Business 39: 131-140.
25. Keim DB (1985) Dividend Yields and Stock Returns: Implications of Abnormal January Returns. Journal of Financial Economics 14: 473-489.
26. Litzenberger RH, Ramaswamy K (1982) The Effects of Dividends on Common Stock Prices: Tax Effects or Information Effects? Journal of Finance 37: 429-443.
27. Granger CWJ (1988) Some Recent Development in a Concept of Causality. Journal of Econometrics 39: 199-211.
28. Johansen S, Juselius K (1990) The Full Information Maximum Likelihood Procedure for Inference on Cointegration With Applications To The Demand For Money. Oxford Bulletin of Economics and Statistics 52: 169-210.
29. Pesaran MH, Pesaran B (1997) Working with Microfit 4.0: An interactive econometric software package (DOS and Windows versions). Oxford: Oxford University Press.
30. Stock JH, Watson M (1993) A simple estimator of cointegrating vectors in higher Order integrated systems. Econometrica 61: 783-820.
31. Newey WK, West KD (1987) A simple, positive semidefinite, heteroskedasticity and autocorrelation consistent covariance matrix. Econometrica 55: 703-708.
32. Leeper EM, Gordon DB (1992) In Search of the Liquidity Effect. Journal of Monetary Economics 29: 341-369.
33. Brunner K (1961) Some Major Problems in Monetary Theory. American Economic Review 51: 47-56.
34. Cagan P, Gandolfi A (1969) The Lag in Monetary Policy as Implied by the Time

Pattern of Monetary Effects on Interest Rates. American Economic Review 59: 277-284.

35. Chen NF, Roll R, Ross SA (1986) Economic Forces and the Stock Market. Journal of Business 59: 383-403.
36. Christiano LJ, Eichenbaum M (1992a) Liquidity Effects and the Monetary Transmission Mechanism. The American Economic Review 89: 346-53.
37. Christiano LJ, Eichenbaum M (1992) Liquidity Effects, Monetary Policy and the Business Cycle. National Bureau of Economic Research.
38. Dhakal D, Kandil M, Sharma SC (1993) Causality between the Money Supply and Share Prices: a VAR Investigation. Quarterly Journal of Business and Economics 32: 52-74.
39. Duca JV (1995) Should Bond Funds be added to M2?. Journal of Banking and Finance 19: 131-152.
40. Effa B (2011) Endogeneous Money Supply and Bank Stock Returns: Empirical evidence Using Panel Data. Applied Financial Economics 25: 345-356.
41. Engle RF, Granger CWJ (1987) Cointegration and Error Correction: Representation. Estimation and Testing. Econometrica 55: 251-276.
42. Fama EF, French KR (1993) Common Risk Factors in the Returns on Stocks and Bonds. Journal of Financial Economics 33: 3-56.
43. Friedman M (1961) The Lag in Effect of Monetary Policy. Journal of Political Economy 100: 447-466.
44. Friedman M, Schwartz AJ (1963) Money and Business Cycles. Review of Economics and Statistics 40: 52-64.
45. Gibson WE (1970a) The Lag in the Effect of Monetary Policy on Income and Interest Rates. Quarterly Journal of Economics 84: 288-300.
46. Gibson WE (1970b) Interest Rates and Monetary Policy. Journal of Political Economy 78: 431-55.
47. Granger CWJ (1969) Investigating Causal Relationship by Econometric Models and Cross Section Special Methods. Econometrica 37: 425-435.
48. Moore BJ (1988) Horizontalists and Verticalists: The Macroeconomics of Credit Money. Cambridge: Cambridge University Press.
49. Kraft J, Kraft A (1977) Common Stock Prices: Some Observations. Southern Economic Journal. 43: 1365-1368.
50. Kraft J, Kraft A (1977) Determinants of Common Stock Prices in Time Series Analysis. Journal of Finance 32: 417-425.
51. Moore BJ (1989) The Endogeneity of Credit Money. Review of Political Economy 1: 64-93.
52. Moore BJ (1988) Horizontalists and Verticalists: The Macroeconomics of Credit-Money. Cambridge: Cambridge University Press.
53. Parhizgari AM, Duong N (2011) M1, M2 and the US Equity Exchanges. Frontiers in Finance and Economics 8: 112-135.
54. Pesando JE (1974) The Supply of Money and Common stock Prices: Further Observations on the Econometric Evidence. Journal of Finance 29: 909-922.
55. Rochon LP (2006) Endogenous Money, Central Banks and the Banking System: Basil Moore and the Supply of Credit. Complexity, Endogenous Money and Macroeconomic Theory, UK.
56. Ross SA (1976) The Arbitrage Theory of Capital Asset Pricing. Journal of Economic Theory 13: 341-360.
57. Rozeff MS (1974) Money Stock Prices: Market Efficiency and the Lag in Effect of Monetary Policy. Unpublished doctoral dissertation. Graduate School of Management, University of Rochester.
58. Toda HY, Yamamoto T (1995) Statistical inference in vector autoregressions with possibly integrated processes. Journal of Econometrics 66: 225-250

15

The Impact of Competitive Devaluation on the Foreign Trade of Turkey

Parisa Fathi* and Mustafa Ersungur S

International Economy, IIBF Economics DepartmentAtaturk University, Erzurum,Turkey

Abstract

Exchange rate system, although it is an important factor in determining the real value of the currency of a country, economy, inflation, devaluation, interest rates vs. foreign trade, such as the affect in many ways. In the study, competitive devaluations and trade relationship is investigating in Turkey. The relationship between foreign trade and competitive devaluations, cumulative method ARDL approach to study is to investigate where there is a long-term relationship between the variables and factors related to long-term model and error correction is estimated between 1965-2014 periods for TB. The results indicate that positive and significant correlation between TB and RER and also between TB and GDP there is, and significant and negative correlation between TB and P, as well as between TB and G there is. Long-term variable coefficient equals 0.80.

Keywords: Devaluation; Foreign trade; ARDL

Introduction

In this study, we determine the impact of competitive devaluations in Turkey's foreign trade with econometric analysis. Competitive devaluation is usually a mover to close the current account deficit of a fiscal policy. While devaluation, decreases the export prices of currency and increases the price of imported goods of national currency. The purpose of devaluations on one hand by encouraging exports is to increase foreign exchange earnings and on the other by reducing domestic demand for imported goods is to save foreign exchange. To make a good result of devaluations in improving the current account balance, it depends on the Marshall-Lerner condition, $e_m + e_x \geq 1$. This situation by assuming an infinite traction of supply, means that the total domestic demand for imported goods(e_m) and foreign demand for exports(e_x) is greater than one. The bigger the total traction than one, the larger the impact of exchange rate adjustment in the external balance will be. The success of devaluations to keep domestic prices depends on no changing in the price of domestic goods in foreign countries as well as consumer habits. However, if the trade deficit depends on structural factors such as low productivity in the national economy, the lack of production and technology and lag of management, the success of the devaluation of national currency in foreign balance will be limited [1]. After the devaluation of the domestic currency, being the total value of traction less than one in the short term, lead the effect of J curve to be one. According to this approach, immediately after the devaluations, first the balance of foreign trade distorted more and the improvement occurs with a certain delay. In the context of summarized theoretical explanations above, it is believed that changes in the variable exchange rate affect the trade balance.

Theoretical Foundations

For the first time Maggie interpreted this phenomenon based on Marshall-Lerner condition Because of the weakening national currency, the real value of import and export volume does not change, but imports more expensive than before, and thus the trade balance worsens the situation. Because by weakening the national currency, the real value of import and export volume does not change, but imports get more expensive than before thus the trade balance situation get worse. Over time, both the suppliers and consumers reacted to the weakening of the national currency and import and export values based on the relative price of domestic goods began to modulate and the trade balance situation improve. In other words, weakening the national currency with intervals affect the trade balance. The Chart of reaction trade balance delay to weaken the national currency, which resembles the letter J, called J-curve effect."

National currency devaluation has two quantity and value effects. The effects of devaluation, represents the exports increasing and imports decreasing. And the impact of its value represents an increasing in import costs according to the domestic currency. In practice it is found that the effect of value which causes deterioration in the trade balance may occur before the quantity effects which improve the trade balance. As mentioned above, this situation is known as the J-curve effect. Because in this case, the trade surplus curve will be drawn as J-curve.

Literature Review

Rezaei Abyaneh Bahareh [2], studied on the asymmetric effects of exchange rate fluctuations on export prices in Iran. And reached the conclusion that export prices reaction is asymmetric to increase and decrease the value of money. So the reaction of export prices according to the negative shock of exchange rate (devaluation) is more than positive shocks (increasing the value of money).

Kazerouni Ali and Mojiri Hadi [3] studied the effect of National currency devaluation on Iran's trade balance with six selected business partner. According to the experimental results between Iran, China and the United Arab Emirates in the short term, the effect of J curve has been confirmed, while it doesn't apply in the other countries (France, Germany, South Korea and Switzerland). In addition to that, J Curve only has been confirmed between Iran and the Emirates in the longer term and rejected in order to the other studied countries.

In this study Carmen and Reinhat [4] has examined the relationship between currency devaluation, relative prices and international trade.

***Corresponding author:** Parisa Fathi, International Economy, IIBF Economics Department Ataturk University, Erzurum, Turkey
E-mail: parisafathi78@yahoo.com

According to the obtained results, relative prices play an important role in determining trade flows, but sometimes there is no systematic relationship between trade balance and relative prices.

Mahesh Kumar and Chaulagai [5] has tested j-curve hypothesis for Nepal and concluded that devaluation is ineffective in correcting the lack of business in Nepal.

Tirsit Genye [6] has studied the impact of devaluation on Ethiopia's economic growth. And according to these studies it is conducted that devaluation has a negative effect on gross domestic product (GDP) of Ethiopia.

Data and Empirical Findings

Reveals the laws of economics as digital and a variety of economic issues to be examined numerically, the econometric methods are needed to assist in obtaining the correct economic decision. In the study, to establish a close relationship between theory and practice is applied econometric analysis. The results achieved by the results of the econometric analysis of the results achieved in other studies in the literature to assess whether it is in the same direction. In the study, to examine the impact of competitive devaluations in Turkey's foreign trade, it covers the years 1965-2014 data for the period between [7]. Data were taken from the World Bank and the model is as follows:

$$\ln TB_t=\beta_0 + \beta_1 \ln GDP_t + \beta_2 RER_t + \beta_3 \ln G + \beta_4 P + u_t$$

Variables used are as follows:

LNTB: was defined as the logarithm of the ratio between exports of goods (X) to imports of goods (M).

RER: the official exchange rate (official market) US dollar at the beginning of the domestic currency (ER), the US wholesale price index (WPIUS) and i in the country's consumer price index (CPI).

LN GDP_t: was defined as logarithm of the national output,

P: was defined as the inflation.

LNG: was defined as logarithm of the government expenses.

In order to evaluate the reliability of variables Dickey Fuller test is used (Table 1).

Dynamic model

Our model for dynamic pattern is as follows:

$$LTB = \alpha + \sum_{j=1}^{q} \mu_j LGDP_{t-j} + \sum_{j=0}^{p_1} \beta_{1i} LG_{t-j} + \sum_{j=0}^{p_2} \beta_{2j} RER_{t-j} + \sum_{j=0}^{p_3} \beta_{3j} P_{t-j} + T + V_t$$

Dynamic model is based on the results (Table 2), while RER and GDP positive and significant, G is negative and significant. So the reduction of the nominal value of the Turkish currency increased exports and reduced imports to Turkey, this also increase the trade balance is Turkey. Turkey's GDP increased that is an increase in both export and import, since the increase in exports greater than imports increase the country's trade balance [8]. Fiscal policy that is more in the form of increased government spending, investment and private consumption increased, leading to an increase in aggregate demand and this increased demand for imports and the trade balance will worsen (Table 2).

Convergence test

Dynamic model, to understand the long-term convergence is considered T-statistical model.

According to Schwarz Byzn criteria for being considered the optimum number of delays, the dependent variable (TB) is a pause, so we have:

$$t = \frac{\sum_{j=1}^{q} \lambda_j - 1}{\sum_{j=1}^{q} S_{\hat{\lambda} j}} = \frac{.53013\text{-}1}{.18391} = \text{-}2.56$$

Where t is calculated absolute values from the absolute value provided by benerje (Associated with the process, the 90% confidence level, are for 2.042) is large. H0 hypothesis is rejected, and the results show that the 90% confidence levels between the variables of the model are thought to be stable long-term relationship [9].

Estimates of long-term relationships

Table 3, shows ARDL provide a long-term model with coefficient calculated. According to the obtained results, RER variable factors, has a positive and significant effect on the balance of payments. Assuming all other variables remain constant, if RER one percent increase, TB, 0.10601 percent increase. Just the same, the GDP variable, on TB, there is a significant and positive effect, if a percent of GDP is increase, 0.40142 percent increase in TB. G variable factors, has a negative and significant impact on the balance of payments. So if G one percent increase, TB, 0.51402 per cent decrease because when government spending increases and this will lead to an increase in aggregate demand and this increased demand for imports and the trade balance will worsen. Inflation (P) in the long term significant negative impact on trade balance (TB) Because when a country's domestic prices rise this increase imports and decrease exports, the trade balance is reduced as a result [10].

Estimation of error correction model (ECM)

Error correction model, the relationship between the dependent variable and independent variables represent in the short term. ECM (-1) factor estimate for the model, -0.80 were obtained and show that each year 80 percent of short-term ımbalance TB close to the long-term stability [11].

Tests: The estimated model, to investigate abuses and violations of

Variables	GDP	RER	G	P	TB
	1. difference	1. difference	1. difference	1. difference	1. difference
Test statistics	-3.753	-4.392	-2.217	-7.915	-7.057
Critical values					
1% level	-4.262	-4.356	-2.636	-3.646	-3.653
5% level	-3.552	-3.595	-1.951	-2.954	-2.951
10% level	-3.209	-3.233	-1.610	-2.615	-2.617

Regression analysis results of all data according to the level of significance of 5% is statistically significant.

Table 1: Unit root test.

Variable name	Factor	T-statistics
LTB (-1)	0.53013	2.8826 (0.008)
LTB (-2)	-0.32962	-2.5686 (0.017)
LG	-0.65572	-3.9296 (0.001)
LG (-1)	0.59085	3.7892 (0.001)
LG (-2)	-0.34608	-3.3516 (0.003)
LGDP	0.32093	2.4428 (0.023)
P	-0.0012543	-1.9652 (0.062)
RER	0.84758	2.5371 (0.018)
C	0.68968	1.8696 (0.674)
T	-0.011980	-2.3989 (0.025)
R^2=0.72		

Table 2: The results dynamic pattern model.

Variable name	Factor	T-istatistik
LG	-0.51402	-2.9224 (0.008)
LGDP	0.40142	2.2727 (0.033)
P	-0.00157	-2.1382 (0.043)
RER	0.10601	2.4596 (0.022)
C	0.86264	2.0066 (0.057)
T	-0.01498	-2.5077 (0.020)

Table 3: Results of a long-term review model.

non-classical assumption is need for the implementation of some of the tests in this study and the results are brought to the Table 4.

According to the obtained results at the level of 10%, no serial autocorrelation and variance heterogeneity deficiency hypothesis is not detectable. As a result, the model is valid classical assumptions.

Stability testing of the coefficient: CUSUM and CUSUMQ tests: If the cumulative residual and cumulative residual square diagrams are between two straight lines (95% confidence interval) are, the null hypothesis that there is no structural breaks will be accepted and if figures are from outside the confidence interval, presence of structural breaks will be accepted [12].

According to Figure 1, the coefficients of both models has been stable over the period examined.

Results

In this paper, the impact of competitive devaluation on the trade

Test statistic	Lagrange coefficients	Prob.	F statistic	Prob.
Autocorrelation test	0.64244	0.725	0.20847	0.813
Heterogeneity of variance test	3.5934	0.1661	1.2831	0.298

Table 4: Test classic assumptions in the model search.

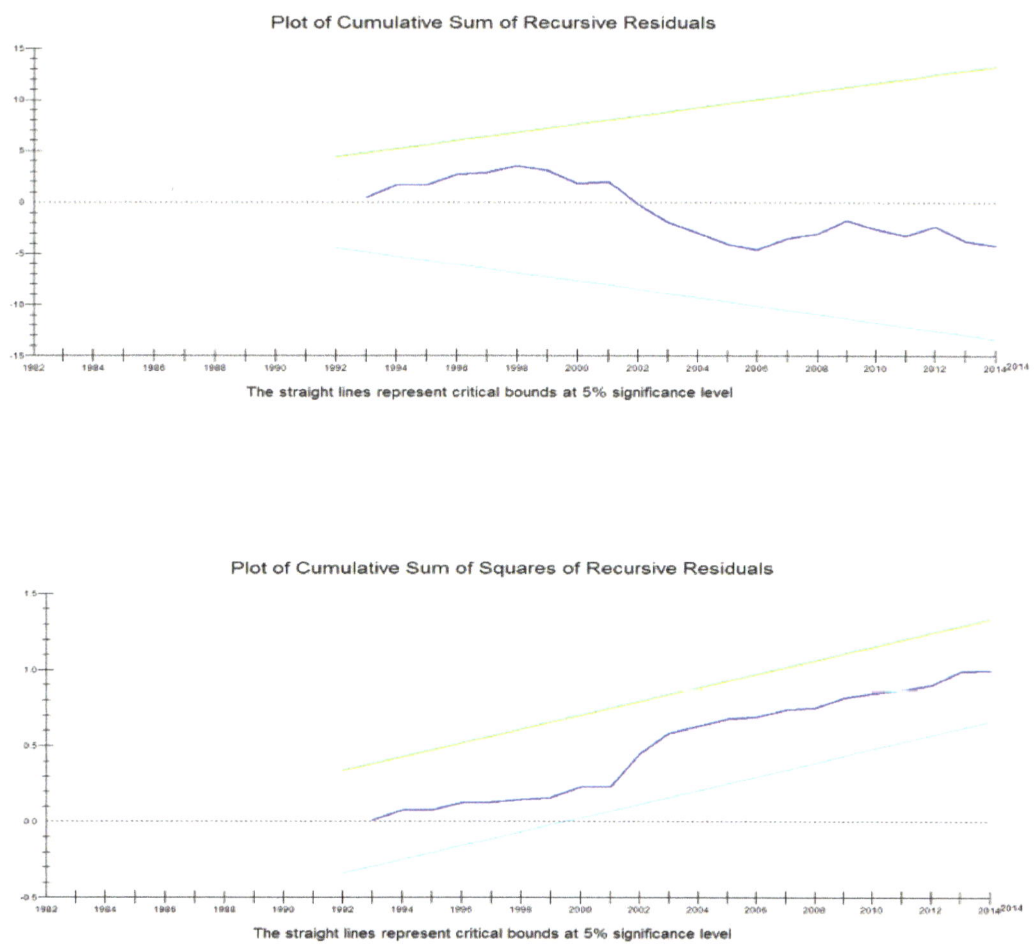

Figure 1: Chi-cumulative and cumulative residual waste Charts.

balance of Turkey, using co-integration ARDL approach for the long-term relationship between variables is used and factor related to long-term models and error correction on the trade balance for the period 1965-2014 have been estimated. The estimated model is considered five variables: 1-Logarithm of the trade balance 2-Real exchange rate 3-Inflation 4-Logarithm of GDP 5-Logarithm of government spending. The results of long-term relationships indicates that log of governments expenditure, log of GDP, inflation and real exchange rate are factors affecting the logarithm of Turkey's trade balance. As government spending leads to an increase in aggregate demand and increase aggregate demand is also increasing import demand, and increase in import demand led to a deterioration of the trade balance of country [13]. On the other hand there is inflation reduces the effect of devaluation on the trade balance, because inflation is an increase in export prices and this led to a decline in exports and increased imports, and the trade deficit will eventually be. As well as an increase in the real exchange rate is an increase in the price of foreign goods, and this will reduce imports and raise exports, and ultimately lead to an increase in the trade balance. Increase in GDP also due to an increase in exports as well as imports, but in Turkey's exports increased more than imports, that the trade balance would be better. Here is the GDP effect on the trade balance is more than the actual exchange rate.

In the short-term analysis of a causal relationship between the model variables from short-term to long-term joint was observed.

References

1. Seyidoglu H (2009) Uluslararas Iktisat, Istanbul: Guzem Can Yayınları 24.
2. Bahareh RA (2011) Asymmetric effects of exchange rate fluctuations on export prices, pp. 14-20.
3. Ali K, Hadi M (2011) The effect of devaluation on the trade balance of trade with six selected partner (Auto Regressive Distributed Lag), Iran Journal of Economic Research Winter 13: 77-102.
4. Reinhat CM (1995) Devaluation, Relative Prices, and International Trade: Evidence from Developing Countries. MPRA Paper No. 6974.
5. Chaulagai MK (2015) Testing the J-Curve Hypothesis:A Case of Nepal. NRB economic review 17-36.
6. Genye T (2011) Currency Devaluation and Economic Growth, The case of Ethiopia, Stockholm University.
7. Bahmani-Oskooee M, Alse J (1994) Short-run versus longrun effects of devaluation: error correction modeling and cointegration. Eastern Economic Journal 20: 453-464.
8. Bahmani-Oskooee M, Kandil M (2009) Are Devaluations Contractionary in MENA countries? Applied Economics 41: 39-150.
9. Barson WH (1983) Economic Structure and Policy for External Balance. IMF Staff Papers.
10. Diaz-Alejando CF (1963) A Note on the Impact of Devaluation and Redistribution and the Redistributive Effect. Journal of Political Economy 71: 577-580.
11. Krugman P (1999) Balance sheets, the transfer problem, and financial crises. IT.
12. Anne DK (1983) Exchange Rate Determination, Cambridge University Press.
13. Dominic S (1987) International Economics, Macmillan.

Role and Impact of Reward and Accountability on Training Transfer

Ahmed U[1]*, Abdul Majid AH[1], Mohd Zin ML[1], Phulpoto W[2] and Umrani WA[3]

[1]School of Business Management, University Utara Malaysia, Malaysia
[2]SZABIST, Karachi, Pakistan
[3]Sukkur Institute of Business Administration Sindh, Pakistan

Abstract

Drawing upon the element of training transfer, this present study investigates whether the reward and accountability act as influencing components for transfer of training. Questionnaire technique of the quantitative research approach was used for the primary data collection from the participants with different managerial positions from the various organizations coming to attend the training programs at National Institute of Labor Administration and Training (NILAT) Karachi, Pakistan. A total of 200 questionnaires were distributed in the numerous training programs at NILAT through using simple random sampling out of which, 128 were returned and 11 were further discarded. The final analysis of 117 respondents revealed a significant relationship between accountability and training transfer whereas the findings outline an insignificant relationship between reward and training transfer. The research indicates that accountability can significantly enhance the transfer of training whereas reward has proved to be insignificant in terms of training transfer, which is contrary to the previous research findings. Discussion to findings is provided along with particularized implications for management.

Keywords: Impact; Reward; Accountability; Training; Transfer

Introduction

Human resource management as a business function plays an imperative role in helping business to responsively manage the work force. Core responsibilities that come under human resource department include recruitment, training, compensation and performance management [1].

As mentioned by Burke [2] and Hutchins that organizations have found it decisively important to invest in people through training to provide them skills that would make the organization successful. Rothwell et al. [3] highlights training to be the most significant HR role as it helps an organization in equipping its employees with skills and capabilities, necessary for the competitive achievement of organizational objectives. The authors further suggest that companies invest millions on training their staff as they have realized that it's one of the major factors that can help businesses to sustain and survive profitably in the 21st century.

Training is referred as a designed activity or set of activities to aid employees` learning of work associated skills, behaviors and attitudes [4]. In simple terms, training is a process that involves information sharing to learn the skills and attitudes necessary to perform a particular task or group of tasks. According to Martin [5] that training is a systematic process that provides opportunity to learn basic and advanced skills and competencies to effectively perform a certain course of action.

Transfer of training can be elucidated as the usage and implementation of newly learned skills and behaviors at the workplace. Notable researchers have studied to outline factors that influence the transfer of acquired knowledge. The study however, by Baldwin et al. [6] is termed to be the most comprehensive and concrete on the topic. The model has outlined three important factors that can substantially influence training transfer and they are trainee characteristics, training design and work environment.

Managers in the work settings have an important role to play in the entire transfer of training process as Clarke [7] has underlined that facilitation and support by the managers encourages training transfer. However there have been studies that propose numerous other factors that influence training transfer such as Saks et al. [8] many employees fail to transfer newly learned skills to the workplace.

As organizations have started realizing that the organizing and conducting training programs are not enough as long as initiatives to ensure the transfer of the learned skills is taken into consideration. Therefore, there has been a serious emphasis of companies to establish systems, procedures and policies that could motivate employees to transfer training [9].

Statement of problem

Edward [10] underscores that accountability works as a driving force for encouraging training transfer and promoting positive change in a work setting. Saks et al. [8] also outlined that accountability boost responsibility and hence increase the transfer of learning to the workplace. Yet research on the impact of accountability on training transfer is very limited [11].

According to Yamnill et al. [12] that rewards can be intrinsic as well as extrinsic and employees satisfactorily transfer learned skills at the workplace when they are adequately rewarded. According to American Society for Training and Development (ASTD) that US companies alone spend $125 billion dollars on training and development initiatives [13]. The report also states that there are further investments made to push employees to transfer skills at the workplace. To what extent rewards effectively support and facilitate training transfer in the context of Pakistan has not been studied yet as per our knowledge. More importantly, which of these organizational factors plays a more important role in training transfer is also not clear.

***Corresponding author:** Umair Ahmed, School of Business Management, University Utara Malaysia, Malaysia, E-mail: umairahm@gmail.com

This paper therefore aims to outline as to how accountability and reward influence training transfer. The study aims to outline as to what extent accountability and rewards will impact on training transfer and to what extent the findings will be in parallel to the research studies conducted in the other geographical locations and work settings.

Literature Review

Transfer of learning

Blume et al. [14] have argued that the transfer of learning is an ever stretched issue in the area of psychology and education. The argument concerning to transfer of training started receiving attention around 100 years ago and the focus has remained on nature, context and prevalence [15]. The issue of learning transfer is critical as it outlines the failure of individuals towards improving their behavior and performance on the job which means that training is unlikely to affect the organizational performance [16].

Saks et al. [8] have also discussed similar problem in a survey that sampled training professionals from 150 organizations. The results of the survey indicated that nearly 34% of the employees failed to transfer the training immediately to the workplace. However, 62% become successful in transferring learning immediately on the job and 44% manage to do so after six months.

In response to this problem, numerous researchers have studied and explored strategies that could facilitate training transfer. However, most of the research studies have focused on individual and situational factors that influence training transfer following a particular training program [14]. Majority of the research projects conducted on transfer of training revolves around individual level of analysis through focusing on any particular training program. However, transfer of training is related and thus can also be examined from organizational perspective to explore what and how organizations can facilitate responsive transfer of training. As Baldwin et al. [6] has underlined that difference in the organizational climate (for instance support) varies the extent of transfer of training material on the job which is why, Ford et al. [17] have highlighted and recommended the need for transfer research to pin point organizational perspective and its potential influence on training transfer and accountability and reward are one of the key organizational components.

This research is therefore focusing on the organizational characteristics such as accountability and rewards to explore their impact on training transfer.

This is the reason why the transfer training theorists have started coining the term 'transfer system'. According to Holton [18] factors influencing transfer system includes person, training program and the organization. Rouiller et al. [19] explored the relationship between organizational transfer climate and transfer of training through the measure with situations and scenarios that could support or facilitate in the process of transfer of training at the workplace. With a sample of Assistant Managers from a growing fast food organization, they found that organizational transfer climate plays a significant role in the promoting transfer behavior across 102 units. It's one of the few empirical studies conducted to explore the imparity of positive organizational transfer climate for training transfer from a training program to a workplace.

Evaluation of the transfer features and issues critically require sound understanding of what is meant by transfer through establishing command over the factors that affect training transfer [6]. The model presented by them outlines three major factors (Figure 1).

Mental ability is considered to be one of the significant factors with regards to learner`s characteristics. As Burke [2] has underlined that previous researches provide evidence suggesting that trainees/learners with higher mental ability are capable of transferring the acquired knowledge more responsively compared to others.

Mathieu et al. [20] have established motivation as the key element in pre, during and post training activities as it keeps the learner persistent and boosts passion for practically performing those activities. These results are in parallel with the findings of Noe [21] that highlights that motivation for learning always facilitates trainees to apply knowledge in the practical world setting. Motivation however can be intrinsic and extrinsic. As Rouiller et al. [19] found that both components are critical for transfer of acquired knowledge to the workplace. Training is training content design and its deliver which includes TNA-Training need assessment, training content design, methods applied for delivery also influences the transfer [2]. Key motivation to attend any training program develops when a training program is designed to fill gap between the actual skills and job required or desired skills [22].

According to Taylor [23] that behavior modeling facilitated training transfer when combined with rewards and sanctions by the organization. Work environment also makes critical contribution in training transfer. Salas et al. [9] have also underlined that realistic practice situations and schemes help trainees to actively transfer learning and new skills.

Work environment has an important role to play in the training transfer. Rouiller et al. [19] suggest that transfer climate consists of elements in work settings that hold back or encourage the use of new skills. the authors also suggest that work settings consists of situational cues which means peer support, manager goals and targets, equipment availability, opportunity to practice etc and consequences comprises of punishment, feedback (+ ve and – ve) on the applied new skills and knowledge [9,12]. According to Clarke [7] that supervisors and peers individually play a healthy role in contributing towards training transfer. Hawley et al. [24], found that networking with peers and exchange of ideas concerning the training content helped trainees in boosting transfer within 6 months after training. Holton et al. [25] investigated upon supervisor support, peer support, training validity and found that organizational transfer climate plays a critical role in this regard. Clarke [7] also mentions that for successful training transfer, trainees require appropriate tools, equipment and opportunity to apply learned skills at the workplace.

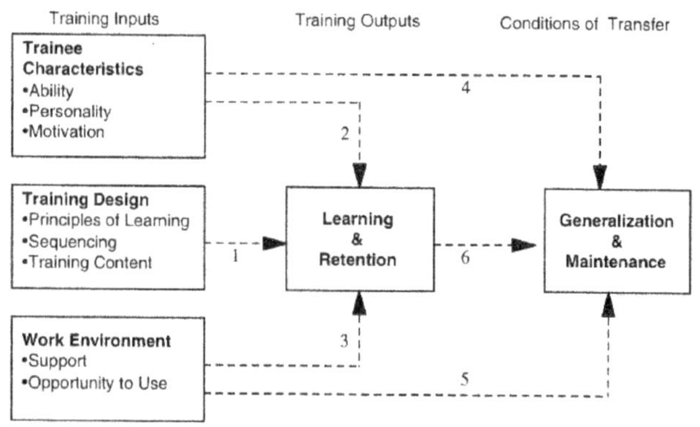

Figure 1: Adapted from, BaldwinTT, FordJK, Personnel Psychoogy 41.

Since the focus of this study is on the impact of accountability and reward on training transfer, the discussion and review of the other influencing components has been kept limited.

Accountability and training transfer

Accountability in the research studies related to training define it as the degree to which the organization, environment and its top management assumes the trainee to learn and use the learned knowledge and skills on to the job with responsibility for doing so [26].

Edward [10] found that senior management in an organization can achieve transfer of training also through increasing employee accountability. The research also found that employee accountability is the driving tool for enhancing training transfer and performance change at the workplace. Research by Saks et al. [8] in which they study found that accountability mechanisms for training proved as a significant predictor of training transfer. Also the research by Tannenbaum [20] as cited by Saks et al. [8] mentioned that making trainees to prepare a post training report or taking them for an assessment makes them fee accountable for their learning which apparently pushes them to transfer.

However, studies on the impact of accountability on training transfer are very scarce [11]. The authors argue that major models on the training transfer have notably missed to focus on accountability. Transfer models by Baldwin et al. [6] or even the ulti level integrated training transfer model by Machin [27] which mentions numerous individual and organizational level variables but does not include accountability. Therefore, the role and impact of accountability on training transfer remains a bit ignored.

Dr. Coates, CEO of Performance Support Systems writes in his review on Enhance the Transfer of Training that researches have outlined that a very low number of training participants actually change their behavior after receiving training, resulting in 70-90% of investment wastage. The review further mentions that transfer of training is a serious concern of businesses these days therefore he suggests businesses to insist upon training transfer through accountability. The employees should be made accountable for the change in their behavior and work once trained and future training decisions should also be based on the ROI- return on the previous training investments through improved performance they provide [28].

Hutchins [29] conducted a research study of the training transfer practices where training professionals of an ASTD center (name not mentioned) were sampled; distributed 413 surveys questionnaires and received 172 back. The research specifically contained items related to accountability to explore its potential effect on training transfer. The research outlined that majority of training professionals outlined that the training practices that were followed by accountability measures at the work place enhanced training transfer. The research also concluded that post training results are best achieved when the top management highlights the training transfer concerns and holds the middle and operational level management accountable to ensure the trainees apply newly learned knowledge and skills at the workplace. The research also underlines a significant impact of performance appraisal followed by rewards and recognition as a motivating organizational factor for the transfer of training.

So the relive of the literature outline that accountability is one of the important organizational variables that can potentially play a predictive role towards training transfer but has not been empirically researched to a greater extent.

Reward and training transfer

Armstrong [30] suggests that, reward is recognition of the contribution of people towards an organization by financial and non-financial means. In the business perspective it can also be viewed as a valuable entity given to an employee in the return of his/her service, efforts and organizational achievements. Yamnill et al. [12] mention that rewards are intrinsic as well we extrinsic and employees satisfactorily transfer learned skills at the workplace when they are adequately rewarded.

Holton et al. [18] conducted a research to explore the effect and significance of 16 different factors that possess potential to influence the training transfer at the workplace through sampling 328 respondents from 6 companies and received 106 questionnaires back and the research found rewards to be a significant predictor of training transfer. The research also found that when employees are rewarded (financially or non-financially) for their enhanced performance after training, the workers feel that the organization recognizes their efforts and values their performance. Noe et al. [21] in their article explained that if an individual expects that he/she will gain equity in pay or through other rewards by attending a particular training then there are greater chances of the occurrence of learning and transfer on the job. Employee training transfer can be supported by organizations and supervisors through recognition, encouragement and rewards [31].

Ryan [32] of Madison performance group suggests that the recent corporate trends in the business sectors have strongly suggested that training alone is not enough. Businesses have learned that an integrated formula of relevant objectives, rewards and incentives offerings motivate employees to use new skills learned. So aligning desired behaviors with the incentives is critical for training transfer. The review also outlines that managers can conveniently communicate goals and aligns performance through using a reward system. However, Xiao [33] conducted a research on training of female workers in four electronic manufacturing companies where the research found that verbal recognition and praise in addition to tangible reward also motivate training transfer. The research also explored that management ideology and practices are also critical for the maximization of training outcomes.

Summary of these entire studies highlight a certain relationship between accountability, rewards and training transfer. However, this present paper analyzes as to what extent the previous study results are consistent with regards to the targeted sample of this study.

Methodology, Population and Sampling Procedure

Simple random sampling technique was used to select individuals with an equal opportunity to participate in the research. A total of 200 questionnaires were distributed during various trainings programs (from January to April, 2014) at NILAT out of which 128 responded. A total of 11 questionnaires turned out to be inappropriately filled; making a total of 117 questionnaires worthwhile for further analysis.

NILAT is a public sector training body that offers training programs concerning to human resource, labor laws, health and various soft skill areas. The participants belong to different managerial positions from public and private sector organizations that were selected as respondents for this study.

Survey technique of the quantitative research approach was used in the primary data collection. Questionnaires were distributed amongst the participants coming from various organizations to attend training programs at the National Institute of Labor Administration and Training (NILAT), Karachi Pakistan.

Measurement (Rephrase accountability first and reward)

Training transfer was measured through items from Holton [34]. Impact of accountability on training transfer was measured through items adopted from an investigation of training activities and transfer of training in organizations by Saks et al. [8]. The impact of rewards on training transfer was measured through items adopted from learning and transfer system inventory by Holton et al. [25,34].

The items were measured by 5 Likert scales with 1 referring to strongly disagree to 5 denoting as strongly agree. Basic demographic information was also collected from the participants that included gender, age, total years of work experience and length of service in the current organization.

Findings

Out of 117 respondents, 100 (85.5%) were male and 17 (14.5%) were female. In terms of the age range of the participants, 7 (6%) of the respondents were from 18-25; 68 (58.1%) from 26-35; 21 (17.9%) from 36-45; 17 (14.5%) belonged to 46-55 and 4 (3.4%) associated them with the age range of 56 and above.

In connection to the total years of work experience 16 (13.7%) responded to have 0 to 5 years of work experience; 46 (39.3%) had experience of 6-10 years; 17 (14.5%) turned out to be having a total experience between 11-15 years; 13 (11.1%) participants were with years of experience between 16-20 and 25 (21.4%) responded to have experience of 21years and above.

The profile with regards to the length of service in the current organization indicated that 27 (23.1%) of the participants have served between 0-5 years; 49 (41.9%) between 6-10 years; 10 (8.5%) between 11-15 years; 9 (7.7%) between 16-20 and 22 (18.8%) have served for 21 years and above.

From the descriptive analysis, results indicated that accountability has a higher mean (2.799), than the reward (2.576). The mean for training transfer is 3.410. Based on these it seems that the respondents agree to most of the statements on each of these three variables respectively (Table 1).

Correlation

According to Malhotra that the correlation is the most commonly used tool for measuring the strength between the two variables. To assess the relationship, the pearson value must fall within the range from - 1 to + 1. The research has underlined that accountability is positively correlated and statistically significant with training transfer (p= 0.186, sig=0.045) whereas reward is correlated but not statistically significant. (p=0.048, sig=0.609) (Tables 2 and 3).

Results show that value of sig=0.034 which is less than 0.05 and t value is 2.15 therefore the relationship between accountability and transfer of training is significant. This indicates that the accountability is a useful factor for transfer of training in this context.

Variable	N	Mean	Std. Deviation
Training Transfer	117	3.410	.660
Accountability	117	2.799	1.123
Reward	117	2.576	.994

Table 1: Descriptive statistics.

	Training transfer
Training transfer- Pearson correlation	1
Sig. (2-tailed)	
N	117
Accountability- Pearson correlation	.186*
Sig. (2-tailed)	.045
N	117
Reward- Pearson correlation	.048
Sig. (2-tailed)	.609
N	117

*Correlation is significant at the 0.05 level (2 tailed)

Table 2: Correlations.

	t	Sig
(constant)	17.471	.000
Accountability	2.15	0.034
Reward	-.892	.374

Dependent variable: Training transfer.

Table 3: Coefficients.

Results show that value of sig=0.374 which is greater than 0.05 and t value is - .892 therefore there is no significant relationship between reward and transfer of training. This suggests that reward is an ineffective factor compared to accountability.

Discussion and Implications

This study specifically aimed to investigate and identify the strength of relationship between the independent variables i.e., accountability and reward and dependent variable, i.e., training transfer. The overall objective was to explore how much both the factors help in enhancing the training transfer at the workplace. Since training transfer is an issue in organizations as discussed earlier in the studies conducted previously; this study strives to fill the information gap for businesses as to how potential enterprises can responsively encourage training transfer through rewards and accountability.

The research has found a significant relationship between accountability and training transfer and the results are in parallel with the research findings of [10,28,29].

On the flipside, the results clearly outline that there is an insignificant relationship between reward and training transfer which is in contrast with the findings of [12,18,30-32,34].

Moreover, the research also highlights a considerable point from the statistical analysis that there is a significant different in terms of the statistical correlation of accountability with training transfer against versus the statistical correlation of rewards with the training transfer.

The study results delineate critically useful implications concerning to the role of organizational components on training transfer.

The research findings suggest that accountability can play a critically healthy role in facilitating and increasing training transfer. The findings suggest that organizations aiming to attain much out from their training investments need to develop a systematic accountability procedure that could make people to be responsible for applying the newly learned skills and knowledge at the workplace. Top Management can play an imperatively significant role in training transfer by implementing companywide policies and procedures to ensure training transfer happens. This can be done through involving people into discussion forums once they return back from the training program(s) or putting them to submit progress report, mentioning how and to what extent they have successfully managed to apply the newly learned skills and information. Supervisory roles can also play a critical part in this regard through motivating people to transfer and ensure what people have learned during the training program(s) is effectively in exercise at the workplace.

The findings also forward implication for the top management to regard employees from varied levels differently. Since the sample of the research consisted of management professionals and office rank employees, the research concludes accountability to be more important to them for training transfer compared to reward. This shows that responsibility motivates and stimulates officer ranked individuals more for training transfer. It can also be seen that the making people responsible for the transfer of newly learned skills to the workplace is more effective than motivating them to do so through rewards. As Hafiza [35] suggest that reward may or may not contribute towards employee motivation.

Moreover, organizational politics and unfair reward system also make it ineffective as Nohria [36] in the Harvard Business Review Suggest that Rewards do not work effectively when they are dominated by politics and status matters; which may be the case of some of the participants [37-39]. So the management needs to ensure that its reward system is based on fair and objective grounds.

Conclusion

The study empirically tested to examine the relationship of accountability and reward with training transfer. The results found that training transfer can be positively enhanced through accountability. Through making people accountable of applying the newly learned skills to the workplace, transfer of training can be responsively enhanced.

The study also found that that employee rewards can also play their part in encouraging training transfer but not greater as compared to accountability. However, previous research studies have found notable impact of rewards on training transfer. Further research in this area is therefore encouraged as companies allocate billions of dollars for rewarding employees to develop and transfer so that the organizational objectives are competitively achieved. It closing, it is expected that the current research findings will encourage numerous researchers to focus on the impact of accountability on training transfer and would also motivate to further explore and verify the contrary results between reward and training transfer for concrete understanding.

References

1. Dessler G (2012) A Framework for Human Resource Management. (7th edn.) NJ, Prentice Hall.
2. Burke LA (2008) A Study of Best Practices in Training Transfer and Proposed Model of Transfer. Human Resource Development Quarterly 19: 107-128.
3. Rothwell WJ, Kazanas HC (2004) Improving On-the-Job Training. (2nd edn.) CA, John Wiley and Sons.
4. Saks AM, Haccoun RR (2010) Managing Performance through Training and Development. (5th edn.) Ontario, Nelson Education.
5. Martin V (2006) Managing Projects in Human Resource Training and Development. Kogan Page, London and Philadelphia.
6. Baldwin TT, Ford JK (1988) Transfer of Training: A Review and Directions for Future Research. Personnel Psychology 41: 63-105.
7. Clarke N (2002) Job/Work Environment Factors Influencing Training Transfer within a Human Service Agency: Some indicative support for Baldwin and Ford`s Transfer climate Construct. International Journal of Training and Development 6: 146-162.
8. Saks AM, Belcourt M (2006) An Investigation Of Training Activities and Transfer of Training In Organizations. Human Resource Management 45: 629-648.
9. Burke LA, Hutchins HM (2007) Training Transfer: An Integrative Literature Review, Human Resource development Review 6: 263-296.
10. Edwards JS (2013) Factors Affecting Training Transfer in Supervisors and Hourly Employees in a Maufacturing Organization. PhD Thesis, Southern Cross University.
11. Burke LA, Saks AM (2009) Accountability in training transfer: Adapting Schlenker's model of responsibility to a persistent but solvable problem. Human Resource Development Review 8: 382-402.
12. Yamnill S, McLean GN (2001) Theories Supporting Transfer of Training. Human Resource Development Quarterly 12: 195-208.
13. Paradise A (2007) State of the Industry: ASTD Annual Review of Trends in Workplace Learning and Performance. Alexandria, VA, ASTD.
14. Blume BD, Ford JK, Baldwin TT, Huang JL (2010) Transfer of Training: A Meta Analytic Review. Journal of Management 36: 1065-1105.
15. Barnett SM, Ceci SJ (2002) When and Where do we Apply What we Learn? A Taxonomy for Far Transfer. Psychological Bulletin 128: 612-637.
16. Kozlowski SWJ, Gully SM, Brown KG, Salas E (2001) Effects of training goals and goal orientation traits on multidimensional training outcomes and performance adaptability, Organizational Behavior and Human Decision Processes 85: 1-31.
17. Ford JK, Weissbein DA (1997) Transfer of training: An updated review and analysis. Performance Improvement Quarterly 10: 22-41.
18. Holton E (2000) The Learning Transfer System Inventory (LTSI) translated into French: Internal structure and predictive validity. International Journal of Training and Development 11: Blackwell Publishing Limited.
19. Rouiller JZ, Goldstein IL (1993) The Relationship Between Organizational Transfer Climate and Positive Transfer of Training. Human Resources Development Quarterly 4: 377-390.
20. Mathieu JE, Tannenbaum SI, Salas E (1992) Influences of Individual and Situational Characteristics on Measures of Training Effectiveness. Academy of Management Journal 35: 828-847.
21. Noe RA, Schmitt N (1986) The influence of Trainee Attitudes on Training Effectiveness: Test of a Model. Personnel Psychology 39: 497-532.
22. Swanson RA (2003) Transfer is just a symptom: The neglect of end analysis. In: Holton EFIII, Baldwin TT (Eds.), Improving the transfer in organizations. San Francisco: Jossey Bass.
23. Taylor PJ, Russ-Eft DF, Chan DWL (2005) A Meta-Analytic Review of Behavior Modeling Ttraining, Journal of Applied Psychology 90: 692-709.
24. Hawley JD, Barnard JK (2005) Work environment characteristics and implications for training transfer: a case study of the nuclear power industry. Human Resource Development International 8: 65-80.
25. Holton EFIII, Bates RA, Ruona WEA (2000) Development of a Generalized Learning Transfer System Inventory. Human Resource Development Quarterly 11: 333-360.
26. Brinkerhoff RO, Montesino MU (1995) Partnerships for training transfer: Lessons from a corporate study. Human Resource Development Quarterly 6: 263-274.
27. Machin MA (2002) Planning, managing, and optimizing transfer of training. In: Kraiger K (Eds.) Creating, implementing, and managing effective training and development, San Francisco, Jossey-Bass.
28. Coates DE (2010) Enhance the Transfer of Training. Info Line Publications.
29. Hutchins HM (2009) In the Trainer`s Voice: A Study of Training Transfer Practices. Performance Improvement Quarterly, Wiley Inter Science 22: 69-93.
30. Armstrong M (2007) A Handbook of Employee Reward Management and Practice. (2nd edn.) London, Kogan Page Limited.
31. Grossman R, Salas E (2011) The Transfer of Training: What Really Matters. International Journal of Training and Development 15: 103-120.
32. Ryan M (2014) Performance Perspectives: Using Reward and Recognition to Improve the Impact of Training.
33. Xiao J (1996) The Relationship between The Organizational Factors and the

Transfer of Training in the Electronic Industry in Shenzhen, China. Human Resource Development Quarterly 7: 55-73.

34. Salas E, Wilson K, Priest H, Guthrie J (2006) Design, Delivery and Evaluation of Training Systems. In: Salvendy G, Handbook of Human Factors and Ergonomics, (3rd edn.) Hoboken, NJ, John Wiley & Sons.

35. Hafiza NS, Shah SS, Jamsheed H, Zman K (2011) Relationship between Reward and Employee Motivation in the Non-Profit Organizations of Pakistan. Business Intelligence Journal 2: 327-332.

36. Nohria N, Groysberg B, Lee LL (2012) Employee Motivation: A powerful New Mode. Harvard Business Review.

37. Bigge ML, Shermis SS (1992) Learning Theories for Teachers. (10th edn.) New York, Harper Collins.

38. Mary BL, Newstorm JW (1992) Transfer of Training, Action Packed Strategies to Ensure high Payoff from Training investments. Reading, Addison-Wesley.

39. Kemal AR (2005) Skill Development in Pakistan. The Pakistan Development Review 44: 349-357.

Structural Factors Affecting International Trade Growth in Iran

Farsi JY[1]*, Moradi MA[1], Jandoust A[2] and Esfandabadi HM[3]

[1]*Department of Entrepreneurship, University of Tehran, Iran*
[2]*Graduate of Entrepreneurship Management, University of Tehran's Faculty of Entrepreneurship, Iran*
[3]*Graduate of Social Sciences, Research Assistant at University of Tehran's Faculty of Entrepreneurship, Iran*

Abstract

Assuming that the future of the country is affected by the activities of nascent ventures today and considering that the establishment of such ventures is one of the aims of governments to improve and ensure a growing economy, it would seem a helpful resolution to encourage infiltration into foreign markets which would result in the prosperity of nascent ventures. Therefore, 32 structural factors affecting the growth of foreign trade were extracted from the related literature and classified according to the context, content and process dimensions. The mental patterns of 40 active exporters were analyzed using the Q-method and the important factors affecting foreign trade were extracted from their mental patterns. The research findings indicate that 9 major factors (international regulations, international policies, developing international infrastructures, developing the infrastructures of the country, service and support, exchange policies; domestic rules and regulations, trends and management) correspond to the three major dimensions. Achieved through reviewing the latest literature, the results can help government policy-makers with decision-making and prioritizing policies for each respective dimension.

Keywords: Welfare growth; Foreign markets; International trade growth

Introduction

Establishing nascent new ventures and stabilizing their commercial activities are among the primary objectives of the governments in achieving sustainable development and social welfare growth. The nourishment of international trade and the facilitation of the related activities can aid the infiltration of additional products into foreign markets and hence the survival of new nascent ventures. Since most of the foreign markets are highly competitive and international trade change and growth is dependent upon changing the conditions in the short run, the role played by structural factors is fundamental in controlling and facilitating the different dimensions of commercial activities and mitigating the effect of the gap between growth strategies [1,2]. While a range of structural factors are aimed at the way processes take place in specific contexts, the identification and application of these factors to growth strategies, as well as the consideration of the interactions among the three dimensions of context, content and process in the overall business environment is regarded as fundamental to governments [3].

The classification of structural dimensions of context, content and process, and the identification of crucial factors in each of the dimensions determines the responsibilities of government decision-makers and sorts out the factors for the top managers in order of priority. Therefore, the major factors affecting the growth of foreign trade are collected from the literature and interviews with experts and categorized into three dimensions. Afterwards, according to the comments made by 40 active commercial institutions, the common mental patterns for 32 factors affecting foreign trade were analyzed using the Q-method. Finally, 9 effective structural factors in the overall environment of international trade in Iran were identified.

Literature Review

The identification of factors affecting business performance requires a careful study of social and commercial structures. To identify the driving factors and promote growth, the structural factors need to be examined and studied in different market environments [4]. Growth strategies depend on structural factors like government policies with permanent effects. Therefore, structural factors have sustainable and immediate effects on domestic and international interactions of organizations and commercial enterprises. These factors include supportive policies, tax cuts and infrastructural development policies administered by governments for commercial development and social growth.

In "Managing Change for Competitive Success" Pettigrew [3] argues that the content, context and process dimensions are the main factors affecting growth (Figure 1).

Content (intentions, objective and goals): What?

Context (domestic and foreign environment): Where?

Process (function and application): How?

Successful changes in this approach are accomplished through

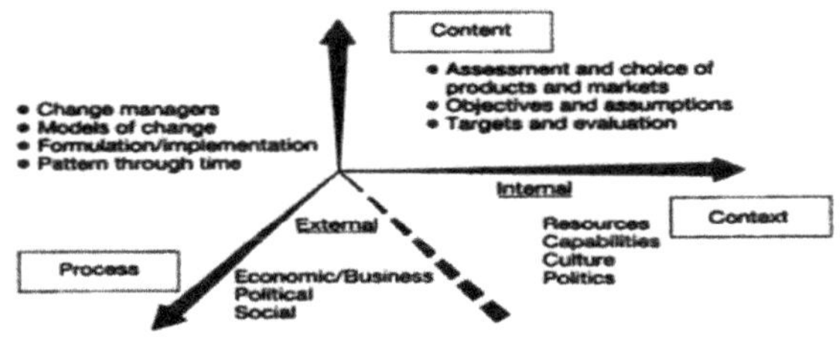

Figure 1: Understanding Strategic Change: three essential dimensions.

***Corresponding author:** Farsi JY, Department of Entrepreneurship, University of Tehran, Iran, E-mail: Jfarsi@ut.ac.ir

emphasizing the interaction between the three dimensions and the way tasks are done in domestic and foreign environments. Therefore, change and growth processes are understood through considering (domestic and foreign) context, content (objectives and assumptions), and process (executive patterns). When it comes to crucial decisions, the most important factor will determine the result of the decisions.

Empirical evidences

Factors: This section deals with the literature related to the factors affecting international trade growth in Iran. Using the SWOT method, a study is conducted to the end of designing a strategic plan for non-oil export development by Trade Promotion Organization of Iran. For data collection, the research used the interview data with non-oil experts conducted in 2006 from the Trade Promotion Organization of Iran on the factors affecting non-oil exports. According to the experts, opportunities, threats, weaknesses and strengths were identified, the main factors of which are shown in Table 1 (Trade Promotion Organization of Iran, 2007) (Table 1).

In another study, Do'ayi et al. used the Delphi method to investigate the factors affecting international trade. They interviewed 25 experts in non-oil exports selected through non-random-snowball sampling.

Their findings revealed that factors such as standardizing business activities, processes and products, developing and advancing IT and stability and national security play a key role in non-oil export growth.

In their study, Fathi and Azizi [5] classified 35 major barriers to political, economic, commercial and inter-organizational development. They prepared and distributed a questionnaire among 500 firms in various industries. Afterwards, the analysis of the collected data from 335 returned questionnaires, point to the importance of low economic security in Iran, low foreign investment, proper management of information systems all over the country and the activities of business, unions, and commerce chambers. They suggest that management functions and systems, business, union and commerce chambers as well as banking systems, the custom organization need to be improved and problems related to financing need to be solved. In another study, Madhooshi [6] argues that factors such as export institutions, lack of knowledge about the laws and regulations of the target country, conflicting export instructions, provincial research centers, seasonal fees, exchange rates, taking foreign agencies are among the major factors in international trade growth in Iran. The major factors affecting businesses in different economic environments which are pointed to in other studies around the globe include: the necessary documents, information about foreign markets, barriers created by governments, foreign competitors [7], the required documents for export, cultural differences, barriers created by governments, competition, exchange rates, taking foreign agencies [8]; high dollar rates, transportation expenses, focusing on foreign markets, government and legal barriers [8] (Baursmichmidt, 1985); government fees, commitment to high quality products and services [9], intense foreign competitions, government support, attractive export and government incentives [10], barriers created by governments, government policies, fees and supports, firm size, experience and network support [9], various standards for products, laws and regulations, government support, exchange rates, taking foreign agencies, political-economic fluctuations, legal and administrative corruption [11], exchange rates, transportation expenses, foreign competitors [12], exchange fluctuations, government support, competitive foreign markets, pricing policies [13], government support, foreign competitors, import tariffs, pricing policies, complex regulations, high exchange rates, government subsidies P [14] and so forth. Some of the above mentioned factors are export drivers and some other factors act as barriers to export growth. The present research aims at identifying the role played by these factors in the context of Iran. The identification of factors affecting export growth in economic environments of other countries could help the identification of opportunities and threats in the way to the path of development. After the modification and localization of these factors, the effect of each factor in mid and long term could be determined (Table 2).

Laws and regulations

The most significant incentives provided by governments for international trade development include: granting subsides to R&D, supervising importations, trade contracts, granting preferential credits and guaranteeing exportations [15]; removing taxes, determining taxes based on each region, postponing tax liabilities [16]; exchange rate stabilization, actual export subsides [17] and removing/facilitating tax payment, income tax on exports, custom fees, importing machineries and equipment for manufacturing export products, subsidy adjustments based on export rates, actual income rates, interest rates, and tax documentations [18].

The characterization of the sample population

Policies: The first systematic initiatives for modifying the export development plans in Iran began in 1998 during the Third Social and Economical Development Plan and was continued in The Fourth Plan. The Fifth Development Plan for the first time includes a completely distinct chapter on foreign trade with a special focus on exportation. This plan also includes target-setting for strategic plans in provinces [19-21].

Therefore, province officials need to consider the Fifth Plan in organizing their future plans. Some of the plans administered in line with export development include the modification of laws and regulations related to export and import which is achieved through forming Exchange Allocation Committee and Order Submission Office for Importation founded in 1979-80.

Other initiatives like adjusting custom tariffs and interest rates, enacting incentives and supportive policies and export incentives for non-oil sector in 2006, removing redundant provisions and clarifying the process of non-oil exports, tax exemptions and special facilities for exporters, modifying the pricing processes for export products,

First category: Opportunities and threats	Second category: Strengths and weaknesses
1. The emergence of powerful competitors such as China, Turkey and India	1. Weak presence in the regional and multilateral treaties
2. Not being accepted in WOT	2. Lack of regulations for export sector and streamlining the processes.
3. The tendency of 25 neighboring countries for importing from Iran as a natural market	3. Lack of coordination between exchange, financial and monetary policies with export development objectives.
4. The possibility of co-production with other countries.	4. Weak transportation despite great opportunities
5. Removing the obstacles and extending relations to more countries.	5. Lack of cooperation between the export organizations in Iran.

Table 1: The SWOT model findings.

Items	Researcher								
	World Trade Organization (2007)	**Do'ayi (2007)**	**Fathi (2007)**	**Madhoushi (2007)**	**Winston (2006)**	**Ahmed (2004)**	**Anderson (1993)**	**Sullivan and Bauerschmidt (1990)**	**Groke and Kreidle (1967)**
Country	Iran	Iran	Iran	Iran	81 countries	Lebanon	Norway	Australia, Sweden, Germany	U.S.A
Firm size	-	-	-	-	Small, middle, large	Small, middle, large	Small, middle	-	Small
market sector	-	-	Electronics	-	Agriculture services	Multiple services	industrial		_
Sample population	-	experts	Various industries	manufacturers	exporter & non-exporter (WTO report)	Exporter entrepreneurs	exporter & non-exporter	Exporter	Exporters
Sampling method		Non-random sampling	consensus	-	-	Stratified-random sampling	Non-random, purposive	Non-random	_
Sample size		25	335	100	8047	20	128	62	_
Data collection method	Interview-Delphi	Interview-Delphi	questionnaire	questionnaire	Interview	Questionnaire-personal interview	personal interview	Electronic questionnaire	Personal interview
Scale	Qualitative	Qualitative	-	-	Jan-00	Likert-5 point scale	Jan-00	Likert-5 point scale	1-0 (cross)
Assessment factors	20	-	35		15	20	-	30	18
Statistical method	-	-	Friedman test	SWOT analysis	probit	Turkey test T-test	F-test	Mean Factor analysis	Frequency (percent)
Factors identified	Removing the legal barriers	Standards for activities	Economic security	Import organizations	Previous export background	Government support	The number of new products	exchange rates	Limited trade possibilities
	streamlining the processes	Processes	Information systems	Few research centers	Providing subsides	Competitive foreign markets	Foreign markets coverage	Transportation expenses	The necessary documents
	Lack of cooperation between exchange policies	Lower manufacture expenses	Management method	Conflicting export regulations	Competitive markets	Pricing system	Expansion in domestic market	Competitive foreign markets	Foreign market information
	Poor transportation		The activities of unions and commerce chambers			High export tariffs			
			Foreign investments			Capital for promotion			

Table 2: The comparison of studies conducted around the world on the factors affecting international trade growth.

Development Plan	Year	target-setting	Achieved (without condensates)	Percent
The First Plan	1989-1993	17.8	11.7	66
The Second Plan	1995-1999	26.4	15.3	58
The Third Plan	2000-2004	28.2	26	92
The Fourth Plan	2005-2009	60 months plan, 52.9	60 months performance 79	149.3

Table 3: The achievement of target-setting in development plans (Billion).

developing export enterprises such as export clusters and improving export organizations, developing the investments in this area through forming joint workshops, attracting foreign investors and focusing more on research particularly in the areas of exporting products and services. The results of the quantitative studies are shown in Table 3.

Other plans include some cultural and educational initiatives. In this regard, the Trade Promotion Organization of Iran has trained about 120556 individuals in 2445 courses at primary-professional-advanced and general levels from 1989 to mid-2010 [22]. Moreover, there are other initiatives that are aimed at policies for developing trade infrastructures such as air, land, and sea transportation and improving culture, supporting packaging and rationalizing the supports. The budget allocation for export awards from 2000-2009 is shown in Table 4.

A review of the table figures demonstrates that there has been a significant increase in the amount of awards in the Fourth Plan [23-25]. 8207 billion Rials paid as export awards during the Fourth Plan could explain the significant increase of the exports during that period (Figure 2).

Despite the pressures and sanctions from foreign countries, the government had a successful experience with regard to non-oil export objectives during 2005-2009 (Trade Promotion Organization of Iran, Trade Program Office).

Figure 3 shows the non-oil export objectives and achievements in Iran's development plans.

As demonstrated in Figure 3, the objectives have been attained above the expected level. Figure 4 shows a four-time growth for non-oil exports during those years.

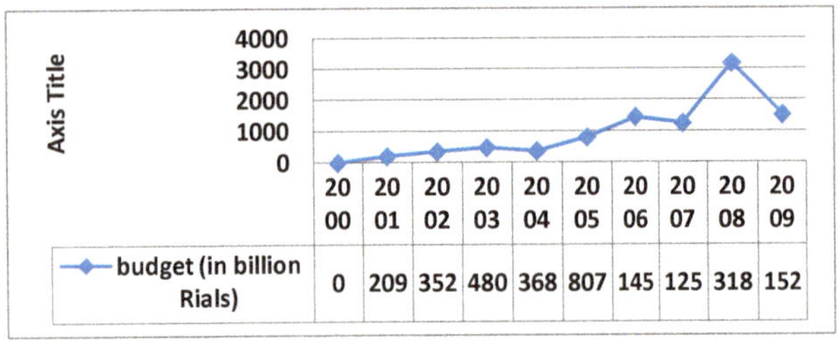

Figure 2: Budget Allocation For Export Awards.

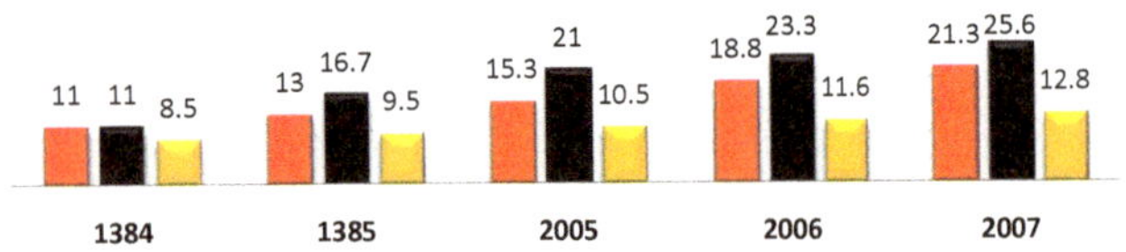

Figure 3: Non-oil export objectives and achievements in Iran's development plans.

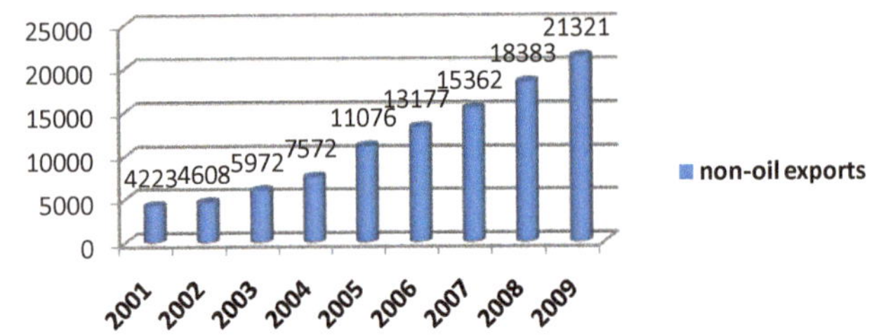

Figure 4: Non-oil exports from 2001 to 2009.

The amount of export award	2000	2001	2002	2003	2004	2005	2006	2007	2008	2009
	0	202	352	480	368	807	1450	1250	3180	1520

Table 4: budget allocation and export awards from 2005 to 2009 Billion (IR Rial).

.Year	Overall objective	Performance		Achievement in comparison with 2010 (percent)	
		With condensates	Without condensates	With condensates	Without condensates
2010	14188	14447	12260	102	86

Table 5: Achievement in comparison with 2010 (percent).

The Figure 4 shows the improvement of export during the Third and Fourth Plans in the non-oil export sector which indicates that the planned objectives have been achieved through development plans. Therefore, given the economic capabilities developed in the country and the new markets in neighboring countries, we need to stabilize this trend and take advantage of the new opportunities (Table 5).

As reported by the Trade Planning Bureau of Iran (Table 5), about 86% of the expected objectives of the year was achieved through non-condensate exports during the first half of the year 2010.

The Conceptual model of the research

There is a range of structural factors that affect the coordination of economic processes i.e. how procedures are accomplished in a given context. Therefore, the conceptual model of the research (Figure 3) adopted from the theoretical model proposed by Pettigrew (Figure 2) has been used for classifying the collected structural factors. The factors affecting international trade growth has been extracted from the related literature and sorted according to the three dimensions of context, content and process.

Contextual structural factors: These include the factors for creating coordination with foreign institutions which affect international trade growth in Iran. External factors consist of political, economic and cultural factors, international infrastructures and internal factors consist of the private sector.

Content structural factors: These include the initiatives carried out by the government for organizing and administering economic policies, infrastructural development, support and promotion.

The procedural structural factors: Rules, trends, institutions and management policies coordinate the decisions made for trade growth and facilitate the process of achieving the goals.

The results of the categorization of the factors into different levels and classes were examined though interviews with experts.

This examination was done to determine whether or not the factors possessed structural features, and to find out if they were related to the subject of the research at hand. Finally, 13 contextual factors, 9 content factors and 10 process factors affecting international trade growth in Iran were identified (Figure 5).

Objective and research questions

The main objective of the research is to identify the structural factors affecting international trade growth in Iran. The research questions include:

1. What are the structural factors affecting international trade growth in Iran?

2. What are the main factors in each of the three dimensions of context, content and process?

Research Methodology

The main factors were extracted from the related literature. The data were changed into short statements after collection. The sample statements were selected using the conceptual model of the research. The collected factors from the related literature include 79 factors in the three dimensions which were organized into a checklist of the structural factors affecting international trade growth in Iran. Afterwards, the correlation between the factors was determined using the Likert scale. The data collected from the test was analyzed using the binomial test. Thirty two Q-sample statements with the highest impacts

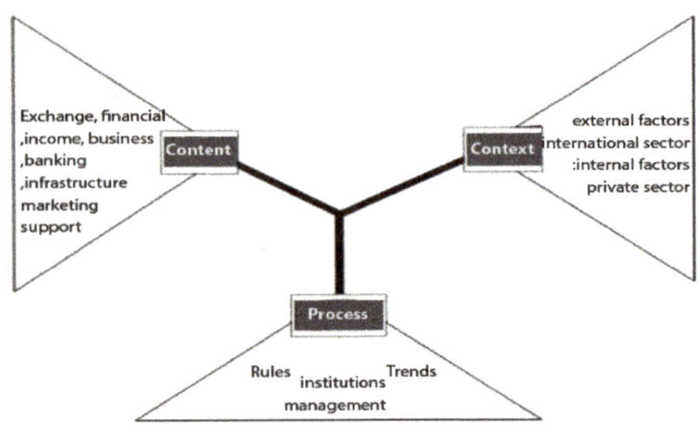

Figure 5: The Conceptual Model For major dimensions and classes.

on international trade were used from the results of the test. Finally, the most important factors in the international trade growth were selected after interviewing with the experts.

The reliability of the collected data was tested using the Cronbach's alpha where the reliability coefficient of 95% was obtained. The validity of the questionnaire items was approved by the experts (Figure 6).

The statistical population

The experts were selected through non-random purposive sampling as three executive chains of executive, academic and government groups which consisted of 13 experts.

Using stratified-random method, 40 respondents were selected from 581 active exporters introduced by the Trade Promotion Organization of Iran.

Empirical results

Q-Sampling statements: The factors affecting international trade obtained from the binomial test, and the interviews with the experts were analyzed where 32 factors with the highest impacts were selected and categorized into the three dimensions (Table 6) and afterwards, used in the questionnaire.

The factors determined through interviews with the respondents (active exporters) were tabulated and grouped using the Q-factor analysis.

Correlation of the viewpoints of the respondents: To determine the correlation of the viewpoints of the respondents and to identify the convergent mental patterns, the cross correlation matrices of the respondents and the effect of each factor with the significant level of 5% was obtained.

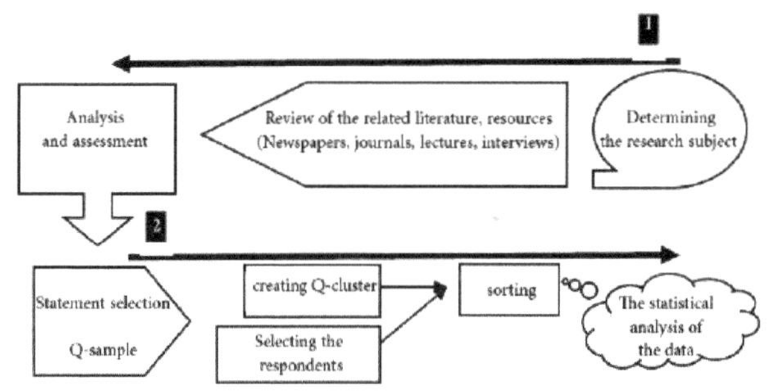

Figure 6: The steps to conducting the Research with Q-Method.

Just like the exploratory factor analysis, the Q-factor analysis is consisted of two phases: Extracting the common mental patterns and classifying them as the first phase and then re-sorting them for interpretation

The Principal Component Analysis is among the most common methods for extracting the factors for conducting the first Q-factor analysis phase.

The results show the level of the relation of each respondent with its corresponding mental pattern group. The number of columns in the factor loading matrix table (with rotation) reveals that the grouping is different from the mental pattern. In other words, each group (column) is composed of individuals with shared statistical classifications (Table 7).

As demonstrated, the table shows the variances for each variable. The variance for the 9th group is 84.8% and the eigenvalue is above (1).

Eigenvalue (the column's total) and the proportion of the variance (the Variance % of the column) for each factor, and their cumulative sum (the cumulative % of the column) is shown in the table.

For example, the eigenvalue for the first group after rotation is 8.865 with the proportion of variance of 23.3% (Table 8).

The grouping of the mental patterns of the respondent: Respondents with different viewpoints were classified using the Q-factor loading. The classification returned 9 groups with shared viewpoints.

Table 8 shows the values for factor loading after rotation.

A factor that was deemed the most important according to the respondents was chosen.

Given the array of factors for each group, and their significant statements, the position of each significant statements was determined in relation to the dimensions of context, content and process.

The most significant factors obtained from significant statements are shown in Table 9.

Contextual factors			
A) International sector			**B) Private sector**
Political factors • International sanctions • Regional conflicts		**Economic factors** • Direct foreign investment • Reputable foreign banks	• **Export-oriented clusters**
• International transportation infrastructures • International shipping • Airlines		**International rules and regulations** • The free trade principle • Quality standards for export products • Intellectual property rights • The laws of the target country	
Technological factor Market information system		**Cultural factor** • The view of other countries to export products	
Content factors			
Exchange policies	**Infrastructure development policies**	**Support services**	**Marketing policies**
• Exchange system • State monopoly in the supply of currency	• Railway transport • Ports • Airline fleet	• Product quality control • After-sale services	• Holding permanent exhibitions for the selected products in neighboring markets • E-marketing
Process factors			

Table 6: Q-sample statements-questionnaire items.

Component	Initial Eigenvalues			Extraction Sums of Squared Loadings			Rotation Sums of Squared Loadings		
	Total	% of Variance	Cumulative %	Total	% of Variance	Cumulative %	Total	% of Variance	Cumulative %
1	16.234	42.72	42.72	16.234	42.72	42.72	8.868	23.337	23.337
2	4.005	10.538	53.258	4.005	10.538	53.258	6.313	16.613	39.95
3	2.904	7.642	60.9	2.904	7.642	60.9	5.887	15.491	55.442
4	1.927	5.072	65.972	1.927	5.072	65.972	2.295	6.039	61.481
5	1.824	4.8	70.772	1.824	4.8	70.772	2.171	5.714	67.195
6	1.688	4.441	75.214	1.688	4.441	75.214	2.169	5.709	72.904
7	1.316	3.464	78.678	1.316	3.464	78.678	1.629	4.287	77.191
8	1.217	3.204	81.882	1.217	3.204	81.882	1.496	3.936	81.127
9	1.114	2.932	84.814	1.114	2.932	84.814	1.401	3.687	84.814

Table 7: The total variance for all the factors (groups).

Individuals	Component								
	1	2	3	4	5	6	7	8	9
p17	0.85								
p8	0.798								
p28	0.794								
p26	0.783								
p24	0.744								
p9	0.737								
p19	0.703								
p2	0.692								
p20	0.682								
p21	0.644								
p37	0.62								
p23	0.586								
p35		0.852							
p14		0.783							
p6		0.753							
p27		0.712							
p12		0.699							
p3		0.634							
p25		0.629							
p13	0.526	0.581							
p32		0.576							
p18			0.936						
p7			0.912						
p29			0.825						
p30			0.693						
p38	0.574		0.656						
p16	0.519		0.522						
p31	0.509		0.516						
p1			0.507						
p10				0.721					
p5				0.708					
p4					-0.82				
p36				0.507	0.599				
p11						0.868			
p22						0.759			
p15							0.875		
p34								0.798	
p33									0.731
Extraction Method: Principal Component Analysis. Rotation Method: Varimax with Kaiser Normalization									
a. Rotation converged in 11 iterations.									

Table 8: factor loading matrix with rotation.

The factors of international rules, domestic rules and regulations, infrastructural development policies, procedures, management, international infrastructural development, exchange policies, support services, and international policies were determined with regard to the significant statements of the shared mental patterns extracted from Table 9.

Factors	Contextual factors		Content factors	Process factors
	International sector	Private sector		
The first factor	International rules			
The second factor				Domestic rules and regulations
The third factor			Domestic infrastructural development policies	
The fourth factor				Procedures
The fifth factor				Management
The sixth factor	International infrastructural development			
The seventh factor			Exchange policies	
The eight factor			Support services	
The ninth factor	International policies			

Table 9: The classification of the 9 factors according to each dimension.

Discussion

The current research was carried out with the aim of identifying the structural process, content and context factors affecting trade growth in the context of international trade in Iran. The findings showed that focusing on international rules, adopting free trade policies for joining the WTO, following qualitative and quantitative standards can positively affect foreign trade growth. However, with regard to undeveloped neighbor countries, it is worth noting that adopting the free trade policy would facilitate importation from these countries and exportation to farther countries. This would result in easier importation and more difficult exportation conditions; because these countries are home to saturated markets and entering their markets requires high competitive expenses to overcome big powerful companies. The long-term effect of international sanction on the economy of Iran is evident. With the formation of a positive atmosphere for economic activities and the increase in the demand from neighboring countries, sanctions could be great barriers to taking advantage of the potential opportunities. Moreover, the decrease in regional tensions could have a positive effect on trade relations with other countries and lessening the sanctions.

Entering into trade relations and mitigating the international tensions could improve the interactions between the economic enterprises of the country and foreign markets. However, this improvement is not possible without the required infrastructures such as the railway system and land transportations. Therefore, focusing on and adopting proper policies by the government in this sector will not only provide a solution to the issues related to the industries, but also will facilitate the domestic and foreign transportations.

Another effective and crucial factor for foreign trade is the exchange policies of the country. It seems that as long as the actual currency rates are not determined, activities related to importations would be more profitable than exportation activities.

Conclusion

The research findings show that observing the international rules and standards, adopting proper policies for developing the international infrastructures, and paying attention to the end effect of the decisions and sanctions from the international organizations plays a vital role in the contextual dimension. With regard to the content dimension, the public top managers need to take actual exchange policies and develop the required infrastructures for developing commerce in the country. Modifying the trade rules and regulations and the current trends and recruiting qualified managers to executive positions could improve the process dimension and enhance the interaction between the three dimensions. This categorization could help the planning of different sectors of the government and developing appropriate strategies for foreign trade.

References

1. Hsiao C (1986) Analysis of Panel Data. Cambridge University.
2. Rynning MR, Andersen O, (1994) structural and Behavioral Predictors of Export Adoption: A Norwegian Study. Journal of International Marketing 2: 73-89.
3. Pettigrew A, Whipp R (1991) Managing Change for Competitive success. Wiley-Blackwell.
4. Kalleberg AL, Berg I (1989) Work and Industry: Structures, Markets, and Processes. Social Forces 68: 244.
5. Fathi S, Azizi SH (2007) The Effect of e-Business on Export Promotion. Journal of Business Research 45: 179-220.
6. Madhoushi M, Tari GH (2007) Non-oil Export Promotion Strategies of Mazandaran Province. Journal of Business Research 195-233.
7. Groke PO, Kreidle RJ (1967) Export! Why or Why Not? Managerial Attitude and Action For Smaller Sized Business Firms. Business and Society 8: 7-12.
8. Kaynak E, Erol C (1989) The Export Propensity of Turkish Manufacturing and Trading House Firms. Journal of Marketing Management 5: 211-229.
9. Gripsrud G (1990) The Determinants of Export Decisions and Attitudes to A Distant Market: Norwegian Fishery Exports To Japan. Journal of International Business Studies 21: 469-485.
10. Leonidas C, Leonidou (2000) Barriers to export management: an organizational and internationalization analysis. Journal of International Management 6: 121-148.
11. Wiig H (2004) Barriers to Export Trade and Investment in Latin America. University of Otago, Dunedin, New Zealand.
12. Sullivan D, Bauerschmidt A (1990) International Internationalization: A test of Johansson and Vahlne's Thesis. Management International Review 30: 19-30.
13. Ahmed JU, Julian CC, Baalbaki I, Hadidian TV (2004) Export Barriers and Firm Internationalization: A Study of Lebanese Entrepreneurs. Journal of Management And World Business Research 1: 11-22.
14. Mir JH (2001) New findings in the International Trade Theory and Policies. Conference Proceedings on Business Export Leap and strategic policies, Business Research and Studies Institute, pp: 1-55.
15. Feinschreiber R (1975) The U.S. Tax Law Provides Two Export Incentives. Columbia Journal of World Business pp: 46-49.
16. Arslan I, WiJnbergen SV (2001) Exportincentives,Exchange Rate Policy And Export Growth In Turkey. The Review of Economics And Statistics 75: 128-133.
17. Jenkins GP, Kuo CY (2007) Evaluating the Relative Impact of Fiscal Incentives and Trade Policies on the Returns to Manufacturing in Taiwan,1955-1995. Asian Economic Journal 21:75-100.
18. Baursmichmidt A, Sullivan D (1985) Common Factors Underlying Barriers to Export: Studies in the U.S. Paper Industry. Journal of International Business Studies 16: 111-123.
19. Iranian Trade Promotion Business planning Office (2008) Foreign trade policy recommendations of the Fifth Development Plan.
20. Iranian Trade Promotion Organization (1997) A report on foreign trade understanding, SWOT, strategies, plans for Non-oil Export Promotion Commission. Iranian Trade Promotion Organization, Tehran.
21. Cavusgil ST (1984) Differences Among Exporting Firms Based on Their Degree of Internationalization. Journal of Business Research.
22. Holly A (2009) Great Expectations: Railroads and U.S. Economic Recovery.
23. Jones RW, Kenen PB (1996) Handbook of international Economics. Amsterdam North–Holland.
24. Kaleka A, Katsikeas CS (1995) Exporting Problems: The Relevance of Export Development. Journal of Marketing Management 11: 499-515.
25. Sullivan D, Bauerschmidt A (1989) Common Factors Underlying Barriers to Export: A Comparative Study in the European and U.S. Paper Industry. Management International Review 29: 17-32.

18

The Comparative Investigation of Investment and Manufacturing Company's Portfolio with an Emphasis on Market Return: The Case of Tehran Stock Exchange

Saeid Jabbarzadeh[1]*, Morteza Motavassel[2] and Parviz Mamsalehi[3]

[1]*Department of Accounting, Urmia Branch, Islamic Azad University, Urmia, Iran*
[2]*Department of Accounting, Osku Branch, Islamic Azad University, Osku, Iran*
[3]*Department in Accounting, Hamedan Branch, Islamic Azad University, Hamedan, Iran*

Abstract

The aim of this study is to conduct a comparative investigation of investment and manufacturing company's portfolio with an emphasis on market return in firms listed in Tehran Stock Exchange (TSE). Statistical sample of the research includes 14 investment firms and 14 manufacturing companies which are studied during the period of 2005 to 2009. Jensen model is used to calculate exceed return over market. The results indicate that both investment and manufacturing companies obtain higher return than market return. However, the return obtained by investment firms is higher than manufacturing companies indicating that investment firms have better performance than both market return and manufacturing firms.

Keywords: Investment and manufacturing companies; Portfolio; Market return; Tehran stock exchange

Introduction

The stock market has an important role in the allocation of resources, both directly as a source of funds and as a determinant of firms' value and borrowing capacity [1]. Sener and Pirinçciler [2] define financial investment as "generally using money in the hope of making more money". One of the factors which affect firm's growth is effective investments. Investments could be in form of increasing firm's capacities (physical assets) or in the form of investment in financial assets such as securities and bonds. Investors would like to evaluate the results of their investments and compare it with other similar investments.

According to Sharp et al. (2006) investment firms are financial mediators that finance by selling securities and invest it in financial assets of other companies to obtain return for their share holders. The main difference of these sorts of firms with other business corporations is that they buy and sell financial assets such and firms securities and bonds instead of buying and selling goods (Behzadi, 2007).

Making investment decisions are an integral and vital part of managing a firm, and thus an efficient investment decision is expected to enhance firm valuations [3]. Evaluation of portfolio performance is vital for investors. If the results of evaluation of portfolio performance are not promising, the reasons must be identified to change investment policies. Evaluation of portfolio performance is also important for traders to make decisions about holding, purchasing and selling investments. In addition, shareholders are looking for shares that have better performance related to other investment firms and market performance [4].

It is expected that investment firms make good investment decisions while they are professional in this and has sophisticated employees to do so. Unfortunately, investment firms have not gain so much development in TSE in the way that only 19 investment firms have been listed in TSE. This may stem from the fact that according to manufacturing firms' charter, they can create investment portfolio while in the most of other countries, this is a specific for investment firms. However, the most critical question that concerns us in this study is whether investment or manufacturing firms could obtain higher return than market return and specifically compare the performance of these two sorts of firms. The results may help potential investors in their investment decisions and also institutional investors to compare their performance. In addition, TSE is considered as an emerging market with some specific characteristic such as high inflation in which firms should obtain higher return than inflation, and also the results could give fresh evidence from emerging markets.

Literature Review

In 1952, Harry Markowitz [5] published his noble work "portfolio selection" in The Journal of Finance. According to him "one type of rule concerning choice of portfolio is that the investor does (or should) maximize the discounted (or capitalized) value of future returns". He proved that by using correlation concept, with changing the amount of funds invested in an asset considering correlation coefficient between returns, risk can be minimized and even in absolute negative one correlation, risk can be decreased to zero. In following, CAPM was developed by W. F. Sharpe. CAPM simplified Markowitz's Modern Portfolio theory, made it more practical. He show that when forming the diversified portfolios consisting large number of securities investors, the calculation of the portfolio risk using standard deviation technically complicated. After these pioneer works, researches developed portfolio performance evaluation [6]. Based on CAPM and risk and return concepts, in 1960s three researchers, Sharpe, Treynor and Jensen developed models to measure portfolio performance.

***Corresponding author:** Saeid Jabbarzadeh, Department of Accounting, Urmia Branch, Islamic Azad University, Urmia, Iran, E-mail: Jabbarzadeh.s@gmail.com

Many studies have applied these portfolio performance evaluation models since then, some of them is mentioned in following.

Hajibozorgi [7] in a research investigated the performance of investment firms in TSE. Studying four investment firms and using measures of annual return, stock price appreciation, bonus share and risk and return, they find that investment firms have a better performance than TSE total index.

Daee [8] investigated as to some investment firms in TSE. By analyzing their problems, stock price trend, financial ratios, beta factor, liquidity absorption find that these firms have a good performance in TSE.

Safari [9] in a research, analyzed the investment portfolio risk and return of insurance companies of TSE. By investigating the performance of portfolio in term of income and portfolio composition and return, he finds that these firms have not an optimal investment portfolio and their performance is not good as to risk and return.

Mashayekh [10] investigated about exceed return of 16 investment firms in TSE using Jensen model. They find that investment firms, on average, obtained higher return than market return. This result holds for short periods either.

Eslamibidgoli et al. [4] investigated the relationship between investment firm's performance with liquidity and firm's size in TSE. Using Jensen, Treynor and Sharp indexes, they could not find evidence to support their two expectations that means they indicate that there is not a significant relationship between investment firm's performance with liquidity and firm's size in TSE.

Ogawa and Suzuki [11] examined investment behavior in the Japanese manufacturing industry using investment revision data to analyze investment behavior from a fresh angle. They tested the martingale investment hypothesis and then the q-theory of investment by looking at the response of stock return and investment to news arriving at firms. The martingale hypothesis was accepted at early stage of investment planning, but not at later stages. They also found evidence for the validity of the q-theory hypothesis. They finally show that investment was responsive to profit rate revision and sales revision, but stock return responded only to profit rate revision.

Cheng et al. [12] studied the relationship between the quality of financial reporting and investment efficiency. They examine the investment behavior of a sample of firms that disclosed internal control weaknesses under the Sarbanes-Oxley Act. They find that prior to the disclosure, these firms under-invest (over-invest) when they are financially constrained (unconstrained). More importantly, they find that after the disclosure, these firms' investment efficiency improves significantly.

Lin et al. [13] investigated as to managerial optimism and investigate the influences of the different levels of managerial optimism on improving the investment efficiency when firms tend to under-invest or overinvest. Their results indicate that an under-invested firm with a CEO that has a high level of managerial optimism can improve the firm's investment efficiency by reducing the degree of underinvestment, further increasing the value of a firm.

Research Hypotheses

Investment firms are professional in investment business; however, it is expected that investment firms obtain more return than other firms. Therefore, following hypothesis is posited:

Hypothesis 1: Investments firms of TSE obtain exceed return on their investments than manufacturing companies.

As before mentioned investment firms are professional in investment business; however, it is expected that investment firms obtain more return than average market return. Therefore, following hypothesis is posited:

Hypothesis 2: investments firms of TSE obtain exceed return on their investments than market return.

Manufacturing firms may have exceed cash holdings. This cash may be invested in other firms to obtain return. In this process, manufacturing firms may hire professional consultants to give advice in investment decisions. Therefore, following hypothesis is posited:

Hypothesis 3: manufacturing companies of TSE obtain exceed return on their investments than market return.

Methodology

Considering that the aim of this study is to describe the position of investment and manufacturing firm's performance through their investments in securities, the study is descriptive research. The research data and information have gathered through two resources: information regarding developing conceptual framework and literature review is gathered by reviewing previous articles and required data of sample firms is collected through TSE database and related software. After data collection, SPSS software is used to testing research hypotheses applying *t*-test method.

The population of this study consist all investment and manufacturing firm's firms listed in TSE which is studied during the period 2005 to 2009. However, sample firms must have following conditions to be included in our sample:

1- Having investment in securities of TSE firms during the studied period.

2- Fiscal year must be ended at the end of Esfand (solar last month).

As a result of these conditions, 14 investment firms and accordingly 14 manufacturing firms are selected to be studied amounting to 140 observation.

Variables definition and measurement

Exceed return: The difference between average portfolio return on investments compared to average expected return on investments. Average portfolio return on investments is weighted average actual return of individual portfolio. Individual investment actual return is calculated using following equation:

$$R_i = \frac{P_{i,t} - P_{i,t-1} + DPS_t + x(P_i - M)}{P_{i,t-1}}$$

R_i: Actual return of investment

$P_{i,t}$: Stock price in time t

$P_{i,t-1}$: Stock price in time t-1

DPS_t: Dividend per share in time t

x: Capital increasing percentage

M: Cash contribution per share

Market return: average market return calculated through price index and cash return using following formulas:

$$\bar{R}_{mt} = \frac{Index_t - Index_{t-1}}{Index_{t-1}}$$

Index$_t$: Index value in time t

Index$_{t-1}$: Index value in time t-1

Jensen's differential return measure: According to Levišauskait [6] "portfolio performance evaluation involves determining periodically how the portfolio performed in terms of not only the return earned, but also the risk experienced by the investor. For portfolio evaluation appropriate measures of return and risk as well as relevant standards". Three portfolio evaluation measures are:

-Sharpe's ratio;

_ Treynor's ratio;

_ Jensen's Alpha.

Sharpe's ratio shows an excess a return over risk free rate, or risk premium, by unit of total risk, measured by standard deviation:

Sharpe's ratio=(řp– řf) / σp,

Here: řp - the average return for portfolio p during some period of time;

řf - the average risk-free rate of return during the period;

σp - standard deviation of returns for portfolio p during the period.

Treynor's ratio shows an excess actual return over risk free rate, or risk premium, by unit of systematic risk, measured by Beta [6]:

Treynor's ratio=(řp –řf) / βp,

Here: βp – Beta, measure of systematic risk for the portfolio p.

One of the common measure of investment performance is Jensen's differential return measure (or alpha). Like Treynor's measure, Michael Jensen proposed this approach based on CAPM. Jensen's Alpha shows excess actual return over required return and excess of actual risk premium over required risk premium. This measure of the portfolio manager's performance is based on the CAPM. According to CAPM, the expected return for portfolio p is expressed as:

E (Rpt)=RFt + βp [E (Rmt) - RFt]

Where E(Rpt)=the expected return on portfolio p in period t

RFt=the risk-free rate in period t

E(Rmt)=the expected return on the market in period t

E(Rmt) – RFt=the market risk premium during period t

βp=the beta for portfolio p.

Comparing the actual return to the predicted return, the difference is the alpha:

αp=Rpt – E (Rpt)=Rpt – { RFt + βp [E (Rmt) – RFt] }.

If the alpha is significantly positive, it suggests that this portfolio has superior performance than that justified by CAPM. On the other hand, a negative value of alpha is evidence of performance below expectations (Lin and Chen, 2006).

Beta coefficient as a measure of systematic risk measurement is calculated by following formula:

$$\beta_i = \frac{COV(r_i, r_m)}{\sigma^2 m}$$

$COV(r_i, r_m)$: is co variation of securities return I to market return

σ^2rm: variation of market return

Empirical Results

Hypotheses test

Main hypothesis: Investments firms of TSE obtain exceed return on their investments than manufacturing companies.

To test this hypothesis, the mean of two samples (investment and manufacturing firms) is compared. The results are shown in Table 1.

According to the results, in 2005, 2006 and 2007 investment firms obtained higher return than manufacturing firms. However, in 2008 and 2009 there is no difference between investment firms and manufacturing firms return. Taking the results of all years, our hypothesis is accepted meaning that investment firms of TSE obtain exceed return on their investments than manufacturing companies.

Sub-hypothesis 1: investments firms of TSE obtain exceed return on their investments than market return.

To test this hypothesis, firstly exceed return is calculated according to Jensen model for each 14 investment sample firms. Then t test is conducted to test this hypothesis which results are shown in Table 2.

The results indicate that in 2005 and 2006, the return of investment firms is higher than market return but in 2007, 2008 and 2009 not. However, taking the results of all years, our hypothesis is accepted that means investments firms of TSE obtain exceed return on their investments than market return.

Sub-hypothesis 2: manufacturing companies of TSE obtain exceed return on their investments than market return.

	Levene Test for Equality of Variances		t- test for Equality of Means				
year	F	Sig.	t	df	Sig(2–tailed)	Mean difference	Error difference
2005	842. 7	010.	000.4	26	.000	2227.73	30524.18
			000. 4	671.21	.001	2227.73	30524.18
2006	322.	575.	612. 3	26	.001	6324. 73	38766. 20
			612. 3	471. 24	.001	6324. 73	38766.20
2007	007.	936.	643. 3	26	.001	7031. 49	64207.13
			643. 3	260. 25	.001	7031. 49	64207.13
2008	424. 6	018.	078.	26	.939	0074. 1	97656. 12
			087.	654. 17	.939	0074. 1	97656. 12
2009	238. 1	276.	611.	26	.546	7035. 11	15146. 19
			611.	511. 19	.548	7035. 11	15146. 19
All years	130.	.721	373.5	26	.000	8538.41	78952.7
			373.5	758.25	.000	8538.41	78952.7

Table 1: The results of t-test for first hypothesis.

	t	df	Sig.(2- tailed)	Mean difference	95% Confidence Interval	
					Of the Difference	upper
					lower	41.6067
2005	162.2	13	.050	20.8110	.0512	66.6974
2006	981.1	13	.069	31.9294	-3.9098	39.7902
2007	596.1	13	.135	16.6564	-5.8698	1844.16
2008	995.	13	.338	5.1041	-5.2679	3590.3
2009	285.1	13	.221	11.3241	-7.7017	29.6274
All years	2.976	13	.011	17.1650	4.7026	

Table 2: The results of t-test for second hypothesis.

	t	df	Sig.(2- tailed)	Mean difference	95% Confidence Interval	
					Of the Difference	Upper
					lower	41.6067
2005	-3.366	13	.500	-52.4117	-86.0484	66.7496
2006	-3.340	13	.500	-41.7030	-86. 6752	39.2097
2007	-3.763	13	.200	-33.0466	-52. 0188	16.1844
2008	.344	13	.737	4.0967	-21.6548	3.3590
2009	-0.22	13	.389	-3.3793	-37.1149	29.6274
All years	-4.717	13	.000	-24.6888	-35.9972	

Table 3: The results of t-test for third hypothesis.

To test this hypothesis, firstly exceed return is calculated according to Jensen model for each 14 manufacturing sample firms. Then t test is conducted to test this hypothesis which results are shown in Table 3.

The results indicate that in 2005, 2006 and 2007, the return of manufacturing firms is higher than market return but in 2007, 2008 not. However, taking the results of all years, our hypothesis is accepted that means manufacturing firms of TSE obtain exceed return on their investments than market return.

Discussion and Conclusion

The aim of this study was to conduct a comparative investigation of investment and manufacturing company's portfolio with an emphasis on market return in firms listed in Tehran Stock Exchange (TSE). In this study three hypotheses are developed to capture the aim of study. First hypothesis assumes that investment firms of TSE obtain more return on their investments than manufacturing companies. To test this hypothesis t test is conducted to compare performance of investments and manufacturing companies. The results show that investment firms obtain more return than manufacturing companies. This result is reasonable while investment firms are professional in this task than manufacturing companies whose mission is to produce goods not invest in securities. The second hypothesis stipulates that investments firms of TSE obtain exceed return on their investments than market return. The results of this hypothesis indicate that as the expectation investments firms of TSE obtain exceed return on their investments than market return. The third hypothesis posits that manufacturing firms of TSE obtain exceed return on their investments than market return. This hypothesis also accepted showing that manufacturing firms of TSE obtain exceed return on their investments than market return. Considering the whole results of the study, it can be concluded that the performance of investment firms on their investments higher than manufacturing firms and they obtain not only more than market return but also more than manufacturing firms. However, taking the results of the study it can be suggested to potential investors to invest in investment firms stock because they obtain higher return than market.

References

1. Tease W (1993) The stock market and investment. OECD Economic Studies No. 20: 41-63.
2. Sener S, Pirinçciler EC (2011) Returns Of Investment Tools In Recession Periods For Turkey. Procedia Social and Behavioral Sciences 24: 72–88.
3. Chen IJ, Lin SH (2012) Will managerial optimism affect the investment efficiency of a firm? Procedia Economics and Finance 2: 73 – 80.
4. Eslamibidgoli G, Tehrani R, Shrazian Z (2005) The investigation of the relationships among investment firms performance based on Jensen, Treynor and Sharp indexes with firms size and liquidity. Financial Researches 19: 3-24.
5. Markowitz H (1952) Portfolio Selection Journal of Finance 7: 77-91.
6. Levišauskait K (2010) Investment Analysis and Portfolio Management. Leonardo da Vinci program project.
7. Hajibozorgi J (2005) The investigation of coordination of investment firms performance and their aims in capital market. M. A. thesis, Allameh Tabatabaee University, Iran.
8. Daee MR (1996) Analysis of investment firms and case studies of some TSE firms. M. A. thesis, Emam Sadeg University, Iran.
9. Safari A (1996) Analytical investigation of portfolio investment risk and return of insurance firms. M. A. thesis, Shahid Beheshti University, Iran.
10. Mashayekh S (2003) Exceed return of active management in investment firms, PHD thesis, Allameh Tabatabaee University, Iran.
11. Ogawa K, Suzuki K (2008) Information, investment, and the stock market: A study of investment revision data of Japanese manufacturing industries. J Japanese Int Economies 22: 663–676.
12. Cheng M, Dhaliwal D, Zhang Y (2013) Does investment efficiency improve after the disclosure of material weaknesses in internal control over financial reporting? Journal of Accounting and Economics 56: 1-18.
13. Lin A, Chen CY (2006) The Impact of Qualified Foreign Institutional Investors on Taiwan's Stock Market, Web Journal of Chinese Management Review 9: 1-2.

Outbound Logistics Performance and Profitability: Taxonomy of Manufacturing and Service Organizations

Matthew J. Liberatore[1]* and Tan Miller[2]

[1]Center for Business Analytics, Villanova School of Business, Villanova University, Villanova, USA
[2]Global Supply Chain Management Program, College of Business Administration, Rider University, Lawrence, USA

Abstract

This paper develops a taxonomy of manufacturing and service firms formed by their emphasis on different key performance metrics to monitor and manage the outbound logistics portion of the supply chain. Furthermore, this study determines whether the use of specific key metrics by firms in these different classifications varies by industry, and what effect, if any, the varying emphases on different key performance metrics within classifications have on firm financial performance. The original data for this study were obtained from SAPs Benchmarking Program for Supply Chain Planning and utilizes performance metrics data from 247 manufacturing and service firms. Cluster analysis was used to develop a taxonomy based on the outbound logistics metrics. Four clusters were found to be distinct and well-formed and emphasize different sets of outbound logistics performance metrics. The clusters were named Inventory Investment Minimizers; Low Cost, Low Service Providers; Planners and Efficient Distribution Spenders; and Heavy Distribution Spenders. This study evaluated whether the emphasis on specific sets of outbound logistics performance metrics tends to be associated with firms in specific industries, and whether differences in firm financial performance, as measured by net operating margin, were found across clusters. This is the first effort to investigate whether a taxonomy of firms can be developed based on the firms' use of different performance metrics to monitor and manage outbound logistics.

Keywords: Outbound logistics; Supply chain performance metrics; Financial performance; Cluster analysis

Introduction

Outbound logistics within the supply chain plays a critical role in a supplier's overall customer relationship management (CRM) process. Outbound logistics can be defined as: "The process related to the movement and storage of products from the end of the production line to the end user" [1]. Most retailers including firms such as Walmart and Target hold their suppliers to very stringent product delivery standards. Failure by a supplier to provide reliable delivery service to its retail customers can result in significant financial penalties and even the delisting (i.e., the elimination) of a supplier's products from a retailer's active product portfolio. Thus, outbound logistics performance represents a major factor in a retailer's decision whether or not to stock a supplier's products (e.g., [2]).

Outbound logistics includes the "last mile" (i.e., the final step of the delivery process) which is often referred to as one of the key make or break steps in the CRM process. Given its critical role, a firm's planning and approach towards outbound logistics can benefit greatly from quantitative "firm performance data" based research, as well as from insights generated by more qualitative perception based data. A few research studies have focused specifically on the link between logistics performance and firm financial profitability. For example, Stapelton et al. [3] discuss how the Strategic Profit Model can be used to determine the effect of adjusting logistical policies on firm financial performance. Additionally, using survey data, Ojha, Gianiodis and Manuja [4] investigate the effect of logistical business continuity planning on firms' operational capabilities and financial performance.

However, despite the importance of the role of outbound logistics in supply chain management, minimal rigorous performance data based research has been done on the direct, stand-alone impact of outbound logistics on such questions as its influence on a firm's profitability and how firms' approaches to outbound logistics differ. Rather, the literature to date tends to group outbound logistics activities into broader studies of supply chain operations where outbound logistics represents just one sub-component. In this research, outbound logistics represents our sole focus. Further, research on supply chain management including outbound logistics also tends to be survey-based (i.e., based on surveys of practitioners' perceptions) rather than performance data based. In this study, we attempt to address this gap by utilizing actual firm performance data.

Since there is no rigorous quantitative published research which evaluates the impact of outbound logistics performance on firm profitability, we review related research on overall supply chain performance. A survey of senior executives found that supply chain is a critical driver of shareholder value and corporate differentiation [5]. Hendricks and Singhal [6] found that supply chain glitches led to strong negative financial impacts on operating income, return on assets and return on sales. Ellinger et al. [7] studied the relationship between supply chain management competency and firm success. They measured supply chain management competency using Delphi-style opinion data from AMR Research's Supply Chain Top 25 rankings, and used Altman's Z-score statistic [8] to measure firm's financial success. They found that firms recognized by industry experts for supply chain management competency have significantly higher Z-scores than their close competitors and industry averages.

Later research focused on the impact of supply chain practices and processes (as opposed to performance) on firm financial performance. Shi and Yu [9] conducted a review of the literature on supply chain

***Corresponding author:** Matthew J. Liberatore, Director, Center for Business Analytics, Villanova School of Business, Villanova University, Villanova, USA
E-mail: matthew.liberatore@villanova.edu

management and firm financial performance. The studies they reviewed utilized either perceptual surveys of supply chain executives or secondary data sources. Their review focused on supply chain practices as contrasted with supply chain performance metrics. They found that sourcing strategy, information technology, supply chain integration and external relationships play important roles in improving financial performance. The authors conclude that, in particular, optimal levels of outsourceabilty, supply chain alignment and integration with IT infrastructure and supply chain relationship management are essential to realize full effective advantage of supply chain management. Using a meta analytic approach of completed studies Leuschner et al. [10] also found a positive and significant link between supply chain integration and firm performance.

Several authors have studied and categorized supply chain performance metrics but have not linked them to firm performance. Supply chain metrics are thought to affect strategic, tactical and operational planning and control, by playing a role in setting objectives, evaluating performance, and determining future courses of actions [11]. Gunasekaran and Kobu [12] provided a literature review of performance metrics in logistics and supply chain management. Gunasekaran et al. [13] developed a framework for supply chain performance metrics and identified a key set of performance metrics and measures for a supply chain. In a later study, Gunasekaran et al. [11] presented a set of supply chain metrics in the context of supply chain activities/processes: plan, source, make/assemble and deliver/customer. They conducted a survey of large UK companies to detemine the importance of these metrics. Their findings led to a supply chain performance framework that includes performance metrics for each supply chain activity/process at the strategic, tactical and operational levels.

Shepherd and Gunter [14] developed a taxonomy of supply chain metrics according to the processes identified in the SCOR model [15]: plan, source, make, deliver and return; whether they measure time, cost, quality, flexibility or innovativeness; and whether they are quantitative or qualitative. Chan and Qi [16] identify six core processes (supplier, inbound logistics, manufacturing, outbound logistics, marketing and sales, end customers) and present an approach for performance measurement that includes input, output and composite measures (such as productivity, efficiency, and utilization).

However, research has not established the link between supply chain performance metrics and financial performance. As stated by Shi and Yu ([9], p.1284) in their review of the literature, "Comparing to the extensive research on SCM's operational performance measurements, our understanding of its financial impact is far from enough." Our research focuses on the financial impact of outbound logistics using outbound logistics performance metrics. It is unclear whether the impact of outbound logistics on firm performance varies by industry or whether there are groups of firms across various industries that perform in a similar fashion. How firms perform across a range of outbound logistics metrics can provide insight into their supply chain operational planning, management and control processes [11]. Whether these differing operational approaches are linked to differences in firm profitability is also unknown. We investigate whether there are distinct groupings of firms formed by their emphasis on key outbound logistics performance metrics and whether these groupings vary by industry, and what effect, if any, these different emphases have on firm financial performance. Cluster analysis is ideally suited to enable us to identify these groupings. We investigate our hypotheses using performance metric and firm profitability data obtained from SAP that comprise a sample of manufacturing and service firms.

Materials and Methods

Research hypotheses

In our research, we sought to determine if firms with similar performance levels and similar emphasis on selected aspects of outbound logistics achieved similar financial operating results. Further, we also wished to explore whether superior performance or relatively heavy emphasis in certain aspects of the outbound logistics process resulted in relatively higher profitability for firms than did superior performance or emphasis in other areas. In other words, our research set out to understand which outbound logistics metrics (and activities) a firm should place more emphasis upon in order to achieve higher profitability.

Interactions with supply chain professionals across a wide range of industries leads us to hypothesize that improvement in outbound logistics should have a positive impact on a firm's financial profitability and that there are differences in outbound logistics performance across industries. However, there remains a dearth of rigorous quantitative analysis that provides specific guidance in this area, motivating this research.

In the manufacturing strategy literature, there have been several studies that have investigated the relationship between competitive priorities and manufacturing strategies (e.g., [17]). Kathuria [18] has studied the relationship between industry, competitive priorities, and performance criteria for small manufacturers. In a related way, we study the relationships between industry, outbound logistics priorities and firm performance. Following the general approach of Kathuria [18], we investigate the relationship between industry, outbound logistics priorities, and performance. Our conceptualization is stated in the form of three hypotheses that are related to the three hypotheses tested in Kathuria [18]:

Hypothesis 1: Firms can be classified into different groups based on their emphasis outbound logistics metrics.

Hypothesis 2: Depending upon the outbound logistics orientation of the groups identified the groups will perform at different levels of profitability.

Hypothesis 3: His group orientation – i.e., the outbound delivery metrics emphasized by a group – is associated with industry membership.

Data

Previous related supply chain studies have used survey-based research that relies on the perceptions or rankings of supply chain executives and practitioners using Likert scale questions (e.g., 1 to 5, poor to excellent). While valuable, these studies are not "objective" or "fact-based" quantitative studies. For this reason, to best achieve our research objectives, we decided to obtain actual performance data on a set of performance levels and costs for outbound logistics.

Variable selection: We sought to develop data on a concise set of variables that covered all components of outbound logistics. For our purposes, we defined outbound logistics as consisting of:

- The management of the inventory produced (to be delivered to the customer)
- The distribution process (i.e., warehousing and transportation)
- The service to the customer (i.e., the actual delivery)

- Capabilities and commitment to demand forecasting and supply chain planning.

Based upon the process and capabilities just defined, we identified the following variables that we wished to include in our study:

1. Inventory carrying costs
2. Obsolete inventory costs
3. Days of inventory on hand
4. Warehousing costs
5. Transportation costs
6. On-time delivery performance
7. Forecast accuracy
8. Supply chain planning costs

In a review of several well-known supply chain management texts, all of these outbound logistics metrics were repeatedly referenced as key performance indicators (e.g., [19-21]. Further, the selection of these metrics ties to the research of Gunasekaran et al. [13]. In their discussion of metrics for the "performance evaluation of the delivery link" category, on-time delivery, total distribution costs, and transportation cost are discussed, among others. Under the "supply chain financial and logistics costs" category total inventory cost and accuracy of forecasting are discussed, among others. Inventory carrying costs, days of inventory on hand, and obsolete inventory costs provide a perspective on a firm's costs of inventory, its commitment to having inventory available for customers and how well a firm plans its inventory. In particular, the level of obsolete inventory a firm may experience offers insight into how well a firm can accurately forecast long-term demand for its products and then execute its plan.

Warehousing and transportation are two primary components of the distribution process. Thus, from a cost perspective, we thought it important to capture both of these cost variables. As we will discuss later, the costs of key activities such as warehousing and transportation can provide different insights, including a perspective on how significant a commitment a firm chooses to make to the distribution process (i.e., the importance of the distribution process to a firm), or alternatively, the efficiency of a firm's distribution process.

Surveys of supply chain practitioners such as those done by the Aberdeen Group (as reported in [22]) invariably show that practitioners rate on-time delivery as the most important measure of a supplier's service to a customer. Therefore, we selected on-time performance as the key service indicator to include in our analysis.

Forecast accuracy is a good barometer of a firm's capability to perform short run planning in a key area – matching demand and supply. Additionally, a firm's forecast accuracy affects other key plans and decisions such as production and delivery plans. Typically, forecast accuracy measures in private industry calibrate the accuracy of relatively short-run forecasts. Some firms measure forecast accuracy two months into the future, while others may use somewhat shorter or longer time definitions. The forecast horizon is often (and ideally) linked to a firm's lead time. However, forecast accuracy is a relatively short-run based planning measure.

To assess a firm's commitment to long term planning, we selected supply chain planning cost, those expenditures related to developing long-term supply chain plans that include those for outbound logistics. Our rationale for including this variable is that one can consider a firm's expenditure level on supply chain planning as a surrogate for the firm's commitment to meeting customers' delivery needs.

We also required a ninth variable, namely, the operating margin of each firm. A firm's operating margin reflects a firm's profitability after the delivery (and sale) of its inventory to its customers. Since outbound logistics covers the delivery and sale of inventory, operating margin is the appropriate measure of profitability for our study.

The data for this study were obtained from SAPs Benchmarking Program for Supply Chain Planning. These data were collected via electronic surveys conducted between 2007 and 2012 from supply chain managers in various manufacturing and service organizations. The respondents were supply chain managers who were asked to provide actual values for the metrics, each of which was explicitly defined in the survey. SAP professionals within their Customer Value organization were responsible for managing the survey, and they checked and validated each data element before including it within the database. Once we received the data set we checked for outliers and incorrect values. We required that each case have a value for operating margin since it is the outcome variable of interest. A total of 247 useable cases comprise the data set. Some of the cases have missing data for one or more outbound logistics metrics.

Missing data analysis: Tsikriktsis [23] states that the treatment of missing data has been overlooked in the OM literature and should be explicitly considered in a discussion of research methods. The deletion of entire cases that have any missing data (called listwise deletion) can have a substantial effect on the size of the data set and a loss of statistical power. As mentioned above, 247 cases in the data set have a value for Operating Margin, while some cases may have one or more of the eight outbound logistics performance metrics missing. A missing data analysis is needed to determine the amount of data that are missing and whether the pattern of missing observations is random or not.

The data set consists of 2,223 data items (9 variables*247 cases), where 330 or 14.84% are missing. For each variable, such as Days of Inventory, separate variance t-tests were run to compare the group of cases with data on another variable (say Obsolete Inventory) with those cases without data on that variable. Of the 9*8=72 tests, only two are significant: Inventory Carrying Cost with Warehouse Management Cost, and Obsolete Inventory with Inventory Carrying Cost, so we conclude that there is no systematic non-random pattern. The definitions of the eight outbound logistics metrics used in this study are given in Table 1.

The amount and pattern of missing data should affect the technique used for replacing missing data values [23]. The possible patterns are non-missing at random (NMAR), missing at random (MAR), and missing completely at random (MCAR). The latter is the best case, and means that the presence of missing data on some variable is unrelated to the values of other variables in the data set. Little's test [24] is the standard for determining whether the data set is MCAR or not. Applying Little's test [24] we find that our data set is MCAR (chi square test statistic=356.491, d. f. 324, p=0.103). Since the data set is MCAR and there are more than 10% missing, Tsikriktsis [23] recommends using pairwise deletion first and either regression or hot-deck methods as a second choice. Pairwise deletion is appropriate for statistical methods such as correlation that require only pairs of data but are inappropriate when full cases are needed as in cluster analysis. Hot deck requires replacing a missing value with an actual value from a similar case in the data set. Linear regression requires developing an equation that is used to estimate the missing value as a function of the other variables in the data set. We chose linear regression since it is more straightforward and less subjective. Linear regression was successfully able to estimate all missing data elements (Table 1).

Operating margin was measured as earnings before interest and taxes (EBIT). Our sample is drawn from a mix of industries as represented by two-digit NAICS codes, and each observation is comprised of data from a single year over the 2007- 2012 time frame. Operating margins can vary across industries and are influenced by prevailing economic conditions. To make the operating margins comparable across the sample, we subtracted the median operating margin for the appropriate industry and year (obtained from Compustat) from the firm's actual operating margin to obtain an adjusted operating margin. The adjusted operating margin indicates how much more (less) profitable a firm in the sample is with respect to their industry during a given year.

Demographics: Table 2 provides the distribution of responding organizations by industry, while Table 3 shows the distribution of annual revenue across the respondents. Manufacturing firms comprise 83.1% of the sample with representation from a variety of industries. The firms in the sample range in annual revenue from under $100 million (7%) to over $5 billion (8%), with the vast majority between $100 million and $5 billion (85%).

Correlation: The correlation matrix for the full data set is given as Table 4. Note that the correlation results without the imputed values are very similar to those shown. Some of the outbound delivery metrics are significantly correlated and a few have relatively high correlation values (Tables 2-4).

Results

Clusters emphasizing multiple metrics

Various researchers have recommended that principal component analysis (PCA) with orthogonal rotation be performed on the data

Metric	Definition
InvCC	Inventory Carrying Cost (% of revenue)
WhMgt	Warehouse Management Cost (% of revenue)
ObsInv	Obsolete Inventory (% of inventory value)
TransSpd	Transportation Spend (% of revenue)
SCPCost	Supply Chain Planning Cost (% of revenue)
On-Time	On-Time Delivery Performance (in %)
ForcAcc	Forecast Accuracy (in %)
DaysInv	Days In Inventory (number of days)

Table 1: Definition of the outbound logistics metrics.

Industry	Frequency (per cent)
Apparel, Leather and Textiles	11 (4.5)
Computers, Electronics, and Electrical Equipment	36 (14.6)
Food, Beverage, and Tobacco	37 (15.0)
Furniture, Wood, Paper and Printing	9 (3.6)
Metals and Machinery	45 (18.2)
Miscellaneous Manufacturing and Mining	21 (8.5)
Miscellaneous Services	9 (3.6)
Petro Chemicals, Plastics, Rubber and Minerals	26 (10.5)
Retail Trade	23 (9.3)
Transportation Equipment	20 (8.1)
Wholesale Trade	10 (4.0)
Total	247

Table 2: Industries of responding organizations.

Range (in millions)	Frequency (Percent)
<50	5 (2.0)
50-100	13 (5.3)
100-250	34 (13.8)
250-500	44 (17.8)
500-1000	50 (20.2)
1000-1500	33 (13.4)
1500-2500	31 (12.6)
2500-5000	17 (6.9)
5000-10000	17 (6.9)
>10000	3 (1.2)
Total	247

Table 3: Distribution of annual revenue of responding organizations.

set prior to performing cluster analysis to adjust for high correlation among variables [25,26]. PCA was performed on the data set using varimax rotation with Kaiser normalization, and resulted in four factors. The four factor scores for each observation were used in the subsequent cluster analysis.

Cluster analysis was applied to develop the taxonomy based on the outbound logistics metrics defined in Table 1. Hierarchical clustering was used to determine the number of clusters and non-hierarchical clustering was applied to determine the membership of the clusters [25,26]. This approach has been applied in other operations management studies (e.g., [18,27]).

Lehmann [28] suggests that the number of clusters should be between n/30 and n/60, where n is the sample size. This leads to a consideration of the number of clusters in this study to between four and eight. The data were analyzed using Ward's method for hierarchical clustering with squared Euclidian distances. Following Hair et al. [26] the agglomeration coefficient was used to determine the number of clusters over the four-to-eight range. The stopping rule is based on the size of the percentage change in the agglomeration coefficient from a larger to a smaller number of clusters. When large increases occur in moving from one set of clusters to the next, the prior cluster solution is selected because the new combination is joining quite different clusters. This approach has been used by several operations management researchers [29,30].

The results show that four clusters is best, with five and six clusters relatively close in agglomeration coefficient values. We then ran k-means clustering for k=4, k=5 and k=6 to determine the cluster membership. Since the results for k-means clustering can depend on the order of the observations, we made a series of additional runs for k=4, k=5 and k=6 where the order of the cases were randomized. The results show that the initial k=4 solution is the most stable. Based on the results, we selected the four-cluster solution.

ANOVA was used to test for differences in the eight outbound logistics metrics between the four clusters. Following the approach used by Kathuria [18] and Zhao et al. [29] to present the results of cluster analysis as used in OM research, Table 5 presents the cluster means, the standard errors, the cluster number(s) from which this cluster was significantly different at the 0.05 level of significance, and the relative rankings of the eight metrics within the clusters. The F-statistics provides strong evidence that one or more of the cluster means differed from the others on all eight metrics at the $p<0.0001$ level, an indication that the clusters are well-formed. However, since the Levene test indicated that the variances are not homogeneous across the clusters for all metrics except for ForcAcc, the Welch test was run since it does not require homogeneity of variances to test for differences in the eight

	InvCC	WhMgt	ObsInv	TransSpd	SCPCost	On-Time	ForcAcc	DaysInv
InvCC		0.309** (0.000)	0.356** (0.000)	-0.096 (0.134)	0.120 (0.060)	-0.146* (0.022)	-0.193* (0.002)	0.469** (0.000)
WhMgt			0.120 (0.060)	0.252** (0.000)	0.023 (0.718)	-0.002 (0.970)	-0.090 (0.160)	0.119 (0.062)
ObsInv				-0.034 (0.598)	0.027 (0.670)	0.028 (0.656)	-0.021 (0.748)	-0.136* (0.033)
TransSpd					-0.002 (0.975)	-0.033 (0.610)	-0.020 (0.750)	-0.112 (0.078)
SCPCost						0.118 (0.064)	-0.049 (0.443)	0.228** (0.000)
On-Time							0.244** (0.000)	-0.205** (0.001)
ForcAcc								-0.110 (0.084)

[a]p-values are in parentheses below estimated coefficients** indicates significance at the 0.01 level* indicates significance at the 0.05 level

Table 4: Correlation matrix for outbound logistics metrics[a].

Metric	Cluster #1 (n=56)	Cluster #2 (*n*=22)	Cluster #3 (*n*=48)	Cluster #4 (*n*=121)	F-stat[a]
InvCC					
Cluster Mean	2.679 (4)[b]	3.498 (3,4)	2.492 (2,4)	1.201 (1.2,3)	33.997***
S. E.	0.22321	0.46409	0.18608	0.06405	
Rank[c]	2	1	3	4	
WhMgt					
Cluster Mean	1.381 (2)	3.815 (1,3,4)	1.440 (2)	1.291(2)	21.881***
S. E.	0.14814	0.63597	0.14822	0.10218	
Rank	3	1	2	4	
ObsInv					
Cluster Mean	5.211 (2)	18.484 (1,3,4)	6.121 (2)	4.228 (2)	57.173***
S. E.	0.51854	2.33187	0.60026	0.29808	
Rank	3	1	2	4	
TransSpd					
Cluster Mean	2.682 (-)	4.060 (3)	2.402 (2)	3.385 (-)	4.086***
S. E.	0.23388	0.5569	0.26436	0.23248	
Rank	3	1	4	2	
SCPCost					
Cluster Mean	0.504 (3)	0.565 (3)	1.315(1,2,4)	0.477 (3)	39.111***
S. E.	0.03455	0.07639	0.12964	0.02621	
Rank	3	2	1	4	
On-Time					
Cluster Mean	74.280 (2,3,4)	90.486 (1)	92.305 (1)	92.107 (1)	64.337***
S. E.	1.77988	1.63391	0.79109	0.57075	
Rank	4	3	1	2	
ForcAcc					
Cluster Mean	66.186 (2,3,4)	77.278 (1)	78.702 (1)	83.087(1)	27.653***
S. E.	1.53348	2.1325	1.67821	1.06474	
Rank	4	3	2	1	
DaysInv					
Cluster Mean	80.216 (2,3,4)	48.155 (1,3)	95.898 (1,2,4)	46.446 (1,3)	51.292***
S. E.	4.07576	6.1397	4.29623	1.99438	
Rank	2	3	1	4	

***p<0.0001

[a]note: In addition to the F-statistic the Welch test was run since the hypothesis that the variances are homogeneous for all metrics across the clusters is not supported (except for ForcAcc); the Welch test is significant at the p <0.01 for all metrics, indicating that for each metric the hypothesis that the cluster means are all equal is not supported

[b]numbers in parentheses indicate(s) the cluster(s) from which this cluster is significantly different at the 0.05 level

[c]ranks are based on highest to lowest values

Table 5: Outbound logistics metrics emphasized by clusters.

outbound logistics metrics between the four clusters. The Welch test was significant at the p<0.01 level for all metrics, verifying the ANOVA results. The Scheffe pairwise comparison of the mean differences at the 0.05 level indicates those cluster means for a given metric that are significantly different from other cluster means. All cluster means for every metric except for two were statistically significantly different from at least one other cluster mean.

Cluster descriptions

Cluster 1: Low Cost, Low Service Providers. The spending on distribution as a percent of revenue of the 56 manufacturing firms that compose Cluster 1 is moderately below the average of all firms (4.1% vs. 4.7% for all firms). In both components of distribution (i.e., warehousing and transportation), the spending of Cluster 1 firms lags the overall firm-wide average by 12% and 13% respectively (Table 5).

Additionally, Cluster 1 firms have below average on-time performance when compared to the average for all 247 firms (74.2% vs. the 88.0% average of all firms). On-time performance is a critical component of delivery service, and therefore, given the very poor performance in this area, this cluster is named low cost, low service providers. Cluster 1 firms also exhibit significantly lower forecasting functionality with an average forecast accuracy of 66.2% vs. the 77.9% sample average.

Interestingly, while Cluster 1 firms have a somewhat higher average inventory carrying cost as a percent of revenue than the average for all firms (2.7% vs. 2.0%), these firms have a somewhat lower average level of obsolete inventory (5.2% vs. 6.1%). On the other hand, Cluster 1 firms' days of inventory (80 days) are significantly higher than the average for all firms (64 days). Thus, overall this cluster exhibits a rather mixed inventory management performance level.

Cluster 2: Heavy Distribution Spenders. The 22 firms that comprise this cluster spend a significantly higher percent of their revenue on the combination of warehousing and transportation than do any of the other clusters. The firms in Cluster 2 spend about 7.9% of their total revenue on these two functions, while no other cluster spends more than 4.7% of their total revenue on distribution. We therefore title this cluster heavy distribution spenders given that they spend over double the percentage of revenue on this function compared to the cluster that spends the least on distribution (Cluster 3), and about 70% more than the average spent on distribution by all 247 firms in the survey. The emphasis of Cluster 2 firms on distribution activities (i.e., on maintaining, controlling and delivering finished goods to customers) results in relatively good on time performance (90.5%) by these companies. However, Cluster 2 firms have only average forecast accuracy (77.2%).

A somewhat surprising area of performance for this cluster is inventory management. Cluster 2 firms' days of inventory on hand (48) are about 16 days below the 247 firm-wide average. At the same time however, the firms in this cluster have average inventory carrying costs as a percent of revenue that are 75% above the overall firm average and obsolete inventory costs that are the highest of all clusters and triple the average of all firms. In summary, Cluster 2 firms exhibit a very mixed overall performance level.

Cluster 3: Planners and Efficient Distribution Spenders. This cluster of 48 firms exhibits the lowest level of spending on distribution (as a percent of revenue) of any of the four clusters. Cluster 3 firms on average expend 18% less on the sum of transportation and warehousing (distribution) than do the 247 firms in all four clusters overall. Cluster 3 firms average 3.8% of total revenue spent on distribution compared to an overall average of 4.7% for all firms. These firms spend the lowest percent of their revenues of any cluster on transportation (2.4%), and a below average percent of their revenues on warehouse operations (1.4% vs. 1.6% overall average).

At the same time, the firms in Cluster 3 spend two times more on supply chain planning (as a percent of revenue) than the overall sample average. Given this combination of relatively low distribution spending, coupled with a strong emphasis on planning, we call these firms planners and efficient distribution spenders. With respect to planning, the cluster with the next highest percent of revenue spent on supply chain planning (Cluster 2) allocates far less than 50% of the relative revenue spent on planning by Cluster 3. There is some evidence that this emphasis on planning contributes to the supply chain execution of Cluster 3 firms. Specifically, Cluster 3 firms exhibit the best on-time delivery performance (92.3%) of the four clusters. At the same time, this group of firms has just minimally above average forecast accuracy compared to the entire set of firms surveyed (78.7% vs. 77.9%).

It is interesting to observe that in terms of inventory costs, Cluster 3 firms are on the relatively high side. Specifically, this group of firms has above average inventory carry costs as a percent of revenue (2.5% vs. 2.0%), while their obsolete inventory costs mirror the average for all 247 firms (both 6.1% as a percent of total revenue). However, Cluster 3 firms average 96 days of inventory on hand, very significantly higher than the overall average of 64 days for all 247 firms in total.

Cluster 4: Inventory Investment Minimizers. The 121 firms in Cluster 4, the largest of the four clusters, have the lowest levels of obsolete inventory (4.2%) expressed as a percentage of revenue. This is over 30% lower than the average of all 247 firms (6.1%), and over 4 times lower than the cluster with the highest percent (Cluster 2). Cluster 4 firms also have the lowest inventory carrying costs (expressed as a percentage of revenue) of any cluster (1.2% vs. 2.0% average for all firms). Further, Cluster 4 firms' average of only 46 days of inventory on hand is lowest among all clusters and is significantly less than the overall average of 64 days among all firms. Overall, all three inventory management metrics indicate that the firms in Cluster 4 focus more on minimizing inventory investment than do firms in the other three clusters, hence the name given to this cluster is inventory investment minimizers.

Interestingly, Cluster 4 firms have the second best (and nearly identical to the best) on-time performance (92.1%) of any cluster and their average exceeds the overall firm average (88.0%) by 4%. Cluster 4 firms also display the highest level of forecast accuracy (83.1%), which exceeds the overall average for all 247 firms of 77.9% by over 5%. Finally, these firms' expenditures on distribution (4.68% of their revenues) is almost identical to the average distribution spending of all firms (4.66%).

The above results support Hypothesis 1 – i.e., that firms can be classified into different groups based upon their emphasis on outbound logistics metrics. And importantly, the results suggest that in general firms emphasize various sets of outbound logistic metrics that reflect their operational planning and control processes in order to meet the needs of the particular markets they serve.

Operating margins and cluster membership

As shown in Table 6, the mean adjusted operating margins of the four clusters range from a high of 5.6% for cluster 3 to a low of 3.4% for cluster 4, a difference of 65%. The operating margin across the entire sample is 4.2%, and so the differences of cluster 3 and 4's means appear substantial. However, as shown in Table 6, the ANOVA test results indicate that the differences across cluster means are not statistically significant. The relatively high standard deviation of operating margins within each cluster relative to their means (high coefficient of variation) appears to be a major contributor to this result. The above results do not support Hypothesis 2 and suggest that there are different emphases on outbound logistics performance metrics that lead to similar levels of firm profitability (Table 6).

Metric	Cluster #1	Cluster #2	Cluster #3	Cluster #4	F-stat[a]
	(n=56)	(*n*=22)	(*n*=48)	(*n*=121)	0.946
OpMarg					
Cluster Mean	0.044	0.048	0.056	0.034	
Std. Deviation	0.06862	0.07101	0.07281	0.08688	
Std. Error	0.00917	0.01514	0.01051	0.0079	
Mean Rank	3	2	1	4	
[a]p=0.419					

Table 6: Operating margin differences across clusters.

Industry	Cluster Number of Cases				Frequency/Percent[c]
	1	2	3	4	
Apparel, Leather and Textiles	1 (2.5)[b]	1 (1.0)	4 (2.1)	5 (5.4)	11/4.5
Computers, Electronics, and Electrical Equipment	12 (8.2)	0 (3.2)	16 (7.0)	8 (17.6)	36/14.6
Food, Beverage, and Tobacco	5 (8.4)	4 (3.3)	3 (7.2)	25 (18.1)	37/15.0
Furniture, Wood, Paper and Printing	0 (2.0)	4 (0.8)	0 (1.7)	5 (4.4)	9/3.6
Metals and Machinery	14 (10.2)	4 (4.0)	7 (8.7)	20 (22.0)	45/18.2
Miscellaneous Manufacturing and Mining	3 (4.8)	2 (1.9)	3 (4.1)	13 (10.3)	21/8.5
Miscellaneous Services	2 (2.0)	0 (0.8)	1 (1.7)	6 (4.4)	9/3.6
Petro Chemicals, Plastics, Rubber and Minerals	10 (5.9)	1 (2.3)	3 (5.1)	12 (12.7)	26/10.5
Retail Trade	4 (5.2)	2 (2.0)	7 (4.5)	10(11.3)	23/9.3
Transportation Equipment	3 (4.5)	4 (1.8)	2 (3.9)	11 (9.8)	20/8.1
Wholesale Trade	2 (2.3)	0 (0.9)	2 (1.9)	6 (4.9)	10/4.0
Total	56	22	48	121	247

[a]Chi Square = 64.779, df = 30, $p < 0.0001$
[b]The numbers in parentheses are the expected cell counts
[c]The percentages are based on the total sample of 247

Table 7: Distribution of Respondents by Industry and Cluster[a].

Industry – cluster relationship

A chi-square test was used to determine whether there is a relationship between cluster membership and the industry grouping in which the firm belongs. Table 7 illustrates the distribution of industries by the four clusters and the test results. The test results indicate that there are significant differences in industry membership across clusters. A comparison of actual vs. expected cell counts indicates that the following clusters have relatively more firms from specific industries as follows:

Cluster 1: Computers, electronics and electrical equipment; machinery and metals; and petrochemicals, plastics, rubber and minerals.

Cluster 2: Furniture, wood, paper and printing; and transportation equipment.

Cluster 3: Computers, electronics and electrical equipment; retail trade.

Cluster 4: Food, beverage and tobacco; and miscellaneous manufacturing and mining.

Apparel, leather and textiles; miscellaneous services; and wholesale trade are the only industries not having relatively more firms in a specific cluster. These are three of the four industries with the smallest numbers of respondents. The above results support Hypothesis 3 and suggest that emphasis on specific sets of outbound logistic performance metrics tend to be associated with firms in specific industries.

Conclusions

This study analyzed the competitive outbound logistics priorities of 247 firms across a wide variety of industries. Our analysis indicates that different groups of these firms emphasize different operational and planning priorities. Specifically, our research suggests that firms across multiple industries can be classified into several statistically distinct groups (or clusters) based on their different performance priorities with respect to outbound logistics. Importantly, our research also found that there were not statistically significant differences in the levels of profitability achieved by our four groupings or clusters of firms, where each group had different outbound logistics priorities. This finding suggests that individual firms cannot rely on one standard approach to outbound logistics. Rather, it indicates that individual firms must develop an approach tailored to their particular supply chain and customers.

The Inventory Investment Minimizers, the largest group representing about 49% of the sample, focus on tightly controlling their inventory investment, carrying and obsolescence costs. The second largest group, the Low Cost, Low Service Providers who comprise 23% of the sample, focus on maintaining low distribution costs and sacrifice on-time service levels in doing so. The Planners and Efficient Distribution Spenders, 19% of the sample, invest more resources on supply chain planning activities and this allows them to provide superior on-time delivery service at relatively low costs. The smallest group in our sample (9%), the Heavy Distribution Spenders, as their name suggests do spend heavily on warehousing and transportation, and this results in good on-time delivery service (Table 7).

An important attribute of a good supply chain manager, and more broadly, a firm with strong supply chain management, is the ability to discern and develop a supply chain operating model that uniquely meets the needs of the individual firm. It is often stated that there is no one supply chain strategy that works for all firms [19,22]. Rather, firms and their managers must assess the requirements and expectations of their customers and suppliers, their internal firm capabilities, as well as their external competitive environment, and all other market forces to develop the optimal supply chain plan for their company. At the same time, there are clearly not an infinite set of viable supply chain operating models that firms may adopt. Supply chain plans ultimately translate into tactics and operational activities in specific areas such as outbound logistics. One implication or interpretation of our Hypothesis 1 is that there are a set of different operational planning and control activities related to outbound logistics that firms may choose between. Our results identified four different clusters (i.e., planning and operational priorities) that the sample firms gravitated towards. Thus, the statistical significance of Hypothesis 1 suggests that firms do choose among a set of distinct priorities in crafting the best outbound logistics operations approach for their particular company.

As noted, the Hypothesis (#2) that different clusters (with different outbound logistics orientations) would have different levels of profitability was rejected. That is, the mean profitability of each of the four clusters are not statistically different. The rejection of this hypothesis offers some interesting implications. First, it suggests that there is no one outbound logistics operational approach that yields levels of profitability superior to all others. Rather, different firms may achieve optimal profits through different outbound logistics approaches. One question this raises is: can we interpret any alignment or compatibility between the acceptance of Hypothesis 1 and the rejection of Hypothesis 2? A possible interpretation that facilitates "compatibility" between these two results is as follows. If one outbound logistics approach was clearly more profitable than all others, one would expect the vast majority of firms to adopt this "more profitable" approach. Further, if the vast majority of firms followed similar outbound logistics approaches, then one would not expect to observe four distinct (and statistically different) clusters. However, our results demonstrated that within our sample, four statistically different groups of firms do exist. In this sense, the acceptance of Hypothesis 1 and the rejection of Hypothesis 2 are compatible and explainable. Specifically, there are a number of different outbound logistics approaches that can potentially be successful. Not every approach however will work successfully for every firm. Therefore, successful firms need to select the approach most appropriate for their particular company.

Turning to Hypothesis 3, it is not surprising that this hypothesis proved to be statistically significant (i.e., true). Again, Hypothesis 3 is that the group orientation – outbound delivery metrics emphasized – is associated with industry membership. Different industries often have different customer delivery requirements and expectations. For example, in the consumer products industry, customers' (e.g., retailers') requirements for on-time deliveries of "commodity" products such as toothpaste, shampoo, etc. are extremely exacting. There are numerous suppliers of these products, and retailers will not accept poor performance from vendors. Prolonged poor on-time delivery performance can result in retailers literally delisting (eliminating) a suppliers' products from their store inventory. In contrast, in industries where a supplier is providing specialty finished products, or perhaps even intermediate goods, mediocre on-time performance will not result in the delisting of a supplier's products.

Days of inventory on hand is another example of a metric where intrinsic differences between industries would lead one to expect differences in outbound logistics. For example, in in the fresh food category of the food industry days of inventory on hand must be constrained due to shelf life limitations. However, shelf life is not a factor affecting outbound logistics performance in many other industries. Thus, product type or product attributes, as well as differences in competitive requirements, lead firms in different industries to their own particular orientation to, and priorities on, outbound logistics operations. The statistical significance of Hypothesis 3 lends credence to this expectation or interpretation.

Unlike previous research this study did not establish a strong connection between differences in supply chain performance and firm financial performance. One possible explanation is that previous research did not investigate the link between supply chain performance metrics and firm performance. For example, in contrast to our use of outbound logistics metrics, D'Avanzo et al. [5] used a variety of data sources in their analysis, including interviews and survey data, as well as three high-level measures: cost of goods sold as a percentage of revenue, inventory turns, and return on assets. Ellinger et al. [7] and the studies reviewed by Shi and Yu [9] utilized either perceptual surveys or secondary data sources, and focused on the connection between firm performance and supply chain practices or competency as contrasted with performance metrics. The meta analytic approach pursued by Leuschner et al. [10] found a postive and significant link between supply chain integration and firm performance. Again, detailed supply chain metrics were not addressed in the studies they considered.

The selection of the eight metrics used in this study ties to the work of Gunasekaran et al. [13]. Each of these outbound logistics metrics were significantly different between at least two of our four clusters, providing some additional support for the discriminating value of the metrics selected. This finding suggests that future studies seeking to examine the link between supply chain performance and firm financial performance should utilize metrics drawn from Gunasekaran et al. [13].

Limitations

While this study offers important insights on priorities and approaches to outbound logistics operations, it also has limitations that lead to potential future areas of study. While our sample covers a broad range of manufacturing and service industries, it is heavily focused on manufacturing firms. The presence of a relatively limited number of service firms (42, or 17% of the sample), might have potentially impacted the formation of the clusters. Future research should address cluster formation based on a more balanced sample of manufacturing and service firms, enabling a comparison of the resulting cluster profiles and those found in this research.

Our sample covers firms who produce and/or sell both finished goods and in some cases intermediate products. In the future, it would be interesting to conduct separate studies of finished goods and intermediate goods producers and suppliers. Differences both within each group and between each group could be evaluated. Another potential area of future study is the more detailed or lower levels of outbound logistics operations and performance metrics appropriate at that level such as those in Gunasekaran et al. [11] or Shepherd and Gunter [14]. For purposes of this study, we focused on the high level or overarching metrics used to monitor and measure overall outbound logistics operations (e.g., total warehouse management costs and total transportation spend). In the future, it would be insightful to explore these activities in greater depth. For example, warehouse management activities and costs can be broken down into major sub-components such as receiving, put-away, storage, picking and shipping. It would be valuable to explore whether different groups of firms place operational emphasis in different lower level areas, and if so, are there discernible differences in outbound logistics performance related to these differing priorities.

References

1. CSCMP (Council of Supply Chain Management Professionals) (2013) Supply Chain Management: Terms and Glossary.

2. Kavilanz P (2010) Dumped! Brand names fight to stay in stores. CNNMoney.

3. Stapleton D, Hanna J, Yagla S, Johnson J, Markussen, D (2002) Measuring Logistics Performance Using the Strategic Profit Model. International Journal of Logisitcs Managmeent 13: 898-107.

4. Ojha D, Gianiodis, Manuja I (2013) Impact of Logistics Business Continuity Planning on Operational Capabilities and Financial Performance. International Journal of Logistics Management 24: 180-209.

5. D'Avanzo R, von Lewinski H, Van Wassenhove L (2003) The link between supply chain and financial performance. Supply Chain Management Review 7: 40-47.

6. Hendricks K, Singhal V (2005) Association Between Supply Chain Glitches and Operating Performance. Management Science 51: 695-711.

7. Ellinger AE, Natarajarathinam M, Adams FG, Gray JB, Hofman D, et al. (2011) Supply Chain Management Competency and Firm Financial Success. Journal of Business Logistics 32: 214-226.

8. Altman E (1968) Financial Ratios, Discriminant Analysis and Prediction of Corporate Bankruptcy. Journal of Finance 23: 589-609.

9. Shi M, Yu W (2013) Supply chain management and financial performance: Literature review and future directions. International Journal of Operations and Production Management 33: 1283-1317.

10. Leuschner R, Rogers D, Charvet F (2013) A meta-analysis of supply chain integration and firm performance. Journal of Supply Chain Management 49: 34-57.

11. Gunasekaran A, Patel C, McGauchey R (2004) A framework for supply chain performance measurement. International Journal of Production Economics 87: 333-347.

12. Gunasekaran A, Kobu B (2007) Performance measures and metrics in logistics and supply chain management: A review of recent literature (1995-2004) for research and applications. International Journal of Production Research 45: 2819-2840.

13. Gunasekaran A, Patel C, Tirtiroglu E (2001) Performance measures and metrics in a supply chain environment. International Journal of Operations and Production Management 21: 71-87.

14. Shepherd C, Gunter H (2006) Measuring supply chain performance: Current research and future directions. International Journal of Productivity and Performance Management 55: 242-258.

15. APICS Supply Chain Council (2015) SCOR.

16. Chan F, Qi H (2006) An innovative performance measurement method for supply chain management. Supply Chain Management: An International Journal (8): 209-223.

17. Miller J, Roth A (1994) A taxonomy of manufacturing strategies. Management Science 40: 285-304.

18. Kathuria R (2000) Competitive priorities and managerial performance: taxonomy of small manufacturers. Journal of Operations Management 18: 627-641.

19. Bowersox D, Closs D, Cooper M, Bowersox J (2013) Supply Chain Logistics Management (4thedn) McGraw-Hill Irwin, New York.

20. Coyle J, Langley J, Novack R, Gibson B (2013) Supply Chain Management: A Logistics Perspective (9thedn) South-Western Cengage Learning.

21. Chopra S, Meindl P (2016) Supply Chain Management: Strategy, Planning and Operation (6thedn) Pearson.

22. Coyle J, Langley J, Gibson B, Novack R, Bardi E (2008) Supply Chain Management: A Logistics Perspective (8thedn) South-Western Cengage Learning p: 149.

23. Tsikritsis N (2005) A review of techniques for treating missing data in OM survey research. Journal of Operations Management 24: 53-62.

24. Little R (1988) A test of missing completely at random for multivariate data with missing values. Journal of the American Statistical Association 83: 1198-1202.

25. Ketchen D, Shook C (1996) The application of cluster analysis in strategic management research: An analysis and critique. Strategic Management Journal 17: 441-458.

26. Hair J, Black W, Babin B, Anderson R (2010) Multivariate Data Analysis, (7thedn) Prentice Hall, Upper Saddle River NJ.

27. Flynn B, Huo B, Zhao X (2010) The impact of supply chain integration on performance: A contingency and configuration approach. Journal of Operations Management 28: 58-71.

28. Lehmann D (1979) Market Research and Analysis. Irwin, Homewood, IL.

29. Zhao X, Sum CC, Qi Y, Zhang H, Lee T (2006) A taxonomy of manufacturing strategies in China. Journal of Operations Management 24: 621-636.

30. Sum C C, Kow L, Chen CS (2004) A taxonomy of operations strategies of high performing small and medium enterprises in Singapore. International Journal of Operations and Production Management 24: 321-345.

20

The Interest Rate Algebra

Yuriy V Kozyr*

Department ofTheoretical Economy and Mathematic Research, Central Economics and Mathematics, Institute of RussianAcademy of Sciences, Moscow, Russia

Abstract

This article considers the structure of interest rate, applied for discounting of risky cash flows. The purpose of the article is a presentation of ways of reflecting inflation and risks in the calculation of risk discount rate.

In introduction on base of well-known dependences is shown that risk premium depends on inflation rate and (for multiplicative-type models) risk free rate.

In the first part of the article three Interest rate algebras are presented. They describe the attitude between nominal discount rate, risk free rate, inflation rate and risk-premium. This algebras can presents in additive-type or multiplicative-type versions and have given risk premium value without detailed description the structure of risk premium.

The second part of the paper has more detailed attitude between risk premium, risk free rate and mathematical expectation of losses because of bankruptcy/default. It is shown that the obtained dependences are slightly different and depends on the initial preconditions calculation: the principle of arbitration or the principle of certainly equivalent.

Keywords: Interest rate; Risk free rate; Risk premium; Probability of lose

Introduction

There are many different interpretations for structure of interest rate: unbiased expectations theory, liquidity preference theory and liquidity premium. Also exist many different models for discount rate valuation, such as CAPM, MCAPM, APM and etc. However most of this model doesn't give possibility of direct connection between such parameters as inflation, real rate and risk premium. This article contains a version of interest rate algebra sets developed by the author and applicable for the interpretation of structure for risk-free (in first part) and risky (in second part) interest rates.

According to the established tradition, the analysis of the structure of interest rate for the purpose of its subsequent use in discounting exercises involves the following relations:

Irving Fisher Expression [1]

$$r = (1+r_r)\cdot(1+i)-1, \tag{1}$$

Where, r - Nominal rate of interest,

rr - Real rate of interest,

i - The rate of inflation for the period,

Furthermore, decomposition of an interest rate into a risk-free component and the risk premium can be expressed as [2-5]:

$$r = r_f + pr, \tag{2}$$

Where, r - The interest rate specific to future cash flows from a project (asset) with a certain investment risk,

rf - Interest rate on risk-free investments,

pr - Risk premium for bearing the risk of investing into similar projects (assets).

In turn, the risk-free rate can be represented in an additive form (following the concept of simple per cents):

$$r_f = r_{fr} + i, \tag{3}$$

Where, rfr - Real interest rate on risk-free investments or in a multiplicative form (following the concept of compound interest):

$$r = r_{fr} + i + pr_{ra}, \tag{4}$$

Where, rfm - Nominal risk-free interest rate used for complex compound interest,

rfrm - Real risk-free interest rate used for complex compound interest.

Thus, the work of the classics of investment theory affords the conclusion that the level of interest rate is a function of the risk-free rate (net of inflation), the rate of inflation, and the risk premium component:

$$r = r_{fr} + i + pr_{ra}, \tag{5}$$

$$r = (1+r_{frm})\cdot(1+i)\cdot(1+pr_{rm})-1, \tag{6}$$

Where, r - Is a nominal rate of interest applicable for discounting cash flows from a risky investment project (i.e., risky cash flows),

rfr - Real (net of inflation) risk-free rate of interest,

prra - Risk premium applicable in an additive-type model, as in (5), given a separate accounting for the inflationary component,

prrm - Risk premium applicable in a multiplicative-type models, as in (6), given a separate accounting for the inflationary component,

rfrm - The value of the real risk-free rate used in multiplicative-type models, as in (6).

***Corresponding author:** Yuriy V Kozyr, Department of Theoretical Economy and Mathematic Research, Central Economics and Mathematics, Institute of Russian Academy of Sciences, Moscow, Russia, E-mail: y_k65@mail.ru

It is evident that there exist the following relations between prra and prrm:

$$pr_{rm} = \frac{pr_{ra}}{1+i+r_{frm}(1+i)} = \frac{pr_{ra}}{1+r_f}, \quad (7)$$

$$pr_{ra} = pr_m(1+r_f), \quad (8)$$

Where, rf - The value of the nominal risk-free rate.

If we decompose the real interest rate rr in expression (1) into the risk-free real rate and the (net of inflation) risk premium (prextrar)[1] (rr=(1+rfr) (1+prextrarm) – 1), the following transformation of the expression obtains:

$$\begin{aligned} r &= (1+r_{frm})(1+pr_{rm}^{extra})(1+i)-1 = \\ &= r_{frm}+i+ir_{frm}+r_{frm}pr_{rm}^{extra}+pr_{rm}^{extra}+ \\ &+ipr_{rm}^{extra}+ir_{frm}pr_{rm}^{extra} = \\ &= r_f + pr_{mr}^{extra}(1+i)(1+r_{frm}). \end{aligned} \quad (1a)$$

The last components in expression (1a) are the observed (ex ante) risk-premia for the respective (i.e., additive or multiplicative) models. These expressions show that the inflation exerts immediate influence on the ex-ante risk premium. Moreover, Expression (1a) indicates that the ex-ante risk premium is also affected by the value of the implied real risk-free rate.

Interest Rate Algebra – 1 (IRA-1)

Expressions (1a) and (1b) demonstrate that the detailed study of the subject of interest rates leads to realization that the number of structural representations for interest rates is not exhausted merely by the expressions (1)-(4). This is due to the following factors:

- A risk-free rate can be represented either in nominal (rf) or real (rfr) terms;
- A risk-free rate may either include some residual risk elements (rf and rfr), or be netted of any such elements (rnf and rnfr);
- A risk-free rate can be determined by the rule of simple (rf, rnf, rnfr) and compound interest (rfm, rnfm, rnfrm);
- The risk premium can be represented differently for the additive (pra) or multiplicative (prm) interest rate models;
- The risk premium can be represented in nominal (pr) or real (prr) terms;
- The risk premium can be used in conjunction with "risk-free rates" which incorporate some residual risk elements - rf, rfr (in this case the risk premium shall be denoted with the "extra" superscript prextra), as well as in conjunction with absolute ("pure") risk-free rates - rnf, rnfr (in this case, the notation for such risk premia does without the «extra» superscript - pr).

Having regard to these circumstances, an attempt is made below to list all possible detailed specifications of the interest rate structure, which can be employed in the context of discounting for risky cash flows (in situations where the risk factor is incorporated in the discount rates, and not through adjusting the cash flows themselves, as the case may be):

[1]To avoid double-counting in practical terms, only that part of the risk premium (prextrara) is to be accounted for in this exercise which is not already implicitly assumed in the risk-free rate, since risk-free rate metrics used in practice, arguably, admit of the presence of a small element of risk in them.

$$pr_{rm} = \frac{pr_{ra}}{1+i+r_{frm}(1+i)} = \frac{pr_{ra}}{1+r_f}, \quad (9)$$

$$pr_{ra} = pr_m(1+r_f), \quad (10)$$

$$r = r_{nfr} + i + pr_{ra}, \quad (11)$$

$$r = r_{nfr} + pr_a, \quad (12)$$

$$r = r_{nf} + pr_{ra}, \quad (13)$$

$$r = r_{fr} + pr_a^{extra}, \quad (14)$$

$$r = r_{fr} + i + pr_{ra}^{extra}, \quad (15)$$

$$r = r_f + pr_{ra}^{extra}, \quad (16)$$

$$r = (1+r_{nfm})(1+pr_{rm})-1, \quad (17)$$

$$r = (1+r_{nfrm})(1+pr_{rm})(1+i)-1, \quad (18)$$

$$r = (1+r_{fm})(1+pr_{rm}^{extra})-1, \quad (19)$$

$$r = (1+r_{frm})(1+pr_{mr}^{extra})(1+i)-1, \quad (20)$$

$$r = (1+r_{nfrm})(1+pr_m)-1, \quad (21)$$

$$r = (1+r_{frm})(1+pr_m^{extra})-1, \quad (22)$$

Where:

r - The nominal rate of interest/return that accounts for risks,

rnfr – Pure real risk-free rate (i.e., one net of all risks and inflation),

rnf - Pure nominal risk-free rate,

i - The rate of inflation,

rf - Nominal risk-free rate, that includes some residual elements of risk in practical terms (residual risk elements),

rfr - Real risk-free rate with some residual risk elements,

rnfm - Pure nominal risk-free rate used in multiplicative-type models,

rnfrm - Pure real risk-free rate used in multiplicative-type models,

rfm - Nominal risk-free rate used in multiplicative-type models, that includes some residual elements of risk in practical terms (residual risk elements),

rfrm - Real risk-free rate used in multiplicative-type models, that includes some residual elements of risk in practical terms (residual risk elements),

prrm - Full risk premium in the multiplicative representation, net of inflation,

prm - Full risk premium in the multiplicative representation, incorporating inflation,

prra - Full risk premium in the additive representation, net of inflation,

pra - Full risk premium in the additive representation, incorporating inflation,

prextram - Partial risk premium over and above the residual risk elements in the risk-free rate rf , in the multiplicative representation (incorporating inflation), prextrarm - Partial risk premium over and above the residual risk elements in the risk-free rate rf , in the multiplicative representation (net of inflation),

prextraa - Partial risk premium over and above the residual risk elements in the risk-free rate rf , in the additive representation (incorporating inflation),

prextrara - Partial risk premium over and above the residual risk elements in the risk-free rate rf , in the additive representation (net of inflation),

rfpr - Risk-free rate with partial account for inflation: rfpr=rfr+αi ,

rnfpr - Pure risk-free rate with partial account for inflation: rnfpr=rnfr+αi ,

prextrapra - Partial risk premium over and above the residual risk elements in the risk-free rate rfpr , in the additive representation (with partial account for inflation): prextrapra= prextrara+(1 - α)i,

prpra - Risk premium with a partial account for inflation applicable in the additive models and to be used in conjunction with the rnfpr risk-free rate partially accounting for inflation: prpra= prra+ (1 - α)i ,

α – a share (fraction) of inflation reflected (included) in the risk-free rate, 0 ≤ α ≤ 1,

(1 – α) - The remaining share (fraction) of inflation reflected (included) in the risk premium.

It can be ascertained that Models in (21) and (22) reflect valid options for inflation accounting -- both in relation to the risk-free rate and the risk premium.

In addition to the basic expressions (9) - (22), reflecting the variety of designs for the calculation of risky discount rate of nominal cash flows also will show how the link between the individual components of the rates:

$$r_f = r_{fr} + i, \quad (23)$$

$$r_{nf} = r_{nfr} + i, \quad (24)$$

$$r_{fr} = r_{nfr} + \Delta_a, \quad (25)$$

$$pr_a = pr_{ra} + i, \quad (26)$$

$$\Delta_a \equiv pr_a - pr_a^{extra}, \quad (27)$$

$$pr_a^{extra} = pr_a - \Delta_a, \quad (28)$$

$$pr_a^{extra} = pr_a - \Delta_a, \quad (29)$$

$$pr_{ra}^{extra} = pr_a^{extra} - i, \quad (30)$$

$$pr_{ra}^{extra} = pr_{ra} - \Delta_a, \quad (31)$$

$$r_{nfrm} = \frac{1 + r_{frm}}{1 + \Delta_m} - 1, \quad (32)$$

$$\Delta_m = \Delta_a \frac{r_{frm}}{r_{fr}}, \quad (33)$$

$$r_{nfm} = (1 + r_{nfrm})(1 + i) - 1, \quad (34)$$

$$pr_m = (1 + pr_m^{extra})(1 + \Delta_m) - 1, \quad (35)$$

$$pr_m = (1 + pr_{mr}^{extra})(1 + i)(1 + \Delta_m) - 1, \quad (36)$$

$$pr_m^{extra} = (1 + pr_{mr}^{extra})(1 + i) - 1, \quad (37)$$

$$pr_{mr} = \frac{1 + pr_m}{1 + i} - 1, \quad (38)$$

$$pr_{mr}^{extra} = \frac{1 + r}{1 + r_{fm}} - 1, \quad (39)$$

$$pr_{mr}^{extra} = \frac{1 + pr_m^{extra}}{1 + i} - 1, \quad (40)$$

Where, Δa - part of the risk premium, which is integrated into the traditional (used) risk-free rate used in additive models,

Δm - part of the risk premium, which is integrated into the traditional (used) risk-free rate used in multiplicative-type models.

Interest Rate Algebra – 2 (IRA-2)

As the dealings in actual professional practice are for the most part limited to the observed "risk-free" rates which contain (or may contain) the admixtures of risk elements (in other words, we have no data on the values of pure risk-free market interest rates rnfr and rnf), practical value attaches only to those Expressions, out of the set of Expressions (9)-(22), which do not contain pure risk-free rates (rnfr and rnf), i.e., to Expressions (12)-(14), (17)-(18), (20)-(21). Since all these Expressions carry the "extra" superscript in the notation for risk premia, it now makes sense to do away with using this superscript for sheer practicality. To avoid confusion in what follows, let us make use of a new notation, removing the "extra" superscript and replacing lower-case letters with the capital ones (it is possible, of course, to continue with using the lower-case letters -- bearing in mind that the applicable value of the risk premium is only partial, as some of its elements have actually been "woven" into the practically observed equivalent for the risk-free rate):

$$R = r_{fr} + i + \mathrm{Pr}_{ra}, \quad (41)$$

$$R = r_f + \mathrm{Pr}_{ra}, \quad (42)$$

$$R = r_{fr} + \mathrm{Pr}_a, \quad (43)$$

$$R = (1 + r_f)(1 + \mathrm{Pr}_{rm}) - 1, \quad (44)$$

$$R = (1 + r_{frm})(1 + \mathrm{Pr}_{rm})(1 + i) - 1, \quad (45)$$

$$R = (1 + r_{frm})(1 + \mathrm{Pr}_m) - 1, \quad (46)$$

$$R = r_{fpr} + \mathrm{Pr}_{pra}, \quad (47)$$

Where, R is an equivalent of r, Pr – of praextra , and Prpra – of prpraextra in terms of notation previously employed in the Expressions (9)-(22).

As seen from the above expressions, IRA-2 assumes a complete absence of risk elements in the risk-free rate. This option algebra, as well as IRA-1, allows for the possibility of presentation of models for valuing the discount rate in multiplicative and additive forms.

Interest Rate Algebra – 3 (IRA-3)

Having regard to the fact that appraisers and investment analysts for the most part limit themselves to the consideration of additive-type interest rate models, the immediately preceding algebra of interest rates (IRA-2) can be further simplified by excluding from it all the multiplicative-type models and leaving in only the additive models. Simultaneously, with the multiplicative models no longer featuring in the algebra, we shall exclude from the ensuing expressions all "a" subscripts denoting the membership in the additive-type model class.

As a result, this new, simplest, algebra set features only additive models in the following representations:

$$r = r_{fr} + i + pr_r, \quad (48)$$

$$r = r_f + pr_r, \quad (49)$$

$$r = r_{fr} + pr \quad (50)$$

$$r = r_{fr} + \alpha i + (1-\alpha)i + pr_r = \\ = r_{fpr} + pr_{pr}. \quad (51)$$

where r is the equivalent of R, prr - of Prra, pr - of Prra, prpr - of Prpra in terms of notation previously used in the Expressions (41) – (43), (47), namely:

r – Is the nominal rate of interest applicable for discounting after-tax cash flows from a risky investment project (risky cash flows),

rfr - Real (i.e., net of inflation) risk-free interest rate (essentially reflecting the above mentioned "usurious" (i.e., "net-net-net") interest),

prr - Real (net of inflation) risk premium,

pr - Nominal risk premium that includes the inflationary component,

ά - A share (fraction) of inflation included (reflected) in the risk-free rate rfpr,

(1 - ά) - The remaining share (fraction) of inflation included (reflected) in the risk premium prpr.

As seen from the above expressions, in the General case, inflation can be taken into account as the risk-free rate and the risk premium. However, it is important to avoid double counting: in other words, inflation can only redistribute between the risk-free rate and a risk premium.

Accounting for Default and Insolvency Risks (IRA-4)

Let us now take up the subject of the impact of risk on discount rates from a different standpoint. The lack-of-arbitrage-opportunities condition can be expressed as follows:

- In additive form:

$$r_1 \cdot (1-p_d) + (-k) \cdot p_d = r_f, \quad (52)$$

- In multiplicative form:

$$[1 + r_1(1-p_d)] \times [1 + (-k)p_d] = 1 + r_{fm}, \quad (53)$$

Where, pd - Probability of insolvency/default (or, of a shortfall in payments, put simply), k – losses given default (as a fraction of the amount outstanding),

rf - Risk-free rate used in additive-type models,

rfm - Risk-free rate used in multiplicative-type models,

r1 - Expected return on investment into shares, at a favourable outcome.

On the basis of Expressions (52), (53) it is possible to obtain an expressions linking the above-mentioned expected return with the risk-free rate and the parameters of risk:

$$r_1 = \frac{r_f + p_d \cdot k}{1 - p_d}, \quad (54)$$

$$r_{1m} = \frac{r_{fm} + p_d \times k}{1 - p_d(1 + k - kp_d)}. \quad (55)$$

Expressions (54)-(55), in turn, is amenable for the quantification of the risk premium:

-Given the additive specification for the risk-free rate and the risk premium:

$$pr_{a1} = r_1 - r_f = \\ = \frac{r_f + p_d \cdot k}{1 - p_d} - r_{fa} = \\ = \frac{p_d(k + r_f)}{1 - p_d}, \quad (56)$$

- Given the multiplicative specification for the risk-free rate and the risk premium:

$$pr_{m1} = \frac{1 + r_{1m}}{1 + r_{fm}} - 1 = \\ = \frac{p_d \times (k + r_{fm}(1 + k - kp_d))}{(1 - p_d(1 + k - kp_d)(1 + r_{fm})}. \quad (57)$$

On the other hand, the relation between the risky rate and risk parameters can be obtained from a different consideration:

$$\frac{1}{1+r} = \frac{1 - p_d \cdot k}{1 + r_f}, \quad (58)$$

Where, the numerator in the right-hand side of this equation reflects the adjustment to expected cash flows that transforms them into their certainty equivalents. Solving Equation (58) for r results in the following expression for the risky rate:

$$r_2 = \frac{r_f + p_d \cdot k}{1 - p_d \cdot k}, \quad (59)$$

Where r_2 - Is the estimate for risky rate obtained on the basis of Condition (58).

Expression (59) also allows for deriving an expression for the risk premium:

- For the additive relation between the risk-free rate and the risk premium:

$$pr_{a2} = r_2 - r_f = \\ = \frac{r_f + p_d \cdot k}{1 - p_d \cdot k} - r_f = \\ = \frac{p_d \cdot k \cdot (1 + r_f)}{1 - p_d \cdot k}, \quad (60)$$

- For the multiplicative relation between the risk-free rate and the risk premium:

$$pr_{m2} = \frac{1 + r_2}{1 + r_f} - 1 = \frac{p_d \cdot k}{1 - p_d \cdot k}. \quad (61)$$

Despite their similarity, the Expressions (54) and (59) are not identical. The author of this Paper is hard put to give a conclusive explanation to the disparity between the formulas; however, it can be assumed that its nature is associated with the fact that in real life the number of possible event scenarios is significantly above the two outcomes implied in the initial lack-of-arbitrage hypothesis. Also it should be noted that when the value of the parameter "pd" is not equal to zero, and the value "k" is equal to zero, the boundary conditions of the Expression (54) are broken, since "r" becomes greater than "rf".

In this regard, and as of the writing, there is a reason to repose greater trust in the Expression (59).

Subsequent to deriving these formulas, the author of this Paper found in the literature [6] an expression similar (even to the point of notation) to one in (54), which, as suggested in the source, can be used for estimating returns on risky bonds. The respective passage from the work of W. Sharpe is reproduced below:

"How high should a default risk premium be for a bond? According to one model [7], the answer depends both on the probability of default and on the possible financial losses of bondholders given the default. Consider a bond whose probability of default is constant every year (provided that the payments for previous years have been met). Let the probability of default during a given year be denoted as pd. Assume that, if the payments are remiss on the bond, the owner of each bond recovers a part, equal (1 - λ), of its market price in effect a year ago. According to this model, the bond shall be fairly priced, if its yield to maturity, "y", and equals to:

$$y = \frac{\overline{y} + \lambda p_d}{1 - p_d}, \qquad (15.4i)\ (62)$$

Where, y denotes the expected yield to maturity of the bond. The difference, d, between the expected yield to maturity "y" and the expected [baseline] yield has been previously alluded to as the default risk premium. Using the expression (15.4), we can see that this difference for fairly priced bonds should be equal to:

$$d = y - \overline{y} = \left(\frac{\overline{y} + \lambda p_d}{1 - p_d}\right) - \overline{y}. \qquad (15.5)\ (63)$$

(End of the quote).

In conclusion, it bears mentioning that cash flow discounting can be exercised in one of the two following ways:

• Each period payment is discounted using a discount rate specific to that period;

• A single discount rate is used for all periods - which correspond to the "duration" of expected cash flows. The problem encountered with this approach is the difficulty of giving simultaneous/summary estimation to a set of rates in the form of an average expected interest rate (scoping over the investment horizon) – estimation which would not fail to reflect all the possible risks in the capital market.

Conclusion

On a final note, it is necessary to sum up the principal point covered in this paper.

• First of all, separation of components of risky interest rate on risk-free rate and risk premium can be done in a relatively correct ways and still plenty of wrong ways. Perhaps this is why so often errors in assessing the values of the discount rate, when often overlooked factors, or are counted twice.

• Secondly, the risk premium applied when calculating the nominal discount rates, in addition to risk factors, also depends on the level of risk-free interest rates and inflation (see (1a), (54), (55), (59)).

• Thirdly, the value of the risk premium has a nonlinear dependence of the expected losses/damages/bankruptcy or loss of the shortfall in expected revenues (see (56), (57), (60), (61)).

•Fourthly, model estimates of the risk premium should correspond to the used model of the calculation of the discount rate (see (54)-(57, (59)-(61)).

•Finally, taking into account the existing «backlash» in the values of the nominal risky interest rates under equal values of the input parameters of the model (because of the differences in models (54), (55), (59)), it should be acknowledged that at the time of writing, the minimum error values calculation risky rate is from 5% to 10% (in relative percentages).

Received in this article the results can hope to reach a more accurate calculations and the avoidance of errors in estimating discount rates.

References

1. Fisher I (1930) The Theory of Interest. New York.
2. Sharpe WF (1964) Capital Asset Prices: A Theory of Market Equilibrium under Conditions of Risk. Journal of Finance pp: 425-442.
3. Lintner J (1965) The Valuation of Risk Assets and Selection of Risky Investments in Stock Portfolios and Capital Budgets. Review of Economics and Statistics 47: 13-37.
4. Lintner J (1965) Security Prices, Risk, and Maximal Gains from Deversification. Journal of Finance 20: 587-615.
5. Mossin J (1966) Equilibrium in a Capital Asset Market. Econometrica 34: 768-783.
6. Sharpe WF, Alexander GJ, Bailey JV (1999) Investments. 5th ed. Prentice Hall International Inc. USA. Pp: 432-433).
7. Pye G (1974) Gauging the Default Premium. Financial Analysts Journal 30: 423-434.

Technical Market Anomalies: Leveraged ETF Trading with Daily and Intraday Temporal Functionalities

Vasiliki A Basdekidou[1]* and Artemis A. Styliadou[2]

[1]*Special Research Fund Account (ELKE), Aristotle University of Thessaloniki, Greece*
[2]*School of Law, Aristotle University of Thessaloniki, Greece*

Abstract

The main target of this paper is to discuss a short-term trading strategy for ETF instruments (as technical market inefficiencies; "momentum effects") and for this purpose, temporal warning dynamics and triggering trading functionalities (TTF) for the daily time-domain (short-term trading) are introduced. The proposed trading strategy is not a fully documented trading system, because it is derived, as well as it has been back-tested on USA Markets sample data (2000-2016) with an initial formal definition and documentation. According to the back-tested sample data, leveraged ETF short-term trading, with a strategy based on these TTF functionalities, offer great profit opportunities. The current paper contributes to corporate finance literature by examining, analyzing and defining these TTF functionalities. For this purpose, four categories of shareholders are regarded: The long-term investors, the short-term swing traders, the short-term momentary speculators, and the intraday speculators. Paper concludes that, in daily and intraday leveraged ETF trading, the short-term swing traders -if they apply the proposed TTF in their trading plans and strategies- are benefit at the expense of momentary and intraday speculators, while the long-term investors in leveraged ETFs are always the big losers.

Keywords: Equity issue timing; Corporate ownership; Liquidity; Market timing; ETF; Temporal Trading functionalities (TTF); Technical market anomalies

Introduction

The main target of the current paper is to discuss a short-term (daily and intraday) trading plan for these instruments characterized as leveraged Exchange-Traded Funds (ETF). Leveraged ETFs are trading instruments that use a combination of derivatives and debt instruments to double (2x) or triple (3x) the movement of an underlying asset or index that it tracks. Obviously, they are not securities and by owing to their leveraged nature, these funds are incredibly volatile, dangerous and risky. ETF could be characterized as technical market inefficiencies (anomalies) because of the great "momentum effect" involved in their trading. Obviously, ETF trading contradicts the well-known "efficient-market hypothesis". Nowadays, leveraged ETFs instruments have grown in popularity with the day trading crowd because these funds can generate returns very quickly (provided of course, that the trader is on the right side of the trade) [1].

The proposed leveraged ETF strategy is actually just a trading "plan" and not a documented trading system, because it is derived, as well as it has been back-tested on USA Markets sample data (2000-2016) with a primitive formal definition and an initial documentation. Security and instrument trading could be regarded as a time-based historical living system with a number of trading functions (e.g. open/close position), price action patterns (e.g. gaps, cups), temporal warning dynamics signals (e.g. on-open gaps, morning cups), triggering signals (e.g. pivotal breakouts, bullish candlestick patterns); all of them incorporating temporal functionalities related to the particular stock or ETF instrument. In the daily and intraday time-domain, various time-frames charts are used as the visual representation of instrument's or stock's price action (e.g. [2-min], [5-min], [30-min], [1-hour]).

In this paper, a temporal (timing) warning dynamics functionality for the daily time-domain and with a number of time-frames ([2-min], [5-min], [30-min]) is introduced (short-term trading). This functionality is regarded as a 2nd level function (i.e. functions of functions; because of the timing involved) with great trading opportunities, and it is defined – for the first time in the corporate finance literature- as a Temporal Trading Functionality (TTF). The leveraged ETF trading, with this TTF functionality offer great trading opportunities for the institutions, the individual (non-commercial) market investors, the swing traders, and the momentary and intraday speculators. Data analysis shows that on Market's opening and during the first 60 minutes of the trading session, shareowners significantly increase their security shareholding; hence, the involved trading volatility is increased, offering great trading and profit opportunities.

Paper contributes to corporate finance literature by examining and defining this TTF functionality for leveraged ETFs. For this purpose, four categories of shareholders are regarded: The long-term investors, the short-term swing traders, the short-term momentary speculators, and the intraday speculators. Paper concludes that, in daily and intraday leveraged ETF trading, the short-term swing traders -if they apply the proposed TTF in their plans - are benefit at the expense of momentary and intraday speculators, while the long-term investors are always the big losers (if involved in ETF trading).

Literature Review

Trading is regarded as a temporal historical living system [2,3] with a number of leveraged TTFs and time-based company initiatives operating as trading functions [4-6] resulting in excellent trading strategies with great profit opportunities [7-12].

In their studies, Myers, and Majluf [13], Jensen [14], Baker, and Wurgler [15], Baker, et al. [16], Hartzell, and Starks [17], Samba, and Mbassi [18], and Chung, and Ariff [19] argue that trading "time" is regarded only as a function of a well-designed long-term trading strategy. While, Cesari, et al. [20] argues on the effects of share-holding and stock liquidation on the timing transactions on opening and closing

***Corresponding author:** Vasiliki A Basdekidou, Special Research Fund Account (ELKE), Aristotle University of Thessaloniki, Greece
E-mail: Vasiliki.Basdekidou@gmail.com

positions and Demiralp, et al. [6] state that old-issue security returns and passive trading, are both strongly connected to the coexisting old-issue changes in corporate holding for a time period up to 3 years after the IPO time. Chemmanur, et al. [21] and Gipson, et al. [22] support that long-term passive-trading investors (as opposed to non-commercial short-term investors and traders) are able to receive more security portions hoping on better future returns (profit) and their post-transactions somewhat greatly exceed a passive "Buy-and-Hold" trading planning by the shareholding investors. Cenar and Turcas [23] discuss, under the prism of a comparative analysis, profitability indicators involved in investments. Alti, and Sulaeman [24], Anghel, and Man [25] and Zaman [26] point to how company issuing initiative is influenced by corporate and non-commercial trading. In their paper, they support the position that high stock returns and profit trading trigger equity derivation only if it is connected with a great pre-issue corporate investor demand, as it is regarded consistent by new corporate holdings (swing momentary traders). The Alti and Sulaeman [24] clarify their results as logical and dependable with company initiatives using the corporate investor demand as a gauge of market's interest. In the above articles and, generally, in corporate finance literature review, no more details for short-term TTF functionalities were given.

In contrast to the above papers, the current article agrees that the trading data are consistent particularly in nowadays IT era, and produce profit with such expectations, as far as the "timing" for ETF is regarded as intraday TTF functionality. Obviously, nowadays, trading equities (stocks), as well as instruments (leveraged ETFs) or non-equities (options, warrants, Forex, etc.), must obey the swing and volatile securities markets rules; and in this domain trading "timing" is very important even for the "buy-and-hold" investors (trading leveraged 3x ETFs; Gold, Silver, WTI Oil, and Natural Gas ETNs; etc.).

In this domain, the main target of the current article is to investigate the influence of "timing", as a TTF functionality, in trading leveraged ETFs. Actually, we investigate that TTF "timing" in conjunction with a number of warning dynamics signals like on-open gup-ups, bullish price action patterns (uprising triangles, cups), etc., would result in a profitable trade. It is notable that, the TTF "timing" could be regarded as a 2-d function. For instance, in intraday trading 3x leveraged ETFs: 1-d for the morning "timing" and the other 1-d for the price action's breakout "timing" during the trading session. This 2-d TTF "timing" could be regarded as a not lagging technical analysis indicator, because all news and price action trends have been already incorporated.

The rest of the article is organized as follows: the next section ("Data and Research Methodology") describes the shareholding data as the corporate shareholding variables for the TTF-based methodology. Following, the section "The Temporal Trading Functionality (TTF)" tries an initial definition of the TTF term by examining the relation between leveraged ETF "timing" and institutional and non-commercial security purchases, as well as the impact of corporate and non-commercial holdings on TTF functionality. Finally, the section "Conclusions and Discussion" summarizes the conclusions and discusses paper's innovations and contributions.

Data and Research Methodology

For the current paper, the shareholding information, the changes in insider holdings and some sample profit/losses trading data (1990-2016) - used in this paper as the shareholding and profit variables-came from many resources: The Barron's information databases and sources, a Wall Street Journal affiliate [27]; The StockCharts.com initiative; The Securities and Exchange Commission/SEC notices, releases and announcements; The Commitments of Traders (CoT)/ CFTC speculative net positions reports; The Yahoo! Finance insiders data feed; the SEC EDGAR database; The individual filings at: http://www.sec.gov/cgi-bin/srch-edgar; The SEC's Forms 4 (CEO) and 14a (Directors and Officers); and The Thomson Financial corporate holdings SEC's Form 13f database [4].

The United States SEC requires that all institutions with a total position greater than $100 million of securities or equities positions greater than 10,000 shares or positions in individual shares greater than $200,000, must report their holdings, using the SEC's Form 13f, quarterly. In this paper, these numbers were used to estimate total corporate holdings and position changes in a sample four-day period.

Also, current paper identifies long- and short-term corporate investors, traders and speculators, based on their average "ETF turnover" portfolio, into a four-day period. The term "ETF turnover" is defined, for the purpose of this paper, as a measure of stock liquidity; calculated by dividing the total number of shares traded over this four-day period by the average number of shares outstanding for that period). Obviously, the higher the "ETF turnover" number, the more liquid the ETF trading instrument in the last four days [28].

The presented analysis is based on a four-day period (sample statistics); and the traders involved in trading were sorted into four categories according to their temporal (time-based) corporate holdings as the percentage of total shares outstanding at the end of each of these four days.

Therefore, in the first category, the institutions ranked in the bottom fourth after having the lowest "ETF turnover" were placed; they are classified as long-term investors (LT investors). In the second category, the institutions ranked in the top fourth after having the highest "ETF turnover" were placed; they are classified as short-term swing-trading traders (ST_1 traders). Then, the rest domain is divided into two equal categories (third and fourth category). In the third category, the short-term momentary traders were placed (ST_2 short-term speculators); and finally, in the forth category, the detected intraday individual or institution speculators were placed (ST_3 intraday speculators).

The back-tested statistics for the sample four-day period are presented in the following Table 1, which displays the summary numbers of 3x leveraged ETF trading and Non-ETF trading from 1st January 2000 to 30th June 2016 (ETF data were obtained from SEC/ SDC) [4] (Table 1).

Table 1 notes:

Size - Here, the natural logarithm of Sales, instead of the actual sales number, is used; as the appropriate for the irregular price action chart smoothing transformation. In stock market data statistical analysis, the log(sales) transformation is preferred instead of other ones like inverse(sales) and $(sales)^2$.

Return - The Stock return measured over the ETF four-day period.

Market-to-Book is (total assets – book equity + market equity)/ total assets.

LT – is the corporate shareholding with a clear Long-term horizon (Investors). Corporate investors' horizon identification is based on their portfolio "security turnover" over the last four days.

ST – is the momentary corporate ownership with a clear Short-term horizon (Traders and Speculators). The Short-term traders were

	3x Leveraged ETF Trading				Non-ETF Trading				
	Obs.	Mean	Median	St. dev.	Obs.	Mean	Median	St. dev.	Differences
A. Shareholding dynamics data									
Size	4105	4.54	4.54	1.92	90,005	4.70	4.87	2.05	−0.16*
Return	4105	0.50	0.35	1.24	90,005	0.15	0.04	0.87	0.35*
Market-to-book	4105	2.31	1.89	1.59	90,005	1.69	1.25	1.22	0.62*
Total shareholding									
(1) LT investors	4105	8.60	7.92	7.28	90,005	9.55	8.47	9.72	−0.95**
(2) ST_1 traders	4105	12.27	11.46	10.48	90,005	10.10	8.05	11.58	2.17**
(3) ST_2 speculators	4105	14.70	12.41	12.54	90,005	11.35	8.57	12.30	3.35**
(4) ST_3 speculators	4105	16.67	12.09	17.40	90,005	12.88	9.02	13.66	3.79**
B. Shareholding Dynamics Cases									
Continuing cases			**Liquidation cases**			**Initiation cases**			
Old LT investors	1,195		25					0	
ST_1 traders	0		95					0	
ST_2 speculators	0		310					0	
ST_3 speculators	0		375					0	
New LT investors	0		0					90	

*Changes significantly different from zero at 5% level
**Changes significantly different from zero at 1% level

Table 1: Sample shareholding statistics.

divided in three categories: ST_1 are the swing Traders; ST_2 are the short-term speculators; and ST_3 are the intraday speculators.

Continuing Shareholding – This term is referred to corporate investors, as shareowners both at the beginning and at the end of the ETF four-day period.

Liquidations – This term is referred to ownership cases where old LT investors and ST traders own shares at the beginning of the ETF four-day period, but liquidate their holdings by the end of this period.

Initiations – This term is referred to cases where new LT investors –i.e. owning no shares at the beginning of the four-day period- establish new positions during this ETF four-day period and continue their shareholding and after this period.

Difference – The difference in Means between leveraged ETF trading and Non-ETF trading.

The result is a statistically unbalanced panel, covering the sample time period from January 1st 2000 to June 30th 2016, with up to 95,000 observations, including a number of more than 4,000 ETFs. The sample period starts from 2000 because from this year the data (shareholding, transaction, etc.) are available in a digital format with a relatively low cost. While weekly data could allow better and more accurate association of the shareholding ETF changes; time shorter (daily) data were used in particular for two reasons. Firstly, because they help to understand better the changes in ETF ownership during the four-day period; and secondly, they provide flexibility in trading leveraged ETFs without serious throwbacks, which are usually occur in time longer (e.g. weekly) data.

The temporal trading functionalities (TTFs)

In this section, the innovative term Temporal (timing) Trading Functionality (TTF) is introduced and analyzed. Chen, et al. [29] and Hao [5] argue that long-term institutions tend to be passive traders not interested therefore for the ETF/TTF functionalities. On the other hand, short-term momentary, swing, and intraday trading institutions (and speculators as well) are better informed and tend to trade actively the leveraged ETFs to exploit their own informational convenience asset position. Trading these leveraged ETFs is a risky and time sensitive procedure that requires to have

Fed Meetings, Reports, etc	Time-Targets ("timing" trading)
USD rate hike trading	Rate announcement time and rate actual time
Day Trading	first/last 5-minutes in a daily trading session (09:30-09:35 am EST, 03:55-04:00 pm EST)
Fed/FOMC monetary policy meetings	Fed/FOMC meetings decision announcement at 02:00 pm EST
Fed/FOMC monetary policy meetings	Fed/FOMC conferences at 02:30 pm EST
Fed/FOMC monetary policy meetings	Fed/FOMC meetings minutes announcement at 01:00 pm EST
Fed Members Speeches	at 10:00 am EST; at 01:00 pm EST
Non-Farm Payrolls reports	first Friday each month at 08:30 am EST
API reports for WTI (USO) inventories	On Tuesdays at 04:30 pm EST
EIA reports for WTI (USO) inventories	On Wednesdays at 10:30 am EST

Table 2: Company Initiatives, Fed Meetings, Reports and Time-Targets.

and to obey a strict time-based strategy. Hence, in trading, the need for a 2nd level timing function of the ETF trading opportunities is obvious and this is the existential definition of the TTF functionality.

The innovative term "Temporal Trading Functionalities" (TTFs) is defined as an array of temporal (timing) functionalities applied to volatile markets like leveraged ETF, traditional company initiatives like SEO and IPO. These functionalities include "temporal" price action patterns like "gaps" ("Windows" in technical analysis terminology) appearing at a particular period during the daily session; and price action "temporal" pivotal point and lines breakouts completing these temporal price action patterns. Even more, these TTFs temporal functionalities could be documented by time-targets in trading instruments and securities (ETFs, stocks, options, futures, Forex) as follows: define swing, momentary and intraday trading strategies based on specific time-targets; and open/close long/short positions at a specific time-target.

These time-targets could be the Fed/FOMC rate hike announcement time; the Fed/FOMC rate hike actual time; the first/last 5 minutes in a daily trading session (09:30-09:35 am EST, 03:55-04:00 pm EST); the Fed/FOMC meetings decision announcement at 02:00 pm EST, the Fed/FOMC conferences at 02:30 pm EST; the Fed/FOMC minutes timing; the Non-Farm Payrolls reports (NFPs) on the first Friday each month at 08:30 am EST; the API and EIA reports on WTI inventories

Ownership	Shareholding Position (%)			
	Before Time-Target ("timing")	@Time-Target ("timing")	After Time-Target ("timing")	Return (Profit)
Long-term Investors (LT Investors)	1,195 (100%)	1,285 (77.93%)	1,260 (100%)	-30%
Short-term Swing Traders (ST_1 Traders)	0 (0%)	50 (3.03%)	0 (0%)	+45%
Momentary Short-term Traders (ST_2 Speculators)	0 (0%)	122 (7,40%)	0 (0%)	-8%
Intraday Traders (ST_3 Speculators)	0 (0%)	192 (11.64%)	0 (0%)	-7%

Where:
1,195 = No. of the old LT investors (shareowners before Time-Target "timing";
1,285 = 1,195 (old LT investors) + 90 (new LT investors);
1,649 (total No. of shareowners at Time-Target "timing") = 1,285 (LT at Time-Target "timing") + 50 (ST1 at Time-Target "timing") + 122 (ST2 at Time-Target "timing") + 192 (ST3 at Time-Target "timing"); and
1,260 = 1,285 – 25 (old LT investors liquidations).

Table 3: Ownership (No.), Shareholding Position (%) and Trading Results (%).

on 04:30 pm EST (on Tuesdays for API data) and 10:30 am EST (on Wednesdays for EIA data) respectively, etc.

Following, Table 2 (above) presents a small number of initiatives (functions) and the related warning dynamics temporal (timing) TTF functionalities acting actually as time-targets in leveraged ETF short-term, swing and intraday trading (Table 2).

Comparative analysis shows that the TTF temporal functionalities apply better to the following four categories of shareowners:

- Long-term investors ("LT Investors")
- Short-term swing traders ("ST_1 Traders")
- Short-term momentary traders ("ST_2 Speculators")
- Intraday traders ("ST_3 Speculators")

Following, Table 3 (above) presents, in summary, the ownership (no.) and the shareholding position (%), as well as the trading results (profit %) for these four categories of traders. The numbers resulted from the Table 1 sample statistics data (3x leveraged ETF).

As it was expected, the short-term swing traders (ST_1) got the best results thanks to the TTF functionalities (time-based warning dynamics signals and time-based triggering signals) incorporated in their trading plans and strategies. For instance, the [2-min, time-frame] on-open price action gaps (usually the gap-ups and in some cases and the gap-downs) and the [30-min, time-frame] uprising triangles and cups bullish price action patterns for the warning dynamics signals; and the [2-min, time-frame] time-based pivotal points and pivotal lines breakouts accompanied by volume sectional increase, and the morning/noon/evening price action breaks (accompanied by volume increase as well) for the triggering signals.

Conclusions and Discussion

Nowadays, with the internet-based trading era and the advancement of time series data [30], the leveraged ETFs instruments, as technical market inefficiencies (anomalies) with great "momentum effects", offer great temporal trading opportunities for both traders and speculators [32-37].

The current paper follows Zaman [26], Gaspar, et al. [31] and Yan, and Zhang [28], to categorize corporate shareowners according to their income, short or long positions, and investment and trading attitudes, in four categories: long-term investors, short-term swing traders, short-term momentary speculators, and intraday speculators [38,39].

Data analysis shows that even the overnight position in leveraged ETF is risky. Since they use financial derivatives, leveraged ETFs are inherently riskier than their unleveraged counterparts. The additional risks come in the form of counterparty risk, liquidity risk, and increased correlation risk. Meanwhile, traders also have to consider external factors such as the impact of leverage on portfolio volatility. Hence, leveraged ETFs are not appropriate for long-term investors and retirement portfolios trying to maintain a low beta coefficient [40].

In paper's back-tested sample data, the long-term investors suffer a 30% loss of their capital (Table 3). Leverage is a double-edged sword, with a bigger move down being just as possible as a bigger move up. Also, data analysis applied found that short-term swing traders incorporating in their strategies the TTF functionalities (intraday warning dynamics signals, triggering signal) are benefit (+45%) at the expense of investors, short-term and intraday speculators (Table 3).

Paper contributes to corporate finance literature by: (i) the introduction of the innovative term "Temporal (timing) Trading Functionality" (TTF) as a 2nd level timing function of the ETF function; and (ii) the application of TTF functionalities (long/short trading session: 09:30 am-04:00 pm EST, swing and intraday time-based trading strategies) to leveraged ETF trading.

Acknowledgments

The financial support (covering primary the CoT/CFTC and the Barron's and WSJ.com market data expenses) from the EU/LLP Programme "EPOCHE 2013" (with Project No. 2012-1-GR-ERA 10-10609) is gratefully acknowledged.

Conflicts of Interest

The authors have not declared any conflict of interests with the Barron's Market Data and trading strategies discussed herein. What is presented in the article is as balanced, objective and evidence-based as possible.

Primary Author's Bio Profile

Vasiliki A. Basdekidou holds a B.Sc. degree in Economics from the Aristotle University of Thessaloniki (Greece, 2002), a two-year master's degree in Economics (major: Financial Economics) from the University of Macedonia (Greece, 2005) and a Ph.D. in Corporate Finance from the Bulgarian Academy of Sciences – Economic Research Institute (Bulgaria, 2015). She is working at the Special Research Fund Account of the Aristotle University of Thessaloniki for the last 10 years.

References

1. http://www.investopedia.com/terms/l/leveraged-etf.asp
2. Styliadis AD (2007) E-learning Documentation of Historical Living Systems with 3-d Modeling Functionality. Journal Informatica 18: 419-446.
3. Styliadis AD, Vassilakopoulos MG (2005) A Spatio-Temporal Geometry-based Model for Digital Documentation of Historical Living Systems. Journal Information & Management 42: 349-359.
4. Hovakimian A, Hu H (2016) Institutional Shareholders and SEO Market Timing. Journal of Corporate Finance 36: 1-14.
5. Hao GQ (2014) Institutional shareholder investment horizons and seasoned equity offerings. Financial Management 43: 87-111.

6. Demiralp I, D'Mello R, Schlingemann FP, Subramaniam V (2011) Are there Monitoring Benefits to Institutional Ownership? Evidence from Seasoned Equity Offerings. Journal of Corporate Finance 17: 1340-1359.

7. Basdekidou VA (2015) Functionality, Returns and Efficiency before and after the Debt Crisis: An Empirical Analysis of the Greek Stock Market (Unpublished doctoral dissertation). Bulgarian Academy of Sciences – Economic Research Institute, Bulgaria.

8. Pezzani F (2016) The "Shamans" of Finance, Derivatives and "Thalidomide". Bus Eco J 7: 214.

9. Chiraz A (2016) Does the Index Futures Destabilize the Underlying Spot Market? Some Evidence from Frensh Stock Exchange. Bus Eco J 7: 244.

10. Ogden JP, Wu S (2013) Reassessing the Effect of Growth Options on Leverage. Journal of Corporate Finance 23: 182-195.

11. Ulum I, Rizqiyah Jati AW (2016) Intellectual Capital Performance: A Comparative Study between Financial and Non-Financial Industry of Indonesian Biggest Companies. International Journal of Economics and Financial Issues 6: 1436-1439.

12. Edelen RM, Ince O, Kadlec GB (2015) Institutional Investors and Stock Return Anomalies. E-Journal SSRN.

13. Myers SC, Majluf NS (1984) Corporate Financing and Investment Decisions when Firms have information that Investors do not have. Journal of Financial Economics 13: 187-221.

14. Jensen MC (1986) Agency Cost of free cash flow, Corporate Finance, and Takeovers. The American Economic Review 76: 323-329.

15. Baker M, Wurgler J (2002) Market Timing and Capital Structure. Journal of Finance 57: 1-32.

16. Baker M, Stein JC, Wurgler J (2003) When does the Market Matter? Stock Prices and the Investment of Equity-dependent Firms. The Quarterly Journal of Economics 118: 969-1005.

17. Hartzell JC, Starks LT (2003) Institutional Investors and Executive Compensation. Journal of Finance 58: 2351-2374.

18. Samba MC, Mbassi C (2016) Does Financial Development Spur Macroeconomic Policy Efficiency in the Cemac Countries? An Empirical Evaluation. Bus Eco J 7: 216.

19. Chung T, Ariff M (2016) Money Supply, Banking Liquidity and Stock Index Returns: Evidence from Four Major Capital Markets. Bus Eco J 7: 238.

20. Cesari AD, Espenlaub S, Khurshed A, Simkovic M (2012) The Effects of Ownership and Stock Liquidity on the Timing of Repurchase Transactions. Journal of Corporate Finance 18: 1023-1050.

21. Chemmanur TJ, He S, Hu G (2009) The role of Iinstitutional Investors in Seasoned Equity Offerings. Journal of Financial Economics 94: 384-411.

22. Gibson S, Safieddine A, Sonti R (2004) Smart investments by smart money: evidence from seasoned equity offerings. Journal of Financial Economics 72: 581-604.

23. Cenar I, Turcas M (2014) The Comparative Analysis of Profitability Indicators of Companies before and after the Implementation of Investment Projects with non-Refundable Financing. Annales Universitatis Apulensis Series Oeconomica 16: 96-109.

24. Alti A, Sulaeman J (2012) When do high stock returns Trigger Equity Issues? Journal of Financial Economics 103: 61-87.

25. Anghel I, Man M (2014) The Impact of Financial Communicationms on Stock Price. The Case of OMV Petrom S.A. 2004-2013. Annales Universitatis Apulensis Series Oeconomica 16: 15-25.

26. Zaman K (2015) Measurement Issues of Income and Non-Income Welfare Indicators: Assessment of Pakistan's Pro-Poor Growth. International Journal of Economics and Financial Issues 5: 802-811.

27. http://www.barrons.com/data

28. Yan X, Zhang Z (2009) Institutional Investors and Equity Returns: Are Short-term Institutions Better Informed? The Review of Financial Studies 22: 893-924.

29. Chen X, Harford J, Li K (2007) Monitoring: Which institutions matter? Journal of Financial Economics 86: 279-305.

30. Salahuddin M, Tisdell C, Burton L, Alam K (2015) Social Capital Formation, Internet Usage and Economic Growth in Australia: Evidence from Time Series Data. International Journal of Economics and Financial Issues 5: 942-953.

31. Gaspar JM, Massa M, Matos P (2005) Shareholder Investment Horizons and the Market for Corporate Control. Journal of Financial Economics 76: 135-165.

32. Basdekidou VA (2016) IPO Trading with Short-term & Intraday Temporal Functionalities. Bus Eco J 7: 257.

33. Basdekidou VA (2017) Seasoned Equity Offerings as Technical Market Anomalies: Long-term Temporal Trading Functionalities. International Journal of Economics and Finance 9 (1).

34. Malkiel BG (2003) The Efficient Market Hypothesis and Its Critics. Journal of Economic Perspectives 17: 59-82.

35. Timmermann A, Granger CWJ (2004) Efficient Market Hypothesis and Forecasting. International Journal of Forecasting 20: 15-27.

36. Laffont JJ, Maskin ES (1990) The Efficient Market Hypothesis and Insider Trading on the Stock Market. Journal of Political Economy 98: 70-93.

37. Basdekidou VA (2016) Technical Market Anomalies: Nonfarm Employment Report Trading with Binary Options & Temporal Functionalities. Annales Universitatis Apulensis series Oeconomica 18 (2).

38. Driga I, Dura C (2015) Loan-Portfolio Quality and Managerial Efficiency in Banking. Annales Universitatis Apulensis series Oeconomica 17(2):22-30.

39. Gurloveleen K, Bhatia BS (2015) An Impact of Macroeconomic Variables on the functioning of Indian Stock Market: A Study of Manufacturing Firms of BSE500. J Stock Forex Trad 5: 160.

40. http://www.wsj.com

Salesforce Control Systems as Direct Antecedents of Salesperson and Sales Unit Performance

Benet-Zepf A[1]*, Marin-Garcia JA[2] and Küster I[1]

[1]*Universitat de Valencia Valencia, Valencia, Spain*

[2]*ROGLE Research Group. DOE - Universitat Politecnica de Valencia. Valencia. Spain*

Abstract

The impact from sales control systems on individual and organizational effectiveness has been a major issue for scholars since these systems were conceptualized by Anderson and Oliver and Jaworski. Salesperson behavioral performance appears as an antecedent of outcome performance, and both are connected to sales unit effectiveness. This paper focuses on a deep literature review during the period 1983-2014, based on the control systems' typologies found, and summarizes the multiple evidences found, connecting this systems with the salesperson behavioral performance and the outcome performance –and between them-, and both individual results with the sales unit effectiveness, including its managerial implications. After the review of the 142 articles in the field, a cluster of four research directions are identified, namely: (1) the impact of the different variables and activities on the control systems and the performance levels, (2) the methodological variables, (3) the measures of the level control system or performance, and (4) the multisectorial, multicultural and multinational sales environment.

Keywords: Salesforce control; Sales management; Behavior control; Output control

Introduction

Sales departments account for the largest portion of personnel and marketing budget for many firms [1-4], especially in the selling of industrial products, where salespeople (1) are the interface between suppliers and buyers [5,6], (2) represent the service component of the seller's offering [7] and (3) are the only function that generates sales/incomes. The significant role of salespeople on customer satisfaction and financial performance has created a growing interest in the academic world for studying this business area over the last thirty years.

Early studies about salesforce control systems focused on evaluating and understanding the personal characteristics which determinate good sales performance [8-11], while the impact of other variables not controlled by the salesperson had a limited research effort [12]. Subsequently, scholars found that, by adjusting the mode and level of control, managers can affect salesperson efficiency levels [13].

Control systems are the organization's procedures for monitoring, directing, evaluating, and compensating its employees [1], in order to ensure the attainment of desired organizational objectives [14-16]. Managers exercise control through information exchanges with salespeople, where the attitudinal and capacitive standards and the performance goals are established and updated periodically. Information management may be considered the first component, while the evaluation from salesperson's performance results and its impact in rewards or punishments, may be considered the second dimension of supervisory control [17].

Best practices in managing sales organizations may be an important source of competitive advantages [5], however controls under specific conditions (competitive intensity) or contextual factors (low performance documentation, or low procedural knowledge), or mismanagement (sales quotas improperly set), may also cause employees to manipulate data, work against the long-term interest of the organization, and exhibit other dysfunctional behaviors [2,18-20].

Given the range of situations in which the different firms face the commercialization process, many of the studies related to salesforce control systems deal with specific aspects of:

- Certain types of product or industry [9,21-24].
- Distribution types [6,25,26].
- Manager profiles [27-29].
- The selling in an export context [30-36].
- How the cultural environment affects the optimal system [37-39].
- Other contingent matters such as the degree of digitization of the sales activity [40] or the different salesperson profiles.

The applicability of the results of such investigations to other contexts is subject to validation by further work. Our study will focus on those related to the salesperson performance and the sales unit (sales organization) effectiveness, and includes the proposals made by researchers on the work area during the last 32 years (1983-2014).

Although some studies about salesforce management deal with informal controls, most research to date focuses on formal systems. The formalization involves the prescription of rules and processes that salespersons have to follow, and the monitoring, evaluation, and compensation procedures [41]. Quantification by vendors or directors, of valuations on the amount of each of the components of formal controls, has been done successfully in many investigations. However informal controls, despite being equally important in what concerns salesperson behaviors and outcomes [42,43], have not been object of a similar number of empirical investigations.

Recent literature analysis include Verbeke et al.'s (2011) work, who listed the antecedents and moderators of salesperson

***Corresponding author:** Benet-Zepf A, Universitat de Valencia Valencia, Valencia, Spain, E-mail: benet100@gmail.com

performance found after Churchill et al. [8] study, while Darmon and Martin [44] proposed a framework with organizational, personal and environmental variables affecting sales force control systems and salesperson outcomes. In a similar vein, Singh and Koshy's [45] literature review proposes the predictors on salesperson's performance in a business to business context.

The purpose of our research is to summarize and to update the academic literature concerning the direct effects of the salesforce control systems on sales-performance and from both on sales unit effectiveness, including managerial implications and the research directions. We focus therefore in linear relationships between the control systems, the salesperson performance and finally the sales unit outcomes. A theoretical background about the salesforce control systems will be followed by the research methodology and the synthesis of studies about salesperson performance and sales unit effectiveness. A summary of managerial implications and future reserach proposals complete this work.

Each of the empirical research concerning the salesforce control systems has used as the backgroung either of the typologies that have been proposed for these systems [1,2,15]. This paper presents a full description of all classifications proposed to date, intending to be a reference for future work, where researchers can identify and assess the similarities and differences between each of these classifications. As a second contribution, we update the state of knowledge on the direct effects that produce control systems on the salesperson performance and sales unit effectiveness, including a classification of the main reserach directions proposed by the scholars during this period: the impact of different variables on performance levels, the methodologies used in research, the measurement of the degree of control, and the issues about the sale in a global context.

Salesforce Control Systems Typology

Scholars have proposed classifications for control systems usually based on the controlled variable: behavior, activity, capacity, input, outcome, output or compensation. Occasionally the criterion is the degree of formalization [2] or the level of different combinations of the degree of formalization with the level of the controlled variable [46]. Individual criteria identified will be presented hereafter.

In behavior-based control systems the firm assumes risk to gain control, and the management monitors and directs the operations of the salesforce [1]. This system emphasizes the use of field sales managers coupled with fixed salary compensation [3,48], and is typified by high levels of supervisor monitoring, direction and intervention in activities, and subjective and complex methods of evaluating performance, centered on salesperson's job inputs [48]. Under such control system, managers monitor and evaluate inputs from employees who are more likely to take a long term view, take risks in the performance of their duties, and engage in activities as relationship building, which do not result in short-term sales, but are necessary for the long-term success [38,47]. Common tools used in behavior-based systems include group meeting, feedback from managers, training programs, incentive programs, scheduling, and territory management. The variables utilized to evaluate performance are qualitative and subjectively assessed by sales managers and include among other attitude, product knowledge, appearance, planning ability [49], adaptive selling, teamwork, sales presentation, and sales support [16]. Ahearne et al. [50] listed the following service behaviors on relationship quality and share of customer: diligence, information communication, inducements (behavior aimed at personalizing the relationship with a customer), sportsmanship (salesperson's willingness to tolerate less-than-ideal circumstances without demonstrating negativism), and empathy.

Under an outcome-based system, the marketplace pressures salespeople's performance, reducing managerial overhead, and shifting risk to the salesperson, as a laissez faire management [1,48,51,52] that uses incentives to reward salespeople on the basis of their outcomes [53]. Such system may lead (1) to give excessive attention to short-term objectives, (2) to pay less attention to customer's loyalty, (3) to use high pressure techniques in selling, and (4) to reduce the development of long term strategies [47]. For outcome-based systems, less interaction between management and the salesforce is expected, so that sales and profit reports, promotion, salary and bonus [27] are regular tools when meeting or exceeding the performance goals. Sanctions or punishments such as explanation for failure, warnings, probation, or dismissal are taken when performance does not reach the standards in terms of sales volume, market share, new accounts, and customer satisfaction [16,17]. Incentive plans play a prominent role in motivating, directing, and retaining a knowledgeable, skilled, and competent sales force [54,55]. Similarly, Jaworski et al. [46] defined output control as the setting of performance standards that are monitored and evaluated, therefore is considered equivalent to the construct of outcome control [56].

Initially the salesforce control system was represented as a continuum between the two extremes: pure behavior-based and pure outcome-based systems [1,48], and management may elect to position its strategy at various levels between these extremes, resulting in significant consequences in terms of the salesperson's affect, cognition, behavior and performance. Hybrid governance can be created by adopting intermediate levels of ownership, monitoring, direction, subjective evaluation, and results sharing [48,57]. Using this control, firms may position themselves along the continuum and selectively use elements of both systems [58], so that the transition from one form of control to the other would result in fairly smooth changes in the consequences. One main indicator is the proportion of fixed to incentive-based compensation in the overall remuneration plan [39,59].

Measuring the salesforce control has been analysed by different studies from the initial conceptualization from Anderson and Oliver [1]. Based on Babakus et al. [12]'s scale, Panagopoulos and Avlonitis [60] proposed the following 13-item version: monitoring (observe the performance of salesperson in the field, pay attention to the extent to which salesperson travels, regularly review call reports); directing (regularly spend time coaching, discuss performance evaluations, and actively participate in training salesperson on the job); evaluating (evaluate the individual sales results, evaluate the quality of sales presentations made, evaluate the number of sales calls made, and evaluate the profit contribution); rewarding (reward based on their sales results, compensate based on the quality of the sales activities, use nonfinancial incentives to reward the salesperson for their achievements).

The framework from Jaworski [2], and Jaworski and MacInnis identified formal control, as written, management-initiated, and oriented to marketing objectives, and informal control as unwritten, typically worker-initiated, and not necessarily supportive of the marketing objectives controls. The former include input control, as actions prior to salesperson's activity, like selection criteria, recruitment and training programs; process control, focusing on influencing on behavior and/or salespeople's activities, in order to achieve the outcomes; and output control, as setting of performance standards, monitoring, and results' evaluation; while the latter refer to self control, as individual employees taking responsibility for their jobs, based largely on their intrinsic motivation; social or professional control, or control trough peers, where the work unit somehow manages the individuals performance; and cultural control, with norms affecting the individuals as a part of an organization. According to this model, different levels of formal and informal control result in four different combinations [46]: bureaucratic system, similar to behavior-baseed control as management-initiated, written controls, with professional and cultural mechanisms operating in a secondary role; clan system, relying primarily on profesional and cultural mechanisms; high control system, following formal procedures, but also mantaining a collegial work environment and the norms and values of the organization; and low control system, where both formal and informal controls operate as secondary.

Attending to the various results of behavior control on end-performance in different studies: negative [48] and unrelated [3,46], Challagalla and Shervani [15] suggested two different types of behavior control, namely activity and capability control, whose independent operating may explain these diverse results on performance. Activity control refers to the specification of activities, its monitoring and the administering of rewards and punishments according to the performance. Moreover capability control empasizes the development of individual skills and abilities, setting goals, and monitoring these skills and abilities, providing guidance for improvement, and rewarding and punishing on the basis of the levels acquired. Training and apprenticeships, mentoring-coaching and job enrichment programs are specific activities to enhance skills such as negotiation, presentation, or interpersonal communication [17,61].

Piercy et al. [29,35] defined compensation control as the proportion of incentive pay in the total compensation of salespeople, that operates independently of behavior and outcome control. This type of control might take as basis one item extracted from behavior and outcome control (as it may be also conceptulized monitoring control, direction control, or evaluation control) that locates closer to outcome control construct for being based both on low supervision and having the economic retribution as a focal point of the control. The autors' framework starts in behavior and compensation control, and introduces behavior performance and compensation control as antecedents of outcome performance, which might sustain this sharing of characteristics between outcome and compensation control.

Conceptualization of formal controls follows mainly three theoretical approaches: Agency Theory assumes uncertain environments for salespeople [62] and information costs that makes it difficult to monitor behaviors [5], taking compensation policies as benchmark, and being process or behavioral controls operationalizad as fixed compensation (where no risk is shared with the salesperson). Under output or outcome controls salesperson's retribution is at least partially based on the economic performance [1,63]. According to Transaction Cost Theory, management seeks the most efficient solution-either within the company, or outsourcing- to implement governance mechanisms to reduce potential salesperson opportunism [64]. According to this, firm's vertical hierarchy represents process or behavioral control, while output or outcome control is exerted by the market forces that the salesperson has to deal with, bearing the risk and acting as an entrepreneur [1]. This theory recommends behavior-based controls when outcomes are hardly measurable, or to retain valuable salespeople, or with so large salesforces that supervision becomes cost efficient [5,23]. Organizational Theory considers management intervention and influence to characterize each control system, so that process and behavioral controls as based on personal vigilance, and output control as measurement of outcomes [1,63]. Cultural control is especially relevant in salesperson activity under this theory, due to the special and nature of the activities and tasks they have to perform: the organizational values guide salespeople through ambiguious situations [65].

Based on Agency Theory, Joseph and Thevaranjan [54] feature an analytical model where salesperson either expends effort in an internal dimension, coordinating the delivery schedule in activities that mainly reduce costs, where monitoring is relatively inexpensive; or in an external dimension, adding value by differentiating the product in the customer's mind, with the resulting increase in sales or profit, thus working outwardly with an infinite cost of monitoring. Based on two scenarios: a pure incentives world by one side, and monitoring the internal dimension, and incentives for the external dimension by another, the model suggests the optimal blend of incentives and monitoring considering costs and profits.

Control systems mirror three managerial orientations, indicating supervisor's assessment of each procedure [66]. Based on output or outcome control, with an end-results orientation, supervisors leave it up to salespeople to determine the strategies and efforts to achieve the targeted sales and market shares. Moreover, supervisors who specify, monitor, and give feedback about the activities that salespeople have to perform, follow an activity orientation. Finally, capability-oriented supervisors coach –rather than monitor- salespeople in order to enhance their skills and abilities, to perform sales tasks effectively, monitoring progress, and providing appropriate feedback regarding their capabilities.

The management of the control system includes two organizational levels. On one hand, senior management represented in the chief sales executive is responsible for the strategic part, indicating the type of system to be used, setting global goals and defining the way in which salespeople must be monitored, focusing on the overall results in terms of turnover and profit of the sales unit. Furthermore the field sales managers monitor the daily performance and behavioral outcomes at the individual level, playing an essential role in executing the broad control guidelines at a tactical level [67].

All these classifications and conceptualizations have been used to support researchers in order to develop later related antecedents, results and mediators between control systems and other relevant variables from an academic or managerial point of view. In the next point of this study we describe the process of identification and screening of the articles.

Methodology

This work is based on management and control systems of the sales forces, and we have taken the last thirty two years (1983-2014) as research target. Inicial articles on salesforce management are still relevant as theorical backgroung and some of them include empirical conclusions that may add value to the present study.

The search was performed systematically on the following databases: Business Source Premier (EBSCO), Science Direct, Scopus and Web of Science, using as keyword formula: "Management Control" and Sale*, or "Control System*" and "Sale*", or "Output Control" and "Behavior Control".

Title, abstract and keywords were taken as main search field, and some specific criteria have been applied to better screen the results: in Science Direct the results were limited to the "Business,

Management and Accounting" field, in Business Source Premier the search was limited to refereed academic publications, and in Scopus we screened with the subject area of Social Sciences and Humanities, and excluded those with keywords different to our focus (inventory control, mathematical models, computer simulation, stochastic control systems, etc.). Finally we included a review of the 300 most relevant (first) results of Google Scholar to complete the initial gathering of information. According to Baldauf et al. [68] research in conference proceedings has been mainly published in abstract form and relevant research in working paper is not available, therefore we focused on peer-reviewed journals (Figure 1).

Figure 1 displays the literature selection breakdown: from the resulting 1394 references, 303 were deleted as repetitions and 785 were false positives not related with our topic under one author's judgement. The reading from abstracts by all authors dropped unanimously another group of 50 studies (if there were differences of criteria, the article remained in the selection) and lastly all authors examined the content of the 256 remaining studies. The final list considered the 114 articles that under any of the authors' judgement, focused on topics about management and control systems of the sales forces: types, theories related, antecedents, mediators, effects and consequences, under the human resources and the organizational points of view. An additional amount of 28 relevant articles coming from citations in this literature was ultimately included in our study. Almost all the 142 final references were published in the main journals about management, marketing and sales (Table 1), being Journal of Personal Selling and Sales Management, Industrial Marketing Management, Journal of Marketing, Journal of the Academic Marketing Science, Journal of Business Research, and Journal of Marketing Research, the most active papers in this area.

Analysis of Results: Direct Effects of Control Systems on Performance

In this chapter, the relationships found in the literature between the control systems, the salesperson performance and the sales unit effectiveness are introduced. Definitions on each construct and contingent aspects from the empirical investigations are illustrated correspondingly.

Effects on salesperson performance

Performance is an evaluation of activities (behaviors) and accomplishments (outcomes) of employees [1,69] or organizations. Most studies distinguish between the performance of the sales organization or sales organization effectiveness and the salesperson performance, which is further subdivided into behavioral performance and outcome performance [3,12,70,71]. The difference between these two constructs stems from the idea that the individual performance has to be limited to factors under the control of the salesperson, while organizational effectiveness depends on many situational factors including salesperson performance [72].

Salesperson performance includes the evaluation of the behaviors and the outcomes as a result of the individual sales activity. The significance of its evaluation is based on the need of information for effective control in two respects: decisions on rewards and punishments according to salesperson's outcomes, and the monitoring and coaching in order to improve performance [3,26]. Singh and Koshi [45] summarize the groups of variables related to sales performance in cognitive (declarative knowledge and procedural knowledge), personality (autonomy, self-determination, involvement, emotional stability, and agreeableness), situational (buyer-salesperson similarity

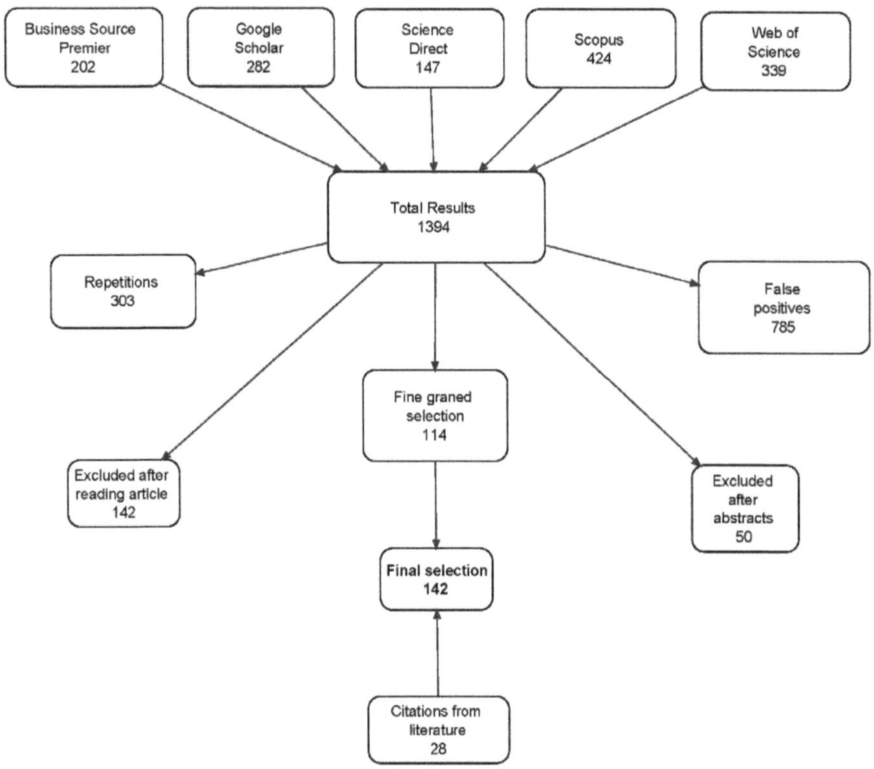

Source: Own elaboration.

Figure 1: Results of each database and later screening.

	1985 and before	1986-1990	1991-1995	1996-2000	2001-2005	2006-2010	2011-2014	Total
Journal of Personal Selling and Sales Management	1		2	2	10	3	4	**22**
Industrial Marketing Management			1	4	1	6	4	**16**
Journal of Marketing		2	4	5	1	1	1	**14**
Journal of the Academy of Marketing Science				1	4	4	3	**12**
Journal of Business Research				1	3	4	1	**9**
Journal of Business and Industrial Marketing					1	5	2	**8**
Journal of Marketing Research	2	1	1	1		1	2	**8**
European Journal of Marketing			1	2	1	2		**6**
International Journal of Research in Marketing				1		3	1	**5**
The Journal of Marketing Management				1	1			**2**
Journal of World Business					1		2	**3**
International Business Review					1	1		**2**
Journal of International Marketing					2			**2**
Marketing Letters				1		1		**2**
Marketing Management					1	1		**2**
Marketing Science	1			1				**2**
The Journal of Product Innovation Management				1		1		**2**
Others	1		3	4	4	8	5	**25**
Total	**5**	**3**	**12**	**25**	**31**	**41**	**25**	**142**
Source: Own elaboration.								

Table 1: Journals that provided the selected articles and years of publishing.

and information needs of the buyer), communication-related (skills in adaptive communication and closing the sales), based on attribution-theory (how people interpret events and how this relates to thinking and behaving), behavioral (cooperating, use of technical knowledge, controlling expenses, creating and mantaining good will, information providing, sales presentations, dealing with customers, and time and territory management), and customer orientation (Figure 2).

Behavioral performance: Behavioral performance is an assessment of salesperson's activities and strategies when executing their job responsibilities including adaptive selling, sales presentations, sales planning, sales support, price negotiations, and involvement in team-based selling efforts [1,12,73]. This performance also contains a component of non-selling activity, such as providing information and controlling expenses [3]. So that five dimensions of salesforce performance are identified: using technical knowledge, providing information, controlling expenses, making sales presentations, and achieving sales objectives [74]. Aulakh and Gencturk [30] identify two sets of behavioral control effects in an international environment: the first includes perceptions of agent compliance (the reception the agent gives to the principal's polices and programs) and flexibility, and the second is relationship flexibility, as the willingness to adjust to changing circumstances.

Behavior-based control and behavior performance is one of the most frequently proven entailments in salesforce management literature. We find support to this link in the field sales managers' sample of Babakus et al. [12] and Grant and Cravens [16] studies from Australian marketers; the British-based researches of Piercy et al. [26,72]; the works of Baldauf et al. [38,67,75] in Austria the United Kingdom, and Australia; the multicultural study in Austria, Bahrain, Greece, India, Israel, Malaysia, Nigeria, Saudi Arabia, and the United Kingdom by Cravens et al. [69]; and the analyzes of Spanish industrial sector from Verano-Tacoronte and Melián-González [76], and Küster and Canales [77] considering fixed salary as a main indicator of a behavioral-based control system. Moreover, two British studies from sales managers of diverse British industrial and consumer products from Piercy et al. [29,78] relate sales manager behavior-based control level together with behavior-based competences, with salesperson behavior performance.

Fang et al. found a weaker effect of activity control and capability control on behavior performance when goal difficulty is high (except for activity control in the American sample), and when goal specificity is high (except for capability control in the American sample), as well as a stronger effect when goal participation is high for the Chinese group. According to Cravens et al. Sales management high control system is more efective on behavior and output performance than the other three control combinations (bureaucratic, low, and clan); while Piercy et al. [28,35] found evidence of this relationship in the Greek sample of their study, but not for the Indian and Malaysian.

Theodosiou and Katsikea [36] considered that higher levels of salespeople and sales manager behavioral performance, were related to sales manager capabilities and behavioral strategies, as well as behavior-based control levels in an export environment. However these same scholars together with Morgan [36] did not support the relationship between the extent of behavior-based control and the behavioral performance in a study based on surveys from British sales executives.

Outcome performance

The results attributed to salesperson's activity represent the outcome performance, which include: sales volume, market share, and new accounts, as well as customer satisfaction and profitability [26]. Customer -orientation [20,79] or relationship -selling [80] foster long-term customer satisfaction, -increasing the firm's long-term profitability-, rather than short-term results. When sales managers set goals and punishments/rewards in outcome control systems, they must assess a balance between short and long-term outcomes. Furthermore, these results may be affected by factors different than salesperson behavioral performance, such as market potential, competitive intensity, workload and product-market scope [38], which explains that over time behavioral performance is gaining more importance when evaluating global individual performance, at the expense of outcome performance. An empirical research in Canada with first-level sales managers, concluded that higher-performing salesforces

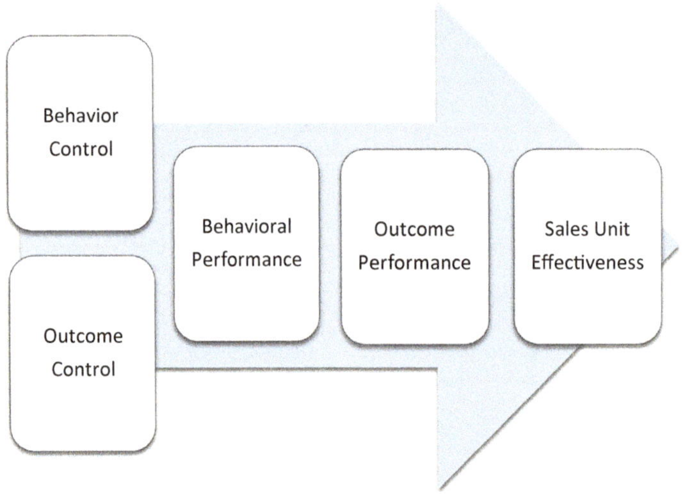

Source: Own elaboration.

Figure 2: Empirical path from salesforce controls to sales unit effectiveness.

possess characteristics thal are typically associated with behavior-based control rather than those with outcome-based control [70]. Given that outcome performance may be substantially attributable to behavioral performance, the literature on salesforce management eventually integrates the both constructs into "salesperson performance" [81].

Jaworski and Kohli [25] found behavioral performance together with positive output feedback and output role clarity as antecedents of outcome performance. Cravens et al. [3] research based on chief sales executives exposed that the achievement of important sales outcomes may be linked with controlling the behaviors of salespeople. Similar results emerged from empirical investigations in Australia [12,16,82] with industrial and consumer markets. This relationship was also supported in the United Kingdom [72], in both Austria and the United Kingdom [38,75], and again in Austria and Australia [67]. Likewise Theodosiou and Katsikea [36] evidenced that export sales manager behavioral performance as antecedent of export sales manager outcome performance.

As previously stated, behavioral control affects positively behavioral performance and thus in turn to outcome performance. Some literature relates both: behavior and outcome controls directly to outcome performance. The former include Cravens et al. [3], Grant and Cravens [16], Piercy et al. [26], Baldauf et al. [38,75], and Verano-Tacoronte and Melián-González [76]; while Fang et al. Proposed that the impact of outcome control on outcome performance is only significant under moderately difficult performance goals. Evans et al. [61] after a research on American salespeople from diverse sectors, concluded that salesperson perceived influence of output controls positively affects a salesperson's outcome performance. Aulakh and Gencturk [30] analysing managers of international operations with agents in foreign markets propose a direct effect of output control on agent's economic performance in this environment.

Reserach in developing countries from Piercy et al. [28] unveiled that outcomes are highest when there is effective interaction between behavior and compensation control, so that behavior control has better consequences when combined with high incentive pay. However, these same authors in a second article [35] find no apparent effect either in behavior or in outcome performance from incentive pay exclusively.

Individual performance: A final group of studies show direct effects of control systems to individual performance as a generic construct, such as Barker [70]'s research on first-level sales managers selected from the largest Canadian companies, that evidenced that higher-performing agents are more likely under behavior-based rather than under outcome-based control systems. Moreover, Piercy et al. [29] identified that higher sales manager levels of behavior control enhance salesperson performance as a direct result, so that appropriate competencies and abilities of field sales managers improve customer relationships, driven by superior salesperson performance. In a similar way, Flaherty et al. [83] connect the deviation from the optimal control profile with a negative influence on individual sales performance, and proposed that managers must be prepared to tailor control to individual characteristics. It will depend on past sales experience, market characteristics and additional strategic considerations. Finally, Holmes and Srivastava [84] designed a straightforward model linking working smart (adaptive selling, developing knowledge in selling situations) and working hard (amount of effort devoted) to the individual performance. The empirical work on the automobile retailing sector evidenced positive effects of both constructs on sales performance.

Interestingly, Slater and Olson [59] followed Miles et al. [85] strategy types: prospectors (continuously seek to locate and exploit new product and market opportunities), defenders (attempt to seal off a portion of the total market to create a stable set of products and customers), and analyzers (occupy an intermediate position between the two extremes by combining the strengths of both the prospector and defender). These authors put forward that prospectors achieve superior performance when utilizing moderate supervisory control, and with outcome-based control systems.

Sales unit/sales organization effectiveness

Sales organization effectiveness is defined as a summary of organizational outcomes for the entire sales organization, or for subsets, such as specific regions, districts, territories, or customer groups [12,72]. Sales volume, market share, profit contribution, customer satisfaction and return on assets are typical bases to measure this term. An empirical study with Austrian field sales managers concluded that sales territory design, particular salesperson characteristics (e.g., intrinsic and recognition motivation, sales support orientation, and customer orientation), and a high behavioral performance (e.g., technical knowledge, adaptive selling, teamwork, sales presentation, sales planning, and sales support), or a high outcome performance are antecedents of upper organizational effectiveness [86]. A similar study with Australian sales managers, considered behavioral performance and sales territory design, together with salesperson organizational commitment, as antecedents of sales organization effectiveness [82].

Contribution of behavioral control on sales unit or sales organization as a direct effect is sustained by Cravens et al. [3] who referred to financial dimension and customer satisfaction; Baldauf and Cravens [86]; Grant and Cravens [82]; Baldauf et al. [38]; Piercy et al. [28,35]; Cravens et al. [69]; and Verano-Tacaronte and Melián-González [76]. Moreover outcome performance as an antecedent of sales organization effectiveness was proposed by Babakus et al. [12]; Bello and Gilliland [31] in a study that focuses on American exporting firms; Piercy et al. [72]; Baldauf et al. [75]; Baldauf et al. [67]; and Piercy et al. [78].

The study of Lambe et al. [87] in the pharmaceutical sector found a positive association between team self-managing behaviors (sales performance, sales activities and selling skills) with selling team performance. Baldauf and Cravens [86] evidenced higher levels of sales unit effectiveness in Austrian organizations whose salespeople display high behavioral or high outcome performance. Similarly, research of Spanish field sales managers [88] proposed that behaviour control, salesperson professionalism, behaviour performance and outcome performance, have a positive and significant impact on salesforce effectiveness, treated as salesforce efficacy and supervisor satisfaction.

Menguc and Barker [55]'s work on sales managers and executives of Canadian firms concluded that the level of incentive pay –as an outcome-based control tool- results in lower financial performance outcomes (sales volume, profitability) when sales volatility is high, or the level of complexity of customer's purchase decisions increases, or the level of monitoring is high.

Finally Piercy et al. [89] in research with salespeople from a publisher of directories in the UK and in the USA, focused on team differences, using sales manager gender as a benchmark: although several positve behavioral effects from teams led by female managers were evidenced (higher intrinsic motivation, job involvement, job satisfaction and organizational commitment, yet lower role conflict, and propensity to leave) lower team's performance levels were perceived by salespeople. However, in a subsequent study of these authors [28,35] with field sales managers from industrial and consumer products and services, found a higher performance both by salespeople as by sales unit, when teams are led by female managers.

Conclusions And Managerial Implications

We find general agreement with the scholars about that behavior-based controls aligned more the salesperson with the long term interests of the company, and that today's markets, competition intensity the outcome-based controls may be more effective in the short term but may lose customer orientation. In most of and reducing costs is increasing, so customer satisfaction is a key factor for a company to continue maintaining its market shares without having to resort to reductions in product prices as main sales pitch. Oliver and Anderson [58] state that salespeople under behavior-based controls work smarter, while those under outcome-based work faster.

Another widespread evidence is that the path between control systems and individual outcome performance flows through behavioral performance [38]. This implies that salespeople with highest outcome standards are those with the best technical knowledge, provide the customer with the better and earliest information, and make the best sales presentations, so that managers expect salespeople to perform well on both dimensions of performance [12].

Behavior-based control with behavioral performance is the most frequent evidenced connection between control systems and individual performance. Sales managers may consider to increasing the level of this type of control for achieving a higher performance. Coaching and working with salespeople in order to develop selling skills and relationship strategies, seem to perform better than commanding, criticizing, and dominating [16,38,70]. Specific managerial activities with strongest link to effectiveness are: (1) to encourage salespeople to increase sales and rewarding them for their achievements; (2) actively participate in training salespeople on the job; (3) regularly spend time coaching salespeople and help them to develop their potential; and (4) discuss performance evaluations with salespeople [86]. Managers, in most effective teams, act more as coaches or communicators, rather than looking for results [88]. So time and resources should be invested in training and developing sales manager's competences to drive superior salesperson performance [78].

High levels of behavior and oucome control simultaneously (high control system) are associated with favourable salesperson consequences regarding job satisfaction, role ambiguity, role conflict, turnover intentions, and organizational commitment [90]. Hybrid systems with elements from outcome- and behavior-based, are the most common choice between firms. Onyemah and Anderson [37] highlight the convenience that all the elements co-aling, sharing the same degree of behavior and outcome components, so that these elements become mutually reinforcing. The decision regarding the point along the continuum falls on the chief sales executive. So good levels of communication between senior management and field sales managers are required for adequate daily monitoring, evaluation and direction of the salesforce.

An effective combination of behavior control and compensation control is another relevant managerial decision. Piercy et al. [28,35] propose high incentive pay with high behavior control as the most efective, while Küster and Canales [77] state that the security of fixed salary plus the motivational variable part fully develops salesperson's abilities generating better outcomes for the salesperson and the company. Cultural differences between countries - especially uncertainty avoidance - will determinate different results in terms of individual and team performance, of the combinations of fixed and variable compensation.

Executive decisions regarding sales unit managers' training appears to have an impact on the final result as well. Manager's training and career development should be an executive priority [82], in ways that enhance managers' skills in behavioral control (directing, evaluating and rewarding) beyond their classical selling and outcome control skills [72].

Studies about sales management in export activities or a global environment have concluded that salespeople control should be customized to each specific culture in order to achieve the highest performance. Under an outcome-based system, a part of the risk is shared with the salesperson, which might lead to negative individual consequences in a high risk-avoidance culture, while behavior-based (process) control builds salesperson trust in high power distance cultures [47]. The complexities of personal selling in overseas activity make behavior control a more difficult and less common tool for export companies [33] especially in psychologically distant markets, where executives should familiarize with market conditions, and exploit the opportunities offered by information technology [36].

Professional control (team self-managing behaviors) has been found as a positive antecedent of sales unit (team) performance [87], and it appears to be an unknown or underused tool for organizations.

Summary Of Research Directions

The main areas of research propositions found in the literature about this topic, contain the following: firstly the impact of the different variables and activities on the control systems and the performance levels [3,12,26,28,29,35]. Baldauf et al. [67] found interesting future research on environmental, organizational and managerial variables that may affect the control strategy; Piercy et al. [26] requested to clarify the congruities and incongruities of the different aspects of control and their relationship with sales organization effectiveness; Baldauf et al. [38] and Piercy et al. [72] focused on the convenience to investigate the behavior-based control extent that lead to higher individual or organizational performance; Cravens et al. [90] refered to the causal links between high control and its consequences; Küster and Canales [88] proposed the study of links between output control on performance and company effectiveness.

Regarding the methodologies, Oliver and Anderson [58] proposed the use of diverse samples and operationalizations, while other authors suggested the studies at different levels. These can include external people, salesperson, sales manager, sales executive, or dyads between them [28,36,70,75,77,78,87,88].

In another hand, most studies on salesforce management are cross-sectional. Therefore longitudinal studies are often requested [5,12,15,17,18,24,29,30-34,37,44,50,55,67,74,76,78,79,89,91-99].

The need to deepen in the measures of the level control system or performance has been highlighted by Piercy et al. [72], who suggested the research on supervisor ratings, self ratings, and sales unit output measures; Barker [70] proposed to refine the measure of outcome performance, and Fang et al. The sales performance in general; Slater and Olson [59] prompted studies about several control variables like average transaction size, number of products handled, number of customers and sales force stucture; and Verano-Tacoronte and Melián-González [76] propounded research on measuring the levels of behavior and output control in hybrid systems.

Finally investigations on multisectorial, multicultural and multinational sales environment issues have been frequently suggested by sales control scholars, as may be the case of studies to verify if the results across one country could be transposed to others [33,38,70,77,83], or the analysis of different combinations of behavior and compensation control in different developing countries [28,35].

Other important constructs widely researched in this area, act as mediators between the control systems and salesperson and sales unit performances, and should be a matter of a particular updated literature review. Such constructs, among others are: satisfaction with territory design [12,16,28,35,38,60], organizational commitment [16,26,98,100,101] interpersonal identification [102] (Ahearne et al. 2013); motivation and attitudes [36], organizational citizenship behavior [4], transformational leadership [96]; intrinsic and extrinsic motivation [103] and role ambiguity, clarity, and conflict [17,93,104-107].

References

1. Anderson E, Oliver RL (1987) Perspectives on Behavior-Based Versus Outcome-Based Salesforce Control Systems. Journal of Marketing 51: 76-88.
2. Jaworski BJ (1988) Toward a Theory of Marketing Control: Environmental Context, Control Types, and Consequences. Journal of Marketing 52: 23-39.
3. Cravens DW, Ingram TN, LaForge RW, Young CE [1993] Behavior-based and outcome-based salesforce control systems. Journal of Marketing 57: 47.
4. Piercy NF, Cravens DW, Lane N, Vorhies DW (2006) Driving organizational citizenship behaviors and salesperson in-role behavior performance: The role of management control and perceived organizational support. Journal of the Academy of Marketing Science 34: 244-262.
5. Krafft M (1999) An empirical investigation of the antecedents of sales force control systems. Journal of Marketing 63: 120-134.
6. Robertson DC, Anderson E (1993) Control System and Task Environment Effects on Ethical Judgment: An Exploratory Study of Industrial Salespeople. Organization Science 4: 617-644.
7. Bradford K, Brown S, Ganesan S, Hunter G, Onyemah V, et al. (2010) The embedded sales force: Connecting buying and selling organizations. Marketing Letters 21: 239-253.
8. Churchill GA, Ford NM, Hartley SW, Walker OC (1985) The Determinants of Salesperson Performance: A Meta-Analysis. Journal of Marketing Research (JMR) 22: 103-118.
9. Futrell CM, Swan JE, Todd JT (1976) Job Performance Related to Management Control Systems for Pharmaceutical Salesmen. Journal of Marketing Research 13: 25-33.
10. Jackson DW, Keith JE, Schlacter JL (1983) Evaluation of Selling Performance: A Study of Current Practices. Journal of Personal Selling & Sales Management 3: 43.
11. Verbeke W, Dietz B, Verwaal E (2011) Drivers of sales performance: a contemporary meta-analysis. Have salespeople become knowledge brokers? Journal of the Academy of Marketing Science 39, 407-428.
12. Babakus E, Cravens DW, Grant K, Ingram TN, LaForge RW (1996) Investigating the relationships among sales, management control, sales territory design, salesperson performance, and sales organization effectiveness. International Journal of Research in Marketing 13, 345-363.
13. Mallin ML, Asree S, Koh AC, Hu MY (2010) Antecedents to managerial trust and sales control in Malaysian salesforce. International Business Review, 19, 292-305.
14. Auh S, Mengue B (2007) Performance implications of the direct and moderating effects of centralization and formalization on customer orientation. Industrial Marketing Management 36: 1022-1034.
15. Challagalla GN, Shervani TA (1996) Dimensions and Types of Supervisory Control: Effects on Salesperson Performance and Satisfaction. Journal of Marketing 60: 89-105.
16. Grant K, Cravens DW (1996) Examining sales force performance in organizations that use behavior-based sales management processes. Industrial Marketing Management 25: 361-371.
17. Challagalla GN, Shervani TA (1997) A Measurement Model of the Dimensions and Types of Output and Behavior Control: An Empirical Test in a Salesforce Context. Journal of Business Research 39: 159-172.
18. Ramaswami SN (1996) Marketing Controls and Dysfunctional Employee Behaviors: A Test of Traditional and Contingency Theory Postulates. Journal of Marketing 60: 105-120.
19. Saini A, Krush M (2008) Anomie and the Marketing Function: The Role of Control Mechanisms. Journal of Business Ethics 83: 845-862.
20. Schwepker CH, Good DJ (2004) Marketing Control and Sales Force Customer Orientation. Journal of Personal Selling & Sales Management 24: 167-179.
21. Ahearne M, Rapp A, Hughes DE, Jindal R (2010) Managing Sales Force Product Perceptions and Control Systems in the Success of New Product Introductions. Journal of Marketing Research 47: 764-776.
22. Atuahene-Gima K, Li HY (2002) When does trust matter? Antecedents and contingent effects of supervisee trust on performance in selling new products in China and the United States. Journal of Marketing 66: 61-81.

23. Lapierre J, Skelling J (2005) Salesforce control system in high-tech contexts: do environment and industry matter? Journal of Business & Industrial Marketing 20: 297-306.

24. Pappas JM, Flaherty KE (2008) The effect of trust on customer contact personnel strategic behavior and sales performance in a service environment. Journal of Business Research 61: 894-902.

25. Lusch RF, Jaworski BJ (1991) Management Controls, Role Stress, and Retail Store Manager Performance. Journal of Retailing 67: 397.

26. Piercy NF, Cravens DW, Morgan NA (1998) Salesforce performance and behaviour-based management processes in business-to-business sales organizations. European Journal of Marketing 32, 79-100.

27. Bingham FG, Quigley CJ (1995) The Effect of Gender on Sales Managers' and Salespeople's Perceptions of Sales Force Control Tools. Journal of Marketing Management 5: 62-70.

28. Piercy NF, Low GS, Cravens DW (2004) Consequences of sales management's behavior-and compensation-based control strategies in developing countries. Journal of International Marketing 12: 30-57.

29. Piercy NF, Cravens DW, Lane N (2012) Sales manager behavior-based control and salesperson performance: the effects of manager control competencies and organizational citizenship behavior. Journal of Marketing Theory and Practice 20: 7-22.

30. Aulakh PS, Gencturk EF (2000) International principal-agent relationships: Control, governance and performance. Industrial Marketing Management 29: 521-538.

31. Bello DC, Gilliland DI (1997) The effect of output controls, process controls, and flexibility on export channel performance. Journal of Marketing 61: 22-38.

32. Katsikea ES, Theodosiou M, Morgan RE, Papavassiliou N (2005) Export market expansion strategies of direct-selling small and medium-sized firms: Implications for export sales management activities. Journal of International Marketing: Summer 13: 57-92.

33. Katsikea E, Theodosiou M, Morgan RE (2007). Managerial, organizational, and external drivers of sales effectiveness in export market ventures. Journal of the Academy of Marketing Science 35: 270-283.

34. Katsikea E, Theodosiou M, Perdikis N, Kehagias J (2011) The effects of organizational structure and job characteristics on export sales managers' job satisfaction and organizational commitment. Journal of World Business 46: 221-233.

35. Piercy NF, Low GS, Cravens DW (2004b) Examining the effectiveness of sales management control practices in developing countries. Journal of World Business 39: 255-267.

36. Theodosiou M, Katsikea E (2007) How management control and job-related characteristics influence the performance of export sales managers. Journal of Business Research 60: 1261-1271.

37. Onyemah V, Anderson E (2009) Inconsistencies Among the Constitutive Elements of a Sales Force Control System: Test of a Configuration Theory--Based Performance Prediction. Journal of Personal Selling & Sales Management 29: 9-24.

38. Baldauf A, Cravens DW, Piercy NF (2001) Examining the consequences of sales management control strategies in European field sales organizations. International Marketing Review 18: 474-508.

39. Segalla M, Rouzies D, Besson M, Weitz BA (2006) A cross-national investigation of incentive sales compensation. International Journal of Research in Marketing 23: 419-433.

40. Johnson DS, Bharadwaj S (2005) Digitization of selling activity and sales force performance: An empirical investigation. Journal of the Academy of Marketing Science 33: 3-18.

41. Agarwal S (1999) Impact of job formalization and administrative controls on attitudes of industrial salespersons. Industrial Marketing Management 28: 359-368.

42. Krafft M, DeCarlo TE, Poujol FJ, Tanner JF (2012) Compensation and Control Systems: A New Application of Vertical Dyad Linkage Theory. Journal of Personal Selling & Sales Management 32: 107-116.

43. Wang G, Dou W, Zhou N (2012) The interactive effects of sales force controls on salespeople behaviors and customer outcomes. Journal of Personal Selling & Sales Management 32: 225-243.

44. Darmon RY, Martin XC (2011) A new conceptual framework of sales force control systems. Journal of Personal Selling & Sales Management 31: 297-310.

45. Singh R, Koshy A (2010) Determinants of B2B salespersons' performance and effectiveness: a review and synthesis of literature. Journal of Business & Industrial Marketing 25: 535-546.

46. Jaworski BJ, Stathakopoulos V, Krishnan HS (1993) Control combinations in marketing: conceptual framework and empirical evidence. Journal of Marketing 57: 57-69.

47. Atuahene-Gima K (1997) Adoption of new products by the sales force: The construct, research propositions, and managerial implications. Journal of Product Innovation Management 14: 498-514.

48. Oliver RL, Anderson E (1994) An empirical test of the consequences of behavior-and outcome-based sales control systems. The Journal of Marketing 58: 53-67.

49. Jackson Jr DW, Schlacter JL, Wolfe WG, Hawes JM (1995) Examining the Bases Utilized for Evaluating Salespeoples' Performance. Journal of Personal Selling & Sales Management 15: 57-65.

50. Ahearne M, Jelinek R, Jones E (2007) Examining the effect of salesperson service behavior in a competitive context. Journal of the Academy of Marketing Science 35: 603-616.

51. Basu AK, Lal R, Srinivasan V, Staelin R (1985) Salesforce Compensation Plans: An Agency Theoretic Perspective. Marketing Science 4: 267-291.

52. Stathakopoulos V (1996) Sales force control: A synthesis of three theories. Journal of Personal Selling & Sales Management 16: 1-12.

53. Miao CF, Evans KR (2012) Effects of formal sales control systems: A combinatory perspective. International Journal of Research in Marketing 29: 181-191.

54. Joseph K, Thevaranjan A (1998) Monitoring and incentives in sales organizations: An agency-theoretic perspective. Marketing Science 17: 107-123.

55. Menguc B, Tansu Barker A (2003) The performance effects of outcome-based incentive pay plans on sales organizations: a contextual analysis. Journal of Personal Selling & Sales Management 23: 341-358.

56. Brown SP, Evans KR, Mantrala MK, Challagalla G (2005) Adapting motivation, control, and compensation research to a new environment. Journal of Personal Selling & Sales Management 25: 155-167.

57. Anderson E, Onyemah V (2006) How Right Should the Customer Be? (cover story) Harvard Business Review 84: 59-67.

58. Oliver, RL, Anderson E (1995) Behavior-and outcome-based sales control systems: Evidence and consequences of pure-form and hybrid governance. Journal of Personal Selling & Sales Management 15(4): 1-15.

59. Slater SF, Olson EM (2000) Strategy type and performance: The influence of sales force management. Strategic Management Journal 813-829.

60. Panagopoulos NG, Avlonitis GJ (2008) Sales force control systems: A review of measurement practices and proposed scale refinements. Journal of Personal Selling & Sales Management 28(4): 365-385.

61. Evans KR, Landry TD, Li PC, Zou S (2007) How sales controls affect job-related outcomes: the role of organizational sales-related psychological climate perceptions. Journal of the Academy of Marketing Science 35: 445-459.

62. Tremblay M, Côté J, Balkin DB (2003) Explaining sales pay strategy using agency, transaction cost and resource dependence theories. Journal of Management Studies 40: 1651-1682.

63. Eisenhardt KM (1985) Control: Organizational and economic approaches. Management science 31: 134-149.

64. Mallin ML, O'Donnell E, Hu MY (2009) The role of uncertainty and sales control in the development of sales manager trust. Journal of Business & Industrial Marketing 25: 30-42.

65. Lopez T, McMillan-Capehart A (2009) Elements of salesperson control: an organization theory perspective. Journal of Business & Industrial Marketing 24: 98-107.

66. Kohli AK, Shervani TA, Challagalla GN (1998) Learning and performance orientation of salespeople: The role of supervisors. Journal of Marketing Research pp: 263-274.

67. Baldauf A, Cravens DW, Grant K (2002) Consequences of sales management

control in field sales organizations: a cross-national perspective. International Business Review 11: 577-609.

68. Baldauf A, Cravens DW, Piercy NF (2005) Sales management control research-synthesis and an agenda for future research. Journal of Personal Selling & Sales Management 25: 7-26.

69. Cravens DW, Piercy NF, Low GS (2006) Globalization of the Sales Organization: Management Control and Its Consequences. Organizational Dynamics 35: 291-303.

70. Barker AT (1999) Benchmarks of successful salesforce performance. Canadian Journal of Administrative Sciences/Revue Canadienne des Sciences de l'Administration 16: 95-104.

71. Jaworski BJ, Kohli AK (1991) Supervisory feedback: Alternative types and their impact on salespeople's performance and satisfaction. Journal of Marketing Research pp: 190-201.

72. Piercy NF, Cravens DW, Morgan NA (1999) Relationships between sales management control, territory design, salesforce performance and sales organization effectiveness. British Journal of Management 10: 95-111.

73. Piercy NF, Cravens DW, Lane N (2007) Enhancing Salespeople's Effectiveness (cover story). Marketing Management 16: 18-25.

74. Behrman DN, Perreault WD (1982) Measuring the performance of industrial salespersons. Journal of Business Research 10: 355-370.

75. Baldauf A, Cravens DW, Piercy NF (2001) Examining business strategy, sales management, and salesperson antecedents of sales organization effectiveness. Journal of Personal Selling & Sales Management 21: 109-122.

76. Verano-Tacoronte D, Melián-González S (2008) Human resources control systems and performance: the role of uncertainty and risk propensity. International Journal of Manpower 29: 161-187.

77. Küster I, Canales P (2011) Compensation and control sales policies, and sales performance: the field sales manager's points of view. Journal of Business & Industrial Marketing 26: 273-285.

78. Piercy NF, Cravens DW, Lane N (2009) Sales management control level and competencies: Antecedents and consequences. Industrial Marketing Management 38: 459-467.

79. Joshi AW, Randall S (2001) The indirect effects of organizational controls on salesperson performance and customer orientation. Journal of Business Research 54: 1-9.

80. Guenzi P (2003) Antecedents and consequences of a firm's selling orientation. European Journal of Marketing 37: 706-727.

81. Grant K, Cravens DW, Low GS, Moncrief WC (2001) The role of satisfaction with territory design on the motivation, attitudes, and work outcomes of salespeople. Journal of the Academy of Marketing Science 29: 165-178.

82. Grant K, Cravens DW (1999) Examining the antecedents of sales organization effectiveness: an Australian study. European Journal of Marketing 33: 945-957.

83. Flaherty KE, Pappas JM, Allison L (2014) The influence of an optimal control system on salesperson performance and championing. Industrial Marketing Management 43: 304-311.

84. Holmes TL, Srivastava R (2002) Effects of job perceptions on job behaviors - Implications for sales performance. Industrial Marketing Management 31: 421-428.

85. Miles RE, Snow CC, Meyer AD, Coleman HJ (1978) Organizational strategy, structure, and process. Academy of management review 3: 546-562.

86. Baldauf A, Cravens DW (1999) Improving the Effectiveness of Field Sales Organizations. Industrial Marketing Management 28: 63-72.

87. Lambe CJ, Webb KL, Ishida C (2009) Self-managing selling teams and team performance: The complementary roles of empowerment and control. Industrial Marketing Management 38: 5-16.

88. Küster I, Canales P (2008) Some determinants of salesforce effectiveness. Team Performance Management 14: 296-326.

89. Piercy NF, Cravens DW, Lane N (2001) Sales Manager Behavior Control Strategy and Its Consequences: The Impact of Gender Differences. Journal of Personal Selling & Sales Management 21: 39-49.

90. Cravens DW, Lassk FG, Low, GS, Marshall GW, Moncrief WC (2004) Formal and informal management control combinations in sales organizations - The impact on salesperson consequences. Journal of Business Research 57: 241-248.

91. Homburg C, Bornemann T, Kretzer M (2014) Delusive perception-antecedents and consequences of salespeople's misperception of customer commitment. Journal of the Academy of Marketing Science 42: 137-153.

92. Lo D, Ghosh M, Lafontaine F (2011) The Incentive and Selection Roles of Sales Force Compensation Contracts. Journal of Marketing Research 48: 781-798.

93. Miao CF, Evans KR (2013) The interactive effects of sales control systems on sales person performance: a job demands-resources perspective. Journal of the Academy of Marketing Science 41: 73-90.

94. Miao CF, Evans KR (2014) Motivating industrial salesforce with sales control systems: An interactive perspective. Journal of Business Research 67: 1233-1242.

95. Onyemah V (2009) The effects of coaching on salespeople's attitudes and behaviors A contingency approach. European Journal of Marketing 43: 938-960.

96. Panagopoulos N, Dimitriadis S (2009) Transformational leadership as a mediator of the relationship between behavior-based control and salespeople's key outcomes An initial investigation. European Journal of Marketing 43: 1008-1031.

97. Piercy NF, Cravens DW, Lane N (2003) Sales Manager Behavior Control Strategy and Its Consequences: The Impact of Manager Gender Differences. Journal of Personal Selling & Sales Management 23: 221-237.

98. Piercy NF, Low GS, Cravens DW (2011) Country differences concerning sales organization and salesperson antecedents of sales unit effectiveness. Journal of World Business 46: 104-115.

99. Sarin S, Challagalla G, Kohli AK (2012) Implementing Changes in Marketing Strategy: The Role of Perceived Outcome- and Process-Oriented Supervisory Actions. Journal of Marketing Research 49: 564-580.

100. Avlonitis GJ, Panagopoulos NG (2007) Exploring the influence of sales management practices on the industrial salesperson: A multi-source hierarchical linear modeling approach. Journal of Business Research 60: 765-775.

101. Pettijohn C, Pettijohn LS, Taylor AJ, Keillor BD (2001) Are performance appraisals a bureaucratic exercise or can they be used to enhance sales-force satisfaction and commitment? Psychology & Marketing 18: 337-364.

102. Ahearne M, Haumann T, Kraus F, Wieseke J (2013) It's a matter of congruence: How interpersonal identification between sales managers and salespersons shapes sales success. Journal of the Academy of Marketing Science 41: 625-648.

103. Miao CF, Evans KR, Zou S (2007) The role of salesperson motivation in sales control systems - Intrinsic and extrinsic motivation revisited. Journal of Business Research 60: 417-425.

104. Cravens DW, Grant K, Ingram TN, Laforge RW, Young C (1992) In Search of Excellent Sales Organizations. European Journal of Marketing 26: 6- 23.

105. Medina-López C, Marín-García JA, Alfalla-Luque R (2010) Una propuesta metodológica para la realización de búsquedas sistemáticas de bibliografía (A methodological proposal for the systematic literature review). WPOM-Working Papers on Operations Management 1, 13-30.

106. Ouchi WG (1979) A conceptual framework for the design of organizational control mechanisms. Management Science 25.

107. Piercy NF (2006) The Strategic Sales Organization. Marketing Review 6: 3-28.

Optimal Design of New Generation Fiscal Rules: Coping with the Business Cycle and Discretionary Tax Reductions

Strawczynski M*

Department of Economics and School of Public Policy, Hebrew University of Jerusalem, Israel

Abstract

While business cycles are crucial for determining the dynamics of government budget deficits, it is rare to find an analysis of optimal fiscal rules that are designed to cope with the asymmetric behavior of fiscal variables during the cycle. In this paper I characterize the dynamics of budget deficits along the cycle: i) in recessions marginal propensity to spend is higher than the coefficient of marginal tax revenues, causing an increase of the deficit over GDP; ii) in expansions tax revenues soar allowing for a deficit reduction; however, marginal spending is still high and consequently a full cycle implies an increase in the deficit. Then, I present a model in which fiscal rules are designed to cope with a political bias that is based on two components: the cyclical bias and discretionary tax reductions. According to my analysis, the new generation fiscal rules should be based on a combination of expenditure and revenue rules, which are newer than budget deficit rules and are becoming widespread. According to my empirically calibrated simulation, this combination of rules succeeds on avoiding the political bias and is more cycle-friendly than a budget deficit rule.

Keywords: Cycle; Fiscal policy; Fiscal rules

Introduction

Following the recent global economic crisis and the resulting high budget deficits, countries are adopting and strengthening fiscal rules [1]. The main motive for that policy change is to provide credibility to the fiscal consolidation policy in order to improve the likelihood of transition to lower fiscal deficits. While the literature has studied the importance of the implementation of fiscal rules, and the pattern of fiscal policy during the cycle, it is puzzling to note that there are at most few papers connecting between these two phenomena. So far the papers were focused on checking the impact of fiscal rules on the cycle, and not in the role that the cycle plays for designing an optimal fiscal rule. Since policy-makers are looking today for the next-generation fiscal rules, filling this gap is a crucial task.

Another unexplored issue in the literature is related to discretionary statutory tax reductions. Reducing tax rates can be used by politicians as a tool for gaining popularity, while at the same time the budget balance may be threatened[1]. One of the reasons for the lack of research on this field was the inexistence of data on statutory tax rates. Recently, Vegh and Vuletin [2] have presented a statutory tax rates database for industrial and developing countries. Interestingly, they found that the vast majority of statutory tax changes in industrial countries are actually tax reductions: they constitute 75 percent of personal statutory income tax changes (of a magnitude of 2.8 percent), 67 percent of statutory corporate tax changes (of a magnitude of 2.6 percent) and 13 percent of V.A.T. tax changes (of a magnitude of 1.6 percent)[2].

In recent decades, several OECD countries have gradually adopted budget and expenditure rules; in late years, revenue rules are becoming more widespread. The increase of fiscal rules from fewer than five countries in the 1970s and 1980s to 30 countries after the 1990s [3] may partially be explained by the effectiveness of numerical fiscal rules in curtailing budget deficits in different parts of the world at different levels of government, such as, USA [4-6], Latin America [7] and Switzerland [8][3].

At the same time, both policymakers and researchers are aware of the possible effect of adopting fiscal rules alongside the benefits of budgetary discipline[4]. The main concern, according to the Keynesian view[5], is that rules for balancing budgets are expected to deepen recessions. Nevertheless, based on a sample of American states, Alesina and Bayoumi [6] found that fiscal rules have not increased output volatility. More recently, several papers detect no evidence that fiscal rules amplify economic fluctuations (Gali and Perotti [9], for the EMU countries, Fatas and Mihov [10] for the USA, and Badinger [11] for the OECD countries). Schunk and Woodward (2005) at the states level, and Debrun [12] at the national level, show that Procyclicality can be avoided if rules are originally designed to preserve the operation of automatic stabilizers. These authors show that expenditure rules are more cyclical friendly than budget and debt rules.

A different strand of the literature analyzes the behavior of fiscal policy along the cycle. The picture arising from this literature has been corroborated by different papers and it points out to an asymmetrical pattern along the cycle. Hercowitz and Strawczynski [16] showed that advanced economies run a countercyclical fiscal policy during

[1]Another source for political manipulations is tax exemptions, usually given to firms to avoid corporate taxes. Studying these changes is beyond the scope of the present paper.

[2]Potentially V.A.T. reductions can be more popular than direct tax reductions since consumption is related to all individuals in society. However, a high income or corporate statutory tax reduction is more attractive for politicians than a small statutory V.A.T. reduction, because of two reasons: i) the visibility of the statutory tax reduction; ii) the income and corporate tax reduction can be targeted on the median voter.

[3]See also Guichard et al. [13], who found that both expenditure and budget rules anchor successful fiscal consolidations.

[4]Kopits [14] provides a list of arguments for and against budget rules.

[5]From a neo-classical point of view, balance budget rules may impose costs due to a sub-optimal path of tax rates [15].

***Corresponding author:** Michel Strawczynski, Department of Economics and School of Public Policy, Hebrew University of Jerusalem, Israel
E-mail: Michel.strawczynski@mail.huji.ac.il

recessions, which is not corrected during expansions; the availability of tax revenues in expansions helps governments reducing the deficit, "hiding" the inherent bias caused by the two phases of the cycle. According to these authors the asymmetric behavior of expenditure in advanced economies, cause a spending bias - which arises after the completion of a full business cycle. This pattern has been confirmed by Balassone, Francese and Zotteri [17] for the budget deficit and the debt. The asymmetry of collecting revenues was confirmed for particular taxes like the corporate tax [18,19].

An important question is how to design budget rules that minimize the cyclical bias, which is related to the interaction between the cycle and political forces that work asymmetrically in the different phases of the cycle. It is important to stress, in this context, that as shown by Von Hagen and Harden [20] one of the main purposes of fiscal rules is to deal with the well-known "common pool problem", which implies that ministers put pressure on increasing spending when tax revenues increase. This phenomenon is clearly related to the business cycle, since tax revenues soar at expansions, which may enhance the potential harm of the common pool problem. Moreover, according to Kim and Watson (1998), the average duration of expansions is 33.3 months, compared to 10 months for recessions - which enhances the probability that political forces can profit expansions for increasing expenditure. Note also that an additional way to be benevolent with potential voters is by implementing tax reductions. Tax reductions maybe implemented in expansions and in recessions; in the latter, because of Keynesian considerations[6].

Consistently with existing empirical findings on the cyclicality of fiscal variables, I analyze the design of fiscal rules based on asymmetric behavior along the cycle: in expansions tax revenues are abundant and the pressure for increasing spending and reducing statutory tax rates materializes[7], while in recessions maintaining the increase in spending or reducing tax rates imply a high deficit, which is problematic since rating agencies may penalize such a policy by reducing country's debt rating.

An important question related to policy is: how should the next generation budget rules look like so as to cope with these issues? What is the right combination of rules?

The paper is organized as follows. In section 2 I describe existing fiscal rules and present a model for analyzing the cyclical pattern of spending and revenues. This model allows me to characterize three types of fiscal rules: budget deficit rule, expenditure rule and revenue rule. In Section 3 I perform an empirical analysis of the expenditure and revenue functions for a sample of OECD countries. The traditional analysis is extended to learn about the role of tax reductions (of V.A.T. and top income tax rates) on government budget deficits, during recessions and expansions. In section 4 I extend the analysis in order to analyze the impact of fiscal rules on government budget deficits. Section 5 summarizes and concludes.

New Generation Fiscal Rules: A Combination of Rules

Review of existing rules

It is well known that the main benefit of fiscal rules is that they allow the Finance Minister to cope with the "common pool problem", which implies that ministers tend to promote their partisan agenda. Fiscal Rules put a cap on these activities, and consequently allow governments to avoid a deficit bias, which is problematic since it raises the government debt.

In the past, the way to cope with this bias was by using only a balanced budget deficit approach - which put a cap on budget deficit. However, as time went by, governments started to understand that since expenditure is at the heart of the common pool problem, it is necessary to put a cap on expenditure. Historically, this development is reflected in the fact that until 1992 there were 16 budget rules that increased to 56 in 2013. Expenditure rules were used since the very beginning, and they substantially increased in the nineties (Figure 1). It is interesting to note that revenue rules were almost inexistent at the beginning of the nineties, and they are becoming widespread as time goes by. This historical development raises the question about the right combination of budget rules: while theoretically expenditure and revenue rules imply an over identification, in practice it seems that governments need a combination of rules. Figure 2 shows the existing combinations by different countries.

From this figure we learn that countries that apply one rule, they use a budget rule (52 countries compared to 5 countries with an expenditure rule and no countries with a revenue rule). When using two rules, the single existing combination includes budget and expenditure rules. Finally, there are 6 countries that use all three rules - which - once countries accept a combination of rules as a right remedy- seems to be an important option that has been increasing along time. In Table 1 I show the list of countries imposing three rules, the time of adoption and a description of the type of rule.

Note that the description of revenue rules remarks two points related to a deficit bias (one of them also related to the cycle): i) if taxes are reduced there should be an alternative revenue source; ii) if

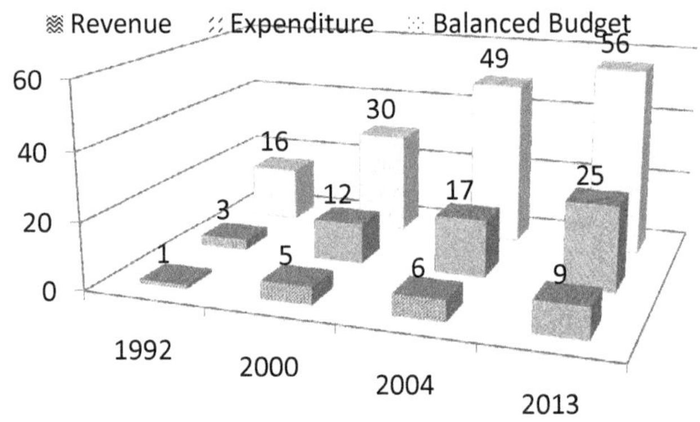

Figure 1: Development of fiscal rules.

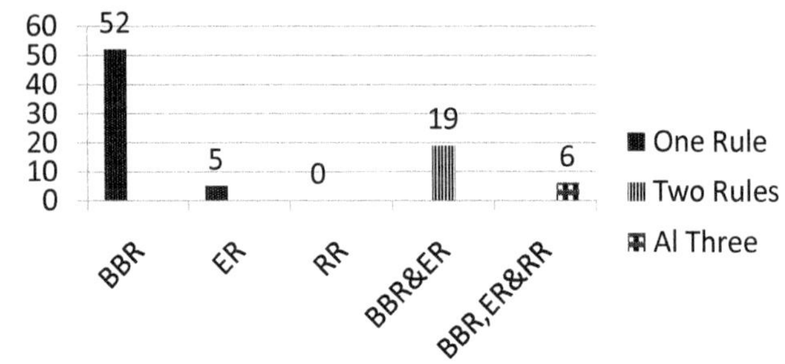

Figure 2: Combinations of fiscal rules.

[6]As in the case of the global crisis; see Spilimbergo et al. (2010).

[7]A paper that is based on this characteristic at the spending side is Talvi and Vegh [21]. For a paper that shows the procyclical behavior of statutory tax rates see Strawczynski [22], who documents this behavior in Israel, and Vegh and Vuletin [2] who document this behavior for developing countries.

Country	BBR implementation	ER implementation	RR implementation	Type of RR
Australia	1985	1985	1985	Not raise tax revenues as a % of GDP
Belgium	1982	1993	1995	Growth of revenues in line with GDP Growth
Denmark	1992	1994	2001	Direct and Indirect taxes cannot be raised
France	1992	1998	2006	Define ex-ante the allocation of revenues higher than expected
Lithuania	2004	2008	2008	Excess revenues must be used to reduce deficit
Netherland	1992	1994	1994	Tax relief must be compensated by a tax increase

Table 1: Countries with three rules.

revenues are higher than expected (i.e., in expansions), they should not be used to increase expenditure[8]. In the next sub-section I present a model that incorporates these issues.

Cyclical bias, tax reductions and fiscal rules

For writing a model of fiscal variables I need the specifications of the tax and expenditure functions as a percent of GDP. The classical approach is to assume that taxes and expenditure are linear functions of GDP, which implies in the long-run that these ratios are constant. However, these simple assumptions are at odd with observed behavior of fiscal variables. Buchanan and Wagner [23] identified a long-run trend of increasing public expenditure as a percent of GDP[9]. Hercowitz and Strawczynski [16] document a similar phenomenon that is related to the cyclical behavior of spending. In fact, a novel way of formalizing this observed pattern was performed by Bertola and Drazen [24] who considered the case in which the spending over GDP ratio is a random walk with an upward drift that is corrected from time to time once it arrives to a trigger point[10]. This approach means that basic fiscal variables as a percent of GDP have an upward trend (corrected from time to time), which can be achieved by using a non-linear relationship between spending and taxation and the GDP.

Following this approach, assume first that the revenue side is given by:

$T=t(Y)\,Y=(A_i+B_iY)Y\,Y$, where i=E (expansions), R (recessions) (1)

Where a small t represents the aggregate tax rate; i.e., the tax rate is progressive[11] through a linear function that has different coefficients A and B in expansions and recessions[12]. This feature characterizes tax functions in advanced economies - and will be corroborated in the empirical analysis.

Note that under this function:

$$\frac{\partial T}{\partial Y}=A_i+2B_iY \qquad (2)$$

Concerning expenditure, assume that the higher the GDP, the higher the political willingness of ministers to spend, and assume that the propensity to do so [represented by g(Y)] is different in expansions and recessions[13]:

$$G=g(Y)\,Y=(C_i+D_iY)\,Y\text{ , i=E, R} \qquad (3)$$

Note that:

$$\frac{\partial G}{\partial Y}=C_i+2D_iY \qquad (4)$$

For simplicity assume that there is a uniform probability of 0.5 to be in a recession and 0.5 to be in an expansion, with a fixed variance. We assume that in times of recessions the propensity to spend is higher or equal than the coefficient of marginal tax revenues; while for expansions the coefficient of marginal taxation is higher than the propensity to spend (these assumptions will be tested empirically):

$$D_R\ge B_R, D_E\le B_E \qquad (5)$$

Concerning tax revenues, following Sobel and Hecombe [26] we shall expect that $B_E>B_R$. Concerning expenditure, the relationship between the coefficients in expansions and recessions depends on whether the political bias described by Talvi and Vegh [21] is relevant, a fact that was not yet documented empirically. If the bias exists we shall find that $D_E>D_R$; if it does not, we shall find that $D_E=D_R$. These relationships between the coefficients will be tested empirically in the next section.

We further assume that when the GDP is at its trend value, the budget deficit as a percent of GDP is balanced:

$$\frac{DEF(\bar{Y})}{\bar{Y}}=\frac{G(\bar{Y})}{\bar{Y}}-\frac{T(\bar{Y})}{\bar{Y}}=0.5\left[(C_E+C_R-A_E-A_R)+(D_E-B_E+D_R-B_R)\bar{Y}\right]=0 \qquad (6)$$

This implies:

$$A_E+A_R-C_E-C_R=(D_E-B_E+D_R-B_R)\bar{Y} \qquad (7)$$

This condition means that in times of recessions there is a deficit bias, due to the propensity of ministers to increase spending at the same pace, at the same time that the GDP declines; in expansion the opposite is true: in principle, the deficit bias goes down. The methodology shown here has the advantage of being stable in the long run: opposed to Balassone, Francese and Zotteri [17] where a full cycle implies an explosive deficit, in my model the structure imposes that the bias is balanced in the long run. In the following equations, I will introduce to the model a new feature: politicians tend to reduce taxes at different opportunities that can be "hidden" during expansion times, given the budget surplus. These tax reductions give a role to fiscal rules, which are intended on assuring convergence to budget balance in the long run.

The bias at the different parts of the cycle is represented by:

$$\frac{\partial DEF}{\partial Y}=C_i-A_i+2Y(D_i-B_i)=\text{def}(Y) \qquad (8)$$

Evaluating this expression at the trend value of Y, means that the deficit bias is equal to:

$$\frac{\partial DEF}{\partial}\Big|(Y=\bar{Y})=(D_E-B_E+D_R-B_R)\bar{Y} \qquad (9)$$

Without losing generality, we assume that the parameters are such

[8]A well-known example of a rule designed to avoid using cyclical revenues for spending is Chile's rule related to revenues from the sale of copper [25].

[9]These findings are in line with the well-known hypothesis developed by A. Wagner and by Peacock and Wiseman.

[10]Alesina and Drazen (1990) show that this adjustment usually occurs after a continuous worsening macroeconomic situation.

[11]I assume that in the long run the GDP is finite. Thus, the tax rate converges to$A+BY$, that is a fixed number. Since Y is a large number, this feature means that A is expected to be negative and B to be small. In the regressions shown in Section 4, A is represented by the constant term and by dummies for the different decades – which are expected to be negative.

[12]Sobel and Hocombe [26] document the asymmetry of short run and long run tax revenue elasticities along the cycle for the US at the national level.

[13]Talvi and Vegh [21] assume that political forces require increases in expenditure using a non-linear function.

that if they are measured at the trend value the budget as a percent of GDP is balanced both in expansions and in recessions:

$$A_E - C_E = (D_E - B_E)\bar{Y} \quad (10)$$

$$A_R - C_R = (D_R - B_R)\bar{Y} \quad (11)$$

We can look at the bias in a recession, in which $Y_t > \bar{Y}$:

$$Recession\,Bias = C_R - A_R + 2(Y_t + \bar{Y} - \bar{Y})(D_R - B_R) \quad (12)$$

$$= 2(Y_t - \bar{Y})(D_R - B_R) + \bar{Y}(D_R - B_R) > 0$$

Or in percent of gdp:

$$RB\_Y = (D_R - B_R)\left(2 - \frac{\bar{Y}}{Y_t}\right) > 0 \quad (13)$$

Analytically, the bias is composed by the gap between marginal propensity to consume compared to the marginal coefficient for revenues, mitigated by the fact that actual GDP is lower than trend, which implies that the last term in the second parenthesis of the right hand side is higher than 1.

The expansion bias, in which $Y_t > \bar{Y}$ is:

$$Expansion\,Bias = 2(Y_t - \bar{Y})(D_R - B_R) + \bar{Y}(D_R - B_R) < 0 \quad (14)$$

Or in percent of GDP:

$$Expansion\,Bias = (D_E - B_E)\left(2 - \frac{\bar{Y}}{Y_t}\right) < 0 \quad (15)$$

In this case the gap between the coefficients of spending and revenues is negative, and the second term in the parenthesis is lower than 1 - exacerbating the surplus bias.

Consider now discretionary tax reductions - represented by β; those can be implemented in a recession (because of Keynesian considerations) or in an expansion (political bias); note that if it is implemented in an expansion, tax reductions will be lower than the surplus bias so as to 'hide' the deficit bias; as a consequence of this policy, the expansion bias can be positive or negative, as a function of the extent of tax reductions:

$$RB_{Y\beta} = (D_R - B_R)\left(2 - \frac{\bar{Y}}{Y_t}\right) + \beta > 0 \quad (16)$$

$$EB_{Y\beta} = (D_E - B_E)\left(2 - \frac{\bar{Y}}{Y_t}\right) + \beta \; ? \quad (17)$$

Summarizing (9) and (10), we find that after a full business cycle the bias depends on the relative coefficients of reaction of spending and tax revenues to GDP and on the magnitude of β, the tax reductions:

$$RB_{Y\beta} + EB_{Y\beta} = 2(D_R - B_R + D_E - B_E) - \left(\frac{\bar{Y}}{Y_{tR}}(D_R - B_R) + \frac{\bar{Y}}{Y_{tE}}(D_E - B_E)\right) + 2\beta > 0 \quad (18)$$

Assuming asymmetric cyclical coefficients, equation 18 implies the result presented by Balassone, Francese and Zotteri [17] where a full business cycle brings in a positive deficit bias. However, in this case the bias does not result only from the asymmetric cyclical pattern of expenditure; it arises also from the fact that governments reduce taxes. This last result gives a crucial role to revenue rules, which are becoming an increasingly widespread tool in the new generation of fiscal rules.

Note also that this pattern of the bias implies that countries may be interested on imposing fiscal rules at the different stages of the cycle. In a recession, the spending bias and the tax reductions may drive deficits to levels that are unacceptable from the point of view of the country's rating, a phenomenon that would be penalized by international rating agencies. Thus, the rule will avoid paying the cost of having the rating reduced. In expansions, the possibility of "hiding" tax reductions (since overall the budget maybe even in surplus), and the existence of a political bias, call for imposing fiscal rules.

Finally, note that three kinds of rules are generally used by policy-makers to deal with the political bias and with tax reductions [1]: i) budget deficit rules that constrain the deficit (effective mainly in recessions); ii) expenditure rules that constraint the increase in expenditure both in expansions and in recessions; iii) revenue rules, aimed at preventing unbalanced tax reductions.

I now turn to the design of these rules, assuming that they are intended to deal with the political cyclical bias and with discretional statutory tax reductions[14].

Budget Rules

Budget deficit rule

Since it is not binding, the budget deficit rule is not the right tool for coping with political spending or statutory tax reduction in expansions. The budget deficit rule is designed to alleviate the recession bias:

$$Recession\,Bias\,after\,the\,rule = (D_R - B_R)\left(2 - \frac{\bar{Y}}{Y_t}\right) + \beta - \alpha = 0.$$

Where α is the parameter that represents government willingness of avoiding a high deficit.

Expenditure rule

The expenditure rule is intended to reduce the political bias: $D'_i = \gamma D_i$. This rule means that there is a cap on expenditure increase that is binding in both recessions and expansions. The bias at the different phases of the cycle is:

$$Cyclical\,Bias\,after\,the\,rule = (\gamma D_i - B_i)\left(2 - \frac{\bar{Y}}{Y_t}\right) + \beta$$

Where γ is the coefficient of effectiveness of the expenditure rule, and is lower than 1. After the imposition of this rule the cyclical bias can be positive or negative, depending on the severity of the rule.

Revenue rule

The revenue rule is intended to alleviate discretionary tax reductions (i.e., those that are not implemented with a parallel reduction of expenditure). Under this rule we introduce the parameter δ which represents the percentage of tax reductions that can be implemented under the revenue rule. Consequently, under this rule tax reductions become $\delta\beta$.

Cyclical Bias, Tax Reductions and Fiscal Rules: An Empirical Analysis

The data

I use a panel of 22 OECD countries[15] during the period 1960 to 2010. The source of my data is the OECD[16]. The rates of change of government expenditure and revenues are computed as the logarithmic

[14]I assume that the decisions on binding rules are taken at the period of budget planning, in which governments have information with respect to the phase of the cycle.

change, deflated by GDP prices. The choice of GDP prices as a deflator is in line with Lane [27]: By using GDP prices, I am able to depict the rise in government wages over domestic prices. Since the matter of wages is one of the main potential political economy forces driving the dynamics of expenditure, it is important to allow it to play a role. Budget deficit is measured by the ratio of nominal government net balance to nominal GDP.

Cyclical bias: parameters estimation

In order to run a simulation we estimate first the expenditure and revenue functions presented in equations 1 and 3 (Tables 2 and 3).

In all regressions I control for variables that are candidates for explaining expenditures (Table 2), and I use the same variables for the tax revenues equation (Table 3). These variables include the population under 15 years old and beyond 65 (pop15+pop65), which are characterized by a high demand for public services; the population (population); dummies for decades in which target rules were implemented in a low scale (Decade60s, Decade70s and Decade80s) in which they take the value of 1 at the specified decade and 0 otherwise; a dummy variable for countries that implemented the policy known as "from welfare to work" (fwtw) which takes the value of 1 for countries and years of implementation[17]; unemployment, that controls for transfer payments (u); budget deficit (defy); and past values of expenditure [g(-1)], budget deficit [deficit(-1)] and tax revenues [tax revenues(-1)][18].

Note that the dummy variables are intended to represent the discrete adjustments that are done by governments from time to time; thus, the coefficients of these variables are expected to be negative. Note also that the coefficient of the variable fwtw is also expected to be negative; moreover, it can be interpreted as the modern correction of the increasing pattern of expenditure - and it is relevant for the period that starts in the nineties and continue until the end of the sample.

I run two specifications that are parallel for both log (g) and log (tax revenues), using panel cointegration after correcting for dependence of variables using the methodology suggested by Pesaran [29]. This correction requires adding the average values of the dependent variable and independent variables for the whole panel sample, as explained by Eberhardt and Bond [30]. I report the W statistic of Im, Pesaran and Shin.

Results are consistent with the model, calling for an interpretation of the parameters of the theoretical model. The main coefficient is the one of log (g)^2 and log(tax revenues)^2, which according to equations 1 and 3 are helpful for estimating the cyclical bias. In Tables 4a-4c I summarize the coefficients and their significance.

Results shown in Table 4a are according to my ex-ante expectations: the test for the model shows 1 percent significance, and most variables are significant and with the expected signs.

Table 4b shows the validity of the inequalities shown in equation 5, according to which in recessions the marginal propensity to spend (measured by the coefficient of squared G) is higher than marginal tax revenues (measured as the coefficient of squared T); and in expansions the opposite result holds: marginal tax revenues are higher than the marginal propensity to spend. While in all regressions the magnitude of the coefficients is according to expected inequalities, only the inequality for recessions is significant at 10 percent; in expansions the coefficients of revenues and expenditure tend to be statistically equal. This result is in line with Hercowitz and Strawczynski [16], who showed that the cyclical effect on deficits is relatively high in recessions, and it is not corrected in expansions.

[15]This list includes all OECD countries except Luxembourg, Mexico, Turkey, and the new members (the Slovak Republic, Poland, Hungary, Korea, the Czech Republic, Chile, Israel, and Slovenia).

[16]The data are from the OECD Annual National Accounts database.

[17]Based on Martin and David [28].

[18]The use of cointegration technique implies keeping to a minimum the number of lagged variables.

Variable	(1)	(2)	(3)	(4)
C	-4.2 (3.1)	-5.1 (3.0)*	-2.5 (2.9)	-2.9 (2.8)
Log(y)*recessions	-0.4 (0.03)***	-0.3 (0.03)***		
Log(y)^2*recessions	0.032 (0.002)***	0.0262 (0.002)***		
Log(y)*expansions			-0.5 (0.03)***	-0.4 (0.03)***
Log(y)^2*expansions			0.0359 (0.002)***	0.0317 (0.002)***
Log(pop15+pop65)	-1.5 (0.7)**	-0.6 (0.6)	0.9 (0.6)	1.0 (0.6)*
Decade60s	-1.1 (0.4)***	-1.3 (0.4)***	-1.2 (0.3)***	-1.4 (0.3)***
Decade70s	-1.2 (0.3)***	-1.4 (0.3)***	-1.3 (0.3)***	-1.0 (0.2)***
Decade80s	-0.8 (0.2) ***	-1.0 (0.2)***	-0.9 (0.2)***	-1.0 (0.2)***
Fwtw	-1.2 (0.2)***	-1.3 (0.2)***	-1.1 (0.2)***	-1.2 (0.2)***
U	-0.1 (0.01)***	-0.1 (0.01)***	-0.1 (0.01)***	-0.1 (0.01)***
Log(population)	2.0 (0.7)***	1.1 (0.6)*	-0.4 (0.6)	-0.6 (0.6)
Tax Revenues(-1)	0.01 (0.003)***	0.06 (0.001)***	0.04 (0.002)***	-0.05 (0.001)***
Average (X)	0.00 (0.00)	-0.03 (0.004)***	0.001 (0.0002)***	-0.001 (0.0005)*
Average (Y)	0.7 (0.2)***	0.9 (0.2)***	0.8 (0.2)***	0.9 (0.2)***
Deficit_y(-1)	0.03 (0.01)***		0.04 (0.001)***	
G(-1)		0.02 (0.004)***		0.001 (0.0003)***
Deficit_y		0.04 (0.008)***		0.04 (0.008)***
Exp_Pct_y		-0.005 (0.002)**		-0.003 (0.002)
Adj. R Squared	0.72	0.74	0.76	0.78
Im, Pesaran and Shin W	-5.2***	-5.4***	-6.3***	-6.9***
Number of observations	918	916	918	916

Table 2: Expenditure functions (Dependent variable: log (g)).

Variable	(1)	(2)	(3)	(4)
C	-32.3 (3.8)***	-32.7 (3.7)***	-29.8 (3.5)***	-30.0 (3.4)***
Log(y)*recessions	-0.3 (0.04)***	-0.3 (0.04)***		
Log(y)^2*recessions	0.027 (0.003)***	0.0248 (0.003)***		
Log(y)*expansions			-0.5 (0.03)***	-0.5 (0.03)***
Log(y)^2*expansions			0.0373 (0.002)***	0.0346 (0.002)***
Log(pop15+pop65)	-4.4 (0.8)***	-3.4 (0.8)***	-1.9 (0.8)**	-1.7 (0.7)**
Decade60s	-2.0 (0.5)***	-2.4 (0.4)***	-2.1 (0.4)***	-2.5 (0.4)***
Decade70s	-2.2 (0.3)***	-3.7 (0.3)***	-2.3 (0.3)***	-2.5 (0.3)***
Decade80s	-1.4 (0.3) ***	-2.5 (0.3)***	-1.5 (0.2)***	-1.7 (0.2)***
Fwtw	-1.8 (0.2)***	-2.1 (0.2)***	-1.7 (0.2)***	-1.9 (0.3)***
U	-0.06 (0.02)***	-0.05 (0.01)***	-0.04 (0.01)***	-0.05 (0.01)***
Log(population)	5.0 (0.8)***	4.0 (0.8)***	2.5 (0.7)***	2.3 (0.7)***
Tax Revenues(-1)	0.004 (0.002)	-0.002 (0.0005)***	0.007 (0.002)***	-0.0008 (0.0005)*
Average (X)	1.9 (0.3)***	2.0 (0.3)***	2.0 (0.3)***	1.9 (0.3)***
Average (Y)		-0.008 (0.001)***		-0.8 (0.1)***
Deficit_y(-1)	0.08 (0.01)***		0.09 (0.01)***	
G(-1)	0.001 (0.0003)***	0.003 (0.0004)***	0.003 (0.0002)***	0.8 (0.1)***
Deficit_y		0.08 (0.01)***		0.1 (0.01)***
Exp_Pct_y		0.008 (0.002)***		0.01 (0.003)***
Adj. R Squared	0.75	0.77	0.79	0.80
Im, Pesaran and Shin W	-3.4***	-3.1***	-4.3***	-4.7***
Number of observations	918	916	918	916

Table 3: Tax revenue functions (Dependent variable: log (tax revenues)).

Equation	(1)		(2)		(3)		(4)	
	B_R	D_R	B_R	D_R	B_E	D_E	B_E	D_E
Coefficient	0.027	0.032	0.0248	0.0262	0.0373	0.0359	0.0346	0.0317

Table 4a: Summary of the coefficients.

Test	B_R- D_R=0		B_E- D_E=0	
Equations	(1)	(2)	(3)	(4)
Probability	0.06*	0.55	0.47	0.13

Table 4b: Wald Test for the Cyclical Coefficients.

Test	D_E-D_R=0		B_E-B_R=0	
Equations	(3)-(1)	(4)-(2)	(3)-(1)	(4)-(2)
Probability	0.04**	0.004***	0.000***	0.000***

Table 4c: Wald Test for the cyclical coefficients.

In Table 4c the Wald test certifies that the coefficient for marginal taxation in expansions is high compared to the one of recessions. This finding was confirmed empirically in the literature, and it is corroborated by the test with a high level of significance (lower than 1 percent). Concerning marginal propensity of spending, results are as expected but with lower significance: while for one specification the coefficient in expansions is higher than in recessions at 1 percent significance, confirming the political bias, in the other specification the significance is found only at a 5 percent level. Thus, the political bias result is weakly confirmed. In terms of the model, the existence of the revenue asymmetry calls for paying special attention to revenues – which may imply using revenue rules.

Note that the constant and all the dummies representing decades, and FWTW, have a negative coefficient (as expected). I also included lagged values of spending and tax revenues so as to control for levels. In the next section I check the behavior of tax reductions, in order to check whether it is a relevant issue.

Tax reductions

One of the most comprehensive studies of the interaction between fiscal rules and cyclicality has been performed by Debrun [12]. These authors consider also revenue rules, and note that they can be cycle-friendly if they avoid using windfalls in expansions, or procyclical if they target a minimum or maximum amount of tax revenues. However, these authors did not consider the possible impact of discretionary tax reductions: if revenue rules are efficient on avoiding discretionary tax reductions in expansions, that would be a positive outcome both from the point of view of cyclical friendliness and avoidance of a structural deficit.

In general statutory tax data is not available, which makes difficult the task of assessing discretionary tax reductions. Recently Vegh and Vuletin [2] studied the behavior of statutory tax rates in a sample of both developed and developing economies, and found that it is acyclical in the first group and procyclical in the second. These authors based their study on the changes in VAT, corporate taxes and the top marginal tax rates of individuals, and did not differentiate among tax increases and reductions[19].

In this sub-section I use the reductions in these three items in order to learn on the cyclical behavior of tax reductions. In order to check the propensity to reduce taxes during the cycle I run a regression where the dependent variable is the group of different sources of tax reductions, and the independent variables are the different phases of the cycle, using cyclical control variables. Since tax reductions are prone to be implemented simultaneously, I use cross-section SUR estimates[20]. The purpose of my analysis is to identify discretionary tax reductions. Thus, I need an identifying strategy. I will consider tax reductions that are parallel to expenditure reductions as "ideological": since they are budgetary balanced, these reductions are a legitimate choice of

[19]Strawczynski [31] used a broader set of taxes for the case of Israel and found that indirect taxation is procyclical, while direct taxation is acyclical.

[20]The SUR technique was used also by Balassone, Zotteri and Francese [17].

politicians and consequently shall not be considered as discretionary; thus, they shall not be a matter to be treated by fiscal rules. Consistently, the dependent variable will include only tax reductions that were not implemented with a parallel reduction of expenditure - which will be considered as discretionary. For this purpose I will check sensitivity by using two definitions: i) DISCR_TAX_RED1 is based on tax reductions that were implemented with no parallel reduction of real expenditure; ii) DISCR_TAX_RED2 is based on tax reductions that were implemented with no parallel reduction of per-capita real expenditure.

In Table 5 I show the results for discretionary tax reductions adding two combinations of fiscal rules: revenue rules and the combination of the three types of rule. Interestingly, the existence of the three kinds of rule moderates discretionary tax reductions, with a coefficient of 0.4 for the first definition (i.e., no parallel real expenditure reduction) and of 0.3 for the second definition (i.e., no parallel per-capita real expenditure reduction) - which will be adopted as a benchmark in the simulation below.

Simulation of fiscal rules

The simulation is performed assuming a symmetric shock and using the coefficients shown in the previous sub-section. I assume that the shock equals to 5 percent of GDP.

Table 6a shows the impact of the shock and the performance of the deficit bias under different rules (Table 6a).

According to the basic setup, and as a consequence of the cycle, there is a political deficit bias, exacerbated by tax reductions. Applying the coefficients of the squared variables for G and T to the benchmark values of G, T and Y, I obtain a recession bias of 1.2 of GDP that is corrected in expansions by 0.6 percent of GDP. Concerning discretionary tax reductions, I estimated them by looking at the reductions of income taxation, corporate taxation and V.A.T. that were implemented with no parallel reduction of per-capita real government expenditure. The average reduction in corporate taxes was 3.6, and in income taxation it was 2.9 (there were no discretionary V.A.T. reductions). Using these estimates and the share of these taxes in tax revenues, I obtained that discretionary tax reductions stand at 0.5 percent of GDP. Consistently with my results in Table 5 and results by Vegh and Vuletin [2], I assume that tax reductions are implemented equally in expansions and recessions. Accordingly, the deficit stands at 3.4 percent of GDP in recessions and 1.5 percent in expansions. Note that while the tax reduction increases the deficit in both phases of the cycle, it becomes visible at recessions, in which the GDP growth is negative.

Imposing a deficit rule means that it will be binding in recessions; in the simulation I use the cap imposed at Maastricht Treaty, which stands at 3 percent of GDP. Thus, the deficit bias in recessions is reduced by 0.4 percent, while in expansions it is not binding and thus it does not affect the deficit bias.

In order to compare between the deficit and expenditure rules, I assume that the expenditure rule is designed ex-ante so as to neutralize the cyclical bias - as estimated in the regressions. Results show that the impact of this rule on the deficit is slightly smaller in recessions (while the whole adjustment comes from the expenditure side) but, as opposed to budget deficit rule, it exists in expansions. In average the deficit is lower, due to the fact that the expenditure rule is designed to cope with the political cyclical bias. Another remarkable aspect is that the expenditure rule is more cycle-friendly than the deficit rule. This result is in line with Debrun [12].

The most notable impact is achieved when imposing a combination of expenditure and revenue rules: since the revenue rule constraints discretionary tax reductions, the deficit bias in recessions is related to the cyclical bias and to the portion of effective discretionary tax reductions under the combination of the rules, which according to the results in Table 5 stands at 30 percent. Under this combination of rules, the deficit bias stands at 2.9 and 1.1 percent of GDP in recessions and expansions, respectively. These figures mean that the combination of rules is efficient on neutralizing the political bias, and that it is binding

Variable/Regression	(1)	(2)	(3)	(4)
Dependent Variable	DISCR_TAX_RED1	DISCR_TAX_RED2	DISCR_TAX_RED1	DISCR_TAX_RED2
C	0.1 (0.05)**	0.14 (0.05)***	0.1 (0.05)**	0.1 (0.05)**
Recessions	0.02 (0.02)**	0.03 (0.02)*	0.02 (0.002)	0.04 (0.002)*
Recessions (-1)	-0.01 (0.02)	-0.02 (0.02)	-0.01 (0.002)***	-0.03 (0.002)
Dlog(exports)	-0.5 (0.2)**	-0.5 (0.2)***	-0.5 (0.2)***	-0.5 (0.3)***
Dlog(unemployment)	-0.01 (0.01)	-0.02 (0.01)	-0.02 (0.02)	-0.02 (0.02)
Output gap	0.08 (0.02)***	0.07 (0.02)***	0.08 (0.00)***	0.07 (0.02)***
Dlog(population)	4.5 (1.8)**	2.5 (1.6)	4.5 (1.8)***	3.2 (1.6)**
Parlament	0.08 (0.04)**		0.08 (0.04)**	0.06 (0.04)*
Rtarget	0.06 (0.04)	0.04 (0.04)		
Rtarget*Btarget*Etarget			0.4 (0.07)***	0.3 (0.06)***
Adj. R Squared	0.03	0.04	0.06	0.06
Durbin Watson	1.9	1.6	1.9	1.9
Sample Period	1975-2010	1075 2010	1975-2010	1975-2010

Table 5: Tax reductions (Cross section SUR regressions).

	Recession	Expansion
Cyclical Bias	3.4	1.5
Deficit Rule	3.0	1.5
Expenditure rule	3.1	1.2
Expenditure and Revenue Rule	2.9	1.1

Table 6a: A simulation of fiscal rules along the cycle simulated deficit bias as a percent of GDP (Chosen parameters: $\alpha = 0.4; \gamma = 0.994; \delta = 0.3$). Assumption: tax reductions are equal in size to the cyclical bias; structural deficit equals the average deficit over the sample.

	A=1, B=1, C=1	A=2, B=0.5, C=0.5	A=0.5, B=2, C=0.5	A=0.5, B=0.5, C=2
Deficit Rule	0.8	0.3	1	1
Expenditure rule	0.7	0.5	0.7	0.75
Expenditure and Revenue Rule	0.4	0.1	0.2	0.89

Table 6b: Social loss under different weights.

in expansions. The ability of coping with the political bias in expansions is an optimal way to react, since it is cycle-friendly. Debrun [12] analyze the different rules according to their characteristics concerning the ability for curtailing the deficit, and the extent of cycle-friendliness.

One of the most well-known formulations for a macroeconomic loss function by a benevolent policy-maker was proposed by Barro and Gordon [32]. It is desired to avoid the deviation of actual unemployment from its natural rate. In the present context, we shall add to the loss function a term that represents the loss of reputation caused by a high debt[21]. Thus, the government would choose the fiscal rules that bring to a minimum the following loss function:

$$Min\,L = K*(DEBT_t - \overline{DEBT}) + H*(u_t - u_N)$$

Where DEBT represents the ratio of general government gross debt to GDP, $\overline{DEBT}$ is the debt target, u_t represents unemployment at time t and u_N is the natural rate of unemployment. In the present case the loss of reputation is represented by the increase of deficits over the cap (which occur during recessions), and by the increase of the structural deficit that is caused by the political bias. The deviations from the natural rate of unemployment are critical in recessions, since at that time unemployment goes up. Thus, the reduced form of equation 19 in the present framework takes the following form:

(1) L=A × (excess deficit over cap)+B × (increase of structural deficit)+C × (cuts in recession)

Where A, B and C are, respectively, the weights given to the different terms. Using different combinations I analyze the strength of the different rules. It turned out that in most cases the combination of expenditure and revenue rules dominates the other options; another clear result is that the budget deficit rule is dominated by the other two options (Table 6b).

Empirical Evidence on Fiscal Rules along the Cycle

Following Kumar [34] I define a fiscal rule here as a numerical target that binds and controls budget deficits and expenditure in annual budgeting—e.g., a budget-balancing rule, expenditure ceilings and caps, revenue rules ("IMF Definition")[22]. According to IMF definition, a target qualifies as a fiscal rule only if it is specified for at least three years (or more); note also that the IMF definition does not include pay-as-you-go targets as a fiscal rule.

Fiscal rules are represented by dummy variables that take the value of 1 during the period beginning at the adoption date of the rule and lasting until the rule is abandoned (otherwise it continues until the end of the sample), and 0 otherwise. The data is freely available at the internet and was facilitated to researchers by the authors.

I considered three different definitions for fiscal rules at the federal level[23]: i) budget balancing rules adopted at the national level (BTARGET); ii) expenditure rules adopted at the national level (ETARGET); iii) revenue rules (RTARGET), which typically require increasing another taxation source when taxes are reduced. The use of this last type of rule is less common, but it has been increasing in recent years. Kumar [34] and Budina [1] stress that the complexity of fiscal finances in modern times imply that the coexistence of the different types of rules is desirable.

Note that these definitions focus on different variables. Budget balancing rules usually affect a deficit by setting a balanced budget target or gradually lowering it, and by cutting expenditure or increasing taxes. Expenditure rules target the rate of increase of government spending; thus, they are more likely to restrain expenditure growth if they are binding[24]. Revenues rules put restrictions on tax reductions, and are intended to strengthen the revenue side of the budget. The choice of these three different definitions allows for testing the efficacy of the different degrees of rules. Moreover, by using interaction variables (defined as the multiplication of the different dummy variables representing the rules), I can test the effectiveness of a combined application of rules. For example, until the end of the period to which the data relates, Netherland implemented all three types of rules, Iceland did not adopt any, and the USA was the only country to abolish an existing budget rule without adopting another.

I performed General Method of Moments (GMM) estimations using year and country fixed effects. Ilzetzki and Vegh [35] emphasize the need to account for potential endogeneity between government expenditure and GDP when studying fiscal policy. To cope with this issue I use exports growth as an instrumental variable for GDP growth. I report robust standard deviations, using White cross-section corrected standard errors.

I used the following control variables to reflect higher sources of demand for government expenditure (public services such as education, child allowances, and old-age pensions, respectively): population growth (DlogPOP) to account for the demand for public services, GDP growth (DlogY) to represent resources, and the growth of the population under 15 years of age (DlogPOP15) and over 65 years of age (DlogPOP65) [36-38].

Dependent Variable:	DEFY			
Period:	1963-2010			
Number of observations	977	977	977	977
C	1.519	1.306	1.305	1.409
	(3.56)***	(2.43)**	(2.44)**	(2.65)***
DlogY	-34.560	-35.541	-35.617	-36.731
	(-3.54)***	(-3.52)***	(-3.53)***	(-3.62)***
DlogPOP	-29.806	24.265	24.925	28.450
	(-0.77)	(0.38)	(0.39)	(0.45)
DlogPOP15+DlogPOP65	15.628	4.786	4.625	3.699
	(1.73)*	(0.40)	(0.39)	(0.32)
DEFY(-1)	-0.185	-0.174	-0.174	-0.179
	(-5.05)***	(-4.24)***	(-4.25)***	(-4.38)***
RTARGET	-0.466			
	(-1.96)**			
ETARGET* BTARGET* RTARGET		-0.719		
		(-1.85)*		
ETARGET* BTARGET* RTARGET(1-YBOOM)			-0.695	
			(-2.10)**	
BTARGET(1-YBOOM)				-0.553
				(-2.01)**
Adj. R2	0.34	0.34	0.33	0.34
Durbin-Watson	2.09	2.08	2.08	2.08

Table 7: The new generation fiscal rule: adding a revenue rule.

[21] A model that solves optimal fiscal policy under the existence of a penalty for the loss of reputation when the debt to gdp ratio is higher than the target is shown by Hercowitz and Strawczynski [33].

[22] For an analysis of different definitions of fiscal rules see Dahan and Strawczynski [22].

[23] Another important dimension is federal vs. state rules. For example, European rules apply to all levels of government. However, learning about the effectiveness of state rules is beyond the scope of the present paper.

[24] Dothan and Thompson (2009) analyze a transparent spending rule governing maximum sustainable rate of spending growth, treating the revenue as given.

Table 7 shows the impact of fiscal rules on budget deficit. Introducing revenue rules reduces the deficit by 0.5 percent. This effect become larger when applied in combination with the other two types of rule: balanced budget and expenditure. Finally, I obtained that the effect of the fiscal rules combination is notable at recessions: the coefficient for these periods is significant. Note that in the ex-ante analysis the tax reduction could be performed in expansions ("hiding") or in recessions (countercyclical policy) [39,40]. This result means that revenue rules, in combination with the other two types of rules, may avoid increasing the deficit in recessions; note that in these periods governments are interested to avoid a high deficit (beyond the automatic stabilizers). The sizable coefficient raises the question of the cycle-friendliness of revenue rules - a question that merits further research (Table 7).

Summary and Conclusions

In recessions the GDP slows down, tax revenues are reduced and the budget deficit goes up. In expansions tax revenues soar and the abundant 'common pool of revenues' stimulates ministers to spend; thus, the correction of the deficit in expansions is not enough to avoid an increase in the deficit after a full business cycle. Fiscal rules, which were created in order to deal with the political bias of the common pool problem, should take into account the impact of the economic cycle on fiscal variables, and be designed so as to cope with the political bias. Note that the political bias does not always show up in real time. A good illustration of this type of phenomenon is the reduction of statutory tax rates: if those are performed in expansions, the exogenous increase in GDP that is characteristic to expansions, compensates for the reduction of tax revenues, and thus it hides the increase of the structural deficit. The right rules to be applied as a reaction to the political bias are the ones that fight it at source: spending and revenue rules. Paradoxically, those are actually less widespread than budget deficit rules (although becoming popular in late years).

In this paper I check whether the pattern of spending and revenues is related to the cycle. Concerning revenues, and in consistence with empirical findings, we shall expect that in good times they rise more than in recessions. The reason for this result is related to progressive taxation: in good times high income individuals advance to subsequent brackets, which implies higher personal income marginal tax rates. Concerning spending, the prevailing hypothesis is that in good times the common pool problem is at place, causing a higher spending compared to recessions. Using a sample of OECD countries between 1963 and 2010, I found very strong support (at 1 percent significance) for the first result and a weaker support (at 5 percent significance) for the second. I also found that in recessions marginal spending is higher than marginal tax revenues, while in expansions they tend to be similar - a result that is in line with Hercowitz and Strawczynski [16].

My next step is to model these facts in order to analyze the possible bias that may arise as a consequence of the interaction of the cycle and the political forces. An additional possible source for a deficit bias is the implementation of discretionary tax reductions, which are defined as those reductions that are implemented without a parallel reduction in expenditure. Discretionary tax reductions can be implemented in recessions as a countercyclical reaction, or in expansions, given the feasibility of hiding the impact of statutory tax reductions on tax revenues in real time. By using V.A.T., corporate and top marginal income tax rates, I show that in OECD countries discretionary tax reductions were implemented mainly in recessions. An examination of the impact of revenue rules on tax reductions show that while these rules limit tax reductions, they allow their implementation in recessions – which in the terminology of Debrun [12] means that they are cycle-friendly.

Fiscal rules can deal with the deficit bias by putting a cap on deficit (balanced budget rules), by putting a limit on spending (expenditure rules) or by limiting discretionary tax reductions (revenue rules). Budina et al. [1] have shown that the combinations of rules are becoming widespread, in order to deal with the source of possible political bias. I run a simulation using the parameters found in the empirical regressions, and found that revenue rules are crucial for limiting the deficit bias caused by discretionary tax reductions. According to the simulation, the addition of a revenue rule is effective on reducing the budget deficit. Moreover, a combination of expenditure and revenue rules is effective for both curtailing the budget deficit and for doing it in a cycle-friendly way[25]. A loss function that combines the political bias and the cycle-friendliness of rules in recessions shows that the combination of expenditure and revenue rules implies a lower loss than the application of a single rule - deficit or expenditure.

Finally, I performed regressions for the general government budget deficit as a function of its main explaining variables, with the addition of fiscal rules. As in previous papers, I found that deficit rules and expenditure rules help for reducing the budget deficit. A new finding is that revenue rules have an additional contribution for reducing the deficit, which becomes more substantial under a combination of the three types of rules.

Acknowledgement

I am thankful to Avi Ben-Bassat, Claude Berrebi, Momi Dahan, Rodrigo Fuentes, Zvi Hercowitz, Chris Huckfeldt, Veronica Mies, Assaf Razin, Karl Shell, Maxim Troshkin, Raanan Sulitzeano-Kenan, and to participants in Seminars at Tel Aviv University, Universidad Catolica de Chile, The Hebrew University School of Government, the Israel Economic Association and the International and Macro Seminar at Cornell University for helpful comments; thanks to Oren Tirosh for his assistance on processing the data.

References

1. Budina N, Tidiane K, Andrea S, Anke W (2012) Fiscal rules in response to the crisis: toward the next generation rule - a new dataset. IMF Working 12: 187.
2. Vegh C, Vuletin G (2012) how is tax policy conducted over the business cycle? NBER Working 17753.
3. Calderon C, Scmidt-Hebbel K (2008) the choice of fiscal regimes in the world. Cent Bank Chile Working 487.
4. Poterba J (1994) State responses to fiscal crises: the effects of budgetary institutions and politics. J Polit Econ 102: 799-821.
5. Alt J, Lowry R (1994) Divided government, fiscal institutions, and budget deficits: evidence from the States. Am Polit Sci Revi 88: 811-828.
6. Alesina A, Bayoumi T A (1996) The costs and benefits of fiscal rules: evidence from US states. NBER Working 5614.
7. Alesina A, Hausmann R, Hommes R, Stein E (1999) Budget institutions and fiscal performance in Latin America. J Dev Econ 59: 253-273.
8. Krogstrup S, Wälti S (2008) Do fiscal rules cause budgetary outcomes? Public Choice 36: 1-2, 123-138.
9. Gali J, Perotti R (2003) Fiscal policy and monetary integration in Europe. Econ Policy, pp. 533-572.
10. Fatas A, Mihov I (2006) The Macroeconomic Effects of Fiscal Rules in the US States. J Public Econ 90: 101-117.
11. Badinger H (2009) Fiscal Rules, Discretionary Fiscal Policy and Macroeconomic Stability: An Empirical Assessment for OECD Countries. Appl Econ 41: 829-847.
12. Debrun X, Laurent M, Alessandro T, Joaquim Ayuso i-C, Manmohan SK (

[25]The friendliness of revenue rules was checked in my paper. The friendliness of expenditure rules was checked and corroborated by Debrun [12].

(2008) National Fiscal Rules. Economic Policy 299-362.

13. Guichard S, Kennedy M, Wurzel E, Andree C (2007) What promotes fiscal consolidation-OECD Country experiences? OECD Papers 7:1.

14. Kopits G (2001) Fiscal rules: useful policy framework or unnecessary ornament IMF Working 1:145.

15. Barro R (1979) On the determination of public debt. J Polit Econ 87: 940-71.

16. Hercowitz, Strawczynski (2004a) Cyclical Ratcheting in Government Spending: Evidence from the OECD. Revi Econ Stat 86: 353-361.

17. Balassone F, Maura F, Stefania Z (2010) cyclical asymmetry in fiscal variables. Empirica 37: 381-402.

18. Creedy J, Norman G (2011) Corporation tax asymmetries: effective tax rates and profit shifting. Int Tax and Public Financ 18: 422-435

19. Bilicka K (2013) Asymmetric behavior of corporate tax revenues in the business cycle. Manuscript, presented at the Annual Conference of the IIPF, Sicily.

20. Von HJ (2006) Fiscal rules and fiscal performance in EU and Japan. SFB/TR 15-Gov efficiency econ sys Discussion 147.

21. Talvi E, Vegh C (2005) Tax base variability and procyclical fiscal policy. J Dev Econ 78: 156-190.

22. Dahan M, Strawczynski M (2013) Fiscal rules and government expenditure composition in OECD countries. J Policy Analysis and Management 32: 484-504.

23. Buchanan J, Wagner R (1978) Fiscal responsibility in constitutional democracy. Stud in Public Choice 1: 79-97.

24. Bertola G, Drazen A (1993) Trigger points and budget cuts: explaining the effects of fiscal austerity. Am Econ Revi 83: 11-26.

25. Frankel J (2011) A Solution to Fiscal Procyclicality: The Structural Budget Institutions Pioneered by Chile. Journal Economía Chilena 14: 39-78.

26. Sobel, Hocombe (1996) Measuring the growth and variability of tax bases over the business cycle. Natl Tax J 49: 535-552.

27. Lane PR (2003) The cyclical behavior of fiscal policy: evidence from the OECD. J Public Econ Elsevier 87: 2261-2675.

28. Martin JP, Grubb D (2001) what works and for whom: a review of OECD countries' experiences with active labor market policies. Swedish Econ Policy Revi 8: 9-56.

29. Pesaran HP (2006) Estimation and Inference in Large Heterogeneous Panels with a Multifactor Error Structure. Econometrica 74: 967-1012.

30. Eberhardt M, Bond S (2009) Cross-section Dependence in Nonstationary Panel Models: A Novel Estimator. Nordic Econometric Conference, Lund (available via the Internet).

31. Strawczynski M (2013) Cyclicality of statutory tax rates. Israel Econ Revi 11: 67-96.

32. Barro R, Roger G (1983) Rules, discretion and reputation in a model of monetary policy. J Monetary Econ 12: 101-121.

33. Hercowitz Z, Strawczynski M (2004b) Fiscal Policy dynamics with a public-Debt Guideline. Israel Econ Revi 2: 91-106.

34. Kumar M, Emanuele B, Andrea S, Carlos C, Daeaheng K et al. (2009) Fiscal rules - anchoring expectations for sustainable public finances. IMF Working Paper, December.

35. Ilzetzki E, Carlos V (2008) Procyclical fiscal policy in developing countries: truth or fiction? NBER Working 14191.

36. Auerbach AJ (2008) Federal budget rules: the U.S. experience. NBER Working 14288.

37. James B, Richard D, Alan D, John VR (2005) the internationalization of public welfare policy. The Econ J 115: C62-C81.

38. Russel D, Kinnon JGM (1993) Estimation and inference in econometrics, Oxford: Oxford University Press.

39. John PM (2000) what works among active labor market policies: evidence from OECD countries' experiences? OECD Econ Studies 30: 79-113.

40. Hagen VV, Jurgen H, Ian J 1995 Budget processes and commitment to fiscal discipline. Eur Econ Revi 39: 771-779.

Why Manufacturers are Less Powerful than Retailers in Trade Circles? A Case Study of Wal-Mart Retailing Business

Shabbir MS*

Centre of Professional Excellence (CPE), BlueArea, Islamabad, Pakistan

Abstract

This paper investigates that from last several years, it became a question mark for the literature of academic and trade circles, why manufacturers are less powerful as compared to retailers. Our study provides a fresh fuel in the existing fire over the United States largest retailing corporation. However, our research provides a new dimension through innovative strategies and theories adopted by Wal-Mart and how retailers become more powerful. For this purpose, we take Wal-Mart as a case study in order to investigate several quarries. What are the reasons which make Wal-Mart so successful, unique, mergence and acquisition innovative capabilities? It also highlights the literary work done by historians on Wal-Mart and to examine the progress and different strategies of Wal-Mart in term of its success in retailing business. It is observed that most of expansion of Wal-Mart Inc. was through joint ventures; however in some countries such as Germany and Canada, it was by acquisition. Moreover, Globalization had a positive effect on Wal-Mart's success and supply chain management system played a major role in its business growth and making it a market leader.

Keywords: Wal-Mart; Trade circles; Innovative strategies; Academic literature; Retailing business

Introduction

There was a long debate how retailers became more powerful than manufactures, however some studies [1-4] suggested that retailors got several benefits from manufacturers such as allowance of slotting, discount of bulk purchase and trade deals and they also took extra discount from manufacturers which increased the market power of retailors and surge their profit also. The answer of the academic literature is controversial whereas, they suggested that such a transference can occurred. While some researchers are not still satisfied such kind of shift can be exist and they made theoretical challenges for themselves [5-7].

The history of Wal-Mart's started from 1930s when a need for discount retailing store arose the major reason for this was Great Depression of 1930. After World War II the concept of grocery super stores got popularity due to low rates, easy access, long working time and colorful advertisement. In 1930s, only few discount super stores were working in United States mainly located in the office building in New York and other major cities. After World War II due to high inflation served a base for discount retailing and Sam Walton noticed the opportunity and availed it (Wong, 2009). In 1940 Sam Walton was running a variety of stores in New York a momentous idea come in to his mind why don't I should bargain from supplier and get extra money and sell goods to supplier at same price in that way to earn more profit [8]. Wal-Mart is a United States public corporation that runs a chain of large discount departmental stores and warehouse stores that operates in various formats around the world. It was found in 1962 by Sam Walton and its Headquartered located is in Bentonville and Arkansas USA [9].

However, the data which reflects fiscal period of five years from 2009 to 2013 provided a snapshot of Wall Mart's performance, where it operated more than 10,700 retail units, approximately 245 and 75% customers work in their stores and operation Management joined hourly associated to Wall Mart's in United States and 27 countries across the world respectively. It also increased respectively 59% and 123% in earning per share and cash flow, which effected positively to their shareholders by $ 60 billion in term of dividend and repurchase of shares. Free cash flow is a non-GAAP measure. Net cash provided by operating activities of continuing operations is the closest GAAP measure to free cash flow. Reconciliations and other information regarding free cash flow and its closest GAAP measure can be found in the Management's Discussion and Analysis of Financial Condition and Results of Operations included in this Annual Report and on our website at http://www.stock.walmart.com [10].

When it comes to our operating segments, Wall mart U.S. is as strong as it has ever been. Last year, we opened our 4,000th U.S. location and added more than $10 billion in net sales, including $4.7 billion in sales growth. We had positive performance and grew market share in a number of our largest categories. Wall Mart International continues to be the growth engine for our company, contributing nearly 30 percent of consolidated net sales, while adding 19 million square feet of new retail space [11].

However, top management of Wal-Mart gave a new strategy of low price and expansion in its products to increase their customers. Wal-Mart Stores emerged to rural Arkansan in 1970s to reshape itself in world's largest economy. Its co-founder, Sam Walton, taught United States to demand for low cost products having best quality or discount store concept. With the passage of time, this company boosts United States Overall productivity, decreased the inflation rate and strengthened the buying power for millions of people of United States. After achieving their desire targets in United States, the top management of company decided to enter in to Asian countries, and

***Corresponding author:** Shabbir MS, Faculty, Centre of Professional Excellence (CPE), Blue Area, Islamabad, Pakistan
E-mail: mshahzad786.pk11@gmail.com

then the company introduced their production with different strategy such as small stores inside the streets and large stores on main streets and this affect was stable on Asian markets [12].

Wal-Mart has 158 distribution centers all across the world. Moreover, Wal-Mart has largest distribution operation in the world. Their logistic setup has a fleet of 6500 tractors, 55000 trailers and more than 7000 drivers. Their regional distribution centers have 12 miles of conveyor belts which can have hundreds of thousands of cases through facility each day [13]. The major activities of Wal-Mart's are

- Purchasing the goods
- Deliver that goods
- Cost control over goods

The other different types of activities were performed for fulfilling the requirement of specific customer [9]. Wal-Mart has a competitive edge in its inventory control procedure, logistics system, and distribution network [14]. The ability to move the goods from one place to others were efficiently and speedy without any disruption result in a great cost reduction which Wal-Mart's achieve. Wal-Mart has exact time information of their products in the stores shelves and when additional products required filling the shelves [15]. The resources of Wal-Mart were consisting on main three categories. First of all, the physical resources which are owned and controlled by the management? Second its human resources, experienced managers, stores managers and logistic staff, and finally the company culture heritage Wal-Mart culture is based on restless effort and focus on constant self-improvement, loyalty and discipline [16].

Key relation of partnership in Wal-Mart was buyer-supplier relationship, in which suppliers were considered as close partners of Wal-Mart. They are also part of the value chain process of each other and it delivered suppliers the chance of accessing itself to a large market. However, it made able the suppliers, who want to take advantages of its broad market, to keep their prices at low cost and the suppliers able to control of their own business and negotiation benefits from Wal-Mart [17]. Wal-Mart customers can be divided into three groups: "brand aspirations", people with low incomes who are obsessed with brand; "price-sensitive effluents" wealthier shoppers who love deals; and finally "value-price shoppers" who like low prices and cannot afford much more [18].

Wal-Mart's business model

Business model describes the organization process of delivers, captures and create value of their goods through a flow chat procedure [19]. Although Elman and Hughes [4] consider four key elements of the business model, the analysis of Wal-Mart's Business Model is given by Osterwalder and Pigneur [19] consist of nine building blocks (Figure 1).

Wal-Mart revenue that generated from its different customer segments are basically come from retail business , such as music downloading, fixed menu pricing. Wal-Mart also earn revenue from selling its own brand, produces by others to cover a segment not cover by other suppliers. Moreover, it takes advantage of selling goods before paying to its suppliers. In year 2012, Wal-Mart delivered a strong financial performance with huge profit. Net sales increased by 5.9% and reach to $443.9 billion, and the consolidated operating income grew by 4 % to $26.6 billion. The diluted earnings per share from Wal-Mart's continued operation were $4.54 per share, from $4.18 in the previous year. However, Wal-Mart's strong financial position which, defines best

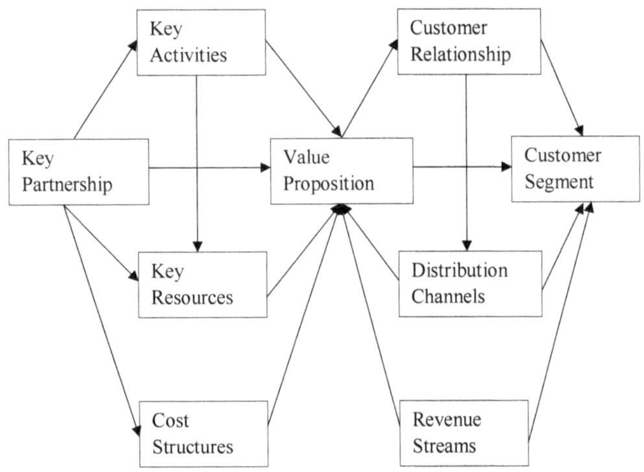

Figure 1: Osterwalder's 9 point decomposition of a Business Model. Source: (Chesbrough, 2010).

their ability to grow. In 2012 Wal-Mart's added 52.2 million square feet through 1,160 additional units previous, including acquisitions in the U.K. and South Africa [20]. The operating ratios of the Wal-Mart five year is shown at Appendix-I, which showed in Wal-Mart's financial performance.

Research question

How retailing business in developing countries can compete with Wal-Mart innovative strategies?

Research objectives

- To explore the factors behind the success of Wal-Mart.
- To study the effect of technological advancement on Wal-Mart operations.
- To analyze the effects of globalization on Wal-Mart growth.

Literature Review

Wal-Mart competitors are generally divided in to two parts Local competitors and foreign competitors. Wal-Mart is giving tough competition to its competitors like Circuit City, Toys R, Home Depot etc and generally put pressure on them to increase the market responsiveness by taking several action in competition to Wal-Mart [21]. Wal-Mart creates a tough competition for its competitors and it was not easy for them to compete with Wal-Mart. Every new Wal-Mart stored decreases local competition, market share and profit margins, and result some businesses to close [22].

According to Warburg (2002) studied by Curie and Jain prices of Wal-Mart is in average of 14% lowest than their competitors [23]. Wal-Mart has 23 miles of retail selling space in the U.S., where 5,500 of its stores consist of 70% of its total which located in United States. Its annual revenues of 2004 were just over $288 billion (Revell, 2005). Wal-Mart is the top US sellers and its sales mainly consist of groceries, music, electronics etc. his company has the largest employees in the United States in private sector with 1.3 million of employees. In 2004 it singly handled 6.5% of total U.S retail sales. Almost 12 million of United States shop from Wal-Mart in every week and in a survey it showed that 84% of United States has done shopping from Wal-Mart in a year 2005 [24].

From the global perspective Wal-Mart is the largest retailing store network in the world. The sales of Wal-Mart is higher than the combines sales of three of its retailing store competitors Carrefour (France), Home Depot (United States), and Metro (Germany). Wal-Mart has been a global leader in retailing business due to many ways, (i) its investment in information technology, (ii) its transformation of supply chain system in to a relationship with its suppliers and customers by establishing its private-label brand and directly purchasing from overseas producers to reduce cost and achieving its policy of "low cost always" another advantage it provides is "one-stop shopping" which make difference from its competitors [14].

Wal-Mart locates its stores in different places, where they consider being profitable after detail study. It includes the possible factors, information about demand for product and cost related to it, the competitive environment and how the competition will be affected after Wal-Mart's entry. Holmes [25] and Jia [22] discuss various demographic factors related to Wal-Mart entry in the market, such as the density and the size of the population, age and income distribution. Now we will study the different strategies due to which the Wal-Marts have maintained its competitive advantage in local and foreign markets.

The mission statement of the Wal-Marts is "Low prices always". They are following their unique mission statement and focus on the business to achieve that mission their low price slogan is good for Wal-Mart as it is paying them even good for shoppers and especially lower income people. Wal-Mart generated savings for customers through cost reduction strategies. One such savings method was done by removing deodorants from boxes. Savings were realized by weight savings in shipping, the purchases of boxes, design and printing for the box. Each box cost approximately five cents. This savings was divided between Wal-Mart and the deodorant companies [26]. Wal-Mart affect the local cost of living standard in two ways (1) the direct effect of the retailer own prices (2) indirect effects due to the retailer competiveness on other merchants (Freeman et al., 2011).

Globalization is another effective and innovative strategy used by the Wal-Mart's. Retail system is becoming global in these days due to its different characteristics such as, new strategic objectives and new capabilities. It is noted that consumers is well- aware and knowledgeable about their needs and wants, more demanding of products and also more search for its required products, values and services from the retailers [27]. Wal-Mart's international stores supply chain is spread around the world such as Canada, Brazil, Mexico, and Costa Rica. Wal-Mart's International stores represent about 45 percent of its total retail outlets [28]. The current goal of Wal-Mart is to increase its international business from its current level of 20-33 of its total revenue which estimated roughly 103 billion by purchasing major interest in 415 retail stores in Latin America and this strategy is followed by Wal-Marts around the globe [29,30].

Information technology is another Wal-Mart's innovative strategy, which plays a major role in Wal-Mart's success. Wal-Mart becomes a leader in technological business process and maintaining the world largest private sector data ware house. However, this data has used mainly by the managers along with suppliers who give access to it for effectively utilizing the coordinated efforts among themselves. Wal-Mart was the first company who build the world first largest satellite communication system. This company is using such data which enabled supply chain coordination process known as collaborative planning, forecasting and replenishment (CPFR) which help them to make coordinated business plans.

Wal-Mart was the first company who used barcode and RFID technology in their store E-recruiting and automated testing system for candidates they got skilled workers all the time. Wal-Mart is not only performing in traditional retailing system but also leading in e-retailing. However, Walmart.com was founded in year 2000 as a joint venture of Wal-Mart Stores and Accel Partners, a leading venture capital firm of that time in Silicon Valley. Walmart.com Inc. is one of the largest e-retailing companies in the world. Walmart.com offers 1.5 million; easy-to-use music downloads digital one-hour photo services, and an adding on innovative strategies to position itself as an online leader [31].

In supply chain procedure Wal-Mart is excellent in working. Wal-Mart slogan is "Low Cost" and they are maintaining that slogan by understanding the importance of controlling cost through supply chain procedure due to this reason Wal-Mart is more focus on pull and demand base supply system instead of traditional push and supply based system. However, the difference in both of them, in pull and demand base system customer determine the requirement of goods while in push and supply system manufacture determine the production requirement and then floated to market [32]. It is a general phenomenon, to every success there are some failures. Wal-Mart's was very successful in those countries around the United States but it became unable to get much success in countries like Germany, Korea and India .One of the reason that these countries customer do not accept Wal-Mart format [33]. Wal-Mart entry in to Pakistan will be the great advantage to Pakistan economy in terms of foreign direct investment (FDI), reducing inflation and job opportunity but a threat to small retailers.

Theoretical Frame Work

From the literature reviews we understand that Wal-Mart has different innovative strategies mentioned at independent variables have result in increase of sales and revenue of Wal-Mart (Figure 2).

Theories applied

From literature review it seems that Wal-Mart is following different theories for growth of their business and increase in sales. The theories manly use are (i) Dunning's theory of the eclectic firm for international expansion (ii) Theory of creative destruction (iii) Theory of networking effect. Dunning's (1981) theory of eclectic firm approach has been widely used for determine FDI and international expansion

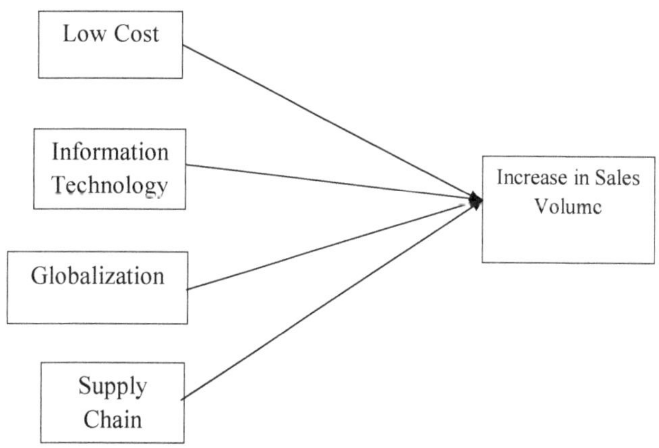

Figure 2: Different innovative strategies mentioned at independent variables have result in increase of sales and revenue of Wal-Mart.

.This theory is applied by Wal-Mart when the company is entering in Germany, Korea and India [33]. The Theory of creative destruction was used by Wal-Mart when the company moves from bar code system to RFID technology. The theory of networking effect is best applied by Wal-Mart in terms of Wallmart.net and CPFR system.

Conclusion and Recommendations

Based on the above literature review and study following is the result of this study. Low Cost retailing has a positive effect on Wal-Mart's growth and success. Information Technology innovation plays a significant role on the success of Wal-Mart's. Globalization has a positive effect on Wal-Mart's success and supply chain management system play a major role in the growth of Wal-Mart's and making it a market leader in retailing business.

On the basis of above study I recommended the following things. No doubt Wal-Mart's strategies are very much effective for United States and its neighborhood countries and the company could not get much success in countries like Germany, Korea and India. However, Wal-Mart's should focus on culture issues rather than low cost strategy. For better result Wal-Mart's should also focus on making strategic alliance for geographic dispersed countries. For developing countries like Pakistan disparately need such kind of companies, so Wal-Mart's entry will lead to prosperity but their motive should not be hostile takeover of other retailing store and making monopoly in the region.

The future area relating to this paper is the RFID technology implications, development and commercial utilization in stores of Wal-Mart and for supply chain process and the use of CPFR technology its benefit and how much it is important for giant retailing super store chains etc. Secondly the effect of e-retailing should be analyzed and how it is affecting the traditional retailing process and future prospects of Wallmart.net in this respect.

References

1. Bowman RJ (1997) Should You Just Say No to Wal-Mart? Distribution 96: 52-54.
2. Buzzell RD, Quelch JA, Salmon WJ (1990) The Costly Bargain of Trade Promotion. Harvard Business Review 68: 141-149.
3. Elman D, Hughes B (1988) How much are Deals Driving BM/HBA? Supermarket Business.
4. Johnson WC (1988) Sales Promotion: It's Come Down to Push Marketing. Marketing News.
5. Kim SY, Staelin R (1998) Retail Power: Is it an Illusion? Working paper, Fuqua School of Business, Duke University.
6. Lariviere MA, Padmanabhan V (1997) Slotting Allowances and New Product Introductions. Marketing Science 16: 112-128.
7. Sullivan MW (1997) Slotting Allowances and the Market for New Products. Journal of Law and Economics 40: 461-493.
8. Frank TA (2006) Everyday Low Vices: How much should we hate Wal-Mart? Washington Monthly.
9. Yunsheng LI (2011) Wal-Mart Business Model Study. IJAEBM Journal 1: 1-5.
10. http://www.stock.walmart.com
11. Wall-Mart's Annual Report, 2013.
12. McWilliams G (2007) Wall Street Journal 3: 1-5.
13. http://www.corporate.walmart.com
14. Basker E (2007) The Causes and Consequences of Wal-Mart's Growth. Economic Perspectives 21: 177-198.
15. Tierney S (2004) The global reach of Wal-Mart. Supply Chain Europe 13: 40-41.
16. Fishman C (2006) The Wal-Mart effect: how the world's most powerful company really works and how it's transforming the American economy. Penguin Press, New York.
17. Parnell JA, Lester DL (2008) Competitive Strategy and the Wal-Mart Threat: Positioning for survival and Success. SAM Advanced Management Journal 73: 14.
18. Barbaro M (2007) It's Not Only About Price at Wal-Mart. The New York Times Company.
19. Osterwalder A, Pigneur Y (2010) Business Model Generation. John Wiley & Sons. Hoboken.
20. Wall-Mart's Annual Report, 2012.
21. Swinyard WR (1997) Retailing trends in the USA: competition, consumers, technology and the economy. International Journal of Retail & Distribution Management 25: 244-255.
22. Jia P (2008) What Happens When Wal-Mart Comes to Town: An Empirical Analysis of the Discount Industry. Econometrica 76: 1263-1316.
23. Bianco, Zellner (2003) Is Wal-Mart too powerful. Business Week.
24. Pew Research Center for the People and the Press (2005) Wal-Mart: A Good Place to Shop but Some Critics Too.
25. Holmes T (2001) Bar Codes Lead to Frequent Deliveries and Superstores. RAND Journal of Economics 32: 708-725.
26. Pittman J (2007) The Wal-Marts Effect: A theological Analysis.
27. Maharajh L, Heitmeyer J (2005) Factors that impact United States retailers expansion into the international market place. Journal of Fashion Marketing and Management 9: 144-155.
28. International Operations Fact Sheet (2007).
29. Longo D (2005) Wal-Mart's on its way to becoming first trillion dollar corporation. Retail Merchandiser 45: 7.
30. Ramshad E (2006) South Korea, E-Mart is no Wal-Mart, s which is precisely why locals love it. Wall Street Journal.
31. Noriega D, Sameer Kumar, Eideon J (2012) International Journal of Productivity and Performance Management 61: 805-830.
32. Blanchard C, Clark L.com (2008) Adding values to service providers: Benchmarking Wal-Mart Benchmarking Journal 15: 166-177.
33. Halepete J, Seshadri Lyer KV, Park SC (2008) Wal-Mart in India: a success or failure? International Journal of Retail & Distribution Management 36: 701-713.

Private Benefits of Control: Contestability versus Coalition

Imen Ben Saanoun[1], Youssef Riahi[2]*, Saoussen Othmani[3] and Mounira Ben Arab[4]

[1]Faculty of Economic Science and Management of Nabeul, University of Carthage, Tunisia
[2]Institute of higher Management of Tunis, University of Tunis, Tunisia
[3]Faculty of Economic Science and Management of Nabeul, University of Carthage, Tunisia
[4]Institute of higher Management of Tunis, University of Tunis, Tunisia

Abstract

Despite the importance of private benefits of control in France and the persistence of concentration of ownership, the link between private benefits of control and ownership structure is still a frequently mentioned and addressed issue in the literature. Our study contributes to the literature by providing an empirical analysis of the harmonies between shareholders and their effect on private benefits of control.

In this paper, we concentrate on this relationship by developing a model where the coalition or the contestability of control influences the size of private benefits of control. On a sample of 44 French listed companies for the period 2001-2011, the empirical analysis produces some interesting results. It demonstrates that the concentrated ownership is a factor that promotes divergence of interests between shareholders. Controlling shareholders hold the most important part of property rights compared to the minority who will further expropriate corporate resources. We conclude that shareholders' agreement is not a good Corporate Governance mechanism because it could be destructive of the firm's value. In other words, if there were no agreement between the two largest shareholders, control and mutual monitoring of each other help to protect minority interests and can positively influence the firm's value.

Keywords: Private benefits of control; Ownership structure; Contestability; Coalition

Introduction

In modern finance, the private benefits of control are a subject of growing interest at the empirical and theoretical level. Several questions arise about the influence of the controlling shareholders on the private benefits and the means used to extract them.

Prior studies found that private benefits of control are due to the opaque portion of the informational environment. Insiders benefit from access to internal information which allows them to create channels to obtain profits [1]. These advantages tend to increase in countries with weak investor protection and when large shareholders possess voting rights greatly exceeding their rights to cash flows [2-4]. Based on the agency theory, the principal is the controlling shareholder and the agent is the smaller holder of capital. In this relationship principal/agent, the first is supposed to take decisions in the interest of the second, seeks to provide various benefits at the expense of minority interests and benefits from their privileged position in the firm. Controlling shareholder receives additional revenue which can be divided into two categories: pecuniary as Excess salaries, perks and larges bonuses and non-pecuniary as the prestige and social status, the ability to employ family members and to appoint them on the board [5,6], the independence from superiors and even personal relationships [4,7].

Private benefits of control are presented as materialization from unfair treatment of shareholders [1]. They can be divided into the benefits of the ownership and other related to the control. From this decomposition, we could designate beneficiaries who are the holders of blocks and managers [8,9]. They are able to affect a number of important corporate decisions, such as investment, the growth, debt and executive compensation [10].

Numerous recent studies have so far suggested that large shareholders control a significant number of firms in many countries, including developed countries [11,12]. In the economies of these countries, controlling shareholders by focusing their property tend to monitor managers and to intervene directly in the decisions of the company. Meanwhile, controlling shareholders can also divert corporate resources for private gains at the expense of other shareholders under the separation of voting and cash flow rights [13].

This situation is particularly important in the case of weak protection of minority rights. In such situation, controlling shareholders whose voting rights greatly exceed their rights to cash flows are frequently encouraged to seek personal benefits at the expense of minority shareholders [2,4,14]. In fact, concentrated ownership often appears to alleviate the agency problems between shareholders and managers [11].

Some researchers point out that when the ownership concentration is above a certain level, large shareholders are motivated to use their voting rights, or to exploit the resources of companies or to enjoy solely of companies advantages in spite of the minority shareholders and managers [2,4,7,14,15]. Controlling shareholders transfer the resources and the interests to other companies under their control [16]. These transfers can also take place for taxation purposes [17]. In fact, by increasing their shareholding, shareholders may practice a more active control and take more important management decisions. They can consequently benefit from shared or private higher benefits of control.

In fact, concentrated ownership often appears to alleviate agency problems between shareholders and managers (La [11,18] endorse that the strong participation of the entrepreneur is associated with a higher valuation of the company and a weakened expropriation of minority shareholders.

The literature on corporate governance has recently begun to

***Corresponding author:** Youssef Riahi, Assistant at Institute of Higher Management of Tunis, University of Tunis, Tunisia, E-mail: youssef.riahi@gmail.com

analyze the strategic interaction among multiple large shareholders. This approach goes beyond the more traditional "large shareholder" framework, where the ownership structure is made up of one dominant owner and many small dispersed investors. The recent Report presented by the European Commission [19] includes agreements among the Control Enhancing Mechanisms (CEMs) employed by European companies to deviate from the "proportionality" (or "one-share-one-vote") principle. In the sample of 464 companies analyzed in the Report, 44% have one or more CEMs, the most common of which are pyramid structures (27% of occurrences of CEMs), followed by multiple voting rights shares (21%) and by shareholders' agreements (14%). The later have a quite significant presence in Italy and Belgium, followed by France and Spain: 23% of the Italian companies included in the sample have shareholders' agreements; the percentage is 31% for Belgium, 18% for France and 13% for Spain.

Bennedsen [20] highlights that a controlling coalition of shareholders can have a larger cash flow stake than an individual owner, inducing it to internalize the consequences of its actions; the same incentive alignment argument points to a positive role for shareholders' agreements. On empirical grounds, Volpin [21] finds that agreements in Italian listed companies lead to a better governance (measured by the sensitivity of managerial turnover to firm performance) and to a higher Q ratio. A contrasting view is provided by Gianfrate [22], analyzing a sample of Italian listed companies: he finds that the announcement of a new agreement is a "bad news" for the stock market; he also finds that agreements are typically used to get a leverage effect (measured as the ratio between board rights and voting rights), enjoyed mostly by the first shareholder.

Laeven [23] using a large sample of companies listed in 13 European countries, show that a more even distribution of voting/cash flow rights among several large shareholders exerts a positive effect on firm value.

A significant number of studies investigated the determinants of private benefits, but the analysis of the coalition as an explanatory factor has not been analyzed until now. For this reason we are trying to offer some insight into understanding this fill this relationship and to explain the effect of shareholders agreements on private benefits of control.

This work contributes to the literature by providing an empirical analysis of shareholders' agreements, which play a significant role in the governance of European corporations. In contrast, we analyze the impact of control contestability over the last decade.

Thus, our theoretical review of the literature will attack particularly three points:

The effect of the control threshold;

The effect of the coalition;

The effect of contestability.

Empirically, we can distinguish few previous researches treating this issue. Our contribution is in the extensions works on the impact of the ownership structure on the private benefits of control. We formulate a model in which the ownership structure is dependent on the existence of a coalition. Indeed, if the coalition, represented by the shareholders' agreement between the two majority shareholders exists, the ownership structure will take the value of the pact. In the opposite case, it will be evaluated by the contestability of control, the difference between the property rights held by the controlling shareholders.

France provides a typical example of a civil law country.

Due both to its weak legal protection rules and to its inefficient law enforcement system, the French judicial environment is deemed not to adequately shield minority shareholders. Furthermore, most French listed firms show a highly concentrated ownership structure and are often controlled through pyramiding and/or double voting shares. Large block-holders either manage the firm directly or tightly monitor delegated managers. The work of Windolf [24] highlights the binary division of firms in France: half of them are being part of the State sphere, the other half being family-controlled companies. The largest shareholder owns control rights in excess of its cash flow rights [12]. The disparity between voting rights and cash flow rights gives the largest shareholder incentives to seek private benefits at the expense of minority shareholders [12,25].

La Porta [11] stipulated that the French legal environment is not effective in protecting the rights of minority shareholders. Thus, the level of expropriation is particularly significant and private benefits are much higher than in other developed countries, often exceeding 28% of corporate values [26].

Our study is made in the period 2001-2011 to benefit from several reforms. The NRE law of 15 May 2001 and the Breton Act of 26 July 2005 reinforce transparency by requiring the inclusion in the annual report a description of the fixed, variable and exceptional components of compensation and benefits.

The rest of the paper is organized as follows: Section 1 covers a literature review of the impact of the existence of controlling shareholders on private benefits of control and discusses the coalition and contestability of controls effects. Section 2 addresses the relationship between block ownership and private benefits of control. Section 3 describes the data and presents the research design. Section 4 summarizes the empirical results. A brief conclusion follows with implications of the findings and suggestions for future research.

Literature Review

Level of control and private benefits of control

There is empirical evidence on the relationship of the separation of ownership and control and the expropriation to minority shareholders. This evidence has been shown to vary among countries. For example, Zingales [27] found that in Italy, expropriation is large and consistent with voting power. Similarly, Franks and Mayer [28] found that in Germany, private benefits of control arise when shareholders have higher voting than cash flow rights. By contrast, evidence from Sweden suggested that separation of ownership and control does not result in substantial expropriation by largest controllers [29]. In the UK, the agency conflict caused by voting controls differs from that generally found in Continental Europe. In the latter, expropriation of minority shareholders might be the key agency problem related to ownership concentration. As there is extensive protection to minority investors in the UK, the agency problem originates from the lack of managerial ownership concentration, which requires codes to prevent managers from benefiting against shareholders [30].

The issue of sharing control has been the subject of a recent focus. From a theoretical perspective, some authors argue that a possession beyond 50% of the voting rights can dominate the society [31]. Recommend that 50% of the control rights are really needed to actually control a corporation.

La Porta [11] studied the control of a sample of the 27 countries in 1995. They noted that in more than 70% of cases, 20% of the voting rights are sufficient enough to isolate controlling shareholder and to exercise control over the company. This level may even be reduced to 10%, and it is sufficient to control a large firm in countries like the United States, the United Kingdom or Japan. According to these authors, the level of current 20% in 75% of cases allow the controlling shareholder to accomplish all the decisions he wishes freely on condition that there is no other shareholders with more than 10% of the rights.

LeMaux [8] analyzed a sample of French companies and used a level of 40% set for a majority stake. He concluded that the expropriation of minority shareholders by a majority coalition is confirmed. He also found that, to the predefined threshold, rather than monitoring managers on behalf outsiders, the controlling shareholders use the powers which they dispose to extract a high level of private benefits.

At this stage, we test the following hypothesis:

H1: The concentrated ownership increases the private benefits of control

The literature on corporate governance has recently begun to analyze the strategic interaction among multiple large shareholders.

Contestability and private benefits of control

Ever since the publication of Berle [32] there has been agreement that the main governance problem in listed corporations, given their dispersed ownership, is the separation of ownership and control in the sense that management controls the firm without any ownership stake. Jensen and Meckling [33] modeled the main agency problem arising from this separation. In the 1980s, the theoretical research of Demsetz and Lehn [5] established a second agency problem in listed corporations that arises between a large shareholder and a widely dispersed ownership.

How a large shareholder affects a firm's performance and valuation has elicited two opposite views. Some have argued that large shareholders have an incentive to seek private benefits of control and expropriate minority shareholders (tunneling). Others claim that incentive large block holders have yields to monitor management good governance since their ownership stakes are high and most of the benefits of good governance will be transferred to their own pockets, with the gains of better performance more than compensating for the costs of monitoring management.

Bloch and Hege also claim that multiple block holders can compensate for the poor legal protection for minorities. They argue that the relevant concept of control is the contestability of the incumbent shareholder's position and that corporate control is contestable if the incumbent cannot increase the level of control rents without losing in a control contest. In their model, the presence of two large block holders acts to limit private rent extraction and attracts the votes of the minority shareholders when proposals are contested.

The non-cooperative competition among the controlling shareholders (the two most important controlling shareholders) plays an important role in mitigating the agency conflict because of the fear of losing control. These authors concluded that private benefits increase with the difference between the proprietary rights held by the two largest shareholders and then the firm value must be assigned [34-36].

According to Burkhart and Lee [37], the contestability of control and partial ownership concentration are two mechanisms for reducing conflict between internal and external shareholders. Thus, the possibility that an outsider person of the society might adversely affect the control could have a disciplinary effect on the controlling shareholders. Into such circumstances, controlling shareholders have an incentive to keep of private benefits of control and to reduce the wealth of the minority and the value of the firm.

Attig et al. [38] have arrived to conclude on a sample de11 65 companies belonging to thirteen countries of Western Europe and eight from Asia, that the existence of several controlling shareholders alleviates agency conflict sand reduces information asymmetry.

In the same sense, Dhillon and Rossetto provide that the presence of a second controlling shareholder can only be beneficial whether it exercise sits oversight role and guidance the company to ward profitable projects, through these votes into General Assembly.

Guti'errez and Pombo [39] also concluded from a study conducted on a sample of 233 non-financial companies in Colombia for a period ranging from 1996 to 2004 that a strong contestability of control between the controlling shareholders helps to limit the extractions of the private benefits.

On a sample of 110 French companies, [40] concluded that firms with more than one controlling shareholder have an average benefit of control lower than firms with no second large shareholder. These results seem to confirm the expectations that the ability of the controlling shareholder to extract private benefits is attenuated in the presence of a second large shareholder. In fact, sharing the control between several large shareholders might reduce the conflict of interests between large and minority shareholders, and hence decrease wealth expropriation [35,38].

Thus, we formulate our second hypothesis as follows:

H2: a strong contestability of control will lead to a decrease in private benefits of controls.

Coalition of control and private benefits

The effect of coalition over private benefits of control has been analyzed by several researchers in different contexts....

Le Maux [8] studied the relationship between the type of control of a listed company and private benefits on a sample of companies in the SBF 120 over three consecutive years (1998, 1999 and 2000). He defined coalition control or control group as an entity composed by managers and controlling shareholders who have access to all the tools and mechanisms for management and control (eg internal audit, strategic decisions ...) and benefit from large information in the controlled company. It examines the coalition control inside Board contesting that "the traditional view of the general assembly, which can be considered a place of strong protests" and confirms the hypothesis of the presence of majority control coalition allows to increase the amount of regulated agreements proofing that the highly concentrated structure significantly explains the private benefits. "

Acting in favor of this coalition, controlling shareholders create asymmetry information and make a barrier to the intrusion of new members to the Board and pay particular attention to the threat of taking external control.

Contrary to what has already been mentioned, Boubaker found in a sample of 510 French listed companies whose third are affected by a shareholders' agreement, that the dummy variable "pact" positively but not significantly influence performance of the company. A year later, in 2006, Roosenboom and Screamed proposed a fairly accurate description of shareholders' agreements on a sample of 299 French companies over the period 1993-1999 and confirm the hypothesis that the existence of an agreement between shareholders positively impacts the value of the firm. Similarly, Mancinelli and Ozkan [41] showed that Italian firms will distribute higher dividends when affected by a voting agreement between shareholders, which reflects on their lower expropriation of minority shareholders.

Gianfrate [22] showed that the event "signature of shareholders Agreement's result in a significantly negative abnormal return, the adverse event" end of a Shareholders Agreement" could be translated as a significantly positive abnormal return.

In 2012, Carvalhal [42] conducted its study on a sample of companies in Brazil and analyzed the effect of agreements between shareholders in listed companies on the value of the company. Their results are that the agreements are intended to reduce conflicts between controlling shareholders and minority, which positively influences the value of the company.

In the same vein, Bargeron [43] highlighted the agreements between the shareholders and found that these agreements are associated with ownership concentration and higher managerial ownership. The results demonstrate that such agreements are not only to reduce information asymmetry; they are rather designed to increase shareholder value and reduce expropriations.

Thus, we will opt for the following hypothesis:

H3: the presence of a coalition decreases the private benefits of control.

Methodology

Our goal is to analyze the impact of the ownership structure on the private benefits of control. To do this, we are dealing with:

- The existence of a controlling shareholder
- The coalition control whose formation is marked by a shareholders;
- The contestability of control which means, the power relationship between the first two shareholders.

Data sources and sample

Our sample is composed of 84 companies belonging to the SBF 250 index for a period of eleven consecutive years from 2001 to 2011, representing all sectors of the French economy. However, various adjustments were necessary to exclude commercial or industrial companies, which have experienced a significant change in scope, banks and insurance companies, with a particular accounting system. Data on the composition of the board of directors and shareholders have been obtained manually from the reference website (www.amf-france.org); otherwise we consult the annual reports.

Recall that the French context is particularly interesting to analyze for different reasons:

Governance mechanisms have seen developments, under the in pulse of reports. Thus listed companies have been motivated by the appointment of independent directors to their boards and multiplied the creation of specialized committees, including compensation committees.

NRE of 15 May 2001 and the Breton Act of 26 July 2005 reinforce transparency by requiring the inclusion in the report of a description of the management of fixed, variable and exceptional component salaries and benefits of the officers.

In order to test our first hypothesis, we use the model [8,16,40]:

$$PBC_{it} = \beta_0 + \beta_1\ CONC_{it} + \beta_2 Q_{it} + \beta_3 TANG_{it} + \beta_4 ROA_{it} + \beta_5 SIZE_{it} + \beta_6 DEBT_{it} + \mu_{it} \quad (1)$$

Where:

PBC: private benefits of control, CONC: refers to the existence of the controlling shareholder, TANG: tangible assets, ROA: return on assets, SIZE: the size of the company, DEBT: leverage, Q: growth opportunities.

To properly analyze and differentiate between controlling shareholders and those interacting in competition, we combine in a single model the dispersion, the concentration of ownership of controlling shareholders with or without coalition. We materialize the control coalition by the existence of a shareholder agreement and in this case the ownership structure will be measured by the ownership of two controlling shareholders who are recorded on pact as C12. Otherwise, we assume that the first two shareholders are competing and the ownership structure will be estimated by the difference between the properties rights of the first two controlling shareholders noted: C1C2.

Drawing on the work of Bloch and Hege, we can develop the following model:

If there is a shareholders' agreement between the controlling shareholders

$$PBC_{it} = \beta_0 + \beta_1\ C12_{it} * CONC_{it} + \beta_2 Q_{it} + \beta_3 TANG_{it} + \beta_4 ROA_{it} + \beta_5 SIZE_{it} + \beta_6 DEBT_{it} + \mu_{it} \quad (2)$$

If not

$$PBC_{it} = \beta_0 + \beta_1\ (C1C2)_{it} CONC_{it} + \beta_2 Q_{it} + \beta_3 TANG_{it} + \beta_4 ROA_{it} + \beta_5 SIZE_{it} + \beta_6 DEBT_{it} + \mu_{it} \quad (3)$$

Private benefits of controls are explained by the structure of ownership in a single equation as follows:

$$APC_{it} = \beta_0 + \beta_1\ C12_{it} * PACTE_{it} * CONCit + \beta_2 C1C2_{it} * (1 - PACTE_{it}) * CONCit + \beta_3 Q_{it} + \beta_4 TANG_{it} + \beta_5 ROA_{it} + \beta_6 TAIL_{it} + \beta_7 DETT_{it} + \mu_{it} \quad (4)$$

The indices i and t represent indicators for individuals and the time index. In our case, the individual index is associated to French companies and the time index presents the period of study (2001-2011).

μ_{it}: present the error term of the regression

Where PBC: private benefits of control, C1C2: the difference between the percentage of common shares owned by the two largest shareholders of French companies C12: the sum percentage of common shares owned by the two largest shareholders of French companies, CONC: refers to the existence of the controlling shareholder, TANG: tangible assets, ROA: return on assets, SIZE: the size of the company, DEBT: leverage, Q: growth opportunities.

Measurement of variables

In the following subsection, we will list the different variables used to test our hypotheses.

Measures of private benefits of control: To measure the extent of private benefits of control, we used the amount of related party transactions and excessive executive compensation. We deliberately chose these two heterogeneous measures to capture maximum illegitimate transfers and not to compare or combine all the results. These two measures of private benefits have the advantage of being observable through the annual reports of companies, due to a legal obligation.

The majority of works on private benefits of control have used indirect measures: the legal system [3,14] and the diversion of the property via versus control [27].

Few studies have estimated the private benefits of control using more direct measures: the value of the voting rights [26,44] Control premiums [15,45], wages excessive executive compensation [40] and related party transactions [40,46].

a. Related party transactions: Le Maux and Dahya [8,46] used the amount of related party transactions as a direct measure of private benefits. In fact, it appears that through related party transactions, not only the leaders, associates with a significant proportion of the voting rights may also impose on the society of which they are shareholders prejudicial convention.

b. Excessive executive compensation: Excessive compensation goes directly to the leader, which is possibly the controlling shareholder of the company, expropriate the company and minority through high remuneration compared to its industry. We will follow the approach of Belanes [40] to estimate the private benefits of control by excessive salary that reflects the excess wages due to expropriation. To determine the amount of overpaid, we calculate the average earnings by sector and excessive compensation which is the difference between the total remuneration and the amount calculated before.

Measures of interest variables

CONC: binary variable that takes 1 if there is a shareholder who holds more than 40% of the capital (the average for our sample of French listed companies), 0 otherwise. This is our measure ewe use for ownership structure.

LeMaux used a dichotomous variable which takes 1 if there is a shareholder holding a proportion more or equal to 40% of the company capital. We will expect that ownership concentration increases the amount of private benefits of control.

C1C2: The difference between the proportions of ownership owned by respectively the first and second controlling shareholder. Bloch and Hege consider that two large shareholders in competition will limit their consumption of private benefits and they came to the conclusion that private profits are increasing with the difference in ownership of the first and second largest shareholder and the value of the firm must be affected [34-36]. Thus, the existence of a second shareholder with a lower proportion compared to that held by the first increases the information asymmetry and the ability to extract the wealth of the firm.

CAOL: A binary variable that takes1 if there is a shareholder agreement between the first and the second controlling shareholder, 0 otherwise. We will expect that the impact of the presence of coalition control materialized by the existence of a shareholder agreement on the private benefits of control is positive. A highly concentrated structure significantly explains the private benefits. We only work on specific and declared agreements to stock exchange authorities by the signatory shareholders [1,8].

C12: This is the proportion of capital held by the first and second largest shareholders. Le Maux, Weifeng et al., and Belanes et al., demonstrated that the private benefits of control are important in firms with concentrated capital. As contestability index is calculated using the proportions of the two largest shareholders, in assessing the ownership structure, we have chosen the ownership of the two largest shareholders.

Measures of control variables: Tangible assets: Rated "Tang" is defined as the ratio between fixed assets and total assets. For holders of the blocks, it is more difficult to divert resources from the company when the assets are observable such as tangible assets [8,15,47].

Debt: Rated "Debt" and measured by total debt to total assets. This is an internal control mechanism. Under the assumption of free cash flow, debt reduces the agency costs related to cash flow available for internal and therefore, private benefits of controls used by controlling shareholders [33].

Growth opportunities: Noted "growth": measured by Tobin's Q that is defined as the ratio between the total market value of the company with the accounting value of the debt by the sum of the book value of equity and the book value of debts. We expect that the controlling shareholders will not encourage increasing their wealth in private benefits when growth opportunities are high [47].

Performance: Noted "ROA": we chose the return on assets ratio as an indicator of the wealth produced, which is the ratio of operating income to total assets (ROA). We assume that higher allows the controlling shareholder of appropriate resources to benefit the firm thus a higher level of private benefits [40].

Size: We chose Neperian logarithm of book value of the total assets of the firm as a size company indicator. We will expect that the relationship between the amount of private benefits of control and firm size is positive insisting that big companies offer more pecuniary and non-monetary benefits, [8,15].

Descriptive statistics and univariate analysis

The following Table 1 provides the descriptive statistics (mean, standard deviation, minimum and maximum) of each variable used in our analysis.

Table 2 describes the values of the variables measuring the amount of private benefits of control and the variables that could have an impact on them. Excessive executive compensation (not divided by total assets) has an average value of 1125. It varies between -1238.11 and 12656 as the minimum and maximum value respectively. Thus, our sample is characterized by leaders who have over their sectors pay. Regarding the second variable, the average value of the regulated agreements is 19,416 with a minimum of 0 and a maximum of 150644.

It was found that the average percentage of common shares owned by the two largest shareholders of French companies is 41.41% and varies from 0% to 99.9%. Thus, on average the two largest shareholders hold half the capital. These statistics allow the proposition that the stock ownership is locked in the hands of the two largest shareholders. The ownership stock of the French firms is closely held by the block holders although the firms of the sample belong to the SBF250 index. In fact, it is argued that there is separation of the control rights from the cash flow rights when companies are listed on the stock exchange, and the non-controlling owners are represented by a large number of minority shareholders. However, this explanation is valid for only a tiny minority of large groups [12].

Size measured by the logarithm of total assets shows an average value of 21, 68 while the average of debts is 57% of total assets. The long-term debt can reach a maximum value of 100% of total assets. Tangible assets are on average of 16% with a minimum of 0 and a maximum of 99%. The rate of return on assets is on average of 5%. It varies between -27% and 59% shown in Table 3.

For our sample composed only of French companies, there is at least one shareholder holding more than 40% in 71% of companies. This rate is similar to that found by Faccio et al., who showed that 64.75% of French companies were dominated by one large shareholder.

Coalitions of control in our study have been materialized by the existence of the pact in almost 38% of our sample. This result seems consistent with Boubaker who noted the presence of shareholder agreements in the third of French companies' sample.

Variables	rating	Measures
private benefits of control PBC	Related party transactions RPT	The amount of related party transactions divided by total assets
	Excessive managerial compensation EXCC	Excessive managerial compensation divided by total assets managé
ownership structure	CONC	A binary variable that takes 1 if there is shareholder who holds more than 40% of the capital (the average for our sample of French listed companies), 0 otherwise.
Coalition	CAOL	A binary variable that takes 1 if there is a shareholder agreement between the first and second controlling shareholder, 0 otherwise.
Ownership Concentration	C12	the proportion of capital held by the first and second largest shareholder.
Contestability of control	C1C2	The difference between the proportions of ownership owned by the first and second controlling shareholder respectively.
Tangible assets	TANG	Fixed assets / total assets
Growth opportunities	Q	(Market value of equity + book value of debt) / (book value of equity + book value of debt)
Leverage	DEBT	total debts to total assets
Return On Assets	ROA	Ratio of profit before interest and tax to total assets
Size of the company	SIZE	Neperian logarithm of book value of the total assets of the firm.

Table 1: Summary table of variables used.

	mean	min	max	SD
RPT	0,0020013	0	0,4001675	0,01558268
RPT*	19.416763	0	150644	125
EXCC	0,0022205	4,449E-07	0,0796369	0,00752021
EXCC*	1125	-1238,11	12656	239
C12	0.41415055	0	0.9958	23,1023888
C1C2	0.55	0	0.63	0.138325
TANG	0,1667085	0,0003871	0,9901343	0,17077753
DEBT	0,5690149	0	0.895234	0.1648682
SIZE	21,688685	16,194408	27,318213	2,1663325
ROA	0,0493278	-.27	0,5976994	0,05080133
Q	1,3844716	0,0101436	7.644888	1,3947438

Source : Variables: RPT - related party transactions, RPT* : related party transactions divided by total assets, EXCC: Excessive managerial, EXCC*: Excessive managerial compensation divided by total assets manager, 0 otherwise. C12:the proportion of capital held by the first and second largest shareholder control, C1C2: The difference between the proportions of ownership owned by the first and second controlling shareholder respectively. TANG: tangible assets, ROA: return on assets, DEBT: leverage, Q: growth opportunities. SIZE : Neperian logarithm of book value of the total assets of the firm.

Table 2: Descriptive statistics of depend and independent variables.

The correlation test shows that there is a positive correlation relationship between the two measures of private benefits of control and (CONC). Such result is compatible to Bebchuk's study, which assumes that firms with high levels of private benefits of control are likely to have more concentrated ownership structure.

This relationship is significant at respectively the level of 1% and 5% for excessive executive compensation and related party transactions. The level of private benefits of control increases with the concentration of ownership. This result is consistent with those of [7,8,15,16].

Our finding contradicts a priori those of Jensen and Meckling who found that the major contribution to rights to benefits by the controlling shareholder increases its commitment to the distribution of dividends and reduces incentives for expropriation, which is likely to disprove our first hypothesis.

Table 4 also points out a negative correlation between the two measures of private benefits of control and assets tangibility. Such correlation is expected because we assume that firms with more tangible assets have lower private benefits of control.

There is a negative correlation between leverage and profitability showing that the most profitable firms' use less debt. However, the correlation between private benefits of control and performance is positive stipulating that most successful companies are those whose controlling shareholders benefit most from their resources.

The results presented in Table 4 show that the concentration of ownership weakens the large size of the firm. This result allows us to confirm the results of Villalonga and Qu that showed that great French companies have more dispersed ownership structures than small and medium companies.

Regression Results and Interpretations

After the realization of econometric tests: Pearson's correlation matrix and vif's test, test for the presence of individual effects, Hausman test and hetero scedasticity test, it would be wise to present the results of our models.

As already mentioned, we use two proxies for private benefits of control: related party agreements and excessive executive compensation both deflated by total assets. We estimate our empirical model by the method of generalized least squares. The estimate of the dependent variable related party transactions allowed us to be more attractive in terms for significance as those found using excessive executive compensation results.

Table 5 shows that the effect of ownership structure is consistent with the univariate analysis and states that the existence of a shareholder

Variables		Observation	Frequency	Percentage
CONC	0	484	138	28.51
	1		346	71.48
COAL	0	484	302	62.39
	1		182	37.60

Source : Variables: CONC- A binary variable that takes 1 if a shareholder who holds more than 40% of the capital (the average for our sample of French listed companies), 0 otherwise, CAOL:A binary variable that takes 1 if there is a shareholder agreement between the first and second controlling shareholder.

Table 3: Descriptive statistics for quantitative variables.

holding more than 40% of capital "CONC" is positive and significant at the 1% level for both measures of the dependent variable. Therefore, the size of private benefits of control increases with the concentration of ownership beyond 40%. Controlling shareholders are expected to benefit from the business under their control to increase their wealth and transfer private benefits outside the company to offset the cost of ownership concentration.

Thus, the concentration of ownership is a factor that promotes the interest divergence of shareholders holding the largest share of property rights over those of minority, increasing the risk of expropriation, there by affirming our first hypothesis.

These results match partly those of Belanes [40] who found that the concentration of ownership in the hands of the top three shareholders has a significant effect on private benefits of control. The results are compatible to the hypothesis that the higher the stock ownership is, the higher is the level of private benefits of control. Such result is already approved by the studies of [7,8,15,16].

Meanwhile, the larger the stock ownership is, the greater are the private benefits in terms of the frequent use of related-party transactions. In fact, when the stock ownership is concentrated enough, the control level is powerful enough. The shareholder is appealed to lonely extract corporate benefits in spite of both minority shareholders and managers [2,3,4,7,15]. Block-shareholders expropriate such private benefits either to increase their own wealth or to provide their controlled companies with necessary funds, or even for tax purposes [16,17]. But above all, block-shareholders are appealed to siphon off higher private benefits of control so as to safeguard their wealth and compensate the cost of concentrating their wealth within one firm and the risk to all lose. In fact, most French firms are family-owned. Founders are often concerned with the survival of their firms and aim at protecting their legacy for future generations and preserve the family wealth accumulated through decades as well.

This result is contradicted in other studies. A holder of blocks may be encouraged to make an effort in monitoring managers since the benefits (in proportion to their ownership of rights to capital), can reasonably offset the cost of this effort. La Porta concluded that the strong participation of the Contractor's rights to the benefits is associated with a higher valuation of the company and a decreasing expropriation of minority shareholders [33].

The estimation results also reveal the significance of tangible assets for both measures of private benefits of control. The presence of tangible assets negatively affects private benefits of control. Controlling shareholders are more difficult to divert the assets of the firm when they are easily observable. These results confirm those of [9,45] who found that the tangible are negatively related to private benefits of control.

Regarding the leverage ratio, it has a negative and significant coefficient for excessive executive compensation and a positive significant coefficient for related party transactions highlighting the influence of the firm leverage depends on the identity of the beneficiary of private profits.

The negative effect of debt on excessive executive compensation is explained by the fact that controlling shareholders choose financing by debtsbecauseloansdonotchangetheownershipstructureofthecompany. This option is particularly relevant to family not wishing the coming of new owners and the loss of control. For related party transactions, the

	EXCC	RPT	CONC	Q	TANG	ROA	TAIL	DETTE
EXCC	1.0000							
RPT		1.0000						
CONC	0.0949***	0.0728**	1.0000					
Q	(0.0083)	(0.0494)	(0.0100)	1.0000				
TANG	(0.1625)***	(0.0669)*	0.0728**	(0.0057)	1.0000			
ROA	0.1505***	0.1228***	(0.0858)***	0.1638***	(0.1181)***	1.0000		
TAIL	(0.1327)***	(0.1181)***	(0.0588)*	(0.0254)	(0.1244)***	0.0258	1.0000	
DETTE	(0.0106)	(0.0420)	(0.0204)	(0.1502)***	0.2744***	(0.2009)***	(0.1627)***	1.0000

Source : RPT - related party transactions divided by total assets, EXCC: Excessive managerial compensation divided by total assets manager, CONC: A binary variable that takes 1 if a shareholder who holds more than 40% of the capital (the average for our sample of French listed companies), 0 otherwise, CAOL:A binary variable that takes 1 if there is a shareholder agreement between the first and second controlling shareholder, 0 otherwise.C12:the proportion of capital held by the first and second largest shareholder control, C1C2: The difference between the proportions of ownership owned by the first and second controlling shareholder respectively.TANG: tangible assets, ROA: return on assets, DEBT: leverage, Q: growth opportunities. SIZE : Neperian logarithm of book value of the total assets of the firm. ***, **, * denote significance at 1%, 5%, and 10% level, respectively.

Table 4: Pairwise Correlations.

	EXCC			RPT		
	coefficient	Z	Value P>|Z|	coefficient	Z	Value P>|Z|
CONC	.0006441***	6.08	0.000	.0004115***	8.01	0.000
Q	-.0002368	-0.66	0.510	-.0027122***	-4.81	0.000
TANG	-.0019059***	-5.62	0.000	-.0004517**	-2.40	0.016
ROA	.0007844***	6.05	0.000	.0008835***	6.83	0.000
SIZE	-.0002181***	-5.51	0.000	-.0004972***	-10.47	0.000
DEBT	-.0001867	-0.54	0.588	.0002339	4.54	0.000
_cons	.0011812	4.69	0.000	.0014197	17.74	0.000
R^2between		26.12%			35.64%	

Source : RPT-related party transactions divided by total assets, EXCC: Excessive managerial compensation divided by total assets manager, CONC: A binary variable that takes 1 if a shareholder who holds more than 40% of the capital (the average for our sample of French listed companies), 0 otherwise, .TANG: tangible assets, ROA: return on assets, DEBT: leverage, Q: growth opportunities. SIZE : Neperian logarithm of book value of the total assets of the firm. ***, **, * denote significance at 1%, 5%, and 10% level, respectively.

Table 5: The impact of the ownership concentration on private benefits of control.

positive relationship can be explained by the fact that through leverage, shareholders will try to transfer the maximum of resources to other firms under their control, through regulated agreements. So, the debt has no longer the disciplinary role of governance, on the contrary, it increases the private benefits of controlling shareholders. These results confirm whose main contribution is that the relationship between the impacts of debt policy on the private benefits of control depends on the identity of beneficiaries.

About growth opportunities, the coefficient of this variable is significant and negative for both proxy variables of private benefits of control, showing that the controlling shareholders try to capture and extract the wealth of the company when growth opportunities are low. However, the coefficient is not significant for excessive executive compensation and significant for related party agreements.

The coefficient of firm size is significantly negative. Such a result shows that the increase in firm size is associated with a decrease in the level of private benefits of control. According to Dyck and Zingales studies [45] we argue that large firms are likely to have a lower level of private benefits of control. In such a situation, the controlling shareholders use all the authority available to them to extract maximum wealth in their favor and at the expense of outside shareholders.

Finally, regarding the return on assets for our two measures of private benefits of control, the coefficient of the variable is significant and positive confirming our expectations. High profitability allows the controlling shareholders to appropriate the resources to benefit the company in many forms such as excessive salaries or related party transactions. This result corroborates those of Le Maux [8].

In previous sections, we investigated the impact of the ownership concentration of private benefits of control based on the existence of a controlling shareholder holding more than 40% of the capital. In what follows, we will enrich our study analyzing the effect of the interaction between the two majority shareholders.

Impact of the coalition or contestability in the private benefits of control

To analyze the effect of the formation of coalition between the controlling shareholders on the extent of private benefits of control, we will refer tomodèle3.

The results presented in Table 6 shows that R2 Between is about 30.29% for excessive executive compensation and 40.13% for related party transaction and there for models have acceptable explanatory power for the total sample.

The results in the Table 6 show the significance of the variable C12*COAL, with a positive sign which is contrary to our expectations, didn't valid our H3 hypothesis which suggests that the presence of the coalition have a negative impact on private benefits and leaves omen the beneficial nature of the coalition as a good governance mechanism.

The coalition majority control there for uses all the powers available to it to extract maximum wealth in his favor and at the expense of outside shareholders. This result is in line with that of Le Maux [9] amount instead of making a reciprocal monitoring on behalf of outside shareholders the main shareholders use the powers they have to extract a high level of private benefits at the expense outside shareholders.

Our findings reinforce those of Gianfrate [22] that the signing of shareholders results in a significantly negative abnormal return, while the opposite event (end of a shareholders' agreement) results in a abnormal return significantly positif. No usalsocontradictVolpin [21] and Ozkan [41] that the shareholder agreements are mechanisms for good governance.

	EXCC			RPT		
	coefficient	Z	Value P>|Z|	coefficient	Z	Value P>|Z|
C12*COAL	.0000838***	3.50	0.000	4.87e-06***	3.05	0.002
C1C2*(1-COAL)	-6.37e-06***	-4.01	0.000	-2.46e-07***	-3.38	0.001
Q	3.32e-06	0.01	0.993	-.0026587***	-4.41	0.000
ROA	-.0022401***	-7.45	0.000	.0005663***	2.84	0.004
TANG	-.0008911***	-7.27	0.000	.0008089***	6.57	0.000
SIZE	.000181***	4.51	0.000	-.0005025***	-10.39	0.000
DEBT	-.0002716	-0.83	0.409	-.0002714***	-5.05	0.000
_cons	.0015296***	5.90	0.000	.0014825***	19.04	0.000
R^2between	30.29%			40.13%		

Source : Variables: RPT: related party transactions divided by total assets, EXCC: Excessive managerial compensation divided by total assets manager,, CAOL:A binary variable that takes 1 if there is a shareholder agreement between the first and second controlling shareholder, 0 otherwise.C12:the proportion of capital held by the first and second largest shareholder control, C1C2: The difference between the proportions of ownership owned by the first and second controlling shareholder respectively.TANG: tangible assets, ROA: return on assets, DEBT: leverage, Q: growth opportunities. SIZE : Neperian logarithm of book value of the total assets of the firm. ***, **, * denote significance at 1%, 5%, and 10% level, respectively.

Table 6: Estimation of the impact of the presence of a coalition and contestability in the private benefits of control.

Moreover, if there is no agreement between the two largest shareholders, the value of the property that will be included in the model is the index of contestability. Its coefficient is significant and negative, which allows us to confirm our second hypothesis.

So when controlling, shareholders have rights to the cash flows with similar size, the contestability is important and the level of private benefits of control will be less. This could be explained by the fact that the controlling shareholders, who are not subject to an agreement and with relatively similar size, are subject to control and reciprocal monitoring each other to protect the interests of minority and positively influence the value of the firm. However, when the relative difference in size between the two shareholders is relatively large it makes the control of the first by the second doubtful. The risk wealth transfer is important and the value of the firm is lower. This outcome is similar to Blochand Hege model predictions and Bennedsen and Wolfenzon [20].

These results seem to confirm the findings of Gutierrez and Pombo [39] who states that strong control contestability between the holders of blocks limits the "tunneling" and extractions of the private profits.

These results confirm those of Blochand Hege, Maury and Pajuste [35] and Attig et al., [38] which have shown that sharing control between controlling shareholders could reduce conflicts of interest between minority and majority. Thus, the contestability of control appears as a factor which limits the appropriation of earnings by controlling shareholders at the expense of minority interests.

Acting on behalf of the coalition, controlling shareholders create information asymmetry to appropriate the benefits of the company. However, the contestability of control allows reducing them.

Conclusion

This paper covers the recent empirical findings and theoretical reasoning for the relationship between ownership structure and private benefits of control. To test the validity of our hypotheses, we conducted an analysis in the French context with a sample of 44 French companies in the SBF 250 over a period of 11 years. Through analysis and detailed overview to the ownership structure of French companies, we could better understand the concept and extraction of private benefits of control channels. We have the advantage of using two direct proxies of private benefits of control: related party transactions and excessive executive compensation corresponding to blocks holder and managers. We contribute to the existing academic literature by demonstrating that the existence of an agreement between the controlling shareholders increases the private benefits of control. However, the contestability of control reduces the diversion of wealth from shareholders control. First, we have highlighted the impact of ownership concentration measured by a binary variable which takes the value1ifthere is a shareholder holding more than 40% of the capital on the private benefits of control for both measures. Our results confirm those of LeMaux [8] who found that the majority control increases the appropriation of earnings. However, we contradict the results of Jensen and Meckling [33], which stipulated that ownership concentration, is a factor that promotes alignment of interests and results in reduced levels of expropriation. Second, we have materialized the coalition by shareholder agreement and we expected that it accentuates the extractions. We concluded that shareholder agreement is a bad governance mechanism enhancing appropriation earnings of the company even by the controlling shareholder or the manager. However, if this latter two does not agree, the power struggle between the controlling shareholders positively affects private benefits of control with controlling and preventing the transfer of wealth. We examined the effect of ownership structure on the private benefits of control by focusing on the consequences of the existence of a shareholders' agreement materializing the formation of the coalition. The fact that most French companies are family firms, motivates us to enrich our study by examining the impact of the type of the controlling shareholders (if they are of the same type or not, institutional or families).

References

1. LeMaux J (2003) Les bénéfices privés : une rupture delégalité entre actionnaires. Finance Contrôle Stratégie 6: 63-92.
2. Grossman SJ, Hart OD (1980) Takeover bids, the free-rider problem & the theory of the corporation. Bell Journal of Economics 11: 42-64.
3. Johnson S, La Porta R, Lopez-de-silanes F, Shleifer A (2000) Tunneling. American Economic Review 90: 22-27.
4. Holderness CG (2003) A survey of block-holders & corporate control. Economic Policy Review 9: 51-64.
5. Demsetz H, Lehn K (1985) The structure of corporate ownership: causes & consequences. Journal of Finance 93: 1155-1177.
6. Ehrhards O, Nowak E (2003) Private benefits & minority shareholder expropriation: empirical evidence from IPOs of German family-owned firms. Working paper, Humboldt University.
7. Weifeng H, Zhaoguo Z, Shasha Z (2008) Ownership structure & the private benefits of control: an analysis of Chinese firms. Corporate Governance 8: 286-298.
8. LeMaux J (2004) Les déterminants de l'ampleur des bénéfices privés : un test sur données françaises. Finance Contrôle Stratégie 7: 195-231.
9. Djebali R, Belanes A, Omri A (2012) Simultaneous Determination of Firm Leverage and Private Benefits of Control in French Firms. International Journal of Economics and Finance.
10. Cronqvist H, Fahlenbrach R (2009) Large shareholders and corporate policies. Review of Financial Studies 22: 3941-3976.
11. LaPorta R, Lopez de Silanes F, Shleifer A (1999) Corporate ownership around the world. Journal of Finance 54: 471-517.
12. Faccio M, Lang LHP (2002) The ultimate ownership of Western European corporations. Journal of Financial Economics 65: 365-395.
13. Burkart M, Gromb D, Panunzi F (1997) Large shareholders, monitoring, and the value of the firm. Quarterly Journal of Economics 693-728.
14. LaPorta R, Lopez-de-Silanes F, Shleifer A, Vishny R (2000) Investor protection & corporate finance. Journal of Financial Economics 58: 3-27.
15. Barclay M, Holderness C (1989) The private benefits from control of public corporations. Journal of Financial Economics 25: 371-395.
16. Tai BY, Liu X, Liu JM (2007) Related-party transactions, corporate performance, and the effectiveness of corporate governance mechanism: evidence from the Chinese stock market. Journal of international business and economics 5: 117-131.
17. Lo WY, Wong MK, Firth M (2010) Can corporate governance deters management from manipulating earnings? Evidence from related-party sales transactions in China. Journal of Corporate Finance 16: 225-235.
18. LaPorta R, Lopez-de-Silanes F, Shleifer A, Vishny R (2002) Investor protection and corporate valuation. Journal of Finance 57: 1147-1170.
19. EU (2007) Report on the proportionality principle in the European Union, External study commissioned by the European Commission, Final Report.
20. Bennedsen M, Wolfenzon D (2000) The balance of power in closely held corporations. Journal of Financial Economics 58: 113-139.
21. Volpin P (2002) Governance with poor investor protection: evidence from top executive turnover in Italy. Journal of Financial Economics 64: 61-90.
22. Gianfrate G (2007) What do shareholder's coalitions really want? Evidence from Italian voting trusts. Corporate Governance 15: 122-132.
23. Laeven L, Levine R (2008) Complex ownership structures and corporate valuations. Review of Financial Studies 21: 579-604.
24. Windolf P (2002) Corporate networks in Europe and the United States. Oxford University Press.
25. Barca F, Becht M (2001) The control of corporate Europe. Oxford University Press.
26. Nenova T (2003) The value of corporate voting rights and control: a cross-country analysis. Journal of Financial Economics 68: 325-351.
27. Zingales L (1994) The value of the voting right: A survey of the Milan stock exchange experience. Review of Financial Studies 7: 125-148.
28. Franks J, Mayer C (2001) Ownership and control of German corporations. Review of Financial Studies 14: 943-977.
29. Bergstrom C, Rydqvist K (1990) Ownership of equity in dual class firms. Journal of Banking and Finance 14: 265–269.
30. Goergen M, Renneboog L (2001) Strong managers and passive institutional investors in the United Kingdom. In: Barca, F., Becht, M. The Control of Corporate Europe, Oxford University Press, Oxford.
31. DeAngelo H, DeAngelo L (1985) Managerial ownership of voting rights: a study of public corporations with dual classes of common stock. Journal of Financial Economics 14: 33-69.
32. Berle A, Means GC (1932) The Modern Corporation and Private Property. MacMillan.
33. Jensen M, Meckling W (1976) Theory of the firm: Managerial behaviour, agency costs & ownership structure. Journal of Financial Economics 3: 305-360.
34. Lehman E, Weigand J (2000) Does the Governed Corporation Perform Better Governance Structures and Corporate Performance in Germany. European finance Review 4: 157-195.
35. Maury B, Pajuste A (2005) Multiple controlling shareholders and firm value. Journal of Banking and Finance 29: 1813-1834.
36. Laeven L, Levine R (2007) Complex Ownership Structures and Corporate Valuations. Review of Financial Studies 1-37.
37. Burkart M, Lee S (2007) The one share -one vote debate: a theoretical perspective. ECGI Finance working.
38. Attig N, Guedhami O, Mishra D (2008) Multiple large shareholders, control contests and implied cost of equity. Journal of Corporate Finance 14: 721-737.

39. Gutierrez LH, Pombo C (2009) Corporate ownership and control contestability in emerging markets: The case of Colombia. Journal of Economics and Business 61: 112-139.

40. Belanes A, Djebali R, Omri A (2011) Private Benefits of Control versus block stock ownership in French firms. Economics and Finance Review 1: 12-30.

41. Mancinelli L, Ozkan A (2006) Ownership structure and dividend policy: evidence from Italian firms. European Journal of Finance 12: 265-282.

42. Carvalhal A (2012) Do shareholder agreements affect market valuation?: Evidence from Brazilian listed firms. Journal of Corporate Finance 18: 919-933.

43. Bargeron LL (2012) Do Shareholder Tender Agreements inform or expropriate shareholders. Journal of Corporate Finance 18: 373-388.

44. Masulis R, Wang C, Xie F (2009) Agency problems at dual-class companies. Journal of Finance 64: 1697-1728.

45. Dyck A, Zingales L (2004) Private benefits of control: An international comparison. Journal of Finance 59: 537-600.

46. Dahya J, Dimitrov O, McConnell J (2008) Dominant shareholders, corporate boards, and corporate value: A cross-country analysis. Journal of Financial Economics 87: 73-100.

47. He Xi, Mingsheng Li, Jing Shi, Twite GJ (2008) Determinants of Dividend Policy in Chinese Firms: Cash Versus Stock Dividends. Electronic Journal.

Permissions

All chapters in this book were first published in BEJ, by OMICS International; hereby published with permission under the Creative Commons Attribution License or equivalent. Every chapter published in this book has been scrutinized by our experts. Their significance has been extensively debated. The topics covered herein carry significant findings which will fuel the growth of the discipline. They may even be implemented as practical applications or may be referred to as a beginning point for another development.

The contributors of this book come from diverse backgrounds, making this book a truly international effort. This book will bring forth new frontiers with its revolutionizing research information and detailed analysis of the nascent developments around the world.

We would like to thank all the contributing authors for lending their expertise to make the book truly unique. They have played a crucial role in the development of this book. Without their invaluable contributions this book wouldn't have been possible. They have made vital efforts to compile up to date information on the varied aspects of this subject to make this book a valuable addition to the collection of many professionals and students.

This book was conceptualized with the vision of imparting up-to-date information and advanced data in this field. To ensure the same, a matchless editorial board was set up. Every individual on the board went through rigorous rounds of assessment to prove their worth. After which they invested a large part of their time researching and compiling the most relevant data for our readers.

The editorial board has been involved in producing this book since its inception. They have spent rigorous hours researching and exploring the diverse topics which have resulted in the successful publishing of this book. They have passed on their knowledge of decades through this book. To expedite this challenging task, the publisher supported the team at every step. A small team of assistant editors was also appointed to further simplify the editing procedure and attain best results for the readers.

Apart from the editorial board, the designing team has also invested a significant amount of their time in understanding the subject and creating the most relevant covers. They scrutinized every image to scout for the most suitable representation of the subject and create an appropriate cover for the book.

The publishing team has been an ardent support to the editorial, designing and production team. Their endless efforts to recruit the best for this project, has resulted in the accomplishment of this book. They are a veteran in the field of academics and their pool of knowledge is as vast as their experience in printing. Their expertise and guidance has proved useful at every step. Their uncompromising quality standards have made this book an exceptional effort. Their encouragement from time to time has been an inspiration for everyone.

The publisher and the editorial board hope that this book will prove to be a valuable piece of knowledge for researchers, students, practitioners and scholars across the globe.

List of Contributors

Jarrett JE
Management Science and Finance, University of Rhode Island, Kingston, RI, USA

Li Y
Doctoral Student (Finance), University of Rhode Island, USA

Byung Woo K
Korea National University of Transportation (KNUT), Korea

Vargas-Hernandez JG
University Center for Economic and Managerial Sciences, University of Guadalajara, Periferico Norte 799, Mexico

Echeagaray JES and Echeagaray TIS
Facultad de Ciencias Economico Administrativas de Mazatlán, Universidad Autonoma de Sinaloa, Av. Universidad s/n Ciudad Universitaria, Mexico

Vasiliki A Basdekidou
Special Research Fund Account (ELKE) Aristotle University of Thessaloniki, Greece

Nurbek Achilov
G-Global Development Community, Kazakhstan

Saibal Kuamr Saha
Assistant Professor, University of Technology and Management, 4th Floor, Bawri Mansions, Dhankheti, Shillong, Meghalaya, India

Kyper E and Prante G
Lynchburg College, Lynchburg VA, USA

Juan Yu and Xia Pan
Sun Yat-sen Universit, China

Jessica Conradie
MBA student, Management College of Southern Africa, South Africa

Adolf Lowies
Director of Research, Management College of Southern Africa, South Africa

Janine Lee Upton
Statistician: Data Analysis Unit, Management College of Southern Africa, South Africa

Li Dai
School of Economics and Trade, Hunan University, China

Peng Zhou
Cardiff School of Management, Cardiff Metropolitan University, Cardiff, CF5 2YB, UK

Yen-Jo Kiang
Department of Business Administration, CTBC Financial Management College, Tainan, Taiwan

Neeraj Kumar Sharma
Baba Ramdas Udaseen Shikshan Sansthan, Hapur, Uttar Pradesh, India

Abiola Babatunde Abimbola
Department of Economics, University of Lagos, Akoka, Nigeria

Ajibola Joseph Olusegun
College of Postgraduate Studies, Caleb University, Imota-Ikorodu, Lagos, Nigeria

Chung T and Ariff M
Taylors University, Subang Jaya, Malaysia

Parisa Fathi and Mustafa Ersungur S
International Economy, IIBF Economics Department Ataturk University, Erzurum, Turkey

Ahmed U, Abdul Majid AH and Mohd Zin ML
School of Business Management, University Utara Malaysia, Malaysia

Phulpoto W
SZABIST, Karachi, Pakistan

Umrani WA
Sukkur Institute of Business Administration Sindh, Pakistan

Farsi JY and Moradi MA
Department of Entrepreneurship, University of Tehran, Iran

Jandoust A
Graduate of Entrepreneurship Management, University of Tehran's Faculty of Entrepreneurship, Iran

Esfandabadi HM
Graduate of Social Sciences, Research Assistant at University of Tehran's Faculty of Entrepreneurship, Iran

Saeid Jabbarzadeh
Department of Accounting, Urmia Branch, Islamic Azad University, Urmia, Iran

Morteza Motavassel
Department of Accounting, Osku Branch, Islamic Azad University, Osku, Iran

Parviz Mamsalehi
Department in Accounting, Hamedan Branch, Islamic Azad University, Hamedan, Iran

Matthew J. Liberatore
Center for Business Analytics, Villanova School of Business, Villanova University, Villanova, USA

Tan Miller
Global Supply Chain Management Program, College of Business Administration, Rider University, Lawrence, USA

Yuriy V Kozyr
Department of Theoretical Economy and Mathematic Research, Central Economics and Mathematics, Institute of Russian Academy of Sciences, Moscow, Russia

Vasiliki A Basdekidou
Special Research Fund Account (ELKE), Aristotle University of Thessaloniki, Greece

Artemis A. Styliadou
School of Law, Aristotle University of Thessaloniki, Greece

Benet-Zepf A and Küster I
Universitat de Valencia Valencia, Valencia, Spain

Marin-Garcia JA
ROGLE Research Group. DOE - Universitat Politecnica de Valencia. Valencia. Spain

Strawczynski M
Department of Economics and School of Public Policy, Hebrew University of Jerusalem, Israel

Shabbir MS
Centre of Professional Excellence (CPE), Blue Area, Islamabad, Pakistan

Imen Ben Saanoun
Faculty of Economic Science and Management of Nabeul, University of Carthage, Tunisia

Youssef Riahi
Institute of higher Management of Tunis, University of Tunis, Tunisia

Saoussen Othmani
Faculty of Economic Science and Management of Nabeul, University of Carthage, Tunisia

Mounira Ben Arab
Institute of higher Management of Tunis, University of Tunis, Tunisia

Index

R

S

T

V

W